Third CIPS-SIGHAN Joint Conference on Chinese Language Processing

(CLP 2014)

AA005686

Wuhan, China
20 - 21 October 2014

ISBN: 978-1-63439-414-7

Printed from e-media with permission by:

Curran Associates, Inc.
57 Morehouse Lane
Red Hook, NY 12571

Some format issues inherent in the e-media version may also appear in this print version.

Printed by Curran Associates, Inc. (2014)

For permission requests, please contact the Association for Computational Linguistics at the address below.

Association for Computational Linguistics
209 N. Eighth Street
Stroudsburg, Pennsylvania 18360

Phone: 1-570-476-8006
Fax: 1-570-476-0860

acl@aclweb.org

Additional copies of this publication are available from:

Curran Associates, Inc.
57 Morehouse Lane
Red Hook, NY 12571 USA
Phone: 845-758-0400
Fax: 845-758-2634
Email: curran@proceedings.com
Web: www.proceedings.com

Preface

As the vast emerging web users generate big data globally, Chinese language resources develop rapidly accompanying with language-specific great interests in academic and industrial applications. CLP2014 targets to harness Chinese language content by reporting recent advancements in technical and linguistic aspects, and drawing interests of global researchers to pursue Chinese processing techniques in this big data age.

CLP2014 is the third conference jointly organized by the Chinese Language Processing Society of China (CIPS) and the ACL Special Interest Group on Chinese Language Processing (SIGHAN). The first conference, CLP-2010, was held on Aug 28-29, 2010 in Beijing, China, in conjunction with COLING 2010. The second conference, CLP2012, hosted by Tianjin University, was held on December 20-21, 2012 in Tianjin, China. CLP2014, hosted by the Central China Normal University, Wuhan, was held on Oct 20-21, 2014.

The series of CLP conference provide a platform for researchers around the world to present their research, share ideas, explore new research directions, and advance the state-of-the-art in Chinese language processing. Continuous efforts of the conference received more and more attention on its characteristics of Chinese language application and studies. The specialty of Chinese language poses challenging task for both linguist and computer scientists, and raises a conference tradition of the international bakeoffs. CLP2014 features four bakeoff tracks: Chinese word segmentation, Chinese Spelling Check, Simplified Chinese parsing, and Personal Attributes Extraction in Chinese Text.

Of the 18 submissions, CLP2014 selected 11 papers through rigorous review process. CLP2014 bakeoffs attract 18 groups to participate and submit 22 papers of both technical and overview papers.

We wish to thank everyone who showed interest and submitted a paper, all of the authors for their contributions, the members of the Program Committee for their thoughtful reviews, the invited speakers for sharing their perspectives on the topic, and all the attendees of the workshop. All of these factors contribute to a truly enriching event!

Le Sun, Chengqing Zong	*CLP2014 General Co-Chairs*
Min Zhang, Levow, Gina-Anne	*CLP2014 Program Co-Chairs*

Organizers

General Chairs:

Le Sun, *Institute of Software, Chinese Academy of Sciences*
Chengqing Zong, *Institute of Automation, Chinese Academy of Sciences*

Program Chairs:

Min Zhang, *Soochow University*
Levow, Gina-Anne, *University of Washington*

Program Committee Members:

Hailong Cao, *Harbin Institute of Technology*
Baobao Chang, *Peking University*
Yidong Chen, *Xiamen University*
Guohong Fu, *Heilongjiang University*
Yanqing He, *Institute of Scientific and Technical Information of China*
Hongying Zang, *Zhengzhou University*
Yuexian Hou, *Tianjin University*
Xuanjing Huang, *Fudan University*
Shujian Huang, *Nanjing University*
Wenbin Jiang, *Institute of Computing Technology, Chinese Academy of Sciences*
Sujian Li, *Peking University*
Yang Liu, *Tsinghua University*
Zhiyuan Liu, *Tsinghua University*
Haoliang Qi, *Heilongjiang Institute of Technology (HIT)*
Bing Qin, *Harbin Institute of Technology*
LikunQiu, *Ludong University*
Weiguang Qu, *Nanjing Normal University*
Yanqiu Shao, *Beijing Language and Culture University*
Xiaodong Shi, *Xiamen University*
Wei Song, *Capital Normal University*
Jinsong Su, *Xiamen University*
Xiaojie Wang, *Beijing University of Posts and Telecommunications*
Houfeng Wang, *Peking University*
Bin Wang, *Institute of Computing Technology, Chinese Academy of Sciences*
Mingwen Wang, *Jiangxi Normal University*
Zhimin Wang, *Beijing City University*
Ting Wang, *The National University of Defense Technology*
Yunfang Wu, *Peking University*
Yunqing Xia, *Tsinghua University*
Tong Xiao, *Northeastern University*
Xiaobing Zhao, *Inner Mongolia Normal University*
Jun Xie, *Institute of Computing Technology, Chinese Academy of Sciences*
DeyiXiong, *Soochow University*
Jinan Xu, *Beijing Jiaotong University*
Zhiming Xu, *Harbin Institute of Technology*
Ruifeng Xu, *Harbin Institute of Technology*
EndongXun, *Beijing Language and Culture University*

Erhong Yang, *Beijing Language and Culture University*
Muyun Yang, *Harbin Institute of Technology*
Tianfang Yao, *Shanghai Jiao Tong University*
Hong Yu, *Soochow University*
Weidong Zhan, *Peking University*
Jiajun Zhang, *Institute of Automation, Chinese Academy of Sciences*
Quan Zhang, *Institute of Acoustics, Chinese Academy of Sciences*
Min Zhang, *Tsinghua University*
HuaRui Zhang, *Peking University*
Zhichang Zhang, *Northwest Normal University*
Dakun Zhang, *Toshiba China*
Yujie Zhang, *Beijing Jiaotong University*
Yu Zhang, *Harbin Institute of Technology*
Yangsen Zhang, *Beijing Information Science & Technology University*
Jun Zhao, *Institute of Automation, Chinese Academy of Sciences*
Tiejun Zhao, *Harbin Institute of Technology*
Shiqi Zhao, *Baidu*
Yanyan Zhao, *Harbin Institute of Technology*
Qiang Zhou, *Tsinghua University*
Yu Zhou, *Institute of Automation, Chinese Academy of Sciences*
Jingbo Zhu, *Northeastern University*
Yaohong Jin, *Beijing Normal University*

Bakeoff Chairs:

*Chinese Word Segmentation:

Huiming Duan, *Peking University*
Zhifang Sui, *Peking University*

*Chinese Spelling Check:

Liang-Chih Yu, *Yuan Ze University*
Lung-Hao Lee, *National Taiwan Normal University*
Yuen-Hsien Tseng, *National Taiwan Normal University*
Hsin-HisChen, *National Taiwan Normal University*

*Simplified Chinese Parsing:
Qiang Zhou, *Tsinghua University*

*Personal Attributes Extraction in Chinese Text:
Ruifeng Xu, *Harbin Institute of Technology*
Jian Xu, *The Hong Kong Polytechnic University*

Publications Chair:

Xiangyu Duan, *Soochow University*

Publicity Chair:

Minhui Dong, *Institute for Infocomm Research, Singapore*
Xianpei Han, *Institute of Software, Chinese Academy of Sciences*

Local Arrangements Chair:

Tingting He, *Central China Normal University*

Table of Contents

Conference Program

Saturday, October 20, 2014

8:30–8:40 **Opening Ceremony**

Invited Talks

8:40–9:35

Research on Chinese discourse rhetorical structure representation scheme and corpus annotation
Guodong Zhou

9:30–10:30

The Construction of language Resource and Knowledge Base for Chinese Language Computing
Zhifang Sui

Research Papers

10:45–11:10

COV Model and its Application in Chinese Part-of-Speech Tagging
Xing Fukun and Song Rou

11:10–11:35

Maximum Entropy for Chinese Comma Classification with Rich Linguistic Features
Xiaojuan Li, Hua Yang and JiangPing Huang

Saturday, October 20, 2014 (continued)

11:35–12:00

Improving Bilingual Lexicon Extraction Performance from Comparable Corpora via Optimizing Translation Candidate Lists
Shaoqi Wang, Miao Li, Zede Zhu, Zhenxin Yang and Shizhuang Weng

13:30–13:55

Ch2R: A Chinese Chatter Robot for Online Shopping Guide
Peijie Huang, Xianmao Lin, Zeqi Lian, De Yang, Xiaoling Tang, Li Huang, Qiang Huang, Xiupeng Wu, Guisheng Wu and Xinrui Zhang

13:55–14:20

Improving Chinese Sentence Polarity Classification via Opinion Paraphrasing
Guohong Fu, Yu He, Jiaying Song and Chaoyue Wang

14:20–14:45

Problematic Situation Analysis and Automatic Recognition for Chinese Online Conversational System
Yang Xiang, Yaoyun Zhang, Xiaoqiang Zhou, Xiaolong Wang and Yang Qin

Saturday, October 20, 2014 (continued)

14:45–15:10

Segment-based Fine-grained Emotion Detection for Chinese Text
Odbal and Zengfu Wang

15:35–16:00

Bilingual Product Name Dictionary Construction Using a Two Stage Method
Yatian Shen and Xuanjing Huang

16:00–16:25

Local Phrase Reordering Model for Chinese-English Patent Machine Translation
Xiaodie Liu, Yun Zhu and Yaohong Jin

Saturday, October 20, 2014 (continued)

16:25–16:50

Sentence Alignment of Historical Classics based on Mode Prediction and Term Translation Pairs
Chao Che and Xiaojun Zheng

Sunday, October 21, 2014

Bake-off Session 1 : Chinese Word Segmentation

8:40–9:05

The CIPS-SIGHAN CLP 2014 Chinese Word Segmentation Bake-off
Huiming Duan, Zhifang Sui and Tao Ge

9:05–9:30

Word Segmenter for Chinese Micro-blogging Text Segmentation – Report for CIPS-SIGHAN'2014 Bakeoff
Lu Xiang, Xiaoqing Li and Yu Zhou

9:30–9:55

Leveraging Rich Linguistic Features for Cross-domain Chinese Segmentation
Guohua Wu, Dezhu He, Keli Zhong, Xue Zhou and Caixia Yuan

Sunday, October 21, 2014 (continued)

Bake-off Session 2 : Personal Attributes Extraction in Chinese Text Task

9:55–10:20

Personal Attributes Extraction in Chinese Text Bakeoff in CLP 2014: Overview
Ruifeng Xu, Shuai Wang, Feng Shi and Jian Xu

10:40–11:05

Personal Attributes Extraction Based on the Combination of Trigger Words, Dictionary and Rules
Kailun Zhang, Mingyin Wang, Xiaoyue Cong, Fang Huang, Hongfa Xue, Lei Li and Zhiqiao Gao

13:30–13:55

An Introduction to BLCU Personal Attributes Extraction System
Dong YU, Cheng YU, Qin QU, Gongbo TANG, Chunhua LIU, Yue TIAN and Jing YI

Bake-off Session 3 : Chinese Spelling Check Task

Sunday, October 21, 2014 (continued)

16:00–16:25

Generative CCG Parsing with OOV Prediction
Huijia Wu

Bake-off Poster

11:05–12:05

An Improved Graph Model for Chinese Spell Checking
Yang Xin, Hai Zhao, Yuzhu Wang and Zhongye Jia

Introduction to NJUPT Chinese Spelling Check Systems in CLP-2014 Bakeoff
Lei Gu, Yong Wang and Xitao Liang

Chinese Spelling Check System Based on Tri-gram Model
Qiang Huang, Peijie Huang, Xinrui Zhang, Weijian Xie, Kaiduo Hong, Bingzhou Chen and Lei Huang

Introduction to BIT Chinese Spelling Correction System at CLP 2014 Bake-off
Min Liu, Ping Jian and Heyan Huang

A mixed approach for Chinese word segmentation
Zhen Wang

Extraction system for Personal Attributes Extraction of CLP2014
Zhen Wang

A Study on Personal Attributes Extraction Based on the Combination of Sentences Classifications and Rules
Nan-chang Cheng, Cheng-qing Zong, Min Hou and Yong-lin Teng

Chinese Spell Checking Based on Noisy Channel Model
Hsun-wen Chiu, Jian-cheng Wu and Jason S. Chang

Sunday, October 21, 2014 (continued)

Research on Chinese discourse rhetorical structure representation scheme and corpus annotation

Guodong Zhou
Soochow University, China
gdzhou@suda.edu.cn

Abstract: It is well-known that interpretation of a text requires understanding of its rhetorical relation hierarchy since discourse units rarely exist in isolation. Such discourse structure is fundamental to document-level applications, such as text understanding, summarization, knowledge extraction and question-answering. In comparison with English, there are only a few studies on Chinese discourse analysis, due to the lack of appropriate theories to Chinese discourse structure representation and large-scale well-accepted corpora. In this talk, I will present a novel discourse structure representation scheme for Chinese, called Connective-driven Dependency Tree (CDT), and describe our adventure in corpus annotation of the Chinese Discourse Treebank (CDTB) of 500 documents, using a top-down strategy to keep consistent with Chinese native's cognitive habit.

BIO: Zhou Guodong received the Ph.D. degree in computer science from the National University of Singapore in 1999. He joined the Institute for Infocomm Research, Singapore, in 1999, and had been an associate scientist, scientist and associate lead scientist at the institute until August 2006. Currently, he is a distinguished professor at the School of Computer Science and Technology, Soochow University, Suzhou, China. His research interests include natural language processing, information extraction and machine learning. Currently, he is an associate editor of ACM Transaction on Asian Language Information Processing(2010.07-2016.06), an editorial member of Journal of Software (Chinese)(2012.01-2014.12) and a vice chair of Technical Committees on Chinese Information/China Computer Federation(2010.12-2016.12), Computational Linguistics/Chinese Information Processing Society of China and Natural Language Understanding/Artificial Intelligence Society of China. Besides, he had been a member of the Editorial Board of Computational Linguistics (2010.01-2012.12).

Proceedings of the Third CIPS-SIGHAN Joint Conference on Chinese Language Processing, page 1,
Wuhan, China, 20-21 October 2014

The Construction of language Resource and Knowledge Base for Chinese Language Computing

Zhifang Sui
Peking University, China
szf@pku.edu.cn

Abstract: With the urgent needs of enhancing the intelligence of the internet, Knowledge engineering is attracting high attention from both industry and academia. Different from the knowledge engineering (such as Dbpedia, Knowledge Graph, YAGO, etc.) based on structured knowledge resources, the task of textual knowledge engineering is to mine knowledge from unstructured natural language texts. One of the critical problems is, there is gap between the shallow structures expressed by natural languages and the deep structures in conceptual knowledge. In this talk we will introduce the building of the multi-level annotated Chinese language resource, the ontology engineering based on encyclopedias and the Web, and the construction of the mapping resource between conceptual relations and their natural language expressions to link linguistic knowledge and the world knowledge together. The ultimate goal is to lay resource foundation for Chinese language computing in the Web scale.

BIO: Zhifang Sui, Professor of Institute of Computational Linguistics, Peking University. Her research focuses on computational linguistics, text mining and knowledge engineering. She has won the National Prize for Progress in Science and Technology for the comprehensive language knowledge base in 2011. Her work is supported by several grants from NSFC and National Key Basic Research Program of China etc.

Proceedings of the Third CIPS-SIGHAN Joint Conference on Chinese Language Processing, page 2,
Wuhan, China, 20-21 October 2014

COV Model and its Application in Chinese Part-of-Speech Tagging

Xing Fukun
Luoyang Foreign Languages University
471003 Henan
xingfukun@126.com

Song Rou
Beijing Language and Cultural
University 100086 Beijing
songrou@126.com

Abstract

This article presents a new sequence labeling model named Context OVerlapping (COV) model, which expands observation from single word to n-gram unit and there is an overlapping part between the neighboring units. Due to the co-occurrence constraint and transition constraint, COV model reduces the search space and improves tagging accuracy. The 2-gram COV is applied to Chinese PoS tagging and the precision rate of the open test is as high as 96.83%, which is higher than the second order HMM, which is 95.73%. The result is also comparable to the discriminative models but COV takes much less training time than them. With symbol decoding COV prunes many nodes before statistics decoding and the search space of COV is about10-20% less than that of HMM.

1 Introduction

Part of Speech (PoS) can provide much useful information for most natural language processing tasks such as word sense disambiguation, chunk detection, sentence parsing, speech synthesis, machine translation and so on. Therefore lots of efforts have been made to build effective and robust models for automatic PoS tagging. According to Doug Cutting (1992), a practical PoS tagger should be "robust, efficient, accurate, tunable and reusable". With regard to efficiency the basic requirement for a PoS tagger is that training and test time should not be too long. And for a robust tagger the tagging accuracy should be as high as possible and can well deal with the sparseness data.

Most of the approaches to PoS tagging can be divided into two main classes, rule-based and statistics-based approach. In rule-based approaches, words are assigned tags based on a set of rules and a lexicon. These rules can either be manually crafted, or learned, as in the transformation-based error-driven approach of Brill (1995).

In the statistics-based approaches HMM is the representative of generative models and is widely used in PoS tagging (Church, 1988; Cutting et al. 1992; Thede & Harper 1999, Huang et al. 2007, etc.) .

Maximum Entropy model and Conditional Random Fields (CRFs) model are the representatives of discriminative models and are also applied in PoS tagging. Thanks to the flexibility of features selection these discriminative models achieve higher precision rates than the generative models in PoS tagging (Adwait, 1996; Lafferty, 2001 etc.). But the training of discriminative models is

Proceedings of the Third CIPS-SIGHAN Joint Conference on Chinese Language Processing, pages 3–10,
Wuhan, China, 20-21 October 2014

time-consuming and requires high-quality computer processing power, which affects their applications in the real tasks.

Concerning all the characteristics of generative and discriminative models, we proposed a new model on the basis of HMM. The new model expand the observation from one single word to n-gram unit and between the neighboring units there is an n-1 gram part, which is shared by the neighboring units. So the new model is called Context OVerlapping (COV) model.

COV is a general sequence labeling model and has been applied to Chinese and English PoS tagging tasks. In these tasks COV achieves better performance than HMM and its performance is comparable to the discriminative models. Meanwhile its training time is much less than the discriminative models, which makes the model more efficient and robust in the real tasks.

The structure of the article is that: the first part will briefly introduce PoS tagging, in the second part we will introduce COV model. The third part will compare COV with HMM. The fourth part will address how to estimate parameters and handle sparseness data. The fifth part is about the algorithm of symbol decoding. The sixth part is about evaluation criteria and the seventh part presents the experiments and results. The final part is some discussions and future work to do.

2 COV Model

COV model is based on HMM. HMM is a form of generative model, that defines a joint probability distribution p(X,Y) where X and Y are random variables respectively ranging over observation sequences and their corresponding state sequences. In order to define a joint distribution, generative models must enumerate all possible observation sequences. For most domains, it is intractable unless observation elements are represented as isolated units, independent from the other elements in an observation sequence. More precisely, the observation element at any given time may only directly depend on the state at that time. This is an appropriate assumption for a few simple data sets, however most real-world observation sequences such as sentences are best represented in terms of multiple interacting features and even long-range dependencies between observation elements. Due to the observation independence assumption the performance of HMM is limited in PoS tagging. For example, here are 2 Chinese sentences:

(1) 市长/n 强调/v 深入/v a 细致/a 的/u 工作/vn 作风/n

(The mayor put emphasis on the careful working style.)

(2) 市长/n 要/v 深入/v a 困难/a 的/u 群众/n 中间/f

(The mayor should care about those people in troubles.)

For the convenience of analysis we assume that in each sentence only “深入”(careful or care) has two parts of speech, adjective (a) or verb (v), and other words only have one PoS. If we use the first-order HMM model to predict the PoS of “深入” the prediction will be like:

$$\hat{Q}_1 = \arg\max_{X\{a,v\}} p(n)p(v|n)p(X|v)p(a|X)$$
$$p(u|a)p(vn|u)p(n|vn)p(\text{市长}|n)p(\text{强调}|v)$$
$$p(\text{深入}|X)p(\text{细致}|a)p(\text{的}|a)p(\text{工作}|vn)$$
$$p(\text{作风}|n)$$

$\hat{Q}_1$ denotes the state sequence of sentence (1) and X denotes the possible state of “深入”. For only “深入” is ambiguous and other words all have only one PoS, the formula can be simplified as:

$$\hat{Q}_1 = \arg\max_{X\{a,v\}} p(X|v)p(a|X)p(\text{深入}|X)$$

And as same as sentence (1) we can get the prediction formula of sentence (2) as:

$$\hat{Q}_2 = \arg\max_{X\{a,v\}} p(X \mid v)p(a \mid X)p(深入 \mid X)$$

Comparing the two formulae, we find that $\hat{Q}_1$ and $\hat{Q}_2$ are the same, which means that HMM tagger will not distinguish between the different PoSs of "深入" in the two sentences. In fact "深入" in sentence (1) is an adjective and in sentence (2) is a verb. So HMM must make one mistake either in sentence (1) or sentence (2). The mistake shows the limitation of HMM in PoS tagging.

In order to overcome the shortcomings of observation independence assumption of HMM and combine more context information into the model, COV model is proposed in this paper. The formalism of 2-gram COV is as follows and the formalisms of other n-gram COV (n>2) models can be gotten according to the 2-gram model.

In the 2-gram COV there is a basic state set $Q = \{q_1, q_2, ... q_s\}$. The observation sequence is S= $w_1 ... w_h$. The corresponding state of a 2-gram observation unit $w_{i-1}w_i$ (2≤i≤h) is a state set $e_i = \{q_{i-1}^j q_i^j\}$, in which q_{i-1}^j is one of the basic states of w_{i-1} and q_i^j is one of the basic states of w_i. The state sequence $q_{i-1}^j q_i^j$ is called one state unit of the observation unit $w_{i-1}w_i$. It is notable that e_i is the state set when the word w_{i-1} and w_i co-occur, which is called Co-occurrence Constraint(CC). When w_{i-1} and w_i co-occur the amount of possible states of $w_{i-1}w_i$ will not be more than the amount of the combination of states of w_{i-1} and w_i.

The search for the state sequence with the highest joint probability can be computed like:

$$\hat{Q} = \arg\max P(Q \mid S) =$$

$$\arg\max P(Q)P(S \mid Q) \approx$$

$$\arg\max_{q_{i-1},q_i}(p(q_1)p(q_2 \mid q_1)\prod_{i=3}^{h} p(q_{i-1}q_i \mid q_{i-2}q_{i-1})$$

$$p(o_1 \mid q_1)\prod_{i=2}^{h} p(o_{i-1}o_i \mid q_{i-1}q_i))$$

Q denotes the state sequence and S denotes the observation sequence. $\hat{Q}$ denotes the final state sequence, whose joint probability is the highest.

For the convenience of computation, we insert 2 "*B*", whose state is "B" at the beginning of the sequence and insert 2 "*E* ", whose state is "E" at the end of the sequence. And then the above formula will be:

$$\hat{Q} = \arg\max_{q_{i-1},q_i}(\prod_{i=1}^{h+2} p(q_{i-1}q_i \mid q_{i-2}q_{i-1})$$

$$\prod_{i=1}^{h+2} p(o_{i-1}o_i \mid q_{i-1}q_i))$$

In this model there is an overlapping part between the neighboring observation units $w_{i-2}w_{i-1}$ and $w_{i-1}w_i$. For w_{i-1} is shared by the neighboring units, the corresponding states units of $w_{i-2}w_{i-1}$ and $w_{i-1}w_i$ should also share the same overlapping state. If $q_{i-2}^k q_{i-1}^k$ is one state of $w_{i-2}w_{i-1}$ and $q_{i-1}^j q_i^j$ is one state of $w_{i-1}w_i$, then only if q_{i-1}^k is the same as q_{i-1}^j then it is possible to transmit from state $q_{i-2}^k q_{i-1}^k$ to $q_{i-1}^j q_i^j$, otherwise there is no transition path from $q_{i-2}^k q_{i-1}^k$ to $q_{i-1}^j q_i^j$. The constraint $q_{i-1}^k = q_{i-1}^j$ is called Transition Constraint (TC).

$\hat{Q}$ is a sequence consisting of h+1 2-gram state units like:

$$B\hat{q}_1, \hat{q}_1\hat{q}_2, \hat{q}_2\hat{q}_3, ..., \hat{q}_{h-1}\hat{q}_h, \hat{q}_h E$$

($\hat{q}_i \in Q$)

It is obvious that the final state sequence can be gotten from the above sequence.

3 Comparisons between COV and HMM

There are 3 different points between COV and HMM.

First, in the nth HMM if each observation has k states and then the amount of the history states will be k^n. But in the n-gram COV the amount of the history states will usually be smaller than k^n because of the Constraint of Co-occurrence. And then the search space of COV will also be smaller than HMM.

Second, in the nth order HMM the emission probability of q_t to o_t is only P($o_t | q_t$). But in the n-gram COV, there are n emission probabilities relevant to q_t and o_t, which are P($o_{t-n+1} \cdots o_t$ | $q_{t-n+1} \cdots q_t$), … , P($o_t \cdots o_{t+n-1} | q_t \cdots q_{t+n-1}$) . For all of these emission probabilities are related to q_t and o_t, these observation units will make constraints on the possible state units.

Third, in the nth order HMM the transition probability from the history state to the current state is P($q_i | q_{i-n}, \cdots q_{i-1}$). But in the n-gram COV the transition path must obey TC, which requires the overlapping part of the neighboring state units must be the same. If the neighboring state units obey TC the transition probability is the same as that in nth order HMM. If the neighboring state units don't obey TC there will be no transition path between them. With TC a great amount of paths are pruned, which makes the search space reduced.

Here is an example to illustrate the lattice building and tagging process by 2-gram COV. In particular, this example needn't any probability computation and can get the final state sequence just with symbol comparing.

1	2	3	4	5
B-*B*	*B*-领导	领导-强调	强调-深入	深入-细致
B-B	B-n	n-v	v-a	a-a
	B-vn		v-ad	ad-ad
	B-v			

6	7	8	9	10
细致-的	的-工作	工作-作风	作风-*E*	*E*-*E*
a-u	u-v	vn-n	n-E	E-E
	u-n			
	u-vn			

Table 1: An example to illustrate COV tagging process (For the space limitation the table is split to two)

In the above table each column is a 2-gram observation unit and the neighboring units share an overlapping part. For example, unit 2 is "*B*-领导"（*B*-leader） and unit 3 is "领导-强调"（leader-emphasizes）, "领导"（leader） is the overlapping part between unit 2 and unit 3. Unit 2 has 3 possible state units, which are "B-n, B-vn, B-v", and unit 3 has only one possible state unit, which is "n-v". With Transition Constraint only if the overlapping part of state unit 2 and state unit 3 is the same there can be a transition path. So in the state units of unit 2 only "B-n" is remained and the state units "B-vn" and "B-v" are all eliminated for their overlapping parts (vn and v) are not the same as the overlapping part of state unit 3 (n). The shadowed grids in the table are all the impossible states and are eliminated. In this example after the symbol comparing and elimination there remains only one path for the sentence and the path is the final tagging result. So this sentence is tagged without any probability computation but only with the symbol comparing. The process of symbol comparing and elimination is called symbol decoding.

Most times there may be more than one possible paths remained after symbol decoding and then the Viterbi algorithm will be applied to get the best tagging sequence. Although HMM also applies Viterbi for decoding, the search space of HMM is bigger than that of COV because COV has eliminated many impossible states in the step of symbol decoding.

4 Parameters estimation and strategy of handling sparseness data

There are 2 main parameters to be estimated in COV:

(1) P_t :State transition probability;

(2) P_e :State emission probability.

We apply the maximum likelihood to estimate these parameters from the tagged corpus. The details of the estimation will not be introduced here.

For the expansion of the observation the sparseness problem in n-gram COV is more serious than that in HMM. COV applies back-off strategy to deal with the sparseness data. The main idea is that if n-gram (n>2) $w_{i-n+1}...w_i$ is not in the n-gram vocabulary, which is gotten from the training corpus, it will be replaced by n-1 gram $w_{i-n+2}...w_i$. And if $w_{i-1}w_i$ is not in the 2-gram vocabulary then the state units of $w_{i-1}w_i$ will be replaced by the combination of states of w_{i-1} and w_i. If w_i is not in the unigram vocabulary it will be handled as same as in HMM.

5 Tagging Procedures and Decoding Algorithm

The main procedures of COV tagging is described in the following flow diagram.

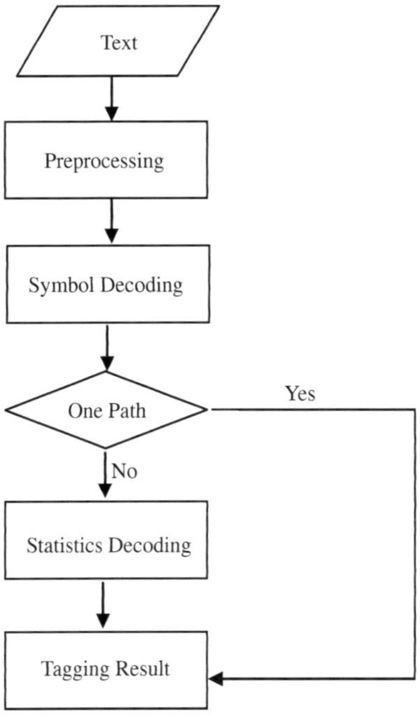

Figure 1: Flow diagram of PoS tagging by COV

There are two steps of decoding in PoS tagging by COV:

(1) Symbol decoding

(2) Statistics decoding

Statistics decoding applies Viterbi algorithm, which is explained in detail by Rabiner (1989) and will not be repeated here.

Here we will describe the symbol decoding algorithm in detail. First we define the suffix and prefix of a state sequence:

Suffix of $q_{i-n+1}...q_i$ is defined as $q_{i-n+2}...q_i$

Prefix of $q_{i-n+1}...q_i$ is defined as $q_{i-n+1}...q_{i-1}$

The symbol decoding algorithm is as follows:

Input: word sequence S=$w_0...w_h$ and all the possible state units of each n-gram unit

---

(1) Comparing the neighboring n-gram state units from left to right.

For any given neighboring observation units $s_{i-1} = w_{i-n}...w_{i-1}$ and $s_i = w_{i-n+1}...w_i$, they have the corresponding state unit sets e_{i-1} and e_i. And each state unit in the set is called state node.

For each node E_{i-1} in the state set of e_{i-1}, a comparison is made between the suffix of E_{i-1} and the prefix of the node E_i in e_i. If they are the same then a parent-child relation is built between the neighboring nodes E_{i-1} and E_i.

If node E_i in e_i has no parent node in e_{i-1} then E_i will be eliminated and if node E_{i-1} in e_{i-1} has no child node in e_i, E_{i-1} will also be eliminated.

(2) Backward from right to left

A. If a node E_{i-1} is eliminated in step (1) for it doesn't have any child node in e_i, then the relation between E_{i-1} and its parent node E_{i-2} will also be eliminated.

B. If the parent-child relation between E_{i-2} and E_{i-1} is eliminated in step A and E_{i-2} doesn't have any child node then E_{i-2} will also be eliminated.

Backward to the left end of the sequence and the process of symbol decoding finishes.

Table 2 Symbol Decoding Algorithm

After symbol decoding the remaining nodes construct a node lattice. If there is only one path from left to right in the lattice then decoding finishes and the state sequence is output. Otherwise Viterbi algorithm is used to calculate and select the most probable path.

6 Evaluation Criteria

We use the following criteria to evaluate the performances of COV.

(1) P_A: Overall precision rate

(2) P_M: Precision rate of the multi-class words,

(3)P_O: Precision rate of OOV (Out Of Vocabulary), not including the personal names, location names and organization names, etc.

(4) P_E: Error reduction rate, comparing with the baseline model.

All the above criteria have been introduced in Kupiec (1992) and Cutting (1992) etc and will not be repeated here.

(5) P_S : State certainty rate

In order to measure the statistics decoding complexity, we define State certainty rate P_S.

$$P_S = \frac{count(Total\_State\_Nodes)}{count(Observations)}$$

Count(Total_State_Nodes) denotes the total number of possible states for all the observations in statistics decoding. Due to the symbol decoding many states have been pruned in COV and the search space for statistics decoding is reduced accordingly. The level of search space reduction can be indicated by the criteria of P_s.

7 Experiments

7.1 Corpus and Preprocessing

The training and test data are all taken from the People's Daily of 2000 year, which has been segmented and manually assigned PoS tags by the Peking university. The division of corpus is as follows:

Group	Usage of corpus	Months	Amount of tokens
1	Training	Feb.	1050934
2		Feb.-June.	6142402
3	Open Test	Jan.	1235628
4	Close Test	Feb.	1050934

Table 3 Division of corpus

The baseline model is the 2nd order HMM, whose results will be compared with that of 2-gram COV.

Before training and tagging the corpus is preprocessed. All the named entities such as personal names, location names, organization names and all the digits are replaced by some particular symbols. For example, personal names are all replaced by "*PerN*".

7.2 Results

	P_A	P_M
2nd order HMM	96.54%	92.76%
2-gram COV	98.29%	96.44%
P_E	50.58%	50.83%

Table 4: Results of the close test.

Corpus of group 2 in table 3 is used as the training corpus.

	Group 1	Group 2
2nd order HMM	94.63%	95.73%
2-gram COV	95.53%	96.79%
3-gram COV	95.63%	96.83%

Table 5: P_A of HMM, 2-gram and 3-gram COV in open test.

The corpus of Group 1 and 2 are used as training corpus.

The above results show that 2-gram and 3-gram COV all outperform second order HMM. And 3-gram COV outperforms 2-gram COV, which indicates that with the expansion of observation the precision rate of COV will not decline but increase.

	Group 1	Group 2
2nd order HMM	90.75%	92.02%
2-gram COV	92.66%	94.24%
P_E	20.64%	27.85%

Table 6: P_M of HMM and COV in open test.

The result shows that COV has a better performance in tagging multi-class words than

HMM.

	Group 1	Group 2
HMM	53.21%	55.07%
COV(2-gram)	92.24%	93.99%
COV (unigram)	53.27%	55.35%

Table 7: P_O of HMM and COV

With regard to the 2-gram OOV, the OOV precision rate of COV is higher than 90%, which indicates that COV can well deal with the OOV problem when the observation unit is expanded.

We have done some experiments to compare the time cost and precision rate among HMM, COV and discriminative models such as MaxEnt and CRFs. For the limitation of computer processing power, we choose the People's Daily of January, 2000 as the training data and the first 5000 paragraphs of the People's Daily of February , 2000 as test data. The taggers are the MaxEnt tagger developed by Standford University and CRF++.

	HMM	COV	MaxEnt	CRF 1	CRF 2
Training time	1mins	2mins	4.6hrs	63hrs	60 hrs
Test time	4mins	8mins	11mins	17mins	11mins
P_A	94.23 %	95.43 %	95.69%	95.67 %	95.80 %

Table 8: Training, test time and PA of different models

The template of MaxEnt is: w-1, w0, w+1, prefix of w0, suffix of w0, length of w0

The template of CRF1 is: w-1, w0, w+1, prefix of w0

The template of CRF2 is: w-1, w0, w+1, prefix of w0, suffix of w0, length of w0

The above data show that the precision rate of COV is higher than HMM, and comparable to the discriminative models. Moreover, training time of COV is much less than the discriminative models and almost at the same level as HMM. High precision rate and low time cost makes COV more competitive and practical than other models.

Training Group	HMM	COV	Reduction of Ps	Reduction rate of Ps
1	1.79	1.66	0.14	7.82%
2	2.03	1.57	0.46	22.66%

Table 9: Ps of 2nd order HMM and 2-gram COV

The above result shows that the search space in statistics decoding of COV is smaller than HMM.

We also count the tokens which can be tagged with symbol decoding.

Training Group	Tokens of Symbol Decoding	Percentage of Symbol Decoding	P_A
1	86187	6.98%	99.24%
2	92174	7.46%	99.42%

Table 10: Results of symbol decoding

The total tokens of test corpus is 1235631.

The above data shows that there are about 7% tokens which can be tagged with symbol decoding and without any probability computation. Moreover, the precision rate of symbol decoding is above 99%, which is much higher than the average precision rate.

The smaller search space and higher precision rate proves the efficiency and robustness of COV in PoS tagging.

We also conducted some experiments of English PoS tagging. The training and test data are from the Wall Street Journal (WSJ) in Penn Tree Bank. We use the texts of group 00 to 19 in WSJ as training data and group 00 to 04 as close test data and group 23 to 24 as open test data. The baseline model is also the 2nd order HMM. Results are as follows.

	P_A of	P_A of	P_M of	P_M of

	HMM	COV	HMM	COV
Close Test	97.85%	98.29%	94.85%	96.44%
Open Test	96.48%	96.79%	93.92%	95.18%

Table 11 Results of English PoS tagging Experiments

The above results show that COV also outperforms HMM in English PoS tagging.

8 Discussion

COV is not only suitable to PoS tagging task. We have applied it to the Chinese word segmentation, sentence boundary detection and chunk detection, in which COV also achieves satisfactory results. COV is not limited to the certain language but can be applied in the tagging tasks of different languages. Comparing with HMM, COV has the advantages of smaller search space and higher tagging precision rate. Comparing with the discriminative models, COV has the advantages of less training time and comparable precision rate. All of these prove that COV is a general, efficient and robust model for sequence labeling.

Meanwhile we also find that it is difficult for COV to combine more context and lexical features as discriminative models can do. For example, COV has not taken the suffix or prefix of a word into the model. In fact such information is important for guessing the PoS of unknown words. In the future we will make efforts to take more context and lexical information into the model and improve its performance.

References

L. Rabiner. 1989. A Tutorial on Hidden Markov Models and Selected Applications in Speech Recognition, Proc. of the IEEE, 77(2).

Church, K. 1988. A stochastic parts program and noun phrase parser for unrestricted text. Proceedings of Second ACL Applied NLP, 136-143.

Scott M. Thede, Mary P. Harper. 1999. Second-order hidden Markov model for part-of-speech tagging. In ACL 37, 175–182.

Eric Brill. 1995. Transformation-based error-driven learning and natural language processing: A case study in part of speech tagging. Computational Linguistics, 21(4):543-565.

Julian Kupiec. 1992. Robust part-of-speech tagging using a hidden Markov model. Computer Speech and Language, 6(3):225-242.

Adwait Ratnaparkhi. 1996. A maximum entropy model for part-of-speech tagging. Proceedings of the Conference on Empirical Methods in Natural Language Processing, pages 133-142.

Doug Cutting, Julian Kupiec, Jan Pedersen, and Penelope Sibun. 1992. A practical part-of-speech tagger. In Proceedings of the 3rd Conference on Applied Natural Language Processing (ACL), pages 133-140.

Scott M. Thede and Mary P. Harper. 1999. A second-order hidden Markov model for part-of-speech tagging. In ACL, pages 175–182.

J. Lafferty, A. McCallum, and F. Pereira. 2001. Conditional random fields: Probabilistic models for segmenting and labeling sequence data. In Proceedings of ICML-01, pages 282-289.

Zhongqiang Huang , Mary P. Harper , Wen Wang. 2007. Mandarin Part-of-Speech Tagging and Discriminative Reranking. In Proceedings of the 2007 Joint Conference on Empirical Methods in Natural Language Processing and Computational Natural Language Learning, pp. 1093–1102.

Maximum Entropy for Chinese Comma Classification with Rich Linguistic Features

Xiaojuan Li
School of Mathematics and Computer Science, Guizhou Normal University
596025763@qq.com

Hua Yang*
School of Mathematics and Computer Science, Guizhou Normal University
College of Chinese Language and Literature, Wuhan University
yanghuastory@foxmail.com

JiangPing Huang
School of Computer, Wuhan University
hjp@whu.edu.cn

Abstract

Discourse relation is an important content of discourse semantic analysis, and the study of punctuation is of importance for discourse relation. In this paper, we propose a method of Chinese comma classification based on maximum entropy (ME). This method classifies the sentence relation based on comma with ME by extracting rich linguistic features before and after the commas in sentences. Experimental results show that this method of sentence relation based on comma is feasible.

1 Introduction

Discourse consists of word, phrase, sentence and sentence group, also known as text or utterance. Discourse relation studies the intrinsic structure of natural language text and understands the semantic relation between the text units, which plays a vital role in language understanding and natural language generation, is a challenge and difficult research hotspot in recent years((Li Yan-cui et al.,2013). Discourse relation is a fundamental work in the research of discourse analysis. Discourse relation means the logical semantic relation, between two text unit (section, clause, sentence, sentence group, paragraphs, etc.) in one discourse, such as coordinative relation, progressive relation, adversative relation (Sun Jing et al., 2014), etc. Defining a hierarchical semantic relationship type system to extend sentence semantic analysis results in that discourse level of semantic information become one of the important ways to solve the discourse semantic analysis, which is benefit to many NLP tasks such as automatic summarization, automatic question answering and machine translation (Zhang Mu-yu et al., 2013).

The commas separates a sentence into two parts, each part is called an argument of the sentence. Discourse relation can be generally classified into explicit relation and implicit relation. Explicit relation recognition is to identify the logical relationship between two arguments in the presence of conjunctions (Sun Jing et al., 2014) while implicit relation recognition is to identify the logical relationship without the presence of conjunctions. Example 1 exemplifies the explicit relation of coordination with the conjunction word "并(and)", and example 2 exemplifies the implicit relation of coordination in the absence of "并(and)", in which conjunction does not appear. For the implicit relation recognition, the absence of conjunction entails methods that can deduce the semantic type from other features in the context before and/or after commas. In previous researches, explicit relation recognition often has a higher precision only based on conjunction, while implicit relation recognition is much more difficult than explicit relation recognition. Some additional information is gradually introduced in addition to lexical features (Zhang Mu-yu et al., 2013).

eg. 1：跳水选手已全部抵达罗马，**并**开始赛前训练。

"All divers have arrived in Rome, and start training before the game."

eg. 2：中国的稳定和发展有利于世界的和平与发展，中国的繁荣与稳定是澳门繁荣与稳定的根本保证。

"China's stability and development are conducive to world's peace and development, China's prosperity and stability are the fundamental guarantee of Macro's prosperity and stability."

Most researches about discourse relation recognition are mainly for English. Although there are some Chinese-oriented research (Jin Mei-xun et al., 2004; Xu Sheng-qin and Li Pei-feng, 2013; Yang ya-qin and Xue Nianwen, 2012), they are mainly concentrated on the analysis and corpus annotation, rarely involving discourse relation recognition; and existing research mostly directly used the English discourse relation system, ignoring the linguistic characteristics of Chinese language itself.

According to the classification of compound sentence theories (Xing Fu-yi, 2001; Lv Shuxiang and

Proceedings of the Third CIPS-SIGHAN Joint Conference on Chinese Language Processing, pages 11–17,
Wuhan, China, 20-21 October 2014

Zhu De-xi, 1952; Shao Jing-min, 2007), in this paper, we propose 9 categories of Chinese comma classification for sentence relation, including Coordination(并列), Interpretation(阐释), Location(地点), Progressiveness(递进), Reliance(凭借), Subsequence(顺承), Time(时间), Purpose(目的), Cause and Effect(因果), and classify Chinese comma into these 9 classes with maximum entropy method (ME), the corpus we used is annotated with a well-established representation scheme for Chinese comma, and the features we used are extracted from the corpus that is based on the sentences' words information on both sides of the comma. We carried out the classification experiment on both the explicit relation recognition and the implicit relation recognition respectively consisted of the 9 categories mentioned above.

The rest of the paper is organized as follows. In section 2, we describe the related work about comma classification research. Section 3 introduces the features we used and other features selecting method used in related work. Section 4 reviews ME method and describe the comma classification method based on ME model. In section 5, we present the process of our experiment and evaluate the experimental result. In section 6, we analyze the causes that lead to the main classification error in different aspects. Finally, a conclusion and future work are put forward.

2 Related Work

As elemental segmentation units of discourse, punctuations provide a new clue for discourse analysis. Many researches about punctuation are closely related with many natural language processing tasks, such as long sentences segmentation, elementary discourse unit recognition, the classification of the relationship between sentences, semantic disambiguation, etc. 16 kinds of punctuations are widely used in Chinese, such as comma, period, question mark, etc. With more than 20 different usages, comma is one of the most common punctuations. Chinese comma can be used to separate coordinate composition or coordinate clause of the sentence, or to separate the words, phrases, clauses which indicate time, place, purpose, condition, or to express a pause between the clauses separated by conjunction (Gu Jing-jing and Zhou Guo-dong, 2014), etc. In recent years, with the progress of the research about punctuation, the study of comma classification gradually caught attention.

Jin and Li (Jin Mei-xun et al., 2004) viewed comma as an important role in long Chinese sentence segmentation, they proposed a method for classifying commas in Chinese sentences by their context, then segmented a long sentence according to the classification results. Element discourse unit (EDU) recognition is a fundamental task of discourse analysis and Chinese punctuation is viewed as a elementary delimiter. Xu Sheng-qin and Li Pei-feng (Xu Sheng-qin and Li Pei-feng, 2013) considered Chinese comma to be the boundary of the discourse units and anchor discourse relations between units separated by comma. They classified comma's role into seven major types and implemented automatic disambiguation of the Chinese comma type. Xue and Yang (Xue Nian-wen and Yang Ya-qin, 2011) held that the central problem of Chinese sentence segmentation was comma disambiguation, and in some context it identifies the boundary of a sentence just as a period, a question mark, or an exclamation mark does. Yang and Xue (Yang ya-qin and Xue Nian-wen, 2012) further pointed out that the Chinese comma signifies the boundary of discourse units and also anchors discourse relations between adjacent text spans, and they proposed a discourse structure-oriented classification of the comma that can be automatically extracted from the Chinese Treebank based on syntactic patterns, and use this method to disambiguate the Chinese comma.

In this paper, we propose a method of sentence relation classification based on rich linguistic features around Chinese comma in sentences. We try to find out the difference among sentence relation types by rich linguistic features, which is found by potential semantic rules derived by statistical method, which is of significance especially for the implicit relation recognition.

3 Features Selection

Currently, few research about sentence relation is based on comma. Sun jing (Sun Jing et al., 2014) classified the discourse relation into four categories: cause and effect(因果), coordination(并列), transition(转折), explanation(解说) with maximum entropy, on the basis of utilizing a set of context features, lexical features and dependency tree features extracted from the corpus of Chinese discourse built by themselves. Lin (Lin Zi-heng et al., 2009) implemented an implicit discourse relation classifier and showed initial results based on the recently released Penn Discourse Treebank. The features they used include the modeling of the context of relations, features extracted from constituent parse trees and dependency parse trees, and word pair features. Zheng (Zheng Lue-xing et al., 2013) presented an approach of Chinese coordination relations recognition based on CRFs. They extracted role information according to their functions in the generation of Chinese coordination relations.

We analyze the feature of different types of sentences, refer to the features proposed in the paper of Li Yancui (Li Yan-cui et al., 2013) and Xue (Xue Nian-wen and Yang Ya-qin, 2011), and propose to learn discourse relation rules through linguistic features of the sentences. This method extract linguistic features from both sides of comma in the sentence. Before extracting the features, the following pre-processing is adopted: 1) segment the sentences into words by using the Chinese lexical analysis system (ICTCLAS) designed by institute of computing technology, Chinese academy of sciences; 2) eliminate the extremely precise POS type for the words, which belongs to the same POS on more general level. For example, "nr" expresses name, "ns" expresses place name), and we use "n" to express the noun, "v" to express verb uniformly, etc.

We call the sentence on the left of the comma as argument 1, denoted as "*l*", and call the sentence after the comma as argument 2 and express it with "*r*". Features we selected and their descriptions are shown in table 1.

Table 1 the selected features and their description

	feature	description
1	f1,f1_p	The first word of argument 1 and its part of speech(POS)
2	f2	Conjunction that connects the clauses on both sides of the comma, if no conjunction appear, f2 =null
3	f3	Difference of clause lengths between argument 1 and argument 2, if the length of argument 1 is greater than the argument 2, f3=1, otherwise f3=0
4	f4,f4_p	The first word of argument 2 and its POS
5	f5_l,f5_r	Whether the *l* and *r* contain a conjunction
6	f6,f6_p	The last word of argument 1 and its POS
7	f7	The POS of the first word combination of argument 1 and argument 2(f1_p+f4_p)
8	f8	Combination of the POS of the first word and last word in argument 1(f1_p+f6_p)
9	f9	Let *x* denote whether the first word of *l* is a conjunction, *x=1* if the first word of *l* is a conjunction, else *x =0*. f9 is the combination of *x* and *POS* of the first word of *l*
10	f10	Feature 10 is analogous to f9, while x denotes whether the last word of *l* is a conjunction.
11	f11	Feature 11 is analogous to f9, while x denotes whether the first word of *r* is a conjunction.
12	f12	f12=1 if the first word and the last word of argument 1 constitute a conjunction, else f12=0

Features of case 1 and case 2 mentioned above are as follows.

1：f1=跳水选手, f1p=n, f2=并, f3=1, f4=并, f4p=c, f5l=0, f5r=1, f6=罗马, f6p=n, f7=n+c, f8=n+n, f9=0+n, f10=0+n, f11=1+c, f12=0

2：f1=跳水选手, f1p=n, f2=null, f3=1, f4=开始, f4p=ad, f5l=0, f5r=0, f6=罗马, f6p=n, f7=n+v, f8=n+n, f9=0+n, f10=0+n, f11=1+v, f12=0

4 Maximum Entropy for Comma Classification

Maximum entropy model (ME) method is to select the model with the maximum entropy that meets some constraint conditions. Maximum entropy model can be applied to classification(Li Hang, 2012, Sang Haiyan et al., 2013).

In our implementation, ME model uses the features listed in table1.

Let C be the set of types of the 9 sentence relation classes we have defined, and *S be the* sentence set, we can calculate $p(c_j \mid s_i)$ through maximum entropy model, which means the probability s_i belongs to c_j, where $s_i \in$ S and $c_j \in$ C. For comma classification problem, c_j with $\arg\max p(c_j \mid s_i)$ will be the class that the sentence s_i belongs to.

The comma classification method is similar to text classification method, their basic idea is to use learning set composed of training samples to train a classifier, to test the performance of the classifier with testing samples in testing set, and use the trained classifier to classify new sentences.

5 Experiments and Evaluation

Corpus used in our experiment is rebuilt from part of CTB 5.0. We annotated it with the information of class. The corpus is divided into explicit relation and implicit relation according to whether the sentences contain conjunction. The distribution of the sample set for each class is shown in table 2 .

The eigenvector expressed with features in Table 1 for each sentence in Table 2 is obtained. All the eigenvectors obtained constitute our data set. The data set is divided into training data set and testing data set with the proportion of 80% : 20%, 10-times 10-fold cross-validation policy is employed. All of above prepared, one of the mallet toolkit classifier--maximum entropy (MaxEnt) classifier is adopted to train and test the final model. The experimental results, i.e., classification precisions for all sentence relation class, are shown in table 3.

Table 2 distribution of sentence relationship

number	categories	data	
		explicit	implicit
1	Coordination(BL)	25	24
2	Interpretation(CS)	25	25
3	Location(DD)	25	6
4	Progressiveness(DJ)	25	11
5	Reliance(PJ)	25	10
6	Subsequence(SC)	12	25
7	Time(SJ)	25	24
8	Purpose(MD)	25	6
9	Cause and Effect(YG)	25	25

We conducted several experiments on different training set size and testing set size. Results show that the unbalance of training set size has a significant effect on the experimental results. So we use the same training set size avoid this instability. As can be seen in table 3, results for four relations (Location, Progressiveness, Reliance and Purpose) are absent. The reason for the absence is that the corresponding precision is unreliable due to the sparseness of related samples in training data showed in Table 2. In addition, the precision for implicit relations is significantly lower than that for the explicit relations.

Table 3 experimental results

category of relationship	explicit precision	implicit precision
Coordination(BL)	56.5%	49.7%
Interpretation(CS)	62.4%	47.3%
Location(DD)	84.9%	--
Progressiveness(DJ)	63.2%	--
Reliance(PJ)	71.2%	--
Subsequence(SC)	--	38.9%
Time(SJ)	43.1%	54.2%
Purpose(MD)	55.5%	--
Cause and Effect(YG)	72%	74.1%
ALL	65.2%	50.6%

6 Analysis

Table 4 shows the details of explicit relation classification, which includes the percentage of the samples that are correctly classified and falsely classified into other classes. Each item in Table 4 is the average calculated from 10 times repeated experiment. Table 5 is corresponding result for implicit relation classification.

As can be seen in Table 4 and Table 5, main errors mainly occur as follows:

（1）For explicit relation, Many Location relation and Time relation are falsely classified into each other; Time relation is cline to be classified into Reliance; Purpose relation is classified into Reliance. The reasons for falsely classification for Location and Time is: the first word in argument 1 is preposition in most cases, and the last word in argument 1 means a location expressed as "f" in some cases, as shown in example 3 and example 4; for the relation of Purpose and Reliance, the reason for falsely classification is that the first word in argument 1 is preposition in most cases, as shown in example 5 and example 6 ; for the relation of Time and Reliance, the reason for falsely classification is that the first word in argument 1 is preposition in most cases and their conjunction is composed of the first word and the last word of argument 1, as shown in example 4 and example 6.

Table 4 details for explicit relation classification

	Interpretation	Location	Progressiveness	Reliance	Time	Coordination	Purpose	Cause and Effect
Interpretation	64%	4%	11%	0	0	14%	4%	4%
Location	0	73%	5%	0	14%	0	5%	5%
Progressiveness	15%	7%	56%	0	0	22%	0	0
Reliance	4%	0	0	83%	4%	0	8%	0
Time	0	28%	8%	12%	44%	4%	4%	0
Coordination	12%	0	16%	0	0	64%	8%	0
Purpose	5%	0	0	20%	5%	5%	65%	0
Cause and Effect	0	0	7%	0	0	0	0	93%

Table5 details for implicit relation classification

	Coordination	Interpretation	Subsequence	Time	Cause and Effect
Coordination	12%	23%	35%	31%	0
Interpretation	37%	56%	7%	0	0
Subsequence	0	6%	71%	24%	0
Time	21%	8%	33%	33%	4%
Cause and Effect	0	4%	0	0	96%

eg. 3：**在**今天的比赛**中**，中国国际大师徐俊迎战队友、国际特级大师叶荣光。（地点）

"In today's competition, the Chinese international master Jun xu will meet his teammate who is an international grandmaster Rongguang Ye."

eg. 4：**在**这一巨大的变革**中**，德国成为最大的得益者。（时间）

"In this huge change, Germany is the biggest beneficiary."

eg. 5：**为**解决庞大资金需求，公司正争取发行股票和尝试更多的融资渠道。（目的）

"To solve the large capital demand, the company is seeking to issue shares and try more financing channels."

eg. 6：**据预测**，今年全球经济增长幅度可达到百分之四点一。(凭借)

"It is predicted that the global economic growth can reach 4.1% this year."

Example 3, 4, 5, 6 represents the Location, Time, Purpose and Reliance respectively. In example 3, the conjunction is the combination of "在" and "中", and the pos-of-part of "在" is preposition, the "中" means location. In example 4 sentence, the conjunction is the combination of "在" and "中", the pos-of-part of this conjunction is same as example 3. In example 5 sentence, the conjunction is "为", and its pos-of-part is preposition. In example 6 sentence, the conjunction is the combination of "据" and "预测", the pos-of-part of "据" is preposition.

（2）Subsequence and other relations class in implicit relations

Implicit relation has no obvious semantic type sign (conjunction) so that it is difficult to determine the existence of relation and the relation type without human's judgment. Subsequence relation is very special that can not be easily differentiated from other relation types even by human, which often result in controversy among annotator, and reduce precision of the implicit relation recognition. For example, the subsequence relation expresses the sentence relation of time, space or logical sequence, etc. However, most other relations involve certain subsequence relation to some degree, resulting in that other relation is easily classified as subsequence in the implicit relation recognition. Example 7 represents the coordination, and example 8 represents the subsequence as shown below.

eg. 7：拉美是一个充满希望的大陆，具有巨大的发展潜力。（并列）

"Latin America is a continent of hope, possessing huge development potential."

eg. 8：《新中东》一书原为英文版，去年秋冬之交出版。（顺承）

"*"The new Middle East" was* English version, and published since the turn of the last autumn and winter."

（3）Coordination, Progressiveness and Interpretation, Coordination and Time

In Chinese, Coordination relation describes the parallelism between clauses or words, which can be split into two independent arguments by the comma. Progressiveness relation always implies that the second argument contains more information. However, in many cases, the conjunction "并" (expressing parallelism in most cases) can also express progressive relationship. No matter in the explicit or implicit relationship recognition, Progressive and Coordinate are easy to be confused with each other because they have similar structure and POS information.

The examples below are two sentences extracted from the corpus, example 9 represents the coordination, and example 10 represents the progressiveness.

eg. 9：两年多来两国经贸合作已顺利起步，**并**取得可观的进展。（并列）

"For more than two years the bilateral economic and trade cooperation has started smoothly, and achieved considerable progress. "

eg. 10：中国已确定了未来五年高技术研究重点，**并**着手制订下世纪的高科技研究计划。（递进）

"China has determined the high-tech research focal point of the next five years, and has began to make plan of high-tech research for next century."

It is difficult to analyze the difference between coordination and progressiveness from above examples, which is one of the causes in classification errors.

7 Conclusions and future work

We proposed the Chinese comma classification based on Chinese discourse relationship corpus. Rich linguistic features have been selected in the classification and sentence relations are classified into 9 categories with maximum entropy method. The experimental results show that the method based on linguistic features for classification of comma is feasible. However, from the result we can see that the overall classification precision still needs to be improved, especially for the implicit relation. In future work, we will further study how to extract more effective features, try to attach great importance to the role of conjunctions, which is vital to distinguish the explicit relation between sentences, and combine these features with the structure of the sentences to improve classification accuracy. In addition, we also need to solve the problem of the small scale of sample set and data sparsity.

Acknowledgement

This paper is supported by Natural Science Foundation Project (61070243, 6133012), Major Project of Invitation for Bid of National Social Science Foundation (11&ZD189), Guizhou High-level Talent Research Project (TZJF-2010-048), Guizhou Normal University PhD Start-up Research Project (11904-05032110011), and Governor Special Fund Grant of Guizhou Province for Prominent Science and Technology Talents (identification serial number "黔省专合字(2012)155号"), China Postdoctoral Science Foundation(2013M531730).

Reference

Li Yan-cui, Feng Wen-he, Zhou Guo-dong. 2013. *Research of Chinese clause identificiton based on comma*. Journal of Beijing University (Natural Science Edition), 2013(01): 7-14.

Sun Jing, Li Yan-cui, Zhou Guo-dong. 2014. *Research of Chinese implicit discourse relation recognition*. Journal of Beijing University (Natural Science Edition), 2014(01): 111-117.

Gu Jing-jing, Zhou Guo-dong. *Chinese comma classification based on segmentation and part of speech-tagging*. 2014. Computer Engineering and Applications.

Jin Mei-xun, Mi-Young Kim, Donggil Kim, Jong-Hyeok Lee. 2004. *Segmentation of Chinese long-sentences using commas*. SIGHAN2004

Xu Sheng-qin, Li Pei-feng. 2013. *Recognizing Chinese elementary discourse unit on comma*. Asian Language Processing (IALP),2013 Internationa. IEEE, 2013: 3-6.

Yang Ya-qin , Xue Nian-wen . 2012. *Chinese comma disambiguation for discourse analysis*. Proceedings of the 50th Annual Meeting of the Asso. Association for Computational Li, 2012: 786-794.

Xing Fu-yi. 2001. *The study of Chinese complex sentence*. Beijing:Commercial Press,2001

Lv Shu-xiang, Dexi Zhu. 1952. *Grammatical rhetoric speech*. Liaoning:Liaoning Education Press,1952

Shao Jing-min. 2007. *The general theory of modern Chinese*. Liaoning:Shanghai Education Press,2007

Lin Zi-heng, Kan Min-yen, Hwee Tou Ng . 2009. *Recognizing implicit discourse relations in the Penn Discourse Treebank*. Proceedings of the 2009 Conference on Empirical Me Association for Computational Li, 2009: 343-351.

Li Hang. 2012. *Statistical learning method*. Beijing: Tsinghua University Press, 2012: 80-87

Sang Hai-yan, Gu Lia-Altenbek, Niu Ning-ning. 2013. *Kazakh part-of-speech tagging method based on maximum entropy*. Computer Engineering and Applications, 2013, 49(11): 126-129,16.

Zhang Mu-yu,Song Yuan,Qin Bing,Liu Ting 2013. *Chinese Discourse Relation Recognition*. Journal of Chinese information, 2013,27(6): 51-57.

Xue Nian-wen, Yang Ya-qin . 2011. *Chinese sentence segmentation as comma classification*. Proceedings of the 49th Annual Meeting of the Asso. Association for Computational Li, 2011: 631-635.

Zheng Lue-xing, Lv Xue-qiang, Liu Kun, Lin Jin. 2013. *Automatic Identification of Chinese Coordination Relations*. Journal of Beijing University (Natural Science Edition),2013,49(1):20-24.

Improving Bilingual Lexicon Extraction Performance from Comparable Corpora via Optimizing Translation Candidate Lists

Shaoqi Wang
University of Science and Technology of China, Institute of Intelligent Machines Chinese Academy of Sciences
Hefei, China
wsq2012@mail.ustc.edu.cn

Miao Li, Zede Zhu, Zhenxin Yang, Shizhuang Weng
Institute of Intelligent Machines Chinese Academy of Sciences
Hefei, China
mli@iim.ac.cn, zhuzede@mail.ustc.edu.cn, xinzyang@mail.ustc.edu.cn, weng1989@mail.ustc.edu.cn

Abstract

In this paper, we propose a novel method to optimize translation candidate lists derived from window-based approach for the task of bilingual lexicon extraction. The optimizing process consists of two cross-comparisons between 1th translation candidate of each target word, and between set of all the 1th candidates and that of each word's 2th to N^{th} ones. Experiment results demonstrate that the proposed method leads to a significant improvement on *accuracy* over window-based approach in bilingual lexicon extraction from both English-Chinese and Chinese-English comparable corpora.

1 Introduction

Bilingual lexicon is a basic resource in the field of Natural Language Processing such as machine translation and cross-language information retrieval (AbduI-Rauf et al., 2009). Parallel corpora (Och and Ney, 2000) are typically applied to automatically extracting bilingual lexicon with high precision, but they are difficult to obtain in several domains. Due to the high cost of acquiring parallel corpora, comparable corpora, which consist of sets of documents in different languages dealing with a given topic or domain and are much easier to collect from the increasingly rich web data (Xiao and McEnery, 2006), become an alternative resource to the task. Based on comparable corpora, researchers begin to use a variety of approaches to exploit them for bilingual lexicon extraction in recent years (Tanaka and Iwasaki, 1996; Fung and McKeown, 1997; Fung and Yee, 1998; Rapp, 1999; Morin et al., 2007; Saralegui et al., 2008; Kun Yu, Junichi Tsujii, 2009). These approaches mainly share a standard strategy based on the assumption that a word and its translation appear in similar context.

These previous work shows that equivalent extraction from comparable corpora is unstable on all but the most frequent words. An explanation for the phenomenon is that translation candidate lists of target words, coming from matrix of context similarities, are always disturbed by lots of noises introduced by many-to-many mapping between the contexts of words in different languages and only more frequent ones keep comparatively robust (Pekar et al., 2006).

Regardless of the polysemy, in the candidate list of a certain target word, there may be only one correct candidate and the rest ones can be regarded as noises. Moreover, the correct candidate of one target word may become the noise in the candidate list of another target one. Therefore, to retain the correct candidate in one list and remove it (viewed as noise) from others' list when it appears, comparison between candidates in each list need to be done.

In this paper, we propose a novel method to remove these noises via optimizing translation candidate lists. The optimizing process is on the basis of cross-comparison which means comparison object lies on different candidate lists. Firstly, we adopt window-based approach to acquire translation candidate lists (Rapp, 1999; Chiao and Zweigenbaum, 2002). Then, we use the proposed two cross-comparisons of similarity. The first one called identical ranking

Proceedings of the Third CIPS-SIGHAN Joint Conference on Chinese Language Processing, pages 18–25,
Wuhan, China, 20-21 October 2014

cross-comparison is the comparison between 1th translation candidate of each target word. The second named distinct ranking cross-comparison is the comparison between set of all the 1th candidates and that of each word's 2th to N^{th} ones. Finally, we conduct the experiments to find target words with different frequencies from both Chinese-English and English-Chinese.

The organization of the paper is as follows: Related work is presented in Section 2. Section 3 is devoted to the introduction of window-based approach. In Section 4, we present the proposed optimizing process. In Section 5 we describe the experimental setup and report the results of bilingual lexicon extraction. Section 6 summarizes the paper with a final conclusion.

2 Related work

Previous work about bilingual lexicon extraction from comparable corpora usually focused on utilizing context similarity. Fung (1995) firstly used context heterogeneity in the task. Subsequently, context vectors were modeled and similarities between source-language and target-language contexts were measured with the aid of a general dictionary by many researchers (Fung, 2000; Chiao and Zweigenbaum, 2002; Robitaille et al., 2006; Morin et al., 2007).

The approaches based on context vectors differ in the way they defined word contexts. Window-based approach uses the window of the compared word to construct context (Rapp, 1999; Chiao and Zweigenbaum, 2002; Dejean et al., 2002; Gamallo, 2007). Apart from that, Syntax-based approach utilizes syntactic information for bilingual dictionary extraction (Otero, 2007).

The above approaches simply yield candidates according to the calculation of vector similarity without any subsequent processing. The proposed method can be viewed as the extension of window-based approach. Different from previous work, we emphasize the optimizing process of translation candidate lists.

3 Window-Based Approach

In window-based approach, some windows of words are firstly considered as forming the context vectors. The approach then translates source words' context vectors by using a general bilingual dictionary, and calculates the similarity between each source and target vector.

3.1 Building Context Vectors

In this step, we first choose a window size β and get β number words from both left and right of every source word w_s in corpora to form the source context information set $I_{w_s} = \{w_{s_1}, \cdots w_{s_{N_s}}\}$. Similarly, we acquire the target context information set $I_{w_t} = \{w_{t_1}, \cdots w_{t_{N_t}}\}$ of target word w_t, where N_s and N_t means the number of words in I_{w_s} and I_{w_t}. The weight $W(w_s, w_{s_k})$ of word w_{s_k} $(1 \le k \le N_s)$, which is represented as follows, is calculated on the basis of mutual information.

$$W(w_s, w_{s_k}) = \ln \frac{count(w_s, w_{s_k})}{count(w_s) \times count(w_{s_k})}. \quad (1)$$

Where $count(w_s, w_{s_k})$ is the number of co-occurrence between w_s and w_{s_k} in all the contexts. $count(w_s)$ and $count(w_{s_k})$ take as values the number of occurrence of w_s and w_{s_k}. We compute weights of every word w_{s_k} $(1 \le k \le N_s)$ in I_{w_s} to form the source context vector $\overrightarrow{V_{w_s}}$. Similar method is adopted to transfer I_{w_t} to the target context vector $\overrightarrow{V_{w_t}}$.

3.2 Vector Similarity

Using a general bilingual dictionary, we map the I_{w_s} into the target language context information $I_{w_s}^{trans}$ whose corresponding context vector is $\overrightarrow{V_{w_s}^{trans}}$: If k^{th} component in I_{w_t} equals to g^{th} component in $I_{w_s}^{trans}$ ($1 \le k \le N_s$, $1 \le g \le N_t$), we assign the value of gth component in $\overrightarrow{V_{w_s}}$ to k^{th} component in $\overrightarrow{V_{w_s}^{trans}}$; if there is no equal word, the value is zero.

By calculating $\overrightarrow{V_{w_s}^{trans}}$ of each w_s and $\overrightarrow{V_{w_t}}$ of each w_t, we create a vector matrix, where rows correspond to $\overrightarrow{V_{w_t}}$, columns to $\overrightarrow{V_{w_s}^{trans}}$ and cells to similarities between each vectors. Finally, we adopt the cosine measure (see equation 2) to calculate the similarities in the matrix and further rank them to generate translation candidate lists.

$$Sim(\overrightarrow{V_{w_t}}, \overrightarrow{V_{w_s}^{trans}}) = \frac{\sum_j v_j v_j^{trans}}{\sqrt{\sum_j (v_j)^2}\sqrt{\sum_j (v_j^{trans})^2}} . (2)$$

where v_j and v_j^{trans} is the component of vector $\overrightarrow{V_{w_t}}$ and $\overrightarrow{V_{w_s}^{trans}}$ respectively.

4 Optimizing Translation Candidate Lists

We take into account top N ranking translation candidates in the total M lists, where M means the number of target words and N means the lowest ranking considered in the section, and optimize them with two cross-comparisons of similarity between each candidate. The optimizing process consists of 2 steps: identical ranking cross-comparison between each first 1th candidate; distinct ranking cross-comparison between all the 1th candidates and each word's 2th to N^{th} ones. The architecture of our method is described in Fig.1.

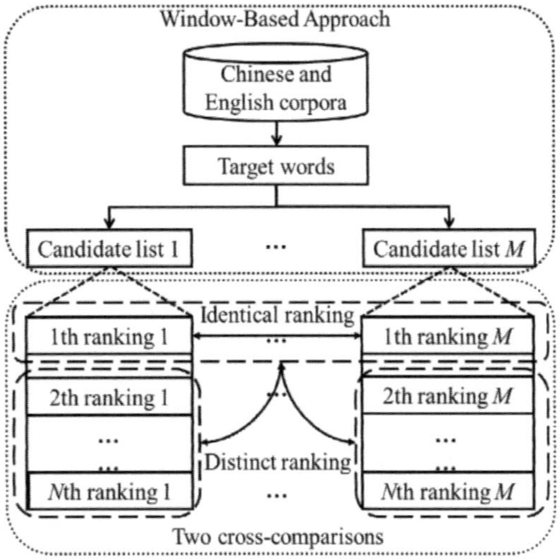

Figure1: Architecture of the proposed method

4.1 Identical Ranking Cross-comparison

Identical ranking cross-comparison relies on the assumption that each target word's 1th candidate is unique. When there are two words having the same 1th candidate, we regard the one with higher similarity as potential correct translation and remove another one defined as noise. This step is presented as follows:

Step1. Choose all the target words' first top ranking candidates $(T^1_{w_{t_1}}, \cdots, T^1_{w_{t_M}})$ and extract their similarities $(Sim^1_{w_{t_1}}, \cdots, Sim^1_{w_{t_M}})$.

Step2. Scan $(T^1_{w_{t_1}}, \cdots, T^1_{w_{t_M}})$. If there exists several equal candidates $(T^1_{w_{t_a}}, T^1_{w_{t_b}}, T^1_{w_{t_c}} \cdots)$ $(1 \le a, b, c \le M)$, jump to Step3. If all the candidates are different, go to Step4.

Step3. Compare the corresponding similarities $(Sim^1_{w_{t_a}}, Sim^1_{w_{t_b}}, Sim^1_{w_{t_c}} \cdots)$. Retain candidate with the highest value and remove others. Jump to Step2.

Step4. Complete identical ranking cross-comparison.

4.2 Distinct Ranking Cross-comparison

In light of hypothesis that all target words' 1th candidates are regarded as optimal translations, the main idea of distinct ranking cross-comparison is that these 1th candidates are assumed as noises when they appear in each word's 2th to N^{th} ones with higher similarities. The following describes this step:

Step1. build a noise set $(T^1_{w_{t_1}}, \cdots, T^1_{w_{t_M}})$.

Step2. use the noise set to scan rest candidates $(T^2_{w_{t_n}}, \cdots, T^N_{w_{t_n}})$ of w_{t_n} (n ranging from 1 to M).

Step3. when $T^j_{w_{t_n}}$ $(2 \le j \le N)$ equals to any element $T^1_{w_{t_m}}$ $(2 \le m \le N)$ in the noise set, remove $T^j_{w_{t_n}}$ if $Sim^1_{w_{t_m}}$ is higher than $Sim^j_{w_{t_n}}$.

4.2 Algorithm Description and Illustration

This part detailedly introduces the proposed method by means of algorithm description. After the description, we illustrate our method with a specific example. Algorithm 1 depicts the identical ranking cross-comparison as follows:

Algorithm 1

Input:
Target words' number M, Lowest ranking N
Unranked Candidate lists from L_1 to L_M
Unranked similarity lists from S_1 to S_M

Output:
New-ranking candidate lists from L_1^{rank} to L_M^{rank}

1: **for** i=1 to M **do**
2: rank Candidate list i:
3: $L_i \rightarrow L_i^{rank} : (T^1_{w_{t_i}}, \cdots, T^N_{w_{t_i}}, \cdots)$
4: $S_i \rightarrow S_i^{rank} : (Sim^1_{w_{t_i}}, \cdots, Sim^N_{w_{t_i}}, \cdots)$
5: end **for**
6: scan $(T^1_{w_{t_1}}, \cdots, T^1_{w_{t_M}})$

while equal candidates exist **do**
    build Set^{i}_{equ}, several sets consist of equal candidates: $(T^{1}_{w_{i_a}}, T^{1}_{w_{i_c}} \cdots), (T^{1}_{w_{i_p}}, T^{1}_{w_{i_q}} \cdots) \cdots$ $1 \le a, c, p, q \le M$
    build $SimSet^{i}_{equ}$: corresponding similarity sets
    Max = sum of Set^{i}_{equ}, i ranging from 1 to Max
    for i=1 to Max **do**
        scan Set^{i}_{equ} and $SimSet^{i}_{equ}$
        find the highest similarity: $Sim^{1}_{w_{i_h}}$
        other $Sim^{1}_{w_{i_x}}$ =0; $1 \le x \le M, x \neq h$
    end for
    re-rank lists, scan $(T^{1}_{w_{i_1}}, T^{1}_{w_{i_2}}, \cdots, T^{1}_{w_{i_M}})$
end while
return all the candidate lists

The following Algorithm 2 realizes the distinct ranking cross-comparison.

Algorithm 2

Input:
Target words' number M
Lowest ranking N
Ranked Candidate lists from L^{rank}_{1} to L^{rank}_{M}
Ranked similarity lists from S^{rank}_{1} to S^{rank}_{M}

Output:
New-ranking candidate lists from L^{rank}_{1} to L^{rank}_{M}

for i=1 to M **do**
    for j=1 to M **do**
        for k=2 to N **do**
            if $T^{k}_{w_{t_i}} = T^{1}_{w_{t_j}}$ & $Sim^{k}_{w_{t_i}} < Sim^{1}_{w_{t_j}}$ **then**
                $Sim^{k}_{w_{t_i}}$ =0;
            end if
        end for
    end for
    re-rank candidate list L^{rank}_{i}
end for
return all the candidate lists

For example, following the above algorithm, we get sorted candidate lists (see Tab.1). In identical ranking cross-comparison, we scan all the 1th candidates in each list (see red square in Tab.1) and find two sets of equal candidates: ('market/0.6162', 'market/0.6097') and ('economics/0.5627', 'economics/0.6492') (see black square in Tab.1) . Through the comparison of similarity, the 'market/0.6097' and 'economics/0.5627' become 'market/0' and 'economics/0'. Then we re-rank the lists and scan again, finding that each 1th candidate is unique. So Algorithm 1 is finished. Tab. 2 shows the re-ranking lists after identical ranking cross-comparison.

In distinct ranking cross-comparison, we build a noise set ('market/0.6162', 'theory/0.6012', 'art/0.4982', 'economics/6492', 'human/0.5627') (see red square in Tab.2) to scan each list's 2th to Nth candidates. Taking the list of word '教育' as example, we first use the noise set to scan the remaining candidates ('economics/0.5220', 'theory/0.5136','education/0.5112','art/0.5078', ···) (see black square in Tab.2) , and then find that 'economics', 'art' and 'theory' exist in the noise set. So we compare the similarity between 'economics/0.6492' and 'economics/0.5220', 'theory/0.6012' and 'theory/0.5136', and 'art/0.4982' and 'art/0.5078'. Thus, 'economics/0.5220' and 'theory/0.5136' with lower value are turned into 'economics/0' and 'theory/0'. Afterwards, we re-rank this list. Tab. 3 presents the finally optimized lists. Correct translations in Tab.1 to Tab.3 are highlighted in bold.

Word	Candidate/Similarity lists					
	1	2	3	4	5	…
市场	**market** **0.6162**	theory 0.5953	art 0.5837	education 0.5716	human 0.5330	…
理论	market 0.6097	**theory** **0.6012**	human 0.5930	family 0.5527	education 0.5326	…
艺术	economics 0.5627	**art** **0.4982**	economy 0.4817	job 0.4721	human 0.4330	…
经济学	**economics** **0.6492**	market 0.5198	art/ 0.5038	education/ 0.4786	state 0.4687	…
教育	human 0.5407	economics 0.5220	theory 0.5136	**education** **0.5112**	art 0.5078	…

Table 1: Ranked lists from window-based approach

Word	Candidate/Similarity lists					
	1	2	3	4	5	…
市场	**market** **0.6162**	theory 0.5953	art 0.5837	education 0.5716	human 0.5330	…
理论	**theory** **0.6012**	human 0.5930	family 0.5527	education 0.5326	nature 0.5008	…
艺术	**art** **0.4982**	economy 0.4817	job 0.4721	human 0.4330	market 0.4291	…
经济学	**economics** **0.6492**	market 0.5198	art 0.5038	education 0.4786	state 0.4687	…
教育	human 0.5407	economics 0.5220	theory 0.5136	**education** **0.5112**	art 0.5078	…

Table 2: Lists after identical ranking cross-comparison

Word	Candidate/Similarity lists					
	1	2	3	4	5	…
市场	**market** **0.6162**	art 0.5837	education 0.5716	job 0.5116	book 0.4930	…
理论	**theory** **0.6012**	human 0.5930	family 0.5527	education 0.5326	nature 0.5008	…
艺术	**art** **0.4982**	economy 0.4817	job 0.4721	book 0.4121	physics 0.4052	…
经济学	**economics** **0.6492**	art 0.5038	education 0.4786	state 0.4687	application 0.4528	…
教育	human 0.5407	**education** **0.5112**	art 0.5078	job 0.4992	state 0.4791	…

Table 3: Final optimized lists

5 Experiments and Analysis

5.1 Experiment Datasets and Setup

We conduct experiments on a Chinese-English corpora derived from the data used in bilingual Wikipedia with 3254 comparable document pairs. The general bilingual dictionary is constructed from an online dictionary which contains 42,373 distinct entries. In addition, we perform the following linguistic preprocessing steps on the comparable corpora: tokenization, lemmatization and removing stop words. After these steps the corpora contain ca. 925,000 Chinese words, and ca. 785,000 English words. The windows size β in building the context vectors is defined as 5, and different sizes are assessed and the above setting turns out to have the best performance in window-based method.

Two experiments are performed on target words with random frequency distribution and certain frequency in order to evaluate the proposed method. During each experiment we also absorb in the extraction performance from both English-Chinese and Chinese-English. The baseline in our experiments is the window-based approach without any optimizing, and we successively use two cross-comparisons in the proposed method and focus on performance respectively.

5.2 Evaluation Metric

We adopt the *accuracy* as evaluation metric. *Accuracy*, which means precision among the top *n* ranking, is a common metric in bilingual lexicon extraction. In this paper, translation candidates in lists from 1th to 20th ranking are kept for automatic and manual evaluation of *accuracy*, and score of *accuracy* is calculated in the following equation:

$$Accuracy = \frac{count_{top_n}}{M}. \qquad (3)$$

Where n means top n evaluation (n ranging from 1 to 20), M means the number of target words and $count_{top_n}$ means the number of correct translation in top n ranking.

5.3 Results and analysis

Experiment 1: target words with random frequency distribution

When we extract bilingual lexicon from English-Chinese, 1000 (M=1000) target words from the Chinese documents are randomly chose. We calculate the vector similarities between these Chinese words and all the English words to generate translation candidate lists, and then optimize them via the proposed method.

Meanwhile, we conduct the experiment of finding translations of 1000 target words from English documents. N in this experiment is assign as 1020. Fig. 2 and Fig. 3 demonstrate the resulting *accuracy* of different methods from two directions.

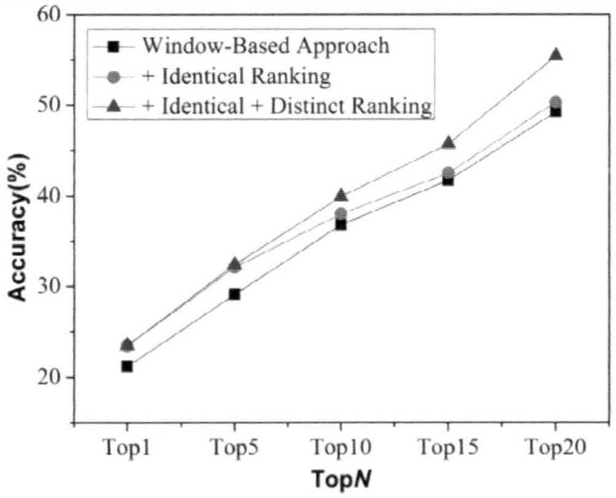

Figure 2: Extraction Results of different methods from English-Chinese

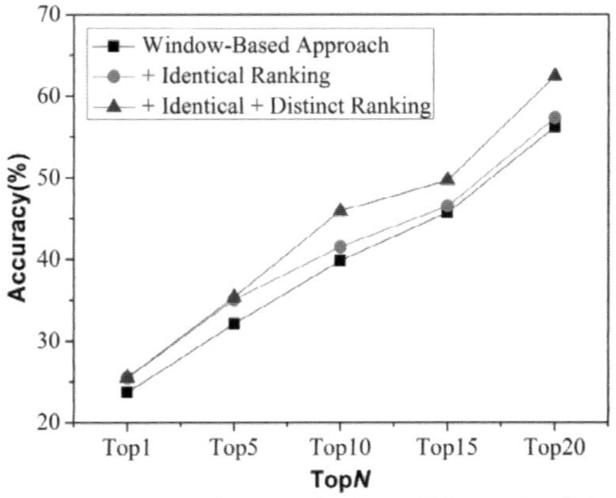

Figure 3: Extraction Results from Chinese-English

The results show that *accuracy* is improved significantly from both English-Chinese and Chinese-English, thereby indicate the robustness and effectiveness of our method. In particular, two steps in the proposed method can gradually improve the *accuracy*. Improvements of *accuracy* in top1 and top5 are mainly attributed to identical ranking cross-comparison as it processes candidate lists' top-ranking area. Distinct ranking cross-comparison can markedly boost *accuracy* in top10, top15 and top20, since it removes noises in larger area of the lists.

Experiment 2: target words with certain frequency

Previous work showed that frequent words' correct translations are easier to be found than infrequent ones (Pekar et al., 2006). Allowing for this fact, we distinguish different frequency ranges to assess the validity of the proposed approach. Target words with frequency more than 400 are defined as high-frequency words (W_H), whereas words with frequency less than 100 are low-frequency words (W_L). The number of target words from either Chinese or English documents is 1000 (M=1000) and N equals to 1020. Extraction performance on *accuracy* beyond W_H and W_L are showed in Fig. 4, Fig. 5, Fig. 6 and Fig. 7.

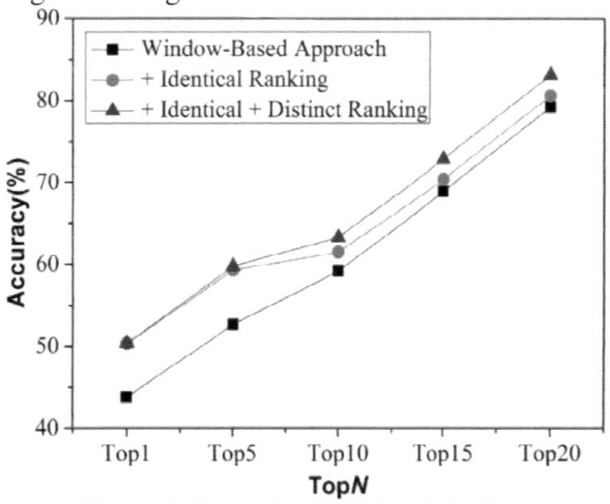

Figure 4: Extraction Results of W_H from English-Chinese

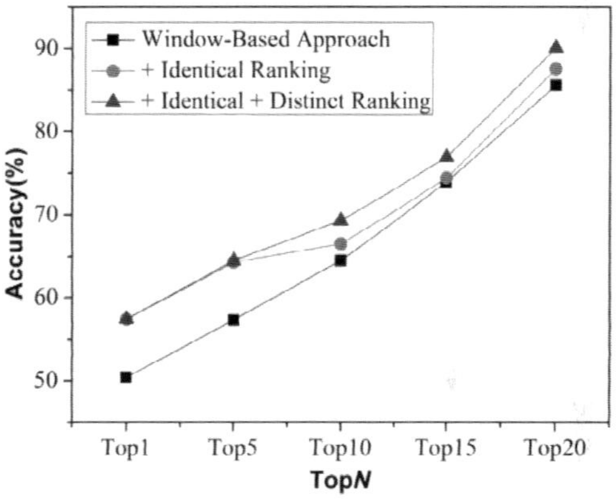

Figure 5: Extraction Results of W_H from Chinese-English

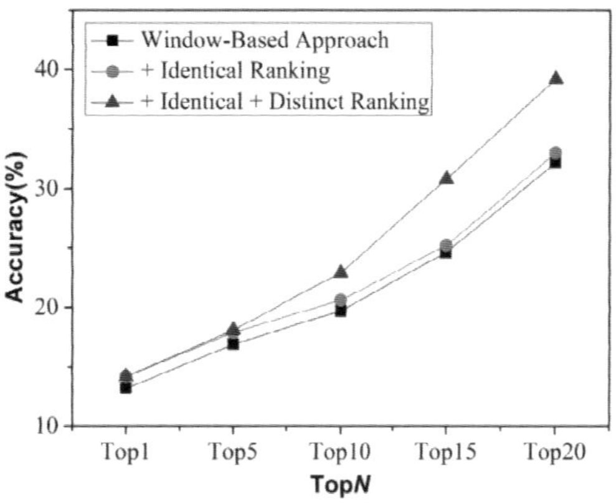

Figure 6: Extraction Results of W_L from English-Chinese

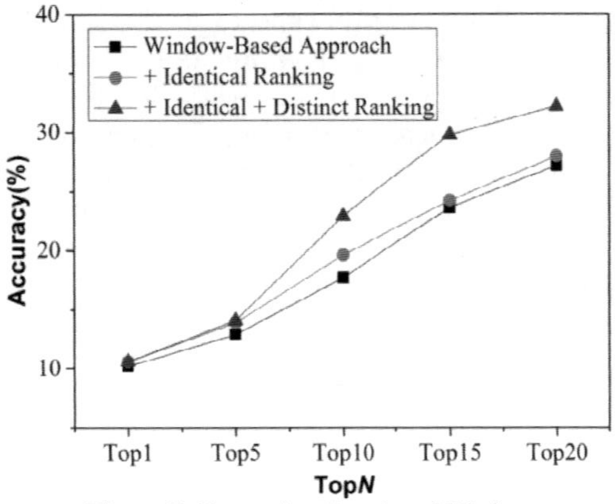

Figure 7: Extraction Results of W_L from Chinese-English

From Fig. 4 and Fig. 5 we have the following observation: *accuracy* improvement effect of identical ranking cross-comparison in top1 and top5 becomes more obvious in the process on W_H. In addition, Fig. 6 and Fig. 7 indicate that in processing W_L distinct ranking cross-comparison promotes *accuracy* in top10, top15 and top20 to a larger extent. The main reason is that for W_H each word's correct translation, which is also high-frequency source word, happens to be noise existing in top-ranking area of other words' lists. This situation leads to increasing number of identical ranking cross-comparison which can eliminate noises more effectively. Meanwhile, for W_L noises in each target word's translation candidate lists are all high-frequency source words, leading high repetition rate between the noises set and top N candidates in the lists. Therefore, distinct ranking cross-comparison can boost most optimal translations which locate in lower ranking before to concentrate in the area between 5th and 20th ranking.

6 Conclusion

In this paper, we address the 'noise' problem in extracting translation equivalent from comparable corpora. To solve the problem, we develop a novel method to optimize translation candidate lists. The optimizing process includes two step cross-comparisons between translation candidate of each target word. Experimental results show that the proposed method can boost *accuracy* significantly and outperform window-based approach in bilingual lexicon extraction from both English-Chinese and Chinese-English. Moreover, identical ranking and distinct ranking cross-comparison can improve the *accuracy* respectively in different ranking area, and their improvements depend on the frequency of target words. Future work may focuses on conducting experiment between the proposed method and syntax-based approach, and eliminating our method's impact on synonyms.

Acknowledgements

The work is supported by the Informationization Special Projects of Chinese Academy of Science under No. XXH12504-1-10 and the Open Projects Program of National Laboratory of Pattern Recognition.

Reference

AbduI-Rauf S, Schwenk H. On the use of comparable corpora to improve SMT performance[C] //Proceedings of the 12th Conference of the European Chapter of the Association for Computational Linguistics. Association for Computational Linguistics, 2009: 16-23.

Chiao Y-C, Zweigenbaum P. Looking for candidate translational equivalents in specialized, comparable corpora[C] //Proceedings of COLING. 2002.

Dejean H, Gaussier E, Sadat F. Bilingual terminology extraction: an approach based on a multilingual thesaurus applicable to comparable corpora[C] //Proceedings of COLING, Tapei, Taiwan. 2002.

Fung Pascale. Compiling Bilingual Lexicon Entries from a Nonparallel English-Chinese Corpus[C] // Proceedings of the 3rd Annual Workshop on Very Large Corpora. 1995: 173-183.

Fung Pascale, Kathleen McKeown. Finding terminology translation from non-parallel corpora[C] //5th Annual Workshop on Very Large Corpora, Hong Kong. 1997: 192-202.

Fung Pascale, Lo Yuen Yee. An IR approach for translating new words from nonparallel, comparable texts[C] //Proceedings of the 17th international conference on Computational linguistics, Montreal, Quebec, Canada. 1998: 414–420.

Fung Pascale. A Statistical View on Bilingual Lexicon Extraction from Parallel Corpora to Non-parallel Corpora[J]. Parallel Text Processing: Alignment and Use of Translation Corpora, 2000.

Hiroyuki Kaji. 2005. Extracting translation equivalents from bilingual comparable corpora[C] //Proceedings of the LREC-2008 Workshop on Comparable Corpora. 2008: 313–323.

Morin E, Daille B, Takeuchi K, Kageura K. Bilingual terminology mining – using brain, not brawn comparable corpora[C] //Proceedings of the 45th annual meeting of the Association of Computational Linguistics, Prague, Czech Republic. 2007: 664–671.

Och F J, Ney H. Improved Statistical Alignment Models[C] //Proceedings of ACL. 2000: 440-447.

Otero P. Learning Bilingual Lexicons from Comparable English and Spanish Corpora[C] // Proceedings of MT Summit XI. 2007: 191-198.

Pekar, Viktor, Ruslan Mitkov, Dimitar Blagoev, Andrea Mulloni. Finding translations for low-frequency words in comparable corpora[J]. Machine Translation, 2006, 20(4): 247–266.

Pablo Gamallo. Learning bilingual lexicons from comparable english and spanish corpora[C] // Machine Translation SUMMIT XI, Copenhagen, Denmark. 2007.

Rapp, Reinhard. Automatic identification of word translations from unrelated English and German corpora[C] //Proceedings of the 37th Annual Meeting of the Association for Computational Linguistics, College Park, Maryland, USA. 1999: 519–526.

Robitaille X. Compiling French Japanese Terminologies from the Web[C] //Proceedings of EACL. 2006.

Saralegi X, San Vicente I, Gurrutxaga A. Automatic generation of bilingual lexicons from comparable corpora in a popular science domain[C] //Workshop on Building and Using Comparable Corpora in LREC. 2008.

Tanaka K, Iwasaki H. Extraction of lexical translations from non-aligned corpora[C] //Proceedings of COLING-96: The 16th international conference on computational linguistics, Copenhagen, Denmark. 1996: 580–585.

Xiao Z, McEnery A. Collocation, Semantic Prosody and Near Synonymy: A Cross-linguistic Perspective[J]. Applied Linguistics, 2006, 27(1): 103-129.

Yu Kun, Junichi Tsujii. Extracting bilingual dictionary from comparable corpora with dependency heterogeneity[C] //Proceedings of HLTNAACL, Boulder, Colorado, USA. 2009: 121–124.

Ch2R: A Chinese Chatter Robot for Online Shopping Guide

Peijie Huang, Xianmao Lin, Zeqi Lian, De Yang, Xiaoling Tang, Li Huang, Qiang Huang, Xiupeng Wu, Guisheng Wu and Xinrui Zhang
College of Informatics, South China Agricultural University,
Guangzhou 510642, Guangdong, China
pjhuang@scau.edu.cn

Abstract

In this paper we present a conversational dialogue system, Ch2R (**Ch**inese **Ch**atter **R**obot) for online shopping guide, which allows users to inquire about information of mobile phone in Chinese. The purpose of this paper is to describe our development effort in terms of the underlying human language technologies (HLTs) as well as other system issues. We focus on a mixed-initiative conversation mechanism for interactive shopping guide combining initiative guiding and question understanding. We also present some evaluation on the system in mobile phone shopping guide domain. Evaluation results demonstrate the efficiency of our approach.

1 Introduction

Spoken dialogue systems are presently available for many purposes, such as, Airline Travel Information System (ATIS) project in the early 1990s (Price, 1990), customer service (Gorin et al., 1997), weather inquiry system (Zue et al., 2000), campus navigation system (Zhang et al., 2004), bus schedules and route guidance (Raux et al., 2003), stock information inquiry (Huang et al., 2004), restaurant recommendation system (Liu, et al., 2008), drug review system (Liu and Seneff, 2011), and spoken route instruction (Pappu and Rudnicky, 2012). These systems have been well developed for laboratory research, and some have become commercially viable.

The next generation of intelligent dialogue systems is expected to go beyond factoid question answering and straightforward task fulfillment, by providing active assistance and subjective recommendations, thus behaving more like human agents (Liu et al., 2010). For example, in the scenario that we envision, on online e-commerce site, an intelligent dialogue system which roles play a conversational shopping guide may suggest which digital camera is a better choice, considering brand, price, pixel, etc.; or suggest which mobile phone is the most popular among teenagers or highest rated by users.

In this paper, we describe our development effort on a Chinese chatter robot, named Ch2R (**Ch**inese **Ch**atter **R**obot) for shopping guide with both intelligent ability and professional knowledge. The challenges of developing such a information guiding dialogue system in Chinese includes: 1) how to provide active assistance and subjective recommendations; 2) how to deal with the diversity and flexibility of Chinese language in question understanding; 3) how to ensure the system with great adaptability which can be easily applied to be a shopping guide in a certain new specialized field.

To tackle the first problem, we propose a mixed-initiative framework. The proposed framework is able to take initiative to obtain users' need, perform passive analysis and understanding of users' questions, and switch between the two modes self-adaptively.

Our solution to the second challenge is to analysis Chinese questions by combining grammar and semantic (Huang et al., 2014). First, hand-crafted sentence compression grammar bases including grammar rules and question type patterns are added to the robot. By sentence compression, the diversity and flexibility of Chinese utterances can be recognized and categorized into limited sentence structures. Then, a question understanding method is proposed by combining grammar based question type pattern recognition and semantic based information extraction and organization.

Proceedings of the Third CIPS-SIGHAN Joint Conference on Chinese Language Processing, pages 26–34,
Wuhan, China, 20-21 October 2014

Finally, we address the last problem by using the design concept of building professional knowledge based on intelligent ability, which combines a variety of human language technologies and intelligent technologies. Such design enables Ch2R with great adaptability, making it easily applied to the shopping guide in a new restricted domain, by adding the semantic knowledge and the detailed commodity information of that specialized field.

An example scenario of Ch2R in mobile phone domain is shown in Figure 1.

(1) **Ch2R**: 您好！ (Hello！)
(2) **User** : 你好！ (Hello！)
(3) **Ch2R**:您想买什么品牌的手机呢?
(Which brand of mobile phone do you want to buy?)
(4) **User** :我要三星的。(I want Samsung.)
(5) **Ch2R**:您打算买什么价位的?
(How much you are going to buy?)
(6) **User** : 2000 块左右的吧。 (About 2000 RMB.)
(7) **Ch2R**:你想要什么输入方式的?
(Which input method do you want ?)
(8) **User** : 触屏手机有什么好介绍?
(Can you recommend some mobile phones with touching screen?)
(9) **Ch2R**:有E120L和I9050。(E120L and I9050.)
(10) **User** : 我也不知道哪个好。
(I don't know which one is better.)
(11)**Ch2R**: 你可以考虑屏幕大小或者摄像头像素。
(Maybe you can consider the screen size or the camera pixel.)
(12)**User** : 哪个屏幕大一点?
(Which one's screen is bigger?)
(13)**Ch2R**: E120L。(E120L.)
(14)**User** :这款摄像头像素高吗?
(Does it has high megapixel camera?)
(15) **Ch2R**:是的， 800 万像素。
(Yes， it has a 8 mega pixel camera.)
(16)**User** : 好的， 就要这款。(Ok, I will buy it.)
(17)**Ch2R**:欢迎下次光临！ (Welcome your next visit!)

Figure 1. Example dialogue of Ch2R.

The purpose of this paper is to describe our development effort, and to present some evaluation results on the system. The remainder of this paper is organized as follows: Section 2 presents the detail framework of Ch2R. The implementation of the mixed-initiative conversation mechanism combining intelligent guiding and understanding within the architecture of our shopping guide robot is proposed in Section 3. The professional knowledge kept by the robot is briefly presented in Section 4. Section 5 shows the preliminary evaluation results of Ch2R in mobile phone shopping guide domain. The paper concludes by outlining future developments and possible applications in Section 6.

2 System Framework

Figure 2 shows the system framework of Ch2R.

In the *sentence preprocessing* component, Chinese word segmentation and part-of-speech tagging are processed by ICTCLAS (Zhang et al., 2003). Wrongly written characters, internet language, nickname of a product, etc. , are also dealt with in this step.

Then, two main parts enclosed by bold dotted lines denote the initiative guiding (branch ①, e.g. line (3), (5) and (7) in Figure 1) and the passive understanding (branch ②, e.g. line (8), (12), and (14) in Figure 1) modes, remaining the situation when no valid information exists after the process of *information extraction* component (branch ③, e.g. line (2), (10), and (16) in Figure 1). In that case, *AIML process*, a process based on the Artificial Intelligence Markup Language (AIML) (Wallace, 2003) is used to handle some simple conversations beyond domain knowledge, some cases potentially to switch to initiative guiding and the state of end. The out of domain utterance processing based on AIML will be discussed in detail later in a separate paper.

In the *information extraction* component, semantic information is extracted from the source utterance by using with the *semantic base*. The extracted semantic information is converted into well organized semantic knowledge in *knowledge organization* component.

For interrogative sentence, i.e. a user question, we use the hand-crafted sentence compression grammar rules to perform sentence compression and employed question type patterns in *question structure recognition* component, matching the only one question type pattern taking along with information for semantic organization and answering for any input question (Huang et al., 2014).

The Ch2R architecture embodies the combination of intelligent ability and professional knowledge. From the intelligent perspective, *sentence compression* and *question structure recognition* components show the ability to understand and analyze questions, *live-table* stands for the ability to memorize, Reinforcement Learning (RL) to update the sequence of the attributes in *live-table* embodies the ability of self-learning, and Case Based Reasoning (CBR) of *AIML process* provides the capacity for logical reasoning. From the professional perspective, *info-table* provides detailed commodity information of a certain specialized field. The semantic knowledge of that field is stored in *semantic base*.

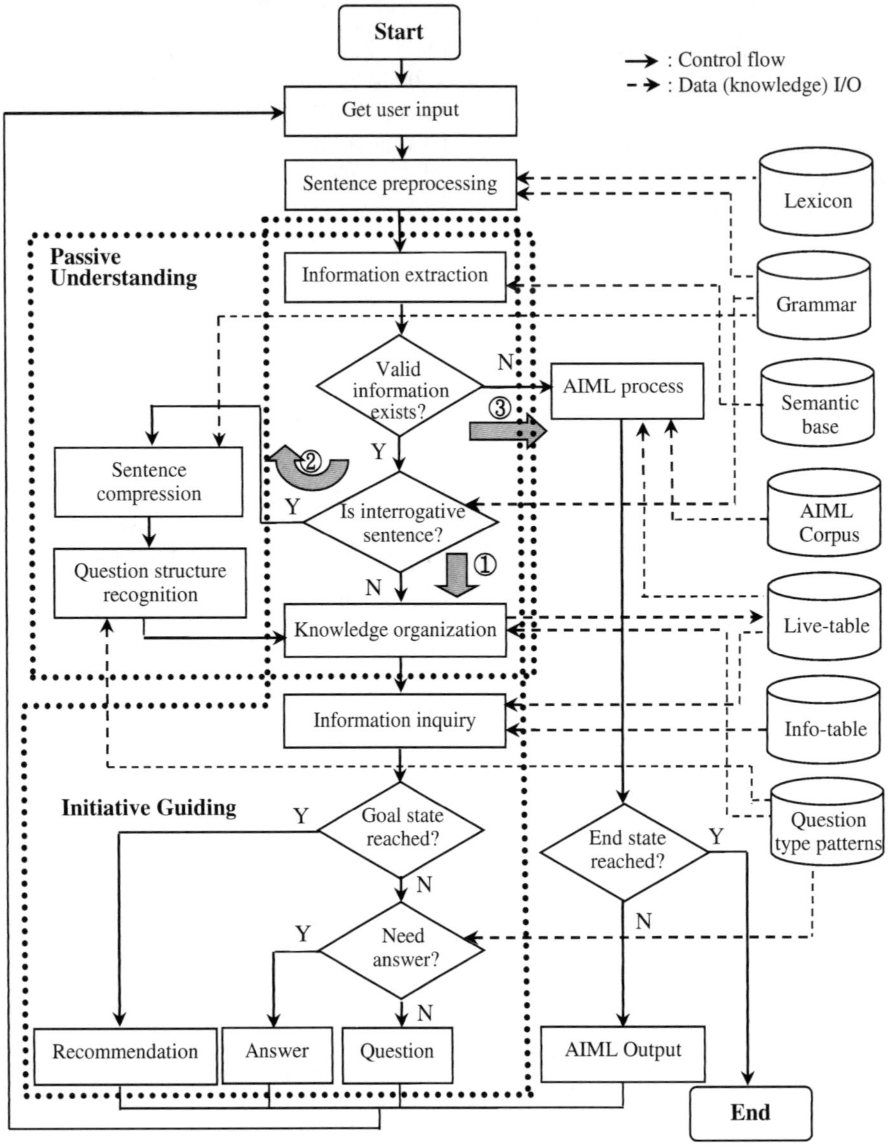

Figure 2. System framework of Ch2R.

3 Mixed-initiative Conversation

3.1 Initiative Guiding

One of the major benefits of Ch2R is that it can provide initiative guiding. We first introduce the *live-table*, and then briefly propose the guiding and recommendation mechanism based on *live-table*.

Live-table: the Ability to Memorize

Live-table is the message storage that acts as the memory of Ch2R. The information of *live-table* is live in the sense that it is active during the whole process of shopping guide. There are three kinds of active information in *live-table,* including the attribute values, the context of the dialogue, and the recommendation list. The meaning representation of Ch2R is similar to other frame-based dialogue system, in which frame had predefined slots that were appropriate for task. Understanding in these systems amounted to extracting specific fillers for each slot (e.g. Brand). Figure 3 shows the update process of *live-table* according to the example dialogue in mobile phone shopping guide from Figure 3 (a).

In our current design, we only keep the last sentences of both chatbot and user to support answering. The long-term memory is kept by the attribute values in *live-table*. So, *live-table* is the basis when Ch2R checks the candidate mobile phones in Information inquiry component.

……
Ch2R: 您想买什么品牌的手机呢?
(Which brand of mobile phone do you want to buy?)
User : 给我看看三星的吧。(I want Samsung.)
Ch2R: 好的，您打算买什么价位的?
(How much you are going to buy?)
User : 3000 块以下的吧。
(Less than 3000 Yuan.)
Ch2R: 您需要高清的摄像头吗?
(Do you need a camera with high megapixel?)
User : 500 万以上。(More than 5 mega.)

(a) Example dialogue in mobile phone shopping guide

属性(Attribute)	**值(Value)**
品牌(Brand)	三星 (Samsung)
价格(Price)	(0, 3000)
摄像头像素 (Pixel_camera)	[5,)
输入方式 (Input_method)	
…	…
颜色(Colour)	
型号(Model)	
Ch2R 最新的话 (Last_S_Ch2R)	您需要高清的摄像头吗? (Do you need a camera with high megapixel?)
User 最新的话 (Last_S_User)	500 万以上。 (More than 5 mega.)
推荐列表 (Recomm_list)	

(b) Live-table

Figure 3. Example of the update process of *live-table*.

Guiding and Recommendation

Effective guiding is achieved by looking up the unconfirmed attributes in the *live-table* to present a question. It is worthwhile to note that the sequence of the attributes in *live-table* is variable, which means the priority of the attributes used in initiative guiding can be changed for users' preference in shopping. A process of Reinforcement Learning (RL) (Kaebling et al., 1996) is used to achieve such flexibility, according to the analysis of the users' questions collected in passive understanding mode.

Ch2R would confirm every attribute, however, this would lead to too many times of interactions with user, and it looks a little mechanical. We address this problem by offering a recommendation in the initiative guiding process once there are only limited numbers of candidates, e.g. 1, 2 or 3 candidates. Such recommendation limits the interactions and can embody the profession of Ch2R in shopping guide.

3.2 Passive Understanding

We now turn to the passive understanding mode. The word passive means that when face to a user's question, the chatbot has to analyze and answer. Actually, we can simply observed that human being, even a three-year-old child can understand many sentences with different structures and make different responses according to different structure of the questions. It reveals that learning and recognition of sentence type structure is the foundation of the ability to understand and analyze questions. After mastering the grammar sentence type structure, once learning semantic knowledge of a certain domain, one can then dialogue in that specialized field.

Therefore, first, hand-crafted grammar bases in Chinese including *grammar rules* for sentence compression and *question type patterns* for question structure recognition are added to the shopping guide robot, which act as the "language acquisition device" suggested by Chomsky (2005). And then we simplify a complex sentence leaving only the structure by sentence compression based on *grammar rules*. Finally, we employed *question type patterns* for question structure recognition, matching the only one question type pattern for any input question (Huang et al., 2014).

Sentence Compression

For all kinds of languages, sentences are diversified and innumerable, but the sentence structures are limited. By sentence compression, the diversity of user inputs can be recognized and categorized into limited sentence structures, i.e. question type pattern. Given an input source sentence of words $x = x_1, x_2, ..., x_n$, a target compression y is formed by removing any subset of these words (Knight and Marcu, 2002). The aim of the sentence compression in our system is to produce a summary of a single sentence that retains the most important structure information while remaining grammatical.

Tree based representation is used in sentence compression. The *Stanford Chinese Parser* [1] (Levy and Manning, 2003) is employed for the tree-based parsing. In order to get a correct syn-

[1] http://nlp.stanford.edu/software/lex-parser.shtml.

tax tree from Stanford Parser, we have to formalize the sentence because Stanford Parse can't understand some sentence structures. Then, we use the hand-crafted sentence compression rules, and rely on recent work in text-to-text generation methods (Cohn and Lapata, 2009; Cohn and Lapata, 2013) to perform sentence compression.

Hand-crafted grammar rules for sentence compression are obtained by analyzing hundreds of question examples with different sentence structures. Because our system use tree based representation in sentence compression, the grammar rules take the forms like (NP (DNP, NP1))->NP(NP1), which states that a NP consisting of a DNP and another NP, denoted as NP1, can be rewritten as NP just consisting of NP1 (without the DNP). Taking a wh-question question, "在你们店有什么 2000 块以下的手机? (Which mobile phones are less than 2000 RMB in your store?)", as example, the sentence compression result is "有什么手机? (Which mobile phones?)". Figure 4 illustrates such example based on the hand-crafted *grammar rules base* used in our system.

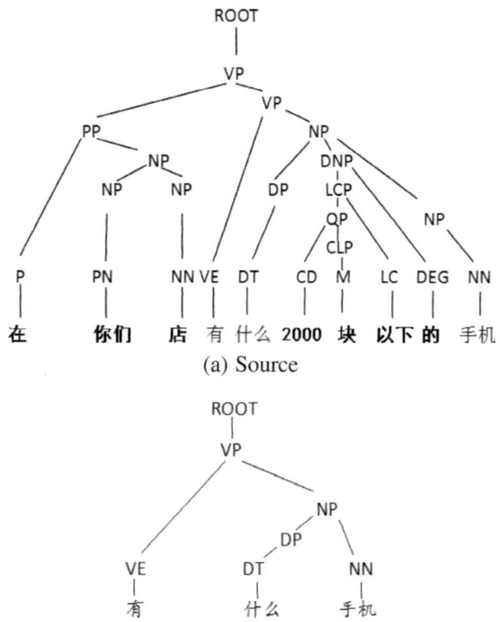

(a) Source

(b) Target

*r*1: (VP(PP, VP1))->(VP1)
*r*2: (NP(DNP, NP1))->(NP1)

(c) Grammar rules used in this example

Figure 4. Example of sentence compression showing the source and target trees, and the grammar rules used. The bold source nodes show the terminals that need to be removed to produce the target string.

Question Type Pattern Recognition

Question type pattern recognition is important for the later steps in information organization and answering. However, building an effective knowledge base of question type patterns is a challenge, especially in Chinese language, which is unlike English, in which question word can basically represents the classification of the interrogative. We design a 4-set question type pattern as {interrogative sentence type, interrogative word type, interrogative phrases, sentence structure}. Taking the compressed sentence, "有什么手机? (Which mobile phones?)", as example, its question type pattern is "(特指问, 什么, 什么/哪*, VP+~+NP) (wh-questions, which, which, VP +~+NP)", where ~ stand for the interrogative phrase. Other questions, such as "有哪些手机? (Which mobile phones?)" and "有哪款手机? (Which mobile phones?)" will be recognized as this question type pattern. Notice that a more complex question, such as "有什么 2000 块以下的大屏幕的手机? (Which mobile phones are less than 2000 RMB and with big screen?)" and an informal user input, such as "有什么 2000 块左右的? (Which are about 2000 RMB?)", will be also recognized as the same question type pattern after sentence compression and question type pattern recognition, which shows good robustness of our design. It also leads to good performance with limited question type patterns (30 question type patterns in our current dialogue system) (Huang et al., 2014).

The procedure of question type pattern recognition is shown in Figure 5.

Due to the inaccuracy of Chinese word segmentation in Stanford Parser, to raise the matching rate, we remark the word tags by employing a more satisfied word segmentation interface in the first step of question type pattern recognition. Given a compressed interrogative sentence, ICTCLAS (Zhang et al., 2003) is introduced to remark the word tags and get the syntax sequence.

In the 4-set question type pattern, the interrogative word type is not used as recognition factor. The similarities of interrogative sentence type, the interrogative phrases and the sentence structure are taken as the three factors for computing the similarity between the compressed interrogative sentence and any question type pattern in *question type patterns base*.

Figure 6 shows how to calculate the similarity between the source syntax sequence and the target syntax sequence, i.e. the sentence structure in a certain question type pattern.

Algorithm 1: Question type pattern recognition
Input: Compressed interrogative sentence *s*
Output: Question type pattern with the highest similarity
Data depend on: *Question type patterns base*

Procedure：
1. get the syntax sequence *ss* of *s*
2. for all question type patterns in data:
   a. judge if *s* has the features of interrogative sentence type in a certain question type pattern. Here is the score c_1.
   b. judge if *s* has the interrogative phrases in a certain question type pattern. Here is the score c_2.
   c. calculate the similarity between *ss* and the sentence structures in question type patterns. The similarity is c_3.
   d. calculate the final similarity $c=c_1*w_1+c_2*w_2+c_3*w_3$, *w* are the weight between 0 and 1.
3. find the highest score *c*, and corresponding pattern is the question type pattern of *s*.
4. return the question type pattern matched.

Figure 5. Algorithm of question type pattern recognition.

Algorithm 2: Sentence structure similarity calculation
Input: Source syntax sequence *x*, target syntax sequence *y*
Output: Similarity score, *100* for maximum
Reference algorithm: Classical Edit Distance

Procedure：
1. for syntax in *x*, do one of the four operation below:
   e. replace a syntax α in *x* with β by score $SR(\alpha) + SR(\beta)$, which is always negative.
   f. add a syntax α to *x* with score $SA(\alpha)$, which is always negative.
   g. delete a syntax α in *x* with score $SD(\alpha)$, which is always negative.
   h. do nothing with a syntax α and get $SN(\alpha)$, which is always positive.
2. transform *x* into *y* with the operations above, figure out the highest score *s*.
3. transform *y* into *y* with the operations above, figure out the highest score *s_max*.
4. return the final similarity score, *100*s/s_max*.

Figure 6. Algorithm of sentence structure similarity.

In step 1 of Figure 6, different syntax has different weight of score. For instance, modal particles, adverbs, punctuation will have a lower weight in score calculation, but nouns, verbs and interrogative words will have a higher weight. In step 2, the highest score is calculated by Edit Distance algorithm (Ristad and Yianilos, 1998).

4 Professional Knowledge

The detailed commodity information and semantic knowledge of a certain restricted domain is the professional knowledge that should be added to Ch2R when applied it to the shopping guide in that specialized restricted domain.

4.1 Info-table: Detailed Commodity Information

Info-table, which is the basic professional knowledge base of Ch2R, provides detailed commodity information of a certain specialized field. There are totally 89 attributes in the Info-table of mobile phone domain, including one as the primary key, and other 88 attributes provide the commodity information in detail. These attributes are selected from major mobile phone e-commerce sites. *Info-table* acts as the complete product information of robot. In other words, it gives the robot more sufficient information than real human in online shopping guide.

4.2 Semantic base: Domain Semantic Knowledge

In *semantic base*, DSem-table stands for the domain semantic knowledge kept by the chatbot. There are totally 77 attributes in the DSem-table of mobile phone domain. Table 1 shows a fragment of it.

Currently, there are three kinds of domain semantic knowledge in Ch2R. The semantic knowledge of the price value is as follows:

1. Conceptual knowledge: "价格/价钱/价位 (price)", "多少钱/多少块钱/多少元钱(how much) ".

2. Qualitative knowledge: "便宜[0,1000) (cheap [0,1000))", "一般[1000,2000) (moderate price [1000,2000))", "较高[2000,) (expensive [2000,))".

3. Quantitative knowledge, which is further divided into two types:

- Approximate number knowledge: "以上/大于(much than)", "以下/小于(less than)", "左右/大概(about/ approximately)", "不超过(not higher than)", "少/低/便宜一点(less/lower/ cheaper)", "高/贵一点(higher/more expensive)".
- Exact quantity knowledge: "数字(0<=数字<20000) +块/元 ((0<=digits<20000)+ RMB/ Yuan)", "数字(0<=数字<20000)+到+数字(0<=数字<20000) ((0<=digits <20000)+RMB /Yuan to (0<=digits< 20000)+RMB/ Yuan)".

属性 (Attribute)	领域语义知识 (Domain semantic knowledge)
品牌 (Brand)	品牌, 牌子, 三星,苹果, 华为, 索尼, 诺基亚,摩托罗拉,小米,魅族,中兴, 黑莓, 步步高,... brand, Samsung, Apple, Huawei, Sony, Nokia, Motorola, HTC, Meizu, ZTE, BBK...
价格 (Price)	价格, 价钱, 价位,多少钱, 多少块钱, 多少元钱, 便宜[0,1000),一般/适中/普通[1000,2000), 较高/贵[2000,), 以上, 以下, 大概/大约, 左右,大于,小于, 不超过, 少/低/便宜一点,高/贵一点,数字(0<数字<20000)+块/元, 数字(0<=数字 <20000)+ 到 + 数 字 (0<= 数 字 <20000). price, how much, cheap [0,1000), moderate price [1000,2000), expensive [2000,), about, approximately, much than, less than, not higher than, less/lower/cheaper, higher/more expensive, (0<=digits<20000)+RMB/ Yuan, (0<=digits<20000)+RMB/ Yuan to (0<=digits<20000)+RMB/ Yuan.
输入方式 (Input method)	输入方式,手写,键盘,触屏,触控,语音输入 input method, handwriting, touch screen, keyboarding, voice input
......	......

Table 1. Fragment of DSem-table (Mobile phone domain).

Another semantic table is ESem-table, which is the evaluating semantic knowledge kept by the service robot. There are totally 11 attributes in the ESem-table of mobile phone domain in current system. Table 2 shows a fragment of it.

属性 (Attribute)	评价性语义知识 (Evaluating semantic knowledge)
外形 (Outline)	外形, 好看,一般,难看,漂亮,时髦,潮流,时尚,经典,过时,老土. outline, good-looking , bad-looking, beautiful, fashion, popular classical obsolete.
性价比 (Rate of quantity and price)	性价比, 高[100, 85),中[85, 70), 低[70, 0). rate of quantity and price, performance-price ratio, high [100, 85), moderate [85, 70), low[70, 0).
热门程度 (Hot degree)	热门, 流行, 受欢迎, 最热. hot, fashion, popular, most popular.
......	......

Table 2. Fragment of ESem-table (Mobile phone domain).

Semantic base is used for semantic information extraction. Taking the source sentence of "有什么2000块以下的大屏幕的手机? (Which mobile phones are less than 2000 RMB and with big screen?)" as example, the extracted semantic information is "价格: 2000块, 以下; 主屏尺寸: 屏幕, 大 (Price: 2000 RMB, less than; Screen_size: screen, big)". Then, the extracted semantic information is converted into well organized semantic knowledge based on the corresponding question type pattern. The extracted semantic information in the above example is organized as " '价格: 2000块,以下'and '主屏尺寸: 屏幕,大' ('Price: 2000 RMB, less than' and 'Screen_size: screen, big')". Generally, knowledge organization of the question type patterns with the same interrogative sentence type will be the same or at less similar.

5 Evaluation

5.1 Screenshot

Figure 7 shows a screenshot of the Ch2R in Web-based application form. Chat log is also shown in the web page which is convenient for customer to look over.

Figure 7. Screenshot of Ch2R in Web-based application form.

5.2 Preliminary Evaluation Resluts

We performed a preliminary system evaluation by logging the interactions of 6 subjects with the system. Each evaluator tests 3 times, i.e. total 18 dialogues. All of the evaluators were familiar with the Ch2R system capabilities, but did not have a detailed knowledge of how to constitute a correct reference answer.

The overall statistical results are shown in Table 3. Branch ①, ② and ③ stand for the turns of initiative guiding, passive understanding and out of domain utterance processing, respectively.

Turns (Avg/Max/ Min)	Turns of Branch ① (Avg/Max/ Min)	Turns of Branch ② (Avg/Max/ Min)	Turns of Branch ③ (Avg/Max/ Min)
13.6/24 /5	5.8/10/3	5.2/11/0	2.6/6/1

Table 3. Overall statistical results.

Total turns	Successfully guiding	Success rate
105	100	95.2%

Table 4. Performance of initiative guiding (Branch ①).

Total turns	Correctly understanding	Success rate
93	84	90.3%

Table 5. Performance of question understanding (Branch ②).

Total turns	Correctly process	Success rate
47	42	89.4%

Table 6. Performance of out of domain utterance processing (Branch ③).

As we can see from Table 3, large gaps between the maximum and the minimum turns of both branch ① and ② show the diversity of the evaluators. Some of them like to ask questions, while some others enjoy system-initiative.

The results for the initiative guiding mode are given in Table 4. Our system provided successful active guiding for 100 of the 105 turns of initiative guiding, and made only 5 cases of failed guiding. One of the errors was due to the change of user intent, i.e., the intent of user was changed but the system failed to catch such change and update the *live-table*. The other four errors that the system made were due to the imperfection of the current *semantic base*, which resulted in incorrectly extracting attribute values in utterances, and thus affected the later guiding.

The results for question understanding are given in Table 5. There are total 96 user questions in the test, 3 of which incorrectly enter the out of domain utterance processing branch due to the imperfection of the *semantic base*. In 93 user questions that entering branch ②, 90.3% were correctly understudied (both correctly semantic information extraction and question type pattern recognition), including some utterances with typing mistakes or ellipsis. We also found that the 93 user questions are only distributed within 12 different question type patterns. That means of the total 30 question type patterns in current system, 18 did not exist in the test. This is mainly because most of the questions in the test are wh-questions and yes-no questions. In 9 incorrectly cases, most of them were due to the inaccuracy brought by part-of-speech tagging and the imperfection of the current *semantic base*. Only 2 errors were due to factors related to the design of the question type patterns.

The results for out of domain utterance processing are given in Table 6. Of the 5 sentences that provided incorrect answers, 4 were also due to the imperfection of the *semantic base*, and thus incorrectly leading the dialogue process entering out of domain utterance processing branch.

6 Conclusions and Future Work

This paper presents the development and preliminary evaluation of a Chinese conversational dialogue system named Ch2R with intelligent ability and professional knowledge for online shopping guide. As we can see from the evaluation results, it can perform well in the mobile phone shopping guide in all kinds of situations including initiative guiding, passive understanding, and out of domain utterance processing. Although still in its primary stage, by combining a variety of human language technologies and intelligent technologies into an integrated framework, it can dialogue like a human being and provide a professional service. Moreover, the design concept of building professional knowledge based on intelligent ability ensures Ch2R with great adaptability. We can easily apply it to the shopping guide of other specialized fields.

There are many possible and promising research directions for the near future. We are implementing new and funny interaction, such as communicate in voice using WeChat. Moreover, a separate component of dialogue management with explicit dialogue model will be added to the system. In addition, we also want to experiment with a larger number and various types of users which will make Ch2R more robust.

Acknowledgments

This work was supported by the Innovation Training Project for College Students of Guangdong Province under Grant No.1056412151, No.1056413096 and No.201410564290.

References

Chomsky N.. 2005. Three Factors in Language Design. *Linguistic Inquiry*, 36(1): 1-22.

Cohn T. and Lapata M.. 2009. Sentence Compression as Tree Transduction. *Journal of Artificial Intelligence Research*, 34(1):637–674.

Cohn T. and Lapata M.. 2013. An Abstractive Approach to Sentence Compression. *ACM Transactions on Intelligent Systems and Technology*, 4(3): 1-35.

Gorin A. L., Riccardi G. and Wright J. H.. 1997. How may I help you?. *Speech Communication*, 23: 113-127.

Huang P.J., Huang Q., Wu X.P., et al.. 2014. Question Understanding by Combining Grammar and Semantic for Chinese Dialogue System. *Journal of Chinese Information Processing*, in presss. (in Chinese)

Huang Y.F., Zheng F., Yan P.J., et al.. 2001. The Design and Implementation of Campus Navigation System: EasyNav. *Journal of Chinese Information Processing*, 15(4):35-40. (in Chinese)

Kaebling L.P., Littman M. L., and Moore A. W.. 1996. Reinforcement Learning: A survey. *Journal of Artificial Intelligence Research*, 4: 237-285.

Knight, K. and Marcu, D.. 2002. Summarization Beyond Sentence Extraction: a Probabilistic Approach to Sentence Compression. *Artificial Intelligence*, 139 (1): 91-107.

Levy R. and Manning C.D.. 2003. Is it harder to parse Chinese, or the Chinese Treebank?. *In Proceedings of the 41th Annual Meeting of the Association for Computational Linguistics (ACL 2003)*, pages 439-446.

Liu J., Xu Y.S., Seneff S. and Zue V.. 2008. CityBrowser II: A Multimodal Restaurant Guide in Mandarin, *In Proceedings of the 9th International Symposium on Chinese Spoken Language Processing (ISCSLP 2008).*

Liu J., Seneff S. and Zue V. 2010. Dialogue-Oriented Review Summary Generation for Spoken Dialogue Recommendation Systems. *In Proceedings of the 11th Annual Conference of the North American Chapter of the Association for Computational Linguistics (NAACL-HLT 2010).*

Liu J., and Seneff S.. 2011. A Dialogue System for Accessing Drug Reviews, *In Proceedings of the IEEE Automatic Speech Recognition and Understanding Workshop (ASRU 2011).*

Pappu A., Rudnicky A.. 2012. The Structure and Generality of Spoken Route Instructions. *In Proceedings of the 13th SIGdial Workshop on Discourse and Dialogue,* pages 99-107.

Price P.J., 1990. Evaluation of Spoken Language Systems: the ATIS Domain. *In Proceedings of DARPA Workshop on Speech and Natural Language,* Hidden Valley, PA.

Raux A., Langner B., Black A., and Eskenazi M.. 2003. LET'S GO: Improving Spoken Dialog Systems for the Elderly and Non-natives. In *Proceedings of the Eurospeech 2003.*

Ristad E.S. and Yianilos P.N.. 1998. Learning String-edit Distance. *IEEE Transactions on Pattern Analysis and Machine Intelligence*, 20(5):522–532.

Wallace R.S.. 2003. *The elements of AIML style.* A.L.I.C.E. Artificial IntelligenceFoundation, Inc..

Zhang H.P., Yu H.K., Xiong D.Y., et al.. 2003. HHMM-based Chinese Lexical Analyzer ICTCLAS. *In Proceedings of the second Sighan workshop affiliated with the 41th Annual Meeting of the Association for Computational Linguistics (ACL 2003)*, pages 184-187.

Zhang L., Gao F., Guo R., et al.. 2004. A Chinese Spoken Dialogue System about Real-time Stock Information.*Computer Applications*, 24(7):61-63. (in Chinese)

Zue V., Seneff S., Glass J., et al.. 2000. JUPITER: A Telephone-Based Conversational Interface for Weather Information. *IEEE Transactions on Speech and Audio Processing*, 8(1): 85–96.

Improving Chinese Sentence Polarity Classification via Opinion Paraphrasing

Guohong Fu, Yu He, Jiaying Song, Chaoyue Wang
Heilongjiang University, Harbin 150080, China
ghfu@hlju.edu.cn, heyucs@yahoo.com, jy_song@outlook.com, chaoyue.wang@yahoo.cn

Abstract

While substantial studies have been achieved on sentiment polarity classification to date, lacking enough opinion-annotated corpora for reliable training is still a challenge. In this paper we propose to improve a supported vector machines based polarity classifier by enriching both training data and test data via opinion paraphrasing. In particular, we first extract an equivalent set of attribute-evaluation pairs from the training data and then exploit it to generate opinion paraphrases in order to expand the training corpus or enrich opinionated sentences for polarity classification. We tested our system over two sets of online product reviews in car and mobilephone domains. The experimental results show that using opinion paraphrases results in significant performance improvement in polarity classification.

1 Introduction

With the explosive growth of the user-generated opinionated texts on the web over the past years, opinion mining has been attracting an ever-increasing amount of attention from the natural language processing community. As a key sub-problem of opinion mining, sentiment polarity classification aims to classify opinionated documents or sentences as expressing positive, negative or neutral opinions, and plays a critical role in many opinion mining applications such as opinion summarization and opinion question answering. Since sentence is usually considered as the smallest semantic unit for expressing the complete opinion, the current study focused on the sentence sentiment classification.

Although recent years have seen a great progress in sentiment classification, lacking large-scale opinion-annotated corpora is still a fundamental issue. On the one hand, statistically-based methods become the mainstream in sentiment analysis. In general, a statistically-based polarity classifier needs an annotated corpus for training. So its performance heavily relies on the training corpus used. On the other hand, to date there are no any large-scale annotated corpora available for achieving reliable training process. Furthermore, opinion mining is usually domain specific. Obviously, it is time and cost consuming to manually construct a large-scale opinion-annotated corpus for each domain.

To address the above problems, in this paper we propose to improve polarity classification by enriching both training data and test data via paraphrasing. We have two motivations for this. Firstly, paraphrasing has proven to be an effective tool for improve the coverage of systems and has been successfully used in many applications such as machine translation, information retrieval and question answering (Bhagat and Hovy, 2013; Heilman and Smith, 2010; Zhao *et al.*, 2013; Fader *et al.*, 2013). However, to date, there has been very limited study on sentiment or opinion paraphrasing. Secondly, unlike opinion corpus annotation, paraphrases are relatively more flexible to acquire using different resources like synonym lexica, bilingual and parallel corpora, and so forth. Therefore, we believe that paraphrasing would be a feasible way to expand the training corpus and at the same time, to alleviate the data sparse problem in statistically-based systems. As such, the purpose of this study is to ascertain the effect of using opinion paraphrases in polarity classification at sentence level. To approach this, we first extract an equivalent set of attribute-evaluation pairs from the training data and then exploit it to generate opinion paraphrases in order to expand the training corpus or enrich opinionated sentences for polarity classification. Based on the generated opinion paraphrases, we also develop a polarity classification system for Chinese under the framework of support vector

Proceedings of the Third CIPS-SIGHAN Joint Conference on Chinese Language Processing, pages 35–42,
Wuhan, China, 20-21 October 2014

machines (SVMs). Experimental results over two sets of online reviews on car and mobilephone products show that using the paraphrases generated by the proposed method can significantly improve the performance of sentence polarity classification.

The rests of the paper proceed as follows. Section 2 provides a brief review of the literature on sentiment classification and paraphrase generation. Section 3 describes in details the proposed method to Chinese sentence polarity classification via paraphrasing. Section 4 reports our experimental results on two sets of product reviews. Finally, section 5 concludes our work and discusses some possible directions for future research.

2 Related Work

Polarity classification is usually formulated as a binary classification problem (Turney, 2002; Pang and Lee, 2008). Most previous studies employ supervised machine learning methods, including naïve Bayes model, support vector machines (SVMs), maximum entropy models (MEMs), conditional random fields (CRFs), fuzzy sets, and so forth (Pang et al., 2002; Pang and Lee, 2008;Fu and Wang, 2010), to perform polarity classification on different linguistic levels such words, phrases, sentences and documents.

Lacking a large scale manually-annotated corpus is one of the major bottlenecks that supervised machine learning methods faced. To break this bottleneck, some recent studies exploit bootstrapping or unsupervised techniques (Turney, 2002; Mihalcea *et al.*, 2007; Wilson *et al.*, 2009, Speriosu et al. 2011, Mehrotra *et al.* 2012; Volkova *et al.,* 2013). Unfortunately, sentiment classifiers based on unsupervised methods usually yield worse performance compared to the supervised ones.

Different from most existing studies, in this study we attempt to enhance Chinese sentence polarity classifier by exploring opinion paraphrasing. We believe that paraphrasing provides us with an option to expand training corpora and to enrich opinion sentences for polarity classification, which would alleviate the problem of data sparseness and lack of annotated corpora for training. At this point, our current study is also relevant to paraphrasing tasks, including paraphrase recognition, paraphrase extraction and paraphrase generation. Although a variety of methods, from dictionary-based methods to data-driven methods (Madnani and Dorr, 2010), have been proposed for paraphrasing. Since in the present study we aim to answer the question whether the use of paraphrasing can enhance polarity classification performance, we do not want to look insight into paraphrasing issues. Instead, we just exploit some simple but efficient paraphrasing techniques to achieve opinion paraphrases for expanding training data and enriching text data for polarity classification, including opinion paraphrase extraction incorporating the Jaccard coefficient based literal similarity with the word embedding based semantic similarity, and opinion paraphrase generation with opinion element substitution.

3 The Proposed Method

3.1 Overview

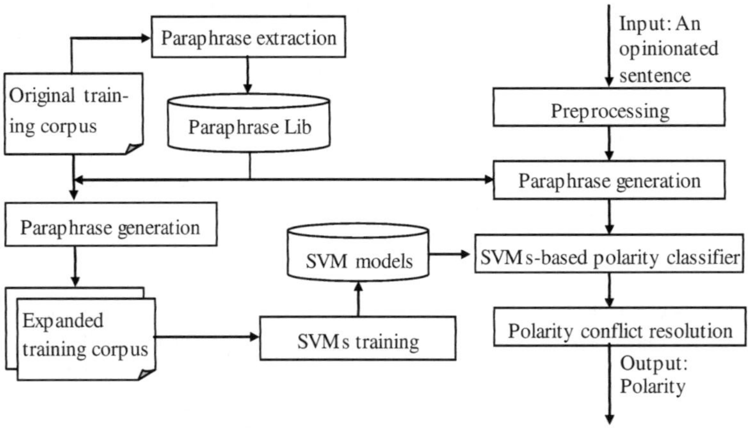

Figure 1. The overall framework of the proposed method to Chinese polarity classification.

Figure 1 presents the general framework for Chinese polarity classification via opinion paraphrasing, mainly including paraphrase extraction, training corpus expansion via paraphrase generation and the SVMs-based polarity classifier with paraphrasing.

Training corpus expansion. For each opinionated sentence from the original corpus for training, we first generate a set of suitable paraphrases and thus expand the training corpus by adding these generated paraphrases into it.

Paraphrase extraction. To achieve opinion element substitution based paraphrasing, we need to extract a set of equivalent attribute-evaluation pairs from the training corpus. In the present study, we incorporate literal similarity and word embedding-based semantic similarity between two coreferred product attributes with the polarity of the paired evaluation expressions to perform attribute-evaluation clustering.

Paraphrase generation. With regard to the focus of the current study, we generate sentential paraphrases by simply substituting opinion elements such as product attributes and their evaluations in the original sentence with their respective semantic equivalents.

SVMs-based polarity classifier. We perform sentence polarity classification using supported vector machines (SVMs) trained from the expanded training data via opinion paraphrasing.

Polarity conflict resolution. To avoid data sparseness, in the present study we perform paraphrasing on the input opinionated sentences in test before polarity classification. As a consequence, this may cause polarity conflicts between the original input sentences and their paraphrases after polarity classification. To address this problem, we employ a rule-based voting method.

In Sections 3.2 to 3.5, we provide the details of our implementation.

3.2 Paraphrases in Product Reviews

Before describing the techniques for paraphrase extraction and generation, it is necessary to clarify what a paraphrase is for product reviews. In linguistics literature, paraphrases are most often referred to as an approximate equivalence of meaning across sentences or phrases (Bhagat and Hovy, 2013). In the present study we characterize opinion paraphrases from the perspective of opinion elements. In general, opinion information consists of five main elements, namely opinion source (viz. opinion holder), opinion target, attribute, evaluation and polarity. Thus, the opinion element perspective defines paraphrases in terms of the kinds of opinion element changes that can take place in an opinionated sentence resulting in the generation of its paraphrases. Considering the characteristics of product reviews, here we focus on product attributes and their relevant evaluations within opinionated sentences in determining whether they are paraphrasing each other. Thus, two opinion sentences that contain the same or similar attribute-evaluation pairs are termed as opinion paraphrases.

With regard to semantic equivalence between attributions and evaluations within opinion expressions, we can thus classify paraphrases in product reviews into four main types, as shown in Table 1. Based on this, given two different opinionated sentences, if they involve identical or coreferred attributions, and at the same time, their corresponding evaluations are identical or approximately equivalent with respect to sentiment polarity, then the two opinionated sentences are considered to be paraphrastic.

Table 1. Categorization of opinion paraphrases in product reviews

Types	Attributes	Evaluations	Examples
1	exactly identical	exactly identical	操控性非常好(The controllability is very good.) 该车的操控性非常好。(The controllability of this car is very good.)
2	exactly identical	semantically equivalent	手感不错 (hand feeling is not bad) 手感好 (hand feeling good)
3	coreferent	exactly identical	性价比真高(The cost-performance ratio is really high) 性能价格比真高(The cost-performance ratio is really high)
4	coreferent	semantically equivalent	质地真不错 (The texture is really good) 材质挺好 (The material is very good)

3.3 Paraphrase Extraction

Since the definition of opinion paraphrase is based on the equivalence of attributes and their corresponding evaluations within opinionated sentences, attribute-evaluation pairs are very important knowledge for substitution-based paraphrase generation. To obtain such knowledge for opinion paraphrasing, we first extract all attribute-evaluation pairs from the training corpus and further cluster them in terms of attribute coreference relation and the polarity. Given two different attribute-evaluation pairs, if the attributes are coreferred each other and at the same time, the relevant polarity are identical, then the two attribute-evaluation pairs are paraphrastic and can be grouped to a cluster.

Due to the fact that polarity information has been manually annotated in the training corpora, attribute coreference resolution becomes the key to attribution-evaluation grouping. To address this problem, we combine two similarity measures, namely the literal similarity based on Jacard coefficient and the semantic similarity based on word embeddings.

(1) Literal similarity. As shown in Equation (1), Jaccard coefficient measures (denoted by *J*) the literal similarity of two attribute expressions A_1 and A_2 by counting the number of identical characters contained in them.

$$SimJ\ (A_1, A_2) = \frac{|\ set\ (A_1) \cap set\ (A_2)\ |}{|\ set\ (A_1) \cup set\ (A_2)\ |} \qquad (1)$$

Where, *set*(*A*) denotes the set of characters that form the attribute *A*.

It should be noted that unlike the classical edit distance, Jaccard coefficient ignores the influence of character location in attributes. Considering two pairs of Chinese attributes (外表, 外形) and (油耗, 耗油), their respective Jaccard coefficients are 0.33 and 1.

(2) Semantic similarity. Literal similarity measures rely on literal matching and work for product attributes with explicit literal connections. However, such information does not always exit in many co-referred feature expressions like 像素 (pixel) and 分辨率 (resolution). To address this problem, we introduce semantic similarity based on word embeddings. Actually, word embeddings map each word to an *n*-dimensional dense vector of real numbers and each dimension has certain latent semantic information (Mikolov, 2012; Mikolov *et al.*, 2013). Obviously, the data size has a strong relationship with the expression of semantic. Thus, we can obtain the similarity between two product attributes by calculating the cosine distance between their relevant vectors, as shown in Equation (2).

$$SimS\ (A_1, A_2) = \frac{\sum_{i=1}^{n} v_i(A_1) \times v_i(A_2)}{\sqrt{\sum_{i=1}^{n} v_i(A_1)^2} \times \sqrt{\sum_{i=1}^{n} v_i(A_2)^2}} \qquad (2)$$

Where, $v_i(A_1)$ and $v_i(A_2)$ ($1 \le i \le n$) denote the respective word embeddings of product attributes A_1 and A_2, and n denotes the number of dimensions in word embedding representation of product attributes.

Table 2 illustrates a sample of equivalent attribute-evaluation pairs extracted from the training corpora.

Table 2. A sample of equivalent attribute-evaluation pairs extracted from the training corpora

Product attributes	Positive evaluations	Negative evaluations
Price:价|价格|价钱|价位|...	*Low*: 合适|适中|实惠|优惠|不高|公道|比较便宜|有优势|值|...	*High*: 高|太高|真高|偏高|有点高|贵|太贵|偏贵|有点贵|不合理|有点无语|...
Acceleration: 加速|加速性|加速能力|...	*Excellent*: 有推背感|一点不软|很好|很给力|令人满意|灵敏|很优秀|...	*Weak*: 差|偏弱|有延迟|很突然|比较没劲|比较没力|...
Touch screen: 触摸屏|触屏|触控|触感|触控|...	*Fast/Sensitive*: 不错|好|很好|灵敏|灵活|快|给力|挺流畅|反应快|好用|灵敏度高|...	*Slow/Insensitive*: 不太灵敏||不是很灵敏|比较慢|有点不灵活|反应太慢|不好用|迟钝|过于灵敏|...

3.4 Paraphrase Generation

Given an opinionated sentence *S*, we generate paraphrases in two steps:

(1) **Opinion element substitution.** We first construct a set of equivalent utterances for each attribution or evaluation in *S* and store them with word lattice. For convenience, here we refer this word lattice as paraphrase word lattice.

The equivalent substitution of attributes or evaluations is essential to opinion paraphrase generation. In the present study, we perform this task by substituting attributes and their evaluations using the extracted attribute-evaluation pairs shown in Table 2.

(2) **n-best paraphrase decoding.** Once the paraphrase word lattice is constructed, our problem is now to score all potential paraphrases within the lattice and select the most probable paraphrases as the equivalent expansion of the input sentence. For simplicity and efficiency of implementation, in this paper we employ bigram

language models to rank the paraphrase candidates and thus decode n-best paths from the paraphrase word lattice. Each path forms a probable paraphrase for the input sentence.

Table 3 shows some generated paraphrases and their bigram scores.

Table 3. Examples of generated paraphrases.

Original sentences	Generated paraphrases	scores
操控性特棒。(The controllability is excellent.)	操控性非常好(The controllability is very good)	1.12e-34
	操控性比较好(The controllability is OK)	6.81e-35
反应有点慢。(The reaction is a bit slow.)	反应比较慢(The reaction is relatively slow)	5.55e-05
	反应迟缓(The reaction is tardy.)	3.70e-05
价格最低！(Lowest price!)	价格合理！(Reasonable price!)	1.29e-11
	价格优惠！(Favorable price!)	8.40e-12

3.5 Polarity conflict resolution

Polarity conflict will arise when an input opinioned sentence and its paraphrases receive different polarity types during polarity classification. The reason may be due to inconsistent generation of paraphrases between the training data and the input opinionated sentences for polarity classification.

In order to avoid polarity conflicts, we employ a simple voting mechanism. Given an input opinionated sentence and its k-best paraphrases generated by the systems, then we have k+1 opinionated sentences for polarity classification. Let i ($0 \leq i \leq k$)be the number of sentences that are classified as positive by the system and j ($0 \leq j \leq k$, and $i + j = k$) be the number of sentences that are negative during polarity classification. Thus, we can take the following three rules to determine the final polarity of the original sentence.

- Rule 1. if $i > j$, then the final polarity is positive.
- Rule 2. if $i < j$, then the final polarity is negative.
- Rule 3. if $i = j$, then the final polarity is the same as that of the original polarity of the input sentence during polarity classification.

4 Experimental Results and Discussions

To assess our approach, we developed a SVM-based sentiment polarity classifier and conducted experiments over car and celphone product reviews. This section reports our experimental results.

4.1 Experimental Setup

The experimental data come from two domains of online product reviews, namely car reviews and mobilephone reviews. Both corpora are manually annotated with multiple linguistic and opinion information, such as word segmentation, part-of-speech tags, opinion elements and polarity classification, and are further divided into training datasets and test datasets, respectively. Table 4 presents the basic statistics of the experimental data.

Table 4. Basic statistics of the experimental data

Dataset	Car			Mobilephone		
	Total	Pos	Neg	Total	Pos	Neg
Training	1904	841	963	2042	1033	1009
Test	913	462	451	1021	516	505

Table 5. The equivalent attribute-evaluation pairs.

Training data	SimJ		SimJ + SimS	
	A-P	A-N	A-P	A-N
Car	137	177	109	161
Mobilephone	88	121	78	107

As shown in Table 5, we have constructed two knowledge bases, namely the equivalent pairs of attributes and their related positive evaluations (A-P pairs for short), and the equivalent pairs of attributes and their related negative evaluations (A-N pairs for short), for opinion paraphrase generation from the two training corpora, respectively. It should be noted that we consider two strategies for attribute clustering during paraphrase extraction, namely attribute clustering with Jaccard coefficient (SimJ for short) and attribute clustering incorporating Jaccard coefficient and the word embeddings based semantic similarity with linear interpolation (SimJ+SimS for short).

Furthermore, in this paper the performance of polarity classification is reported in terms of accuracy.

4.2 Effects of different paraphrasing

Our first experiment intends to investigate the effects of different paraphrasing strategies on polarity classification, including different n-best paraphrase generation and paraphrasing on different data. Note that in this experiment, we consider five cases (viz. n = 1 to 5) during n-best paraphrase generation, and compare the relevant polarity classification results. Furthermore, to better understand the results for different n-best paraphrase generation, we also conducted an investigation on the relationship between the number of generated paraphrases for different data and the value of n in n-best paraphrases. It should be noted that in this experiment paraphrases are generated using equivalent attribute-evaluation pairs extracted with SimJ and SimS, as shown in Table 5. The results are summarized in Tables 6-9.

Table 6. Number of generated paraphrases for the training and test corpora in car domain

n-best	Dataset	Total	Pos	Neg
1	Training	3460	1708	1637
	Test	1702	805	792
2	Training	4914	2469	2296
	Test	2394	1141	1123
3	Training	6361	3229	2949
	Test	3083	1476	1452
4	Training	7796	3983	3596
	Test	3768	1809	1779
5	Training	9224	4735	4238
	Test	4450	2141	2104

Table 7. Number of generated paraphrases for the training and test corpora in mobilephone domain

n-best	Dataset	Total	Pos	Neg
1	Training	3768	1966	1802
	Test	1889	931	958
2	Training	5487	2897	2590
	Test	2751	1342	1409
3	Training	7187	3825	3362
	Test	3603	1749	1854
4	Training	8881	4751	4130
	Test	4447	2152	2295
5	Training	10568	5676	4892
	Test	5287	2555	2732

Table 8. Polarity classification over car reviews with different paraphrasing strategies

n-best	Para. on training data only	Para on test data only	Para. on both training and test data
1	70.09	70.69	70.19
2	70.29	71.60	70.80
3	70.29	71.70	70.50
4	67.98	73.01	69.50
5	67.77	71.70	69.49

The results in Tables 7-8 reveal that the value of n in n-best paraphrase generation appears to be an important influence factor for polarity classification with paraphrases. As n increases, the number of generated paraphrases is going up, and at the same time, the polarity classification accuracy is also rising for the case of performing paraphrasing on the training corpora. But in case of paraphrasing on the test data, the performance in polarity classification does not always rise with the number of generated paraphrases. The reason might be due to the fact larger number of generated paraphrases may introduce more polarity conflicts during polarity classification.

Table 9. Polarity classification over mobilephone reviews with different paraphrasing strategies

n-best	Para. on training data only	Para on test data only	Para. on both training and test data
1	83.45	83.74	83.45
2	84.62	84.62	87.86
3	85.41	85.31	87.76
4	86.19	86.10	89.81
5	85.21	85.50	89.81

4.3 Comparison of polarity classification with/without paraphrasing

As we have mentioned above, paraphrasing provides us with an option for avoiding the problems of data sparseness in open applications. So our last experiment is designed to examine the effectiveness of using paraphrasing in polarity classification. The experiment is conducted by comparing the results produced by the SVMs-classifies with paraphrases to that of the systems trained with the original corpora in Table 5 only (viz. the baseline systems). Furthermore, we consider two strategies, namely SimJ and SimJ&SimS, for paraphrase extraction in this experiment. The results are presented in Table 10.

Table 10. Comparison of polarity classification with/without paraphrasing

Systems	Car	Mobilephone
Baseline	66.06	83.74
Para. on training data based on SimJ	69.99	86.39
Para. on test data based on SimJ	73.72	86.19
Para. both training and test data based on SimJ	70.90	89.62
Para. on training data based on SimJ&SimS	70.29	89.19
Para. on test data based on SimJ&SimS	73.01	86.10
Para. on both training and test data based on SimJ&SimS	70.80	89.81

As can be seen from Table 10, using paraphrases can significantly improve polarity classification performance. Take the system with paraphrasing on the training data only via

SimJ&SimS, the accuracy can be improved by more than 4 and 6 percents for car and mobilephone reviews, respectively, compared to the baseline without using any paraphrases, illustrating in as sense the effectiveness of the proposed method. Furthermore, it can be observed from Table 10 that the system yields better results for mobilephone reviews than for cars. Moreover, the results over mobilephone data shows the performance in polarity classification can be enhanced by incorporating word embeddings based semantic similarity with literal similarity for paraphrase extraction, while the experiments on car reviews do not illustrate similar results. The reason might be due to the fact that car products have more attributes than mobilephone products, which makes it more difficult to cluster product attributes. In addition, more attributes may results in more paraphrases and thus produce more polarity conflicts to polarity classification.

4.4 Polarity conflicts between paraphrases

As we have mentioned above, larger number of generated paraphrases may introduce more serious polarity conflicts to polarity classification. Our third experiment is thus to investigate the problem of polarity classification conflict between paraphrases. This experiment is conducted by counting the number of polarity class conflicts between each sentence in the test data and its paraphrases using different n-best paraphrase generation. In addition, here the system for polarity classification is trained using the expanded training data via 5-best paraphrase generation. The results are summarized in Table 11.

Table 11. Number of polarity conflicts in the test dataset yielded by systems using training datasets with/without paraphrasing

n-best	Car		Mobilephone	
	SimJ	SimJ&SimS	SimJ	SimJ&SimS
1	216	228	40	39
2	224	233	41	47
3	232	238	42	50
4	236	243	46	51
5	237	247	48	51

As can be seen from Table 11, the number of conflicts is also increasing with the rise of generated paraphrases. Also, we can observe from Table 11 that there are more polarity conflicts in the car data than in the mobilephone data. This illustrates again that the larger number of product attributes in car domain might be one potential reason for its relative lower performance in polarity classification, in comparison to the mobilephone domain.

Our in-depth analysis shows that there are three main possible causes for polarity conflicts, as shown in Table 12.

(1) Incorrect paraphrase generation. Wrongly-generated paraphrases possibly lead to polarity conflicts, as illustrated by the first example in Table 12.

(2) Dynamic polarity. In cases of opinionated and paraphrases with dynamic polar words, the classifier does not always works and thus cannot consistently yield correct polarity classes, as the second example in Table 12 shows.

(3) Explanatory opinionated sentence. The evaluation expressions in explanatory opinionated sentences usually have more complicated structures and most often have no explicit polarity words, as shown by the third example in Table 12. It is obviously very difficult for the system to produce correct paraphrases or perform consistent polarity classification for explanatory opinionated sentences (Kim, *et al.*, 2013).

Table 12. Examples of generated paraphrases with contradict polarity.

No.	Paraphrases with polarity conflicts
1	(a) 价格浮动频繁(The price fluctuation is frequent) (b) 价格很不给力 (The price is ungelivable) (c) 价格太高(The price is too high)
2	(a) 内置软件过多(There is too much built-in software) (b) 内置软件很多(There is very much built-in software)
3	(a) 电池一般三天左右(The duration of the battery is about three days) (b) 电池玩一段时间会发烫(The battery will be hot after a period of working) (c) 电池 1880 毫安(The battery capacity is 1880 mAh)

5 Conclusions and Future Work

In this paper, we have exploited opinion paraphrasing to enhance Chinese sentence polarity classification. We have demonstrated that paraphrasing on training corpora and test corpora can result in a significant improvement of performance in polarity classification.

The encouraging results of the present study suggest several possibilities for future research. With regard to the concentrate of our current work, we have only employed very simple techniques to perform paraphrase extraction and generation. To further enhance our system, in future work we intend to exploit a more tailored method to achieve high-quality paraphrases for polarity classification. The present study focuses on Chinese polarity classification. In future, we also plan to extend our current system and apply it to other languages like English.

Acknowledgments

This study was supported by National Natural Science Foundation of China under Grant No.61170148 and No.60973081, the Returned Scholar Foundation of Heilongjiang Province, and Harbin Innovative Foundation for Returnees under Grant No.2009RFLXG007, respectively.

Reference

A. Fader, L. Zettlemoyer, and O. Etzioni. 2013. Paraphrase-driven learning for open question answering. In *Proceedings of ACL'13*, pages 1608-1618.

B. Pang, and L. Lee. 2008. Opinion mining and sentiment analysis. *Foundations and Trends in Information Retrieval*, 2(1-2): 1-135.

B. Pang, L. Lee, and S. Vaithyanathan. 2002. Thumps up? Sentiment classification using machine learning techniques. In *Proceedings of EMNLP-02*, pages 79-86.

C.-C. Chang, and C.-J. Lin. 2011. LIBSVM: A library for support vector machines. *ACM Transactions on Intelligent Systems and Technology*, 2(27): 1-27.

G. Fu, and X. Wang. 2010. Chinese sentence-level sentiment classification based on fuzzy sets. In *Proceedings of COLING'10*, pages 312-319.

M. Heilman, N.A. Smith. 2010. Tree edit models for recognizing textual entailments, paraphrases, and answers to questions. In *Proceedings of NAACL'10*, pages 1011-1019.

M. Speriosu, S. Upadhyay, N. Sudan, and J. Baldridge. 2011. Twitter polarity classification with label propagation over lexical links and the follower graph. In *Proceedings of the First workshop on Unsupervised Learning in NLP*, pages 53-63.

N. Madnani, and B. J. Dorr. 2010. Generating phrasal and sentential paraphrases: A survey of data-driven methods. *Computational Linguistics*, 36(3): 342-387.

P.D. Turney. 2002. Thumbs up or thumbs down?: semantic orientation applied to unsupervised classification of reviews. In *Proceedings of ACL'02*, pages 417-424.

R. Bhagat, and E. Hovy. 2013. What is a paraphrase?. *Computational Linguistics*, 39(3): 463-472

R. Mehrotra, R. Agrawal, and S.A. Haider. 2012. Dictionary based sparse representation for domain adaptation. In *Proceedings of CIKM'12*, pages 2395-2398.

R. Mihalcea, C. Banea, J. Wiebe. 2007. Learning multilingual subjective language via cross-lingual projections. In *Proceedings of ACL'07*, pages 976-983.

S. Volkova, T. Wilson, D. Yarowsky. 2013. Exploring sentiment in social media: Bootstrapping subjectivity clues from multilingual twitter streams. In *Proceedings of ACL'13*, pages 505-510.

S. Zhao, X. Lan, T. Liu, et al. 2009. Application-driven statistical paraphrase generation. In *Proceedings of the ACL-IJCNL'09*, pages 834-842.

T. Mikolov. 2012. Statistical language models based on neural networks. Doctoral Thesis, Brno University of Technology.

T. Mikolov, W. Yih, and G. Zweig. 2013. Linguistic regularities in continuous space word representations. In *Proceedings of NAACL-HLT.'13*, pages 746-751

T. Nakagawa, K. Inui, and S. Kurohashi. 2010. Dependency tree-based sentiment classification using CRFs with hidden variables. In *Proceedings of HLT-NAACL'10*, pages 786-794.

T. Wilson, J. Wiebe, and P. Hoffmann. 2009. Recognizing contextual polarity: An exploration of features for phrase-level sentiment analysis. *Computational Linguistics*, 35(3):99-433

H.D.Kim, M. Castellanos, M. Hsu, C.X. Zhai, U. Dayal, and R. Ghosh. 2013. Ranking explanatory sentences for opinion summarization. In *Proceedings of SIGIR'13*, pages 1069-1072

Problematic Situation Analysis and Automatic Recognition for Chinese Online Conversational System

Yang Xiang[†], Yaoyun Zhang, Xiaoqiang Zhou[‡], Xiaolong Wang, Yang Qin
Key Laboratory of Network Oriented Intelligent Computation,
Harbin Institute of Technology Shenzhen Graduate School, China
[†]**windseedxy@gmail.com** [‡]**xiaoqiang.jeseph@gmail.com**

Abstract

Automatic problematic situation recognition (PSR) is important for an online conversational system to constantly improve its performance. A PSR module is responsible of automatically identifying users' un-satisfactions and then sending feedbacks to conversation managers. In this paper, we collect dialogues from a Chinese online chatbot, annotate the problematic situations and propose a framework to predict utterance-level problematic situations by integrating intent and sentiment factors. Different from previous work, the research field is set as open-domain in which very few domain specific textual features could be used and the method is easy to be adapted to other domains. Experimental results show that integrating both intent and sentiment factors gains the best performance.

1 Introduction

Automatic conversational systems are computer programs that interact with human users based on their knowledge bases. Developers of conversational systems devote plenty of efforts and time in collecting and verifying knowledge so as to maximize the information needs of potential users. However, problematic situations are inevitable due to several reasons (i.e. human verifiers would make mistakes or omissions, or quality of some answers couldn't be judged without certain contexts). So it is necessary to equip a conversational system with an automatic PSR module to keep its performance constantly improved. The program is responsible of monitoring whether the dialogue or some utterances are problematic during interactions and then providing feedbacks to the dialogue managers.

Problematic situations reflect that a human user is not satisfied with answers that a conversational system offers. From one perspective, some of these un-satisfactions can be captured through a human user's dialogue acts. For example, if a user repeats requesting the same question or frequently changes topics, it is likely that the system provides unsatisfactory answers (Chai et al., 2006). From another perspective, some explicit manners (i.e. sentiment-related expressions or dissatisfied feelings) that reflect the change of a user's mentality would also indicate a problematic situation occurs. Some previous systems use surveys to capture users' satisfactions: they let users to vote or evaluate whether the system has perfectly help them complete certain tasks (Hastie et al., 2002; Higashinaka et al., 2010) so as to collect users' satisficing scores. However, for a real-world conversational application, there are very few users who are willing to provide this kind of feedbacks.

The dialogue materials for this research come from a Chinese online chatting robot—BIT, which is developed for chatting and entertainment. It also integrates real-time data query functions about share price, weather report, post-code and telephone area code lookup. In addition to queries about real-time data, the corpus is totally open-domain and the number of topics that a dialogue could be related is unlimited. We annotated problematic situation labels in the utterance level (whether a question-answer pair is problematic/whether an answer is problematic) and took a deeper analysis towards different cases. Finally, we introduce the PSR framework. This framework is simple but efficient: we mapped the user intent and user sentiment categories to two groups of representative features and predicted problematic situations with supervised learners.

Proceedings of the Third CIPS-SIGHAN Joint Conference on Chinese Language Processing, pages 43–51,
Wuhan, China, 20-21 October 2014

Our main contributions stem from the features, domains and language: Unlike most previous researchers who considered only user intent (Chai et al., 2006) or took offline satisfaction scores provided by users as user sentiment (Hastie et al., 2002; Higashinaka et al., 2010), our method integrates intent and sentiment in an online manner, which automatically identifies these two factors and gives the managers real-time feedbacks. The domain of the dialogue is open which is different from (Hastie et al., 2002; Chai et al., 2006). Another contribution is that this is the first work that solves this issue on the Chinese language, which has very different language specific features and resources from English.

We experimented on the corpus through 10-fold cross validation. In each individual fold, we compare our method with two baselines and with four popular classifiers. Results show that integrating both user intent and user sentiment factors gains the best performance with an average F_1 of 0.62 (by SVM).

Following, we first introduce related work o PSR from different perspectives. Introduction to the corpus are arranged next. The feature selections and the recognition framework are proposed in Section 4. Experiments, future work and conclusions constitute the rest.

2 Related Work

Previous researches in this literature differed in research grains, input features and research domains.

2.1 Dialog-level vs. Utterance-level

Most early work focused on the prediction of a complete dialogue. Hastie et al.(2002) predicted problematic dialogues from a series of DARPA Communicator dialogues according to user satisfaction rates, task completion predictors and some interaction based features. Walker et al. (2002) presented their prediction model on the basis of information the system collected early in the dialogue and in real time. Oulasvirta et al. (2006) reported relations between users' satisfaction rates among the goal-level, concept-level, task-level and command-level, and captured a number of qualified user features. Möller et al. (2008) evaluated performance of different models including linear regression models and classification trees on predicting dialog-level user satisfaction in three spoken dialogue datasets.

Although the predictions of progress towards dialogue completion might be used as a cue to the dialogue manager, the results couldn't reflect in which position a dialogue began to become problematic. Chai et al. (2006) proposed the definition of user intent and incorporate a few matching features to predict utterance-level problematic situations (whether an immediate answer is satisfactory). Engelbrecht et al. (2009) employ the Hidden Markov Model (HMM) to model the whole dialogue into a sequence where each node of the sequence corresponds to the quality of the utterance. Higashinaka et al. (2010a; 2010b) also use HMM to model the good/bad sequence and testing the effects of turn-wise and overall ratings. Similar spirit also exists in (Hara et al., 2010). Support Vector Machines (SVM) are used by Schmitt et al. (2011) for the quality prediction on the CMU's Let's Go Bus Information system (Raux et al., 2006) and ASR features are compared in their experiments.

2.2 Features

There are many factors that could affect the performance of judging whether a dialogue is problematic or not, i.e. time attributes like the total time of a dialogue and the time delays between utterances (Hastie et al., 2002; Walker et al., 2002; Möller et al., 2008), dialogue acts that may reflect user intents (Hastie et al., 2002) and users' satisfaction ratings toward the system's performance (Hastie et al., 2002). To avoid the side effects by Automatic Speech Recognition (ASR) and concentrate on the pure textual features in dialogues, several researchers only study the effect of dialogue acts and users' satisfaction ratings (Chai et al., 2006; Higashinaka et al., 2010). However, it has also proved that users' satisfaction ratings could not be always relied on since different groups of users may have different predictive powers (i.e. from novices to experts) (Möller et al., 2005).

2.3 Research Domains

Another main difference among previous researches is domain restriction. Specific domains or tasks simplify the PSR task and features are easy to be defined by employing domain experts. However, this restriction limits the ability of feature adaption from certain domains/tasks to others. In a way, domain-specific knowledge and user surveys are not easy to be adapted. As far as we know, most previous related work restricted their researches on specific domains such as travel plan making (Hastie et al., 2002), restricted scenarios (Chai et al., 2006), bus schedule information (Schmitt et al., 2011), music information (Hara et al., 2010), animal discussion and attentive listening (Higashinaka et al., 2010a; Higashinaka et al., 2010b).

3 Problematic Situation Analysis

This section will first introduce the characteristics of the corpus we construct and then provide definitions and examples for what we have learned from the dialogues.

3.1 Corpus Description

The corpus includes 479 dialogues with totally 3111 QA pairs. The dialogues are extracted from log files of the BIT robot from May to June, 2013. Each dialogue has a specific session ID, identifying that the dialogues are collected from different users or on different time. Chatting (> 2/3), stock real-time inquiries (<1/6) and weather report inquiries (<1/7) account for the largest proportion. The dialogues are almost original which contains a number of curse words (although we have removed some too dirty words), facial expressions (by expressing moods through several punctuations such as ":)"), boring statements (i.e. I am boring uh) as well as duplicate questions, indicating the irregular and informal characteristics of the online chatting contexts. The language of the corpus is Chinese, with very few English utterances (<1/100). The length of dialogues ranges from 1 to 64 QA pairs[1].

To collect users' un-satisfactions, the developers place good/bad comment buttons for each answer but it seems to be useless (seldom users would click the buttons). Through observation, we found that users' behaviors, including the type of both *inquiries* and *responses*, provide important cues to determine whether a user is satisfied with an answer or not. To show this relation, two examples are listed in Table 1.

We asked two annotators to label whether each answer is problematic or not. They gave their judgment according to whether they considered the answer provided by the chatting system was reasonable or not, but ignored whether it was not precise (i.e. a factual answer that is out of date). When labeling the current pair, they were asked to refer to the above interactions so as to take the context restrains into consideration. By using Cohen's kappa coefficient, the inter agreement of the two annotators is $\hat{P}_o \approx 0.933$, $\hat{P}_e \approx 0.602$, and $\kappa \approx 0.833$ which is relatively high. Most conflicts occur when the two annotators have different under standings towards a question or one of them couldn't understand what a question really means. The conflict labels are resolved by a third annotator. Finally, 832 out of 3111 pairs (26.7%) are labeled as problematic, indicating that the chatting system still has a lot of room for improvement.

<table>
<tr><th>Type.</th><th>Question by User</th><th>Answer by BIT</th><th>Explanation</th></tr>
<tr><td rowspan="2">Sentiment-related</td><td>你会…?
(Can you do…?)</td><td>这也不会,那也不会(I can't do anything.) -- problematic</td><td rowspan="2">The second question which is a curse sentence implies that the user is not satisfied with the robot's previous answer.</td></tr>
<tr><td>你真是个废物 (You are really a good-for-nothing.)</td><td>我是比特
(I am BIT.)</td></tr>
<tr><td rowspan="2">Intent-related</td><td>你儿子呢?
(Where's your son?)</td><td>你要闹哪样啊?
(What're you going to do?)
--Problematic</td><td rowspan="2">Adjacent utterances. Repeat questions reflect the unsatisfactory of the user towards the last answer. Probably due to irrelevant answers. On the left, the first answer is irrelavant.</td></tr>
<tr><td>你儿子呢?
(Where's your son?)</td><td>天若赐我辉煌,我必比天猖狂
(If the God favours me, I would be crazier than the God.[Chinese network catchwords]) -- Problematic</td></tr>
</table>

Table 1. Examples of problematic situations in BIT.

3.2 Corpus Deeper Analysis

According to observation, the style of sentences raised by users could be roughly divided into two groups: *questions* and *statements*(corresponding to *inquiries* and *responses* in the previous section). Questions are sentences that send inquiries to the system, indicating that users have some information needs. Contrarily, statements are sentences that reflect no information needs, but could express complains, exclamations or some other affections. We've also observed that a specific group of features is much related to questions while another group is more likely to co-occur with statements.

[1] In this paper, we will use the notion "utterance" and "QA pair" exchangeablely.

	Category	Utterance	Explanation
Int.	switch	1. 中国(China)	The current question belongs to a different topic from the last one. The beginning of a new **dialogue** (other than greeting) is classified to switch.
	retry	2. 中华人民共和国 (People's Republic of China)	The current question has the same idea as the last one but may be expressed in a different style.
	continue	3. 中国首都 (The capital of China)	The current question belongs to the same topic as the last one. The example is a detailed question about the topic "China".
	clarify	4. 中国首都在哪里? (Which city is the capital of China?)	Negotiate with the system to refine or coarsen the last question for a clearer intent.
Sen.	greeting	早上好(Morning) / 亲爱的! (Honey!)	Usually a beginning or ending of a dialog. Intimate speeches are also categorized into greeting.
	criticize/ response	你好聪明!(You are so clever!) / 你说对了(You are right)	Criticism or response towards the last answer. Positive or negative criticisms frequently occur in the corpus, indicating users' (un)satisfactions.
	exclaim/ statement	好烦啊!(It's so boring!) / 我喜欢**. (I love someone.)	Exclaims or statements that the user delivers which are not aiming at the chatbot.
	curse	Dirty words.	Explicit curse words that are inevitable in chatting dialogues. They sometimes show unsatisfactory, but sometimes occur dues to that the user has been ridiculed by the robot.
	order	讲个笑话!(Tell me a joke!)	Order the system to provide information or do something.
	other	。。。/ !!!	Utterances other than the above such as punctuations or symbols that might show speechless(。。。), exclaiming / warning(!!!) or some facial expressions.

Table 2: Examples and definitions for user intent (Int.) and user sentiment (Sen.).

Based on this intuition, we define two concepts as:

User Intent – the action of a user when raising a question, indicating that the user is executing an inquiry to the system.

User Sentiment – the sentiment or affection that a user expresses through his/her utterances, including negative and non-negative.

The definition of user intent follows (Chai et al., 2006). It mainly contains four lower-level types: *switch, continue, retry,* and *clarify*. Switch means to start a new topic or a new dialog. Continue, retry and clarify are restricted in the same topic, with different dialogue acts. User sentiment is associated with the following cases: *greeting, criticize/response, exclaim/statement, curse, order* and *other*. *Other* contains punctuations, facial expressions and special symbols that are frequently used in Chinese daily chatting. Examples with explanations for user intent and sentiment are listed in Table 2.

The annotations towards the lower-level categories have more conflicts (with an average κ about 0.5) than the problematic labels. The disagreements are solved after declaring some issues: 1) if intent and sentiment characteristics both occur, label according to the type of the sentence (question correlates with intent and statement with sentiment) 2) *Criticize*s are towards the system's last response while *curse*s are not.

Problematic situations that originate from the following types are more direct and easier to understand: a) repeat the last question (retry, 4.95%-45.45%); b) change the topic (switch, 32.27%-32.17% with 6.97% at the beginning); c) try to clarify what the user intended to ask (clarify, 1.29%-50%) d) negative criticisms towards the last answer (criticize, 13.79%-15.85%); e) negative words toward the robot (curse, 6.59%-11.7%). The percentages 4.95%-45.45% stand for that *retry* accounts for 4.95% in all, and among all the *retry* cases, 45.45% are problematic. We also have the polarity (negative or non-negative) of each user provided utterance annotated and find that nearly all the negative occur in statements. The rest problematic situations mostly come from the *other* type (8.61%-48.13% with 36.19% facial expressions that the system is not able to recognize), *continue* (8.01%-28.4%), *exclaim* (10.83%-19.58%) and *order* (7.23%-19.55%).

We also notice that in several cases, although users hadn't received satisfactory answers, they didn't mean to negotiate with the system any more, indicating that many users are not patient enough to provide cues. These cases bring about difficulties for the prediction. Another special case we notice is from the disagreements of annotators, that is, sentiment and intent characteristics could co-occur (i.e. repeated *curse*s). This inspires us to synthesize both user intent and user sentiment attributes for an utterance.

4 Recognition Framework for Problematic Situations

Based on a simple dependency analysis for a dialogue, we first map user intent and user sentiment into related feature groups, and then use the features to predict problematic situations.

4.1 Utterance Dependency Analysis

A dialogue could be modeled using a directed graph constituted by the question sequence $\boldsymbol{Q}$ and the answer sequence $\boldsymbol{A}$. In the graph, a node stands for an utterance (question/answer), and edges are drawn from each Q_{i-1} to Q_i, Q_i to A_i, A_{i-1} to A_i and A_{i-1} to Q_i. The edges stand for dependencies or constrains between utterances (Figure 1).

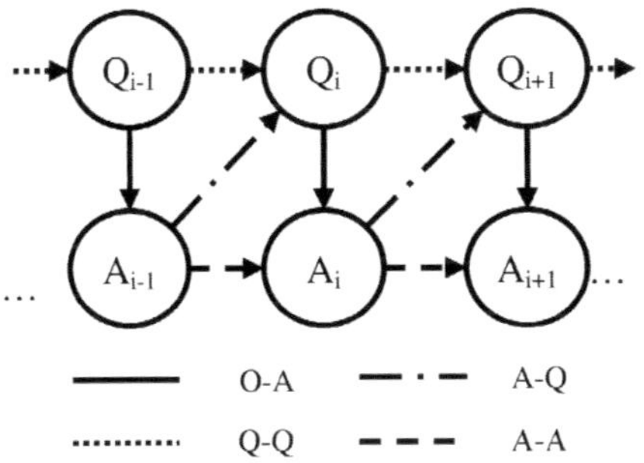

Figure 1. Dependencies or constrains in dialogues

In this work, the edges from A_{i-1} to Q_i and from Q_{i-1} to Q_i are the main dependency types we research. A_{i-1} to Q_i shows the last answer affects the current question in a dialog, always reflected by user sentiment. Constrains between questions are more related to user intent, i.e. the current question would have a high similarity with the last one if one attempts to retry an inquiry. The following example typically shows the two types of constrains:

Q_{i-1}: *Who did you go with yesterday?*

A_{i-1}: *My advantage is that I am handsome.*

Q_i: *Who did you go with yesterday?*

A_i: *If the God favours me, I would be crazier than the God.*

Q_{i+1}: *You are an idiot.*

In the example, the *retry* case from Q_{i-1} to Q_i implies that A_{i-1} should not be a good answer. The negative *curse* Q_{i+1} indicates that A_i may be problematic.

4.2 Mapping to problematic situations

To avoid cascade errors brought about by lower-level classifications, we weaken the category constrains by mapping the taxonomy to related features. The four types for user intent could be distinguished by features considering about similarity between sentences, which descends from *retry*, *clarify* to *continue* and *switch*. For the six types in user sentiment, we define word features, word polarity features and pattern features to make the types distinguished.

In our proposed framework, the automatic PSR problem is simplified into a one level binary classification task in which utterances are modelled with general features, user intent specific features and sentiment specific features. General features are textual and non-textual features that have nothing to do with user intent or user sentiment, including: *whether the answer is from the system's default response list to underdeveloped knowledge*, *whether the question is a real-time inquiry*, *the number of utterances before and follow* (especially to distinguish the beginning or ending of a dialog), *the similarity between the question and its corresponding answer*.

User intent specific features are those extracted from the perspective of user intent, mainly related to the similarity between two adjacent questions. User sentiment specific features are those extracted from the perspective of user sentiment, which focus on whether a user-raised utterance contains any sentiment information.

4.3 Intent Specific Feature Selection

Specifically, we tag whether the current question is *retry* because *retry* always corresponds to a very high similarity which is easy to be identified and many of them are related to problematic situations. We also use the similarity between two questions to distinguish the other types of intents. Typical features are listed in Table 3(NE stands for Name Entity).

The semantic similarity measure between questions (labeled by * in Table 3) is based on a Chinese semantic web, HowNet (Dong and Dong, 2006). The defined semantic similarity in HowNet is a normalized real value ([0,1]) of the shortest path connecting two words in the HowNet Concept Relation Net. Suppose two questions P and Q (word sequence size m and n, respectively), the semantic similarity between them is defined as:

$$ssim(P,Q)=\frac{1}{2}\left(\frac{\sum_{i=1}^{m}P_i}{m}+\frac{\sum_{j=1}^{n}Q_j}{n}\right)$$

where P_i and Q_j are denoted as:

$$P_i=\max(ssim(P_i,Q_1),ssim(P_i,Q_2),...,ssim(P_i,Q_n))$$

$$Q_j=\max(ssim(P_1,Q_j),ssim(P_2,Q_j),...,ssim(P_m,Q_j))$$

$ssim(P_i,Q_m)$ denotes the semantic similarity of the ith word in *Question P* and the mth word in *Question Q*. If two words are the same, the similarity is set to *1*.

The final similarity is defined as:

$$sim(P,\ Q)=\lambda_1 nsim(P,\ Q)+\lambda_2 ssim(P,\ Q)$$

$nsim(P,Q)$ is the normalized real value of the number of words the two questions share. λ_1 and λ_2 are the weighted parameters (set to be *0.5,0.5* in our experiment).

Feature	Description
Exact match (Boolean)	After removing punctuations and stop words.
No. of NEs	By analyzing results of LTP.
NE similarity	The match No. and contents for NEs.
Ques. Similarity	Weighted similarity based on lexicon and semantics*.
Ques. similarity without NEs	Weighted similarity based on lexicon and semantics*.
Target word	The target word in a question.
Dependency similarity	Dependency pattern similarity.

Table 3. User intent specific features.

The target words, name entities and dependency trees are identified or generated by LTP (LTP, Liu et al., 2011). Target words are defined as the direct objects that the root verb governs in a dependency parse tree in questioning sentences. The dependency similarity is computed by counting the number of common dependency relations (normalized to [0,1]).

4.4 Sentiment Specific Feature Selection

User sentiment is a good reflection of a user's current mood. The difficulty lie on that *curse* sentences and negative *criticisms* are not easy to be distinguished, especially for the Chinese language where many sentences have no subjects at all. A solution is that considering both the similar key words between the last answer and the current statement, and whether a second person pronoun (i.e. you/BIT) exists.

This work models the possible relations from sentiments to problematic situations by defining a series of sentiment related features. We employ dictionary-based method (Zhao et al., 2010) to judge the polarity of words in a sentence. Typical features are shown in Table 4.

Feature	Example
Key words	弱智(stupid), 次(weak)
Question word/ question mark	为什么(why), 是什么 (what), 是谁(who), ?
Target word	天气(weather), 人名 (person name)
Ending word	好吗(is it ok?), 吗(modal)
Sent. pattern	你好/真/太傻(you're quite/very/too stupid)
Part-of-Speech	Adjectives, nouns
Polarity	Polarity of a word
Person pronoun	你(you), 比特(the name of the robot)
Dependency	Subject-verb-object (SBV and VOB by LTP)

Table 4. User sentiment specific features.

Cursing sentences or negative criticisms are usually expressed in certain patterns which could be captured through regular expressions after removing adverbs and modals. Adjective and noun words are good indicators for sentiment which could be looked up in sentiment dictionaries. We employ two general Chinese sentiment dictionaries (NTUSD[2] and HowNet) to determine the polarity of a word (including both nouns and adjectives for the consideration of both *You're a fool* and *You're foolish.*). In addition, we tag the sentence as *negative* if it only contains negative words (key words) after removing useless components. Real-time inquiries are special cases that we should filter out through key words matching.

There are also something special that we should consider. Suppose there are three continuous pairs: A->B->C: If the question in B contains negative criticism information but A is a real-time inquiry, we couldn't directly judge A is problematic. A typical example is that the answer is closely related but is not precise (i.e. out of date). Inquiry includes questions about weather,

[2] http://nlg18.csie.ntu.edu.tw:8080/lwku/pub1.html

stock, post code, telephone and identity code in this system.

In addition to un-satisfactions for not achieving the desired answer, *curse/criticism* sentences could also grow out from some other cases: (1) the user has been ridiculed by the system thereby becomes irritated; (2) the user just wants to express his/her feelings to the system through repeated statements. These cases are not directly related to problematic situations, which, however, haven't been well recognized yet, hindering the improvements of the learners.

4.5 The Recognition Framework

We expected that the lower-level category information could be well modeled through features and classifiers. General features, user intent specific features and user sentiment specific features are extracted for each QA pair. Intuitively, the feature groups for user intent and user sentiment have relatively different emphasis and the hybrid features should naturally increase the system's recall.

Suppose the sequences *are* $\boldsymbol{Q}$ and $\boldsymbol{A}$, in which Q_i is to be determined (see Figure 1). The automatic PSR model is described as the follows:

a) Pre-processing: tokenization, POS tagging, parsing, removing stop words, and filtering system specified inquires (weather, stock, post code, telephone and identity code);
b) Extract sentiment specific features for Q_i based on Q_i;
c) Extract intent specific features for Q_i based on Q_{i-1} and Q_i;
d) Tag whether Q_i is *retry* or not, tag whether Q_i is *negative* or not;
e) Determine problematic of Q_i according to sentiment (*retry* or not) and intent labels (*negative* or not), specific features (Table 3 and 4) and general features (§4.2), as well as the labels for Q_{i-1} (*retry, negative,* and *problematic*);
f) Post-processing: For the last QA pair in a dialog, if a same pair exists before and is labeled as problematic, Q_i is labeled problematic.

The reason why we also take the labels of Q_{i-1} into account is based on the fact that the labels of Q_{i-1} may help determine the current label. For example, if the last intent indicates a *retry* and the current question indicates a *switch* (a much lower similarity with the last one), it is very likely that the user has tried at least twice but hasn't received a satisfactory answer. In this case, the previous *retry* could also increase the probability of *switch*, which is helpful for the final determination.

Post processing mainly deals with the last utterance in a dialogue which doesn't have any followings.

5 Experiments and Analysis

To prove the effectiveness of our model, we compare it with two baselines on four classical classifiers through 10-fold cross-validation.

The baselines include the model with general features (GF) and intent specified features (ISF), the model with GF and sentiment specified features (SSF). We name our hybrid model that with hybrid features as GF+ISF+SSF. We report the detailed performance gains of the GF+ISF+SSF model compared with the two baselines with intense experiments on the corpus. General features (GF) only contains little useful information towards our task and has very poor performance, therefore we didn't set it as a baseline. We test the model with SVM, Naïve Bayes, Decision Tree and CRF so as to find out an efficient and stable learner for the task.

GF+SSF			
	Prec.	**Rec.**	$\mathbf{F_1}$
SVM	92.97	44.44	60.05
J48	85.03	22.94	35.85
NB	95.37	22.53	36.37
CRF	89.20	40.06	55.01
GF+ISF			
	Prec.	**Rec.**	$\mathbf{F_1}$
SVM	93.77	43.80	59.57
J48	88.76	21.72	34.67
NB	**96.39**	23.24	36.42
CRF	88.74	44.89	59.46
GF+ISF+SSF			
	Prec.	**Rec.**	$\mathbf{F_1}$
SVM	85.73	49.38	**62.19**
J48	79.15	24.89	37.75
NB	85.97	29.09	43.35
CRF	91.08	**45.02**	60.16

Table 5. Average performance by cross-validation.

10-fold cross validations are performed on the dataset. To specify, the corpus should be divided in the unit of dialogues rather than utterances for the sake of integrating sequential features (i.e. the previous labels). LibSVM (Chang and Lin, 2011), Naïve Bayes and Decision Tree (J48) were provided by the Weka toolkit (Hall, et al.,

fold	Prec.	Rec.	F_1	Percent.	Best	Learner	im-in	im-sen
1	89.21	49.01	63.27	26.69	intent	CRF	-0.03	+6.1
2	84.57	50.51	63.25	30.24	hybrid	SVM	+3.16	+1.74
3	92.41	42.07	57.82	29.51	hybrid	CRF	+0.12	+6.38
4	85.47	47.52	61.08	28.85	hybrid	SVM	+3.16	+3.16
5	84.82	54.92	66.67	28.41	hybrid	SVM	+3.61	+3.61
6	95.42	44.17	60.39	25.94	sentiment	SVM	-0.07	-0.07
7	78.45	55.69	65.14	26.90	hybrid	SVM	+3.12	+3.72
8	85.33	52.46	64.97	32.50	hybrid	SVM	+2.93	+3.42
9	83.03	51.31	63.43	26.90	hybrid	SVM	+5.47	+4.0
10	94.29	39.87	56.05	28.55	sentiment	SVM	+1.3	-0.2

Table 6. Detailed results in 10-fold cross validation.
"im-in" and "im-sen" stand for the improvements of the hybrid model than intent and sentiment specific models. "Percent." stands for the proportion% of problematic utterances in this fold of data.

2009). CRF is provided by CRF++[3], a C++ implementation. Metrics of *precision*, *recall* and F_1 are used for evaluation.

We list results for the average performance of cross-validation in Table 5. From the data we notice, all the four learning models perform well in precision but a little poor in recall (no matter for which model). And the case of Naïve Bayes is especially obvious. According to analysis towards the output, the performance of high precision and low recall mainly due to the following reasons: Firstly, we select features empirically which may generate strong rules: if some condition is satisfied, some conclusion is drawn. Secondly, there are still a number of situations that we couldn't resolve by training our models. For example, not all *retry* result in problematic situations, and sometimes the users' intents are hard to understand. Finally, there are many negative sentences that are not related to problematic situations which could confuse the learners.

We also notice that SVM and CRF have much better results than J48 and Naïve Bayes, implying the effectiveness of the two classifiers. The hybrid model outperforms the two baselines mainly by recall, reflecting the reasonability of considering both user intent and sentiment.

More evidence for the robustness of the hybrid features and the learners can be recognized through a detailed report of the cross validation (Table 6). From the table we observe two important things: one is that SVM performs much more stable than other classifiers, and CRF is not so good as what we have expected, considering there are sequential features; the other is that the hybrid model outperforms other baselines in most cases, and it also has comparative results in other cases (fold 1, 6, and 10).

What we have also noticed is that although Naïve Bayes doesn't achieve a better score in F_1, it always performs well in precision (Table 5). Its characteristics of running fast, easy implemented and with high precision enable the developers to integrate the automatic recognizer in the system and send back precise predictions in real time.

6 Future Work

We left two problems for future work. Firstly, although we have defined lower-level categories for user sentiment and user intent, we failed to well identify each of them. More representative features (maybe word embedding or something else) should be extracted to clearly identify their boundaries. Secondly, there is much noise in the original corpus which may affect the model performance. An automatic sieve should be developed to deal with the noisy information.

7 Conclusion

This paper analyses different problematic situations under the chatting context for the Chinese language. Other than previous work, we propose the problematic situation recognition model from two perspectives—user sentiment and user intent, and test the proposed model on a totally open-domain corpus. Experiments verify that integrating both the two factors gains the best predicting result. More representative features and more efficient approaches will be developed for further improvement.

Acknowledgements

This work is supported in part by the National Natural Science Foundation of China (No. 612-72383 and 61173075). And the foundations of

[3] http://crfpp.googlecode.com/svn/trunk/doc/index.html

Shenzhen(JC201005260118A, ZDSY20120613-125401420, JCYJ20120613151940045, and JC201005260175A).

Reference

Joyce Y. Chai, Chen Zhang, and Tylor Baldwin. 2006. Towards Conversational QA: Automatic Identification of Problematic Situations and User Intent. In Proceedings of COLING/ACL.

C. C. Chang and C. J. Lin. 2011. LIBSVM : A Library for Support Vector Machines. ACM Transactions on Intelligent Systems and Technology, 2(27)1-27.

Zhendong Dong, and Qiang Dong. 2006. HowNet and the Computation of Meaning. River Edge, NJ: World Scientific, 25-76.

Klaus-Peter Engelbrech, et al. 2009. Modeling User Satisfaction with Hidden Markov Model. In Proceedings of the SIGDIAL 2009 Conference. Association for Computational Linguistics.

Sunao Hara, Norihide Kitaoka, and Kazuya Takeda. 2010. Estimation Method of User Satisfaction Using N-gram-based Dialogue History Model for Spoken Dialogue System. LREC.

Mark Hall, Eibe Frank, Geoffrey Holmes, Bernhard Pfahringer, Peter Reutemann, Ian H. Witten. 2009. The WEKA Data Mining Software: An Update; SIGKDD Explorations, Volume 11, Issue 1.

Helen Wright Hastie, Rashmi Prasad, Marilyn-Walker. 2002. What's the Trouble: Automatically Identifying Problematic Dialogues in

DARPA Communicator Dialogue Systems. In Proceedings of ACL.

Ryuichiro Higashinaka, et al. 2010. Issues in Predicting User Satisfaction Transitions in Dialogues: Individual Differences, Evaluation Criteria, and Prediction Models. Spoken Dialogue Systems for Ambient Environments. 48-60.

Ryuichiro Higashinaka, et al. 2010. Modeling User Satisfaction Transitions in Dialogues from Overall Ratings. In Proceedings of the SIGDIAL 2010 Conference.

Ting Liu, Wanxiang Che, Zhenghua Li. 2011. Language Technology Platform. Journal of Chinese Information Processing. 25(6): 53-62.

Sebastian Möller, et al. 2005. Quality of Telephone-based Spoken Dialogue Systems.

Sebastian Möller, Klaus-Peter Engelbrecht, and Robert Schleicher. 2008. Predicting the Quality and Usability of Spoken Dialogue Services. Speech Communication 50.8: 730-744.

A.Oulasvirta, S.Möller, S. Engelbrecht, et al. 2006. The Relationship of User Errors to Perceived Usability of a Spoken Dialogue System. In Proceedings of the 2nd ISCA/DEGA Tutorial and Research Workshop on Perceptual Quality of Systems, Berlin.

A. Raux, D. Bohus, B. Langner, A. W. Black, and M. Eskenazi. 2006. Doing Research on a Deployed Spoken Dialogue System: One Year of Let's Go! Experience. In Proceedings of the International Conference on Speech and Language Processing.

Alexander Schmitt, Benjamin Schatz, and Wolfgang Minker. 2011. Modeling and Predicting Quality in Spoken Human Computer Interaction. In Proceedings of the SIGDIAL 2011 Conference.

Marilyn A. Walker, et al. 2002. Automatically Training a Problematic Dialogue Predictor for a Spoken Dialogue System. Journal of Artificial Intelligence Research, Vol.16(1): 293-319.

Yanyan Zhao, Bing Qin, and Ting Liu. 2010. Sentiment Analysis. Journal of Software, 21(8): 1834-1848.DARPA Communicator Dialogue Systems. In Proceedings of ACL.

Segment-based Fine-grained Emotion Detection for Chinese Text

Odbal
Dept. Of Automation, University of Science and Technology of China
Institute of Intelligent Machines, Chinese Academy of Sciences
wdbl@iim.ac.cn

Zengfu Wang
Dept. Of Automation, University of Science and Technology of China
Institute of Intelligent Machines, Chinese Academy of Sciences
zfwang@ustc.edu.cn

Abstract

Emotion detection has been extensively studied in recent years. Current baseline methods often use token-based features which cannot properly capture more complex linguistic phenomena and emotional composition in fine grained emotion detection. A novel supervised learning approach—segment-based fine-grained emotion detection model for Chinese text has been proposed in this paper. Different from most existing methods, the proposed model applies the hierarchical structure of sentence (e.g., dependency relationship) and exploits segment-based features. Furthermore, the emotional composition in short text is addressed by using the log linear model. We perform emotion detection on our dataset: news contents, fairly tales, and blog dataset, and compare our proposed method to representative existing approaches. The experimental results demonstrate the effectiveness of the proposed segment-based model.

1 Introduction

Emotion detection aims to identify fine-grained emotion categories (e.g., happy, angry, disgust, fear, sadness and surprise) of a given text, and it is a challenging and difficult problem with applications throughout natural language processing.

Currently, the most widely used probability models for emotion classification are supervised based machine learning algorithms, such as Naive Bayes (NB) and Support Vector Machine (SVM) etc,. Researchers have trained the classifier depends on corpus-based features, mainly unigrams, combined with lexical features (Alm et al, 2005; Aman and Szpakowicz, 2007; Katz, et al, 2007). Nevertheless, these methods used in the emotion classification system concentrate on token based features and do not include any linguistic or contextual information, which often yields poor performance. Therefore, recent studies have investigated the approach using contextual information around emotional words to identify fine grained emotion classes. (Das and Bandyopadhyay, 2010) observe that the emotion word, POS, intensifier and direct dependency features play an important role in extracting emotional expressions as well as tagging sentences with emotions and intensities. (Diman Ghazi et al., 2012) propose an approach which takes the contextual emotion of a word and the syntactic structure of the sentence into account to classify sentences by emotion classes. However, these works still use token-based features, which cannot address the problem of the emotional composition, especially those that are the expression-level representations.

There has been previous work using composition rules and statistical methods to handle sentiment composition. (Moilanen and Pulman, 2007) propose a theoretical composition model, and evaluate a lexical dependency parsing post-process implementation, which treat both negation and intensifier via three models: sentiment propagation, polarity conflict resolution and polarity reversal. (Choi and Cardie, 2008) incorporate structural inference motivated by compositional semantics into the learning procedure for subsentential sentiment analysis. (Socher et al., 2011, 2012) present matrix-vector representations with a recursive neural network. The model is built on a parse tree where the nodes are associated to a vector. The matrix captures how each constituent modifies its neighbor. (Baptiste Chardon et al,. 2013) propose a computational model that accounts for the effects of negation and modality on opinion expressions. However, it is not as clear how to use a compositional treatment to classify fine grained emotion classes. Sentiment composition combines

Proceedings of the Third CIPS-SIGHAN Joint Conference on Chinese Language Processing, pages 52–60,
Wuhan, China, 20-21 October 2014

individual positive and negative words or phrases, and the final polarity of a sentence is positive or negative. Nevertheless, it is more challenging and difficult to make categorization into distinct emotion classes for the higher level of classification in emotion recognition task. In order to facilitate our discussion, consider the following examples:

1.不过在教堂里,站在讲台上的牧师却是大叫大嚷,非常生气. (But inside the church the pastor stood in the pulpit, and spoke very loudly and angrily.)[anger]

2.迷信使她的血一会儿变冷,一会儿变热.(Superstition made her alternately shudder with cold or burn with the heat of fever.)[fear]

3.骑在桦木条上的那个蜡人忽然变得又高又大了.他像一阵旋风似地扑向纸花那儿去,说:"居然把这样的怪想头灌进一个孩子的脑子里去!全是些没有道理的幻想!"这蜡人跟那位戴宽帽子的枢密顾问官一模一样,而且他的那副面孔也是跟顾问官一样发黄和生气.可是那些纸花在他的瘦腿上打了一下,于是他缩做一团,又变成了一个渺小的蜡人.(All at once the wax doll which rode on the carnival rod seemed to grow larger and taller, and it turned round and said to the paper flowers, "How can you put such things in a child's head? they are all foolish fancies;" and then the doll was exactly like the lawyer with the broad brimmed hat, and looked as yellow and as cross as he did; but the paper dolls struck him on his thin legs, and he shrunk up again and became quite a little wax doll.)[anger]

In the first example, we can use the key words "大叫","大嚷"(spoke very loudly), and "生气"(anger), to easily identify the emotion classes of the sentence. However, in the second example, we cannot use the words "血"(blood), "变冷"(make cold), "变热"(make burn) or the phrase "血变冷" and "血变热" to easily detect the final emotion category of the sentence. "血" and "变冷" carry "fear" category, and the words "血" and "变热" can be classified as "joy", but the final emotion label of the sentence is "fear". In the last example, there are four types of emotion classes for sub-sentential segments, for example, "蜡人变得又高又大"(the wax doll seemed to grow larger and taller)[joy], "怪想头"(such things) [surprise], "没有道理的幻想!"(foolish fancies)[anger], "生气"(anger) [anger], and "一个渺小的蜡人"(a little wax doll)[sad], but the overall emotion of the short text is "anger".

These examples demonstrate that a sentence or short text exists several expression-level emotion labels, and the words or constituents interact with each other to yield the overall emotion label, which cannot be easily resolved by token-based methods. To solve this problem, we present segment-based supervised learning approach to investigate how to recognize the overall emotion tag of a sentence or short text. Closer to our current purposes is the work of (Nakagawa et al, 2010). It employs a conditional random field (CRF) for sentiment classification of Japanese and English subjective sentences using dependency tree-based method. In their method, the sentiment polarity of each dependency subtree, which is not observable in training data, is represented by a hidden variable. The polarity of the whole sentence is calculated in consideration of interactions between the hidden variables. However, this research doesn't work on the fine grained emotion recognition and it is unable to deal with multiple consecutive tokens (e.g., a phrase).

In this paper, we employ semi-Markov conditional random fields (semi-CRFs) for segment-based emotion detection. Semi-CRFs (Sarawagi and Cohen, 2004) are more powerful than CRFs in that they can assign labels to segments instead of tokens; hence, features can be defined at the segment level. To our knowledge, segment-based fine-grained emotion recognition for Chinese text has not been attempted. Our learning framework can be determined in a three-step process: (1) segment the input sentence or short text into some dependency subtrees and then (2) employ the semi-CRFs with various context informed features to assess the emotion classes of the constituents of the segment, and (3) exploit a composition learning model to combine the segment level emotion labels. We evaluate the proposed model on our construction dataset, which consists of news content, fairy tales and blog dataset, and the experimental results show that segment-based learning algorithm works well in our experimental data.

2 Related Work

Supervised learning method has been well studied and used in fine-grained emotion detection with promising results. (Alm et al., 2005) explores the text-based emotion prediction problem empirically, using supervised machine learning. (Das and Bandyopadhyay, 2010) deals with the extraction of emotional expressions and tagging of English blog sentences with Ekman's six basic emotion tags and any of the three intensities: low, medium and high. Baseline system is developed based on WordNet Affect lists and dependency relations. SVM based supervised framework is employed by incorporating different word and context level features. (Chaffar and Inkpen, 2011) adopts a supervised machine learning approach to recognize six basic emotions (anger, disgust, fear, happiness, sadness and surprise) using a heterogeneous emotion-annotated dataset which combines news headlines, fairy tales and blogs. (Saif Mohammad, 2012) uses word-level affect lexicons to provide significant improvements in sentence-level emotion classification. (Purver and Battersby, 2012) describe a set of experiments using automatically labeled data to train supervised classifiers for multi-class emotion detection in Twitter messages with no manual intervention. (Diman Ghazi et al., 2012) present a method which enables us to take the contextual emotion of a word and the syntactic structure of the sentence into account to classify sentences by emotion classes.

Other related studies on this task are emotion resource construction. (Xu et al., 2010) adopts a graph-based algorithm to build Chinese emotion lexicons for public use. (Patra et al., 2013) uses the Potts model for constructing emotion lexicon annotated with Ekman's six basic emotion classes. There are also studies that analyzed the deeper level information, such as color-concept-emotion associations (Volkova et al., 2012); emotion causes detection (Chen et al., 2010); and learning hashtags to improve emotion classification performance (Qadir and Riloff, 2013). In sentiment composition, the presence of modalities is generally used to combine the individual positive and negative word (Moilanen and Pulman, 2007; Choi and Cardie, 2008; Nakagawa, 2010; Socher et al., 2011, 2012; Chardon et al,.2013). There is a few works on the higher level of composition in emotion recognition task.

Different from above approaches, we use a segment-based method for the fine-grained emotion detection. To use the strengths of segment-based features, we propose to employ the semi-Markov Conditional Random Field, which was previously used in information extraction to tag continuous segments of input sequences and outperformed conventional CRFs in the task of named entity recognition and opinion extraction (Sarawagi and Cohen, 2004; Okanohara et al., 2006; Andrew, 2006; Yang and Cardie, 2012). We describe this model in the following section.

3 Segment-based Emotion Detection using semi-CRF

In this section, we first introduce the semi-Markov conditional random field and then elaborate the proposed segment-based emotion detection model.

3.1 Semi-CRF

In this subsection we briefly review the semi-Markov conditional random field. We follow the definitions in (Sarawagi and Cohen, 2004). Let $s = s_1^m =< s_1, \cdots, s_m >$ denote a segmentation of an observed sequence x. To represent all the information associated with each segmentation, we define s_i as $s_i =< t_i, u_i, y_i >$, which consisting of three components: a start position t_i, an end position u_i, and a label y_i. We assume that segments have a positive length bounded above by the pre-defined upper bound L ($1 \leq u_i - t_i + 1 \leq |x|$) and completely cover the sequence x without overlapping, that is, s satisfies $t_1 = 1$, $u_m = |x|$, and $t_i + 1 = u_i + 1$ for i = 1, ..., m-1. For emotion detection, a valid segmentation of the sentence " 善良的姑娘细心地照顾这只弱小的猫" might be $s =< (1, 3, happy), (4, 6, happy), (7, 11, sad) >$, corresponding to the label sequence $y =< happy, happy, sad >$.

Then, Semi-CRF defines a conditional probability of a state sequence y given an observed sequence x by:

$$p(y, s|x) = \frac{1}{Z(x)} exp(\sum_{i=1}^{m} \sum_{t=1}^{|s|} \lambda_i f_i(x, s, y)) \quad (1)$$

where $f_i(x, s, y) = f_i(y_{j-1}, y_j, x, s_j)$ is a feature function and Z(x) is the normalization factor as defined for CRF. The model parameters are a set of real-valued weights $\lambda = \{\lambda_j\}$, each of which represents the weight of a feature.

$$Z(x) = \sum_{s'} exp(\sum_{i=1}^{m} \sum_{t=1}^{|s|} \lambda_i f_i(x, s', y)) \quad (2)$$

The inference problem for semi-CRF can be solved by using a semi-Markov analog of the usual Viterbi algorithm. An implementation of semi-CRF is available at http://crf.sourceforge.net.

3.2 Segment-based Emotion Detection Model

In this subsection, we will describe our segment-based emotion detection model (see Figure 1).

Assume that we are given a sequence of observations $x = x_1^J =< x_1, \cdots, x_J >$ and we would like to infer a corresponding label y^t, where $y^t \in y$ is one of the Ekman' s six basic emotion types such as happiness, sadness, fear, surprise, anger and disgust. Every emotion class is regarded as a possible emotion tag for the input sentence or short text with a posterior probability $p(y|x)$.

Our proposed segment-based approach can be determined in a three-step process: at first, a sentence or short text is divided into non-fixed length segments. We construct segment units from the dependency parse tree of each sentence, and then build up possible segment candidates based on those units. More specifically, the dependency subtrees that contain the path from the root node (e.g., core verb 照顾(take care of)) to leaf node are selected for the candidate segmentation. For instance, let us consider the subjective sentence "善良的姑娘细心地照顾这只弱小的猫"(Good girl carefully take care of the small cat). The dependency parse tree of this sentence is illustrated in Figure 2. We can select four dependency subtrees (善良的姑娘,照顾) (good girl, take care of), (细心地,照顾) (carefully, take care of), (照顾,这只,猫) (take care of, the cat), and (照顾,弱小的猫) (take care of, the small cat) as the candidate segmentations. The reason that the dependency representations are chosen as the segment unit is, compared with phrase-structure tree, it can describe more complicated structure information of a sentence (such as the long distance dependency relation). Then, we use the segmentation strings as observations and supply various context-informed features as inputs to the semi-CRF to assess the emotion classes of the segment. That is, instead of determining y directly from x, we introduce hidden variables $z = (z_1, \cdots, z_m)$ as intermediate decision variables, where $z_i = (s_i, y_i)$ and $y_i \in \{$ happiness, sadness, fear, surprise, anger, disgust, none $\}$, so that y_i represents whether s_i is a phrase with happiness, sadness, fear, surprise, anger, or disgust, or none of the above. In the above example, we can obtain the emotion label of each segment $y =< happy, happy, happy, sad >$. At last, once we determine the intermediate decision variables, we use a probabilistic model based on log linear model to combine expression-level emotion categories. For simplicity, we decompose the probability by introducing two probability distribution models: expression-level emotion detection model and emotion tag distribution model. Specifically, for the segment-based emotion detection problem, the discriminate function can be defined as follows:

$$
\begin{aligned}
p(y^t|x) &= \sum_{s,y} p(s_1^K|x) \cdot p(y_1^K|s_1^K, x) \cdot p(y^t|y_1^K, s_1^K, x) \\
&= \sum_{s,y} \prod_{k=1}^{K} p(y_1^K, s_1^K|x) \cdot p(y^t|y_1^K)
\end{aligned}
\quad (3)
$$

There are two probability distributions:

- Expression-level emotion detection model: $p(y, s|x)$. This model describes the distribution of the sequence of segmentation $s_i(1:k)$ and its corresponding emotion tag $y_i(1:k)$. This distribution can be calculated directly by the semi-CRF model.

- Emotion tag distribution model: $p(y^t|y_1^K)$. This model describes the probability distribution of the emotion classes. Where y_1^K is expression-level emotion tag and y^t indicates the overall emotion tag. This distribution can be calculated by similar n-gram model.

In this study, we use the maximum a posteriori estimation with Gaussian priors for parameter estimation. The inference problem can be solved by the Viterbi algorithm.

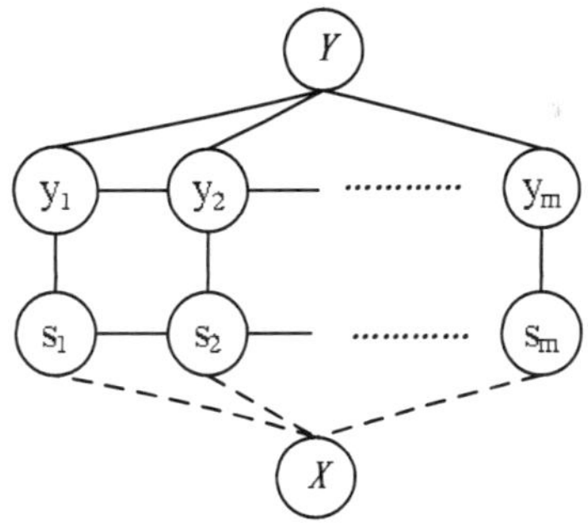

Figure 1: Graphical presentation for semi-CRF segment based model

3.3 Feature Design

We reused features in the original token-based model based on unigram, POS tags, emotion word lists and context-informed dependency relations.

Bag-of-words: Surface forms of word unigrams and bigrams in the sentence are used as features.

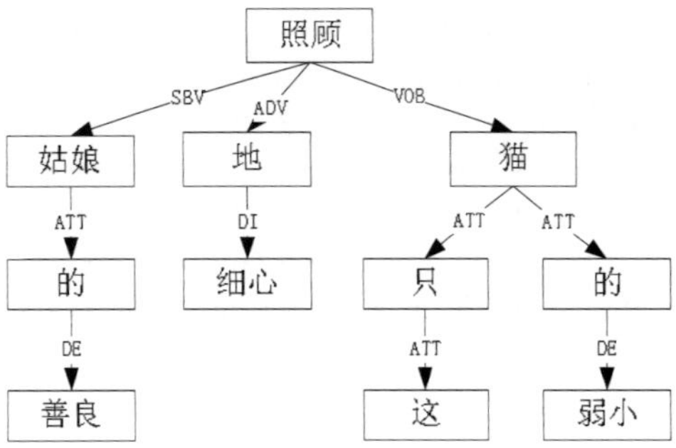

Figure 2: A dependency parse tree example. There are four segment units in the sentence

Part-of-speech: The part-of-speech (POS) of the current word and the surrounding words are used as a feature for emotion classification.

Content bag-of-words: N (noun), V (verb), JJ (adjective) words by POS is used as features.

Emotion word lists: This set of features is based on the emotion-word itself. The emotion class of a word can be assigned as the word's prior emotion tag according to the Chinese emotion lexicon, which is a translation and extension version of WordNet-Affect lexicon and its construction details described as section 4.1.

Dependency relations: This set of features is binary indicators of whether the leaf phrase in the dependency parse tree belongs to one of the emotion classes. The dependencies are all binary relations: a grammatical relation holds between a governor (head) and a dependent (modifier). Dependency arcs are stored as 3-tuples of the form $< w_1, r, w_2 >$, denoting occurrences of words w_1 and word w_2 related by the syntactic dependency r.

After parsing the sentence and getting the dependencies, we count the following dependency-tree boolean features for the emotional word, if this sentence have the emotional words:

- Whether the word is in a "neg" dependency (negation modifier): true when there is a negation word which modifies the emotional word.

- Whether the word is in an "amod" dependency (adjectival modifier): true if the emotional word is (i) a noun modified by an adjective or (ii) an adjective modifying a noun.

- Whether the word is in an "advmod" dependency (adverbial modifier): true if the emotional word (i) is a non-clausal adverb or adverbial phrase which serves to modify the meaning of a word, or (ii) has been modified by an adverb.

If the sentence has not any emotional word, we will consider the adjective words and its around words.

4 Experiments and results

4.1 Data Construction

In this subsection, we explain the dataset and lexicon used in our experiments. Table 1 shows the details of the construction dataset, and Figure 3 displays the distribution of the six emotion classes (happy, fear, sad, surprised, angry, and disgust) in the corpora. The various corpora and lexicon have the following origins:

(1) Chinese emotion lexicon. Currently, there is not any open and free existing Chinese emotion lexicon with fine-grained emotion classes. Therefore, the first resource we need to construct is an emotional lexicon of Chinese with various emotion categories. The English WordNet Affect lists (Strapparava et al., 2004) based on Ekman's six basic emotion types have adequate number of emotion word entries. These English words lists can be used to convert to Chinese words using English to Chinese bilingual dictionary or thesaurus. Our final lexicon contains 1810 entries.

(2) News dataset. This news domain corpus is created manually by two annotators. The annotation process proceeds as follows: they have been trained separately and work independently in order to avoid any annotation bias and get a true understanding of the task difficulty. Each annotator marks the sentence level or short text with one of six primary emotions (Ekman, 1992), and then calculate the kappa value to assess such reliability regarding emotion categories with a value of 0.7 or above it indicating complete agreement. Disagreements can be annotated by the third one, then calculate the kappa value.

(3) Alm's translation dataset. This data set is based on Alm's dataset (Alm et al., 2005), which include annotated sentences from fairy tales, and five emotion tags (happy, fearful, sad, surprised and angry-disgusted) from the Ekman's list of basic emotions were used for sentences or short text annotations. The construction process of this dataset proceeds as follows: firstly, we collect English-Chinese parallel corpora of fairy tales, and split the text into individual sentences. Secondly, select Chinese sentences which corresponding translation appeared in Alm's Dataset accord-

Table 1: The dataset entries used in our experiment

Chinese emotion lexicon	Alm's translation dataset	News dataset	Blog dataset	unlabeled corpora
1810	1223	1135	1000	115M

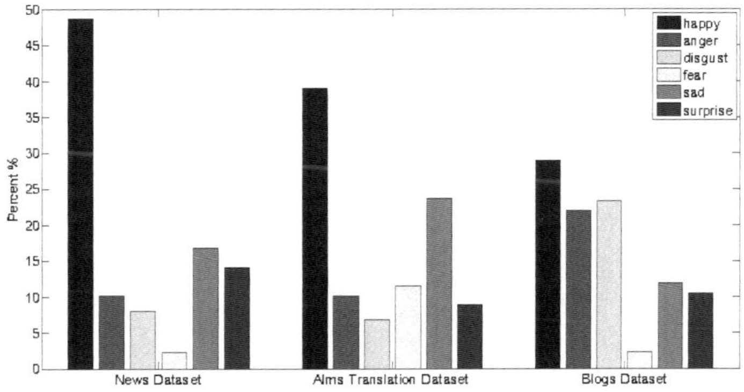

Figure 3: The distribution of the six emotions (happy, fear, sad, surprised, angry, and disgust)in the corpora

ing to sentence alignment strategy. Lastly, annotate angry and disgusted sentences by manually. Since Alm's dataset doesn't separate the angry and disgusted categories.

(4) Blog dataset. This dataset consists of emotion-rich sentences or short text collected from blogs. These sentences or short text are labeled with six emotion tags by two annotators. The annotation process is the same as that of news dataset.

(5) Unlabeled corpora. We downloaded additional 15M Chinese version of children's story from Andersen's and Green's fairy tales and 100M Chinese news dataset to use as the unlabeled set. We haven't select blog corpora, because it is noisy. This allows us to check the performance of each system on the same kinds of data, and the unlabeled set and the test set are in the same domain and have similar underlying feature distributions.

4.2 Preprocessing

Given a labeled or an unlabeled data, we first carry out segmentation and part-of-speech (POS) tagging on each sentence or short text using the Stanford toolkit, and then apply a simple word filter based on POS tags to select content words (nouns, verbs, and adjectives). In next step, we create dependency parse tree produced by the Stanford dependency parser, and construct dependency subtrees. As we all know, the performance of Chinese dependency parser is not very satisfactory. Hence, we modify several wrong results manually. We just want to testify our idea of that the fragments based on dependency grammar are better than tokens.

4.3 Experimental Results

In this subsection, we report experimental results on our dataset which contains news dataset, Alm's translation dataset and blogs dataset. The entries of our dataset are short text or sentence. The news dataset consists of 1135 entries and its average length is 27.09. The Alm's translation dataset consist of 1223 entries and its average length 34.76. The blog dataset contains 1000 entries and its average length is 30.73. The tasks on the Alm's translation dataset may be difficult because the syntactic structures of the sentences are less restricted and highly variable.

Table 2, Table 3 and Table 4 respectively shows the accuracy result of our segment-based method compared to two token-based approach using SVM and MaxEnt, and a segment-based method using CRF models (similar to the work of (Nakagawa et al., 2010)), which employ five kinds of feature sets (BOW, contentBOW, part-of-speech, emotion words and dependency relations) and their combination features, setting 10-fold cross validation as a testing option.

As shown in Table 2-4, we can obtain below conclusions:

(1) We can see that our approach based on the

Table 2: Experimental results on news dataset %

Feature	SVM	MaxEnt	CRF	Our approach
BOW	46.84	46.1	53.29	53.33
contentBOW	48.59	47.8	55	55.74
contentBOW+POS	48.64	47.67	56.78	56.69
contentBOW+Emotion	51.46	50.7	57.41	58.55
contentBOW+Emotion+POS	50.2	47.1	58.53	61.53
contentBOW+Emotion+POS+Dependency	54.45	54.32	59.06	65.12

Table 3: Experimental results on Alm's translation dataset %

Feature	SVM	MaxEnt	CRF	Our approach
BOW	39.59	40.30	35.79	40.09
contentBOW	39.98	40.59	35.87	42.11
contentBOW+POS	40.19	38.82	36.05	43.95
contentBOW+Emotion	45.86	42.26	39.44	46.49
contentBOW+Emotion+POS	46.15	40.98	41.89	48.95
contentBOW+Emotion+POS+Dependency	48.23	45.05	45.68	50.81

Table 4: Experimental results on blog dataset %

Feature	SVM	MaxEnt	CRF	Our approach
BOW	46.09	45.81	44.24	45.62
contentBOW	46.34	46.06	46.33	46.19
contentBOW+POS	46.56	45.93	46.92	47.01
contentBOW+Emotion	47.92	46.03	47.23	47.63
contentBOW+Emotion+POS	48.38	45.77	47.98	48.63
contentBOW+Emotion+POS+Dependency	50.05	48.12	49.61	53.23

segment-based semi-CRF model has the highest accuracy rate for each dataset using the combination features of contentBOW + Emotion + POS + Dependency. Segment-based approach performed better than token-based approach for the news dataset, but without expected results for the Alm's translation and blogs dataset. This result, on the one hand, demonstrates that Semi-CRF is more powerful than CRF, and on the other hand, our emotion tag distribution model gives effective results. For token-based method, SVM gives a better result than MaxEnt for all three of our Chinese corpora.

(2) The accuracy rate of SVM has slightly less than our model, but the results of MaxEnt and CRF is unbalanced. As we notice from table 2 to table 4, CRF gives better results on the news dataset than on the Alm's translation dataset, but the results of MaxEnt on all dataset is worst. The reasons for this result may be due to the bias problem of MaxEnt.

(3) We can observe that using the combination features of contentBOW + Emotion + POS + Dependency has the highest accuracy rate for each dataset and each classifier. There are two types of features achieve significantly improvements: emotion words and the dependency relations, for example, on news dataset, SVM with contentBOW has the accuracy rate of 48.59% and adding emotion words has the accuracy rate of 51.46%, showing the improvements of 2.87%. This is not surprising result since emotion words has key influence to detection of the emotion category of a sentence. However, the words or constituents interact with each other to yield the overall emotion label, there exists expression level emotion. Dependency relationship features can solve this problem and improve the performance of the system,like in the example above,adding Dependency relationship features has the accuracy rate of

54.45%, showing the improvements of 5.86%.

When the baseline system use the content-BOW features, the POS, Emotion and Dependency representation improve the accuracy rates of the SVM, CRF and our classifier for each dataset, but the use of POS representation for the MaxEnt classifier decreased the accuracy rate compared to the Emotion and Dependency representations. One reason lead to this problem might be the quality of the data we use in this experiment.

(4) Overall performances on the news dataset are better than on the Alm's translation dataset and blogs dataset. The reason perhaps is that the syntactic structures of the sentences from Alm's translation dataset are less restricted and highly variable, and the sentences from blogs dataset are noisy, and there exist some linguistic or spelling error.

5 Conclusion

In this paper, we present a segment-based learning approach for fine-grained emotion detection. In this method, the emotion label of each dependency subtree of a subjective sentence or short text is represented by a hidden variable. The values of the hidden variables are calculated in consideration of interactions between variables whose nodes have head-modifier relation in the dependency tree. Differ from the existing token-based approach, the segment-based emotion detection model can simultaneously exploit both the linguistic structure and the expression-level emotion relation embedded in sentences or short text. Three different dataset, which contains news content, fairly tales, and blogs data, is constructed to test our proposed model, and the experimental results show that our approach performed the best on three emotion corpora and make a statistically significant improvement over other classification algorithms, reflecting its potential usage in the emotion detection task.

References

P. Ekman. 1992. *An argument for basic emotions Cognition and Emotion*, 6(3):169–200.

C. Alm, D. Roth, and R. Sproat. 2005. *Emotions from text: Machine learning for text-based emotion prediction, In Proceedings of HLT - EMNLP*, 579–586.

Saima Aman and Stan Szpakowicz. 2007. *Identifying Expressions of Emotion in Text, TSD 2007*, 196–205.

Phil Katz, Matthew Singleton, Richard Wicentowski. 2007. *SWAT-MP: The SemEval-2007 Systems for Task 5 and Task 14, Proceedings of the 4th International Workshop on Semantic Evaluations (SemEval-2007). Prague*,308–313

Karo Moilanen and Stephen Pulman. 2007. *Sentiment Composition, In Proceedings of Recent Advances in Natural Language Processing.*

Yejin Choi and Claire Cardie. 2008. *Learning with Compositional Semantics as Structural Inference for Subsentential Sentiment Analysis, EMNLP 2008*,793–801.

Richard Socher, Jeffrey Pennington, Eric H. Huang, Andrew Y. Ng, Christopher D. Manning. 2011. *Semi-Supervised Recursive Autoencoders for Predicting Sentiment Distributions, EMNLP 2011*,151–161.

Richard Socher, Brody Huval, Christopher D. Manning, Andrew Y. Ng. 2012. *Semantic Compositionality through Recursive Matrix-Vector Spaces, EMNLP-CoNLL 2012*,1201–1211.

Baptiste Chardon, Farah Benamara, Yannick Mathieu,Vladimir Popescu, Nicholas Asher. 2013. *Sentiment Composition Using a Parabolic Model, Proceedings of the 10th International Conference on Computational Semantics (IWCS 2013)* .

Tetsuji Nakagawa, Kentaro Inui, Sadao Kurohashi. 2010. *Dependency Tree-based Sentiment Classification using CRFs with Hidden Variables, HLT-NAACL 2010*,786–794.

S. Chaffar and D. Inkpen. 2011. *Using a heterogeneous dataset for emotion analysis in text, In Canadian Conference on AI*,62–67.

S. M. Mohammad. 2012. *Portable Features for Classifying Emotional Text, 2012 Conference of the North American Chapter of the Association for Computational Linguistics: Human Language Technologies*,587–591.

Matthew Purver and Stuart Battersby. 2012. *Experimenting with Distant Supervision for Emotion Classification, Proceedings of the 13th Conference of the European Chapter of the Association for Computational Linguistics*,482–491.

Ge Xu, Xinfan Meng, Houfeng Wang. 2010. *Build Chinese Emotion Lexicons Using A Graph-based Algorithm and Multiple Resources, In Proceeding of COLING-10*,1209–1217.

Braja Gopal Patra, Hiroya Takamura, Dipankar Das, Manabu Okumura and Sivaji Bandyopadhyay. 2013. *Construction of Emotional Lexicon Using Potts Model, International Joint Conference on Natural Language Processing*,674–679.

Svitlana Volkova, William B. Dolan, Theresa Wilson. 2012. *CLex: A Lexicon for Exploring Color, Concept and Emotion Associations in Language, Proceedings of the 13th Conference of the European Chapter of the Association for Computational Linguistics*,306–314.

Ying Chen, Sophia Yat Mei Lee, Shoushan Li, Chu-Ren Huang. 2010. *Emotion Cause Detection with Linguistic Constructions, Proceedings of the 23rd International Conference on Computational Linguistics (Coling 2010)*,179–187.

Ashequl Qadir, Ellen Riloff. 2013. *Bootstrapped Learning of Emotion Hashtags hashtags4you, Proceedings of the 4th Workshop on Computational Approaches to Subjectivity, Sentiment and Social Media Analysis*,2–11.

Dipankar Das and Sivaji Bandyopadhyay. 2010. *Identifying Emotional Expressions, Intensities and Sentence level Emotion Tags using a Supervised Framework, PACLIC 2010*,95–104.

Diman Ghazi, Diana Inkpen, Stan Szpakowicz. 2012. *Prior versus Contextual Emotion of a Word in a Sentence, Proceedings of the 3rd Workshop on Computational Approaches to Subjectivity and Sentiment Analysis*,70–78.

Sunita Sarawagi, William W. Cohen. 2004. *Semi-Markov Conditional Random Fields for Information Extraction, NIPS 2004.*

Daisuke Okanohara, Yusuke Miyao, Yoshimasa Tsuruoka, Jun'ichi Tsujii. 2006. *Improving the Scalability of Semi-Markov Conditional Random Fields for Named Entity Recognition, ACL 2006*,465–472.

Galen Andrew. 2006. *A Hybrid Markov/Semi-Markov Conditional Random Field for Sequence Segmentation, EMNLP 2006*,465–472.

Bishan Yang, Claire Cardie. 2012. *Extracting Opinion Expressions with semi-Markov Conditional Random Fields, EMNLP-CoNLL 2012*,1335–1345.

C Strapparava, A Valitutti. 2004. *WordNet-Affect: an Affective Extension of WordNet, LREC 2004*,1083–1086.

Bilingual Product Name Dictionary Construction Using a Two Stage Method

Yatian Shen, Xuanjing Huang
School of Computer Science, Fudan University, Shanghai, China
shenyatian@gmail.com, xjhuang@fudan.edu.cn

Abstract

This paper proposes a novel two-stage method for bilingual product name dictionary construction from comparable corpora. In previous work, some researchers study the problem of expanding a set of given seed entities into a more complete set by discovering other entities that also belong to the same concept, it just solves the problem about expansion of entity set in a monolingual language, but the expansion of bilingual entity is really blank problem from comparable corpora. A typical example is to use "Honda-本田"as seed entity, and derive other entities(e.g., "Ford-福特") in the same concept set of product name. We address this problem by utilizing a two-stage approach based on entity set expansion and bilingual entity alignment from comparable corpora. Evaluations using English and Chinese reviewer corpus verify that our method outperforms conventional methods.

1 Introduction

Bilingual lexicons are important resources for bilingual tasks such as machine translation (MT) and cross-language information retrieval (CLIR). Therefore, the automatic building of bilingual product name lexicons from corpus is one of the important issues, however it has not attracted many researchers. As a solution, a number of previous works have been proposed for extracting bilingual product name lexicons from comparable corpora, in which documents are not direct translations but share the same topic or domain. The use of comparable corpora is motivated by the fact that large parallel corpora are only available for a few language pairs and limited domains.

Bilingual product name lexicon is similar to traditional bilingual lexicon extraction, what they are all common on is extract bilingual entity translation pair from comparable corpora, but there is some difference between them. Our problem is: first given an seed set for semantic classes, finding the conceptually entities by extending semantic classes. Then, the bilingual entity translation pairs are extracted from comparable corpora. Traditional bilingual lexicon extraction approaches can only find entity translation pairs from comparable corpora, but not expand semantic set.

Set expansion systems provide us a useful solution to the above problem because they create a more perfect set of name entities by expanding the small number of seed words given for the target domain. Google Sets is a well-known example of a web-based set expansion system. Another prominent work is the SEAL system (Wang and Cohen, 2007; Wang and Cohen, 2008; Wang and Cohen, 2009), which adoptes a two-phase strategy, where they first build customized text wrappers based on the input seeds in order to exact candidate entities from web pages. Then a graph-based random walk approach is used to rank candidate entities based on their closeness to the seeds on the graph. The third method is set expansion by iterative similarity aggregation (He and Xin, 2011), in which a set of given seed entities is expanded into a more complete set. All these methods are entity expansion from monolingual data sources.

Another meaningful work is the bilingual lexicon extraction (Fung and McKeown, 1997; Rapp, 1999; Andrade et al., 2010; Fišer et al., 2011; Daille and Morin, 2005; Vulic et al., 2011; Andrade et al., 2011; Bo et al., 2011). Most of the

Proceedings of the Third CIPS-SIGHAN Joint Conference on Chinese Language Processing, pages 61–69,
Wuhan, China, 20-21 October 2014

previous methods are based on the assumption that a word and its translation tend to appear in similar contexts across languages. Based on this assumption, many methods calculate word similarity using context and then extract word translation pairs with a high context similarity. while their researches aim to generate a general bilingual lexicons, our work is bilingual entity extraction of the same semantic category, these entities are refer to product name.

Considerable progresses have been made in developing high-quality set expansion systems in the monolingual setting. while bilingual product name dictionary construction and extraction still do not attract much research attention. For bilingual product name dictionary construction, there are two major fundamental problems. The first is generating an extensive list of the same semantic entity, while some seed entities of the same concept are given as input. The second problem is to find bilingual entity translation from comparable corpora.

Facing the above problems, we present a novel approach to construct bilingual product name dictionary in this paper. In order to express the simplification, we will replace word "product name" with "entity" each other. Following the common practice, our system proceeds in two stages, which first expands the entity set for the semantic category by giving some bilingual set pairs and then finds bilingual product name translation pair from comparable corpora. Semantic category set expansion is carried out through the bootstrapping algorithm. In this stage ,our goal is to discover relevant entities by giving some entity seed set. In the second stage, we use this assumption that a word and its translation tend to appear in similar context across languages (Rapp, 1999). Our method calculates entity similarity using context and then extract entity translation pairs with a high context similarity. We call this method as context-similarity-based methods. The context similarity is usually computed using machine translation model by mapping contexts expressed in two different languages into the same language space. In the mapping process, information not represented by the seed lexicon is discarded.

The main contributions of this paper are as follows: 1) we propose a bilingual product name extraction method that can get the set of semantic category by bootstrapping. At the same time, we can find bilingual product name translation pairs based on context similarity from comparable corpora. 2) we propose an the algorithm that can not only build set of semantic category by giving some bilingual seed set but also find entity translation pairs from comparable corpora. 3) we construct a dictionary of the bilingual product name from comparable corpora, which do not need fully parallel data that is seldom.

2 Related Work

There is a significant body of related work in the broad space of information extraction and named entity extraction. We will only summarize work most relevant to set expansion and bilingual entity extraction due to the limit of space.

Google sets does set expansion using propriety algorithms which are not publicly available. (He and Xin, 2011) expand seeds by iterative similarity aggregation. (Talukdar et al., 2006) studied the problem of set expansion of open text, which proposes to automatically identify trigger-words which indicate patterns in a bootstrapping manner. (Ghahramani and Heller, 2005) used the method of Bayesian inference to solve the problem of set expansion. In comparison, our approach expands bilingual entity seeds set by using bootstrapping algorithms ,which learn entity candidates and their corresponding patterns iteratively. Our goal is to find the same semantic concept set .

(Fung and McKeown, 1997) present a statistical word feature that is said to the word relation matrix, which can be used to find translated pairs of words and terms from non-parallel corpora across language groups. (Daille and Morin, 2005) proposes a method of extracting bilingual lexicon composed of single-word terms (SWTs) and multi-word terms (MWTs) from comparable corpora of a technical domain. First, this method extracts MWTs in each language, and then uses statistical methods to align single words and multi-word terms by exploiting the term contexts. The alignment of words in translated texts are well established, this algorithm is used to identify word translations (Rapp, 1999). (Andrade et al., 2010) suggest a new method which selects a subset of words (pivot words) associated with a query and then matches these words across languages, a new Bayesian method for estimating Point-wise Mutual Information is used to detect word associations. (Fišer et al., 2011) presents a series of exper-

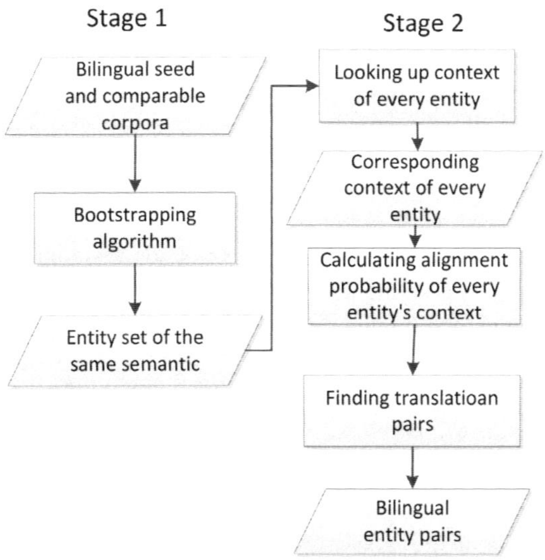

Figure 1: Flow chart of our two-stage system.

iments aimed at inducing and evaluating domain-specific bilingual lexicon from comparable corpora. (Vulic et al., 2011) investigate the algorithm of bilingual topic models, which finds translations of terms in comparable corpora by using knowledge from word-topic distributions. (Andrade et al., 2011) propose to perform a linear transformation of the context vectors, the new word translations are found by context similarity. (Bo et al., 2011) introduce a clustering-based approach for enhancing corpus comparability which exploits the homogeneity feature of the corpus, and preserves most of the vocabulary of the original corpus. (Tamura et al., 2012) proposes a novel method for lexicon extraction that extracts translation pairs from comparable corpora by using graph- based label propagation.

All the methods mentioned above may potentially extract entities translation pairs when context of entities are similarity. We are also based on this assumption, but we are different from the previous models where we use machine translation model to map the context of entity to the same language space, which can improve performance and illustrate robustness.

3 Proposed Method

Figure 1 illustrates the framework of our proposed methods. The proposed method has the following components: Bootstrapping algorithm is used to get entity sets and the patterns for Chinese and English respectively, then we can find entity translation pairs by calculating context similarity and construct bilingual product name lexicon.

Step 1. Using Bootstrapping algorithm gets entity sets and the patterns for Chinese and English respectively.

Step 2. Based on the assumption that the word and its translation tend to appear in similar contexts across languages, we can find translation pair.

Step 3. Construct bilingual product name lexicon.

4 Bootstrapping for Entity Set Expansion

In this paper, we expand seed entity set into a more complete set by discovering other entities that also belong to the same concept set. A typical application is to use seed entities to derive other entities in the same concept set of brands. In order to discover such relevant entities, we expand seed entities to assign semantic similar entities to the same semantic set using plenty of user reviews.

4.1 Growing Seed Dictionary

We focus on the problem of how to grow the seed dictionary and discovering new product names from user reviews. In this section, we use the seed entity to automatically generate semantic lexicons. For the specific case of brand discovery, this initial list used to generate semantic lexicons must contain only names that are unambiguously. We hence remove ambiguous names or phrases that belong to multiple entity types from the dataset, and only choose those entities as entity seed that it owns definite semantic. We used a weakly supervised bootstrapping algorithm that automatically generates semantic lexicons (Thelen and Riloff, 2002).

Bootstrapping algorithms hypothesizes the semantic class of entity by gathering collective evidence about semantic associations from extraction pattern context. For our representation of extraction patterns, we used the AutoSlog system (Riloff, 1996), AutoSlog's extraction patterns represent linguistic expressions that extract a noun phrase in one of three syntactic roles: subject, direct object, or prepositional phrase object. Before bootstrapping begins, we run AutoSlog exhaustively over the corpus to generate an extraction pattern for every noun phrase that appears. In these, noun or noun phrase are entities, we will possibly extract them as production name. The patterns are then applied to the corpora and all of theirs extracted noun phrases are recorded. For every iteration, the top 20 extraction patterns are put into a pattern pool. Every pattern used the R-logF metric that has been used for extraction pattern learning (Riloff, 1996).

All entities in the candidate entity pool are scored and the top five words are added to the semantic lexicon. Bootstrapping algorithm learns pattern that associate entity to their correct expansions, the intuition of our work is that the algorithm learns context that can associate some entities that have the same semantic.

5 Finding Translation Pairs

Translating domain-specific entities from one language to another is challenging because they are often not listed in a general dictionary. In this section, we are based on this assumption that context similarity is helpful since two words with identical meaning are often used in similar contexts across languages(Rapp,1999). Let us briefly recall the main idea for using context similarity to find translation pairs. First, the context pattern of every entity is found because the context of a entity is usually defined by the word which occur around it(bag-of-words model), we use ten forward and backward window of word as context. Second, we use machine translation model to translate context, the context of two entities can be aligned about their probability. At last, if the context of two entities is similar, so they corresponds to entity pairs as bilingual product name pairs. The detail algorithms is as follows:

5.1 Looking Up Context of Every Entity

With the bootstrapping algorithm, we get the set of semantic category entity in English and Chinese comparable corpora. For every entity, we look up their context, and use the method of string matching in the corpora. We use 3 forward and backward window of word as context, That is what we call the context. The context and their corresponding entities have great relevance. As an example, it is easier for us to find some words around "Camera" name,such as the pixel,the screen and cmos, these words are the context of entity, which often appear near the name of camera. By context, we are able to find their corresponding entities.

Algorithm 1 Finding translation pairs in bilingual

Input: $I = (x_i), i = 1, 2, \ldots, l$ in which x_i is the ith entity of the same semantic entity set, BilingualData is bilingual comparable corpora

Output: Entity tanslation pairs

repeat
  for $i = 1\ to\ n$ **do**
    Looking up the context of every entity $context_i$ in BilingualData ;
    Calculating the alignment probability of every entity's context in different languages
    Computing similarity of the context between $context_i$ and $context_j$
    if Similarity($context_i$,$context_j$)is maximal **then**
      For the highest similarity value of context to corresponding entity pair, extracting them as an entity translation pair
    end if
  end for
until no x_i is in the I during iteration

5.2 Aligning the Context of two Entities

To bilingual context, how they are aligned with each other is a major problem. This component is to identify equivalence relation in every entity corresponding to bilingual context. We assume that the same context appears around the same entity. Thus, our aim is to find translation pairs between Chinese and English corpora. Machine translation is commonly used to complete the task. By the tool of machine translation, two different language context of entity is mapped to the same language space.

Many studies on machine translation use GIZA++ as their underlying word-by-word alignment system. Machine translation systems have also benefited from such alignment, performing it at the character level (AbdulJaleel and Larkey, 2003), (Virga and Khudanpur, 2003), (Gao et al., 2005). GIZA++ is a statistical machine translation toolkit freely available for research purposes. The extended version of this toolkit is called GIZA++ and was developed by (Och and Ney, 2003). We employ the word-based translation model to perform context alignment, we get the alignment probability between the context pattern of two different entities. GIZA++ alignment system is trained on parallel corpora English and Chinese reviews, we manually annotate the context of bilingual entity pair on 3000 parallel sentence pairs about car domain reviews. A probability table about the context of bilingual entity pair is generated by training GIZA++ model.

5.3 Entity Translation Extraction

In order to find entity translation pairs in different languages, we use statistical machine translation toolkit GIZA++ to calculate the alignment probability of every entity's context in different languages. A pair of entity is treated as a bilingual product name pair when the alignment probability of their context is high. In this, if the alignment probability of four words which is said to context is greater than threshold, we will think that entity pairs which have this context are bilingual entity pair, We found that the word alignment probability threshold of the context is set to 0.53 is a good choice by experiment.

6 Experiments

6.1 Dataset and Evaluation Metrics

In order to evaluate our approach, we conduct experiments on two real data sets, which are from collection of brand reviews including digital cameras and car domains. For the target language of English, the product dataset contains 9542 reviews which are collected from www.buzzilions.com and www.carreview.com. For the source language of Chinese, the product dataset contains 8432 reviews which are collected from www.Amazon.cn and www.xche.com.cn. For our experiment,we use a Oxford English-Chinese bilingual dictionary to match similarity semantic reviewer sentence, any two of them are used as comparable corpus,the copora are non-parallel, but loosely compara in term of its content. Though the scale of Chinese corpora is large, most of the reviews are short texts and there are a lot noise in the content. For Chinese, we use the ICTLAS 3.0 (Zhang et al., 2003) toolkit to conduct word segmentation over sentences.

To evaluate the effectiveness of our algorithms, we select two semantic entity sets in camera domain and car domain as seeds, where set expansion experiments are conducted . We select these two categories because (1) they are from different domains; and (2) they have different degree of difficulty for finding entity translation pairs.

Language	Domain	#Sentence	#Reviews
Chinese	Camera	2480862	1566
	Car	3526109	2103
English	Camera	1090862	4506
	Car	2563120	5036

Table 1: Statistics on English corpus about Camera and Car domain. # denotes the size of the reviews/sentences

In experiments, each English review is segmented into sentences according to punctuation. Then sentences are tokenized and the part-of-speech of each word is assigned. Stanford NLP tool is used to perform POS-tagging. Next, function words were removed since function words with little semantic information spuriously co-occurred with many words. Table 1 shows the size of each corpora.

We measure the performance on product name translation pair extraction as Top N accuracy (Acc_N), which is the number of test words whose top N translation candidates contain a correct translation equivalent over the total number of test words. We randomly select 50 Chinese words as our test data. We manually evaluate whether translation candidates contained a correct translation equivalent. We do not use recall because we do not know whether the translation equivalents of a test word appear or not in the corpus.

6.2 Example Output

Table 2 lists the top 20 ranked results produced by two stage algorithm for the two domains that we experiment with. In each domain, those terms in boldface are the input seeds. The underlined terms are the results that do not belong to the ground truth set and thus counted as incorrect results. While the remaining terms are correct results expanded from the input seeds.

From Table 2, we can see that in the top-20 ranked results, the "Camera" domain have high precision. "Camera" domain has only two incorrect result, the top-20 results for "Car" domain, however, includes some noisy entities that are incorrect, such as product workshop names ("大众汽车" and "Audi company"), and the similarity concept name ("Honda car" and "福特汽车公司").

6.3 Our Methods VS. State-of-art Methods

To prove the effectiveness of our method, we select the following state-of-art methods as baseline for comparison.

1) Rapp is a typical context-similarity-based method (Rapp, 1999). Context words are words in a window (window size is 10) and are treated separately for each position. Associations with context words are computed using the log-likelihood ratio. The similarity measure between context vectors is the city-block metric.

2) Andrade is a sophisticated method in context-similarity-based methods (Andrade et al., 2010). Context is a set of words with a positive association in a window (window size is 10). The association is calculated using the PMI estimated by a Bayesian method, and a similarity between contexts is estimated based on the number of overlapping words.

3)Tamura proposes a method for lexicon extraction that extracts translation pairs from comparable corpora by using graph-based label propagation (Tamura et al., 2012). They utilize indirect relations with the bilingual seeds together with direct relations, in which each word is represented by a distribution of translated seeds. The seed distributions are propagated over a graph representing relations among words, and translation pairs are extracted by identifying word pairs with a high similarity in the seed distributions.

Camera	Car
富士-FUJIFILM	奥迪-audi
卡西欧-Casio	宝马-BMW
徕卡-Leica	别克-Bulk
柯达-Kodak	福特-Ford
理光-Ricoh	**福克斯-Focus**
索尼-SONY	本田-Honda
奥林巴斯-OLYMPUS	马自达-Mazda
松下-Panasonic	丰田**-Toyota**
佳能-Canon	尼桑-Nissan
尼康-Nikon	丰田皇冠-Toyota Crown
宾得-Pentax	textbf沃尔沃-Volvo
康佳-Konka	大众-Volkswagen
柯尼卡-Konica	马自达6-Mazda6
尼康S2-Nikon S2	日制汽车-Honda
佳能 VTD-Canon VTD	奔驰-Benz
尼康-Konka	本田雅阁-Honda
三星-SAMSUNG	雷克萨斯-Lexus
佳能-Nikon	现代-Hyundai
美能达-Minolta	通用-GM
柯尼卡-Konica	雪铁龙-Citroen

Table 2: Top -20 results by two stage method

6.4 Experiments Results

Table 3 and Table 4 show the performance of each method using Car and Camera review dataset. Table 3 and Table 4 show that the proposed methods outperform the baselines on both datasets. The results show that expansion of bilingual product name by using two stage algorithm is effective .

Rapp's method computed associations with context words using the log-likelihood ratio. The city-block metric is used to compute similarity between context vector. Andrade define context as a set of words with a positive association in a window, Pointwise Mutual Information estimated by a Bayesian method is used to calculate. The similarity between contexts is estimated based on the number of overlapping words. Tamura's method utilize indirect relations with the bilingual seeds together with direct relations, in which each word

Methods	Acc_1	Acc_{10}	Acc_{20}
Rapp	1.6%	2.5%	3.9%
Andrade	1.8%	3.2%	4.1%
Tamura	2.5%	5.8%	7.5%
Ours	4.5 %	8.6%	12.4%

Table 3: Performance statistics on Camera domain by using Top N accuracy (Acc_N).N is 1,10,20 respectively.

Methods	Acc_1	Acc_{10}	Acc_{20}
Rapp	1.5%	2.3%	4.5%
Andrade	1.7%	3.6%	5.1%
Tamura	2.3%	6.2%	8.5%
Ours	4.3 %	9.6%	13.8%

Table 4: Performance statistics on Car domain by using Top N accuracy (Acc_N).N is 1,10,20 respectively.

is represented by a distribution of translated seeds. Then they extracts translation pairs from comparable corpora by using graph-based label propagation. The parameter setting in these three baselines are the same as the original papers. The overall performance results are shown in Table 3 and 4. From these results, we can make the following observations.

1) Ours achieves performance improvement over other methods. This indicates that our method is effective for bilingual product name extraction.

2) Our two stage method outperform Rapp's method, Andrade's method and Tamura's method. The reason is that two stage-based method extract bilingual entity name in a flexible way, we first consider entity set expansion, then find bilingual entity pair by using machine translation methods from comparable corpora, which is not only find the same semantic entity, but also can find entity translation pair, so we can extract bilingual product name on specific domain. but Rapp's method, Andrade's method and Tamura's method only build a general bilingual lexicon.

3) Our method construct context association by utilizing machine translation model between bilingual entity name. Machine translation model have the characteristic of accurate and interpretation, which favor our problems. Our test data, on the other hand, includes many low-frequency words. It is generally true that translation of high-frequency words is much easier than that of low frequency words. The accuracies of the baselines in Table 3 and 4 are worse than the previous reports: 14% Acc_1 and 46% Acc_{10} (Andrade et al., 2010), and 72% Acc_1 (Rapp, 1999).

4) Our methods expand entity name of the same semantic concept by using the bootstrapping algorithm, which is weak-supervised learning algorithm. The algorihtm need not labeled dateset to train model, meanwhile which is easier to implement it, it exceeds Tamura's method,which only considers distribution of translated seeds, then each word is represented by seeds distribution. The seed distributions are propagated over a graph representing relations among words, but constructing a graph is consuming lot of forces, its effect is very low.

6.5 Effect of Seeds Size

In this subsection, we aim to prove the effectiveness and robustness of our algorithms for bilingual entity extraction. We vary the number of input seeds and report the corresponding bilingual entity extraction performance. Specifically, given the 4, 6 and 8 seeds for each of the two domains in the experiments,we aim to test the performance of our two stage algorithm. The results are reported in Table 5, Table 6. The overall trend stands out that the performance of our algorithm with 6 seeds is in general much better and more stable than the case where only 4 or 8 seeds are used as input. We consider three kinds of the characters that the entity seed set have. The seed must be first the most representative of a semantic class, and polysemy of a seed should be avoided, we also consider the coverage of a seed set. This suggests that our algorithm is more robust when a reasonable number of seeds are given, and the performance may fluctuate with very few number of seeds, largely depending on the quality of the seeds given.

6.6 Effect of Translation Model

We can find entity of similar pattern by using GIZA++ model, but the alignment model result in some errors, there are two central reasons. Our test data includes words whose translation equivalence inherently cannot be found. The first of these types are words whose equivalence does not

Number	Acc_1	Acc_{10}	Acc_{20}
4	1.6%	2.5%	4.9%
6	2.7%	4.3%	6.5%
8	2.3%	3.9%	5.5%

Table 5: Performance statistics on Car domain by using Top N accuracy (Acc_N).The number of seeds choose 4,6 and 8 respectively.

Number	Acc_1	Acc_{10}	Acc_{20}
4	2.0%	3.5%	4.9%
6	2.7%	4.5%	7.4%
8	2.5%	4.1%	5.9%

Table 6: Performance statistics on Camera domain by using Top N accuracy (Acc_N).The number of seeds choose 4,6 and 8 respectively.

exist in the English corpus, which is an unavoidable problem for our methods based on comparable corpora. The second reason of errors is word sense ambiguity, which is different in every language, the Chinese word "宝马" means either "horse" or "car" in English, the proposed methods could not identify correct translation pairs. We will leave this word sense disambiguation problem for future work.

7 Conclusions

This paper proposes a novel two-stage method for product name dictionary construction from comparable corpora. The bootstrapping algorithm is used to expand bilingual product name in the first stage, Then in the second stage we find bilingual product name pair by calculating context similarity. The alignment model is used to Calculate alignment probability of every entity's context in different languages. Evaluations using English and Chinese comparable corpora outperforms conventional methods.

In future work, we are planning to investigate the following open problems : word sense disambiguation and translation of compound words in bilingual entity extraction. We are also planning an end-to-end evaluation, for instance, by employing the extracted bilingual product name into an machine translation system.

References

Nasreen AbdulJaleel and Leah S Larkey. 2003. Statistical transliteration for english-arabic cross language information retrieval. In *Proceedings of the twelfth international conference on Information and knowledge management*, pages 139–146. ACM.

Daniel Andrade, Tetsuya Nasukawa, and Jun'ichi Tsujii. 2010. Robust measurement and comparison of context similarity for finding translation pairs. In *Proceedings of the 23rd International Conference on Computational Linguistics*, pages 19–27. Association for Computational Linguistics.

Daniel Andrade, Takuya Matsuzaki, and Jun'ichi Tsujii. 2011. Learning the optimal use of dependency-parsing information for finding translations with comparable corpora. In *Proceedings of the 4th Workshop on Building and Using Comparable Corpora: Comparable Corpora and the Web*, pages 10–18. Association for Computational Linguistics.

Li Bo, Eric Gaussier, Akiko N Aizawa, et al. 2011. Clustering comparable corpora for bilingual lexicon extraction. In *Proceedings of the 49th Annual Meeting of the Association for Computational Linguistics*, pages 473–478.

Béatrice Daille and Emmanuel Morin. 2005. French-english terminology extraction from comparable corpora. In *Natural Language Processing–IJCNLP 2005*, pages 707–718. Springer.

Darja Fišer, Špela Vintar, Nikola Ljubešić, and Senja Pollak. 2011. Building and using comparable corpora for domain-specific bilingual lexicon extraction. In *Proceedings of the 4th Workshop on Building and Using Comparable Corpora: Comparable Corpora and the Web*, pages 19–26. Association for Computational Linguistics.

Pascale Fung and Kathleen McKeown. 1997. Finding terminology translations from non-parallel corpora. In *Proceedings of the 5th Annual Workshop on Very Large Corpora*, pages 192–202.

Wei Gao, Kam-Fai Wong, and Wai Lam. 2005. Phoneme-based transliteration of foreign names for oov problem. In *Natural Language Processing–IJCNLP 2004*, pages 110–119. Springer.

Zoubin Ghahramani and Katherine Heller. 2005. Bayesian sets.

Yeye He and Dong Xin. 2011. Seisa: set expansion by iterative similarity aggregation. In *Proceedings of the 20th international conference on World wide web*, pages 427–436. ACM.

Franz Josef Och and Hermann Ney. 2003. A systematic comparison of various statistical alignment models. *Computational linguistics*, 29(1):19–51.

Reinhard Rapp. 1999. Automatic identification of word translations from unrelated english and german corpora. In *Proceedings of the 37th annual meeting of the Association for Computational Linguistics on Computational Linguistics*, pages 519–526. Association for Computational Linguistics.

Ellen Riloff. 1996. Automatically generating extraction patterns from untagged text. In *Proceedings of the national conference on artificial intelligence*, pages 1044–1049.

Partha Pratim Talukdar, Thorsten Brants, Mark Liberman, and Fernando Pereira. 2006. A context pattern induction method for named entity extraction. In *Proceedings of the Tenth Conference on Computational Natural Language Learning*, pages 141–148. Association for Computational Linguistics.

Akihiro Tamura, Taro Watanabe, and Eiichiro Sumita. 2012. Bilingual lexicon extraction from comparable corpora using label propagation. In *Proceedings of the 2012 Joint Conference on Empirical Methods in Natural Language Processing and Computational Natural Language Learning*, pages 24–36. Association for Computational Linguistics.

Michael Thelen and Ellen Riloff. 2002. A bootstrapping method for learning semantic lexicons using extraction pattern contexts. In *Proceedings of the ACL-02 conference on Empirical methods in natural language processing-Volume 10*, pages 214–221. Association for Computational Linguistics.

Paola Virga and Sanjeev Khudanpur. 2003. Transliteration of proper names in cross-language applications. In *Proceedings of the 26th annual international ACM SIGIR conference on Research and development in informaion retrieval*, pages 365–366. ACM.

Ivan Vulic, Wim De Smet, Marie-Francine Moens, and KU Leuven. 2011. Identifying word translations from comparable corpora using latent topic models. In *Proceedings of ACL*, pages 479–484.

Richard C Wang and William W Cohen. 2007. Language-independent set expansion of named entities using the web. In *Data Mining,2007.ICDM 2007. Seventh IEEE International Conference on*, pages 342–350. IEEE.

Richard C Wang and William W Cohen. 2008. Iterative set expansion of named entities using the web. In *Data Mining, 2008. ICDM'08. Eighth IEEE International Conference on*, pages 1091–1096. IEEE.

Richard C Wang and William W Cohen. 2009. Character-level analysis of semi-structured documents for set expansion. In *Proceedings of the 2009 Conference on Empirical Methods in Natural Language Processing: Volume 3-Volume 3*, pages 1503–1512. Association for Computational Linguistics.

Hua-Ping Zhang, Hong-Kui Yu, De-Yi Xiong, and Qun Liu. 2003. Hhmm-based chinese lexical analyzer ictclas. In *Proceedings of the second SIGHAN workshop on Chinese language processing-Volume 17*, pages 184–187. Association for Computational Linguistics.

Detection on Inconsistency of Verb Phrase in TreeBank

Chaoqun Duan, Dequan Zheng, Conghui Zhu, Sheng Li
MOE-MS Key Laboratory of Natural Language Processing and Speech
Harbin Institute of Technology, Harbin, China 150001
{cqduan,dqzheng,chzhu,lisheng}@mtlab.hit.edu.cn

Hongye Tan
Key Laboratory of Computational Intelligence and Chinese Information Processing of Ministry of Education
Shanxi University, Taiyuan, China 030006
hytan_2006@126.com

Abstract

Annotating linguistic data is often a complex, time consuming and expensive endeavor. Even with strict annotation guidelines, human subjects often deviate in their analyses, each bring different biases, interpretations of the task and levels of consistency. The aim of this paper is to explore a way to find out the inconsistencies in the corpus TreeBank which is used for syntactic analysis through the procedure we study the inconsistencies of verb phrase tagging in the corpus TreeBank. At the same time, we can analyze the inconsistencies of verb phrase tagging which are found in the corpus TreeBank in order that we can find a way to improve the consistency of verb phrase tagging automatically which is effective to improve the quality of corpus.

1 Introduction

Most empirical work in Natural Language Processing (NLP) is based on supervised machine learning techniques which rely on human annotated data of some form or another. But the construction of a corpus is a complicated work. Especially for individuals, it's a more hard assignment. Generally, a large-scale and high quality corpus comes from a team and it requires working in teams and different people is responsible for a particular part of the corpus respectively. Due to that the work is cut into several parts and distributed to different persons, inconsistencies may be generated. Because everyone has an individual understanding about the same case and different people may make the different annotations. All of these may cause inconsistencies, and even errors. When we train our models with a corpus which may contains inconsistencies even errors, the models will not represent the real distribution of the problems precisely. So the work to find the inconsistencies in the corpus and to correct them is useful to improve the precision of the models, which can help us obtain more accurate results in natural language processing.

2 Related Work

At present, the research on corpus consistency is mainly concentrated on the consistency of word segmentation and part-of-speech (POS) tagging. Liu Bo, Zheng Jiaheng and Zhang Hu proposed a method to handle the consistency of word segmentation which is based on the combination of statistics and rules. They also introduced a number of strategies to handle different kinds of inconsistency [5]. Zhang Hu and Zheng Jiaheng put forward a method to check the consistency of part-of-speech (POS) tagging on the foundation of the analysis of the part-of-speech (POS) tagging which is based on the classifications of ambiguity words [11].

Besides the research on the inconsistency of word segmentation and part-of-speech (POS) tagging, some people focused on the research about the ambiguity of structure or function in Chinese corpus gradually as well. The Chinese ambiguities of structure in high frequency are divided into three basic types based on the analysis of structural ambiguity. By analyzing the ambiguities of structure, Yang Sichun and Chen Jiajun found out the causes of structural ambigui-

Proceedings of the Third CIPS-SIGHAN Joint Conference on Chinese Language Processing, pages 70–75, Wuhan, China, 20-21 October 2014 ty, and proposed some strategies to remove them, especially the solution based on examples [12].

This paper aims to find the inconsistencies of verb phrase tagging in the corpus TreeBank. As we all know, some errors always exists in corpus as a kind of inconsistency. So when we find out the inconsistencies in the corpus TreeBank we will lay a foundation of finding out errors in the corpus TreeBank.

3 Terminology

- TreeBank

In this paper, we use the corpus which is named Chinese Treebank 7.0 (CTB7.0). There are 2,448 text files in this release, containing 51,447 sentences, 1,196,329words, 1,931,381 hanzi (Chinese characters). The data is provided in four different formats: raw text, word segmented, word segmented and POS-tagged, and syntactically bracketed formats.

In Chinese Treebank 7.0 (CTB7.0), the frequency of verb phrases is in second dgree, which is only less than the frequency of noun phrase. In addition, the usage of Chinese vocabulary is very flexible and a word always can act as a variety of components of the grammar in different context, especially verb, which causes a lot of grammatical ambiguity in syntactic analysis. So, we choose the verb phrases to find out the inconsistent tagging.

- Verb Phrase

The verb (including verb compound) and aspect sequence forms the verbal head that takes zero or more complement to form a verb phrase.

- Verb Head

The verb (including verb compound) and aspect sequence forms the verbal head.

- Verb Compounds

Although compounding is highly productive in Chinese, it is still considered to be a lexical process. Therefore compounds are treated in a similar fashion as simple monolithic verbs. The challenge is to clearly identify compounds and distinguish them from situations where a phrasal projection is necessary. Due to the lack of a clear standard between compounds and phrases in Chinese, we will adopt the following working criteria for verb compounds where there is a sequence of verbs: (1) they share the argument structure, (2) they share aspect markers, (3) they share modifiers, (4) and they do not fall into the clearly defined raising or control structures.

A classification of verbal compounds are shown in Table 1.

Tags	Explanation
VCD	coordinated verb compound
VCP	verb compounds formed by VV + VC
VNV	verb compounds formed by A-not-A or A-one-A
VPT	potential form V-de-R or V-bu-R
VRD	verb resultative compound
VSB	verb compounds formed by a modifier + a head

Table 1. a classification of verbal compounds

- Aspect Maker

In Chinese, the particles (e.g.了 (le), 着 (zhe), 过 (guo)) are named as aspect maker.

- Inconsistency

In Chinese Treebank 7.0 (CTB7.0), we can find the phenomenon that a verb phrase may have different annotations in different place while they are in the same context. We define this phenomenon as inconsistency.

```
(VP(VV取得)
   (NP-OBJ(NN突破性)
          (NN进展)))
```

```
(VP(VV取得)
   (NP-OBJ(ADJP(JJ突破性))
          (NP(NN进展))))
```

Figure 1. An example of the different tagging of verb phrase in Chinese Treebank 7.0

In figure 1, we can see the annotations of "取得突破性进展" are different. In the top table, the "突破性" was tagged as JJ while in the bottom table, it wsa tagged as NN.

4 Research Method

In this paper, we find out the inconsistencies by comparing the tagging of verb phrase. In this section, we mainly describe the method and the result of experiment.

4.1 The Method Based on Comparison of Tags of Verb Phrases

We divided all of the verb phrases into different categories based on the Chinese characters which were consisted of the verb phrase. Then we compared the annotations of verb phrases which belonged to the same category each other. If we found the different tagging of verb phrases in one category, there might be inconsistency in it.

Procedure.

Our goal is to find out the verb phrases in corpus that they shared the same Chinese characters while their tagging are different.

Step1: Finding verb phrases.

Firstly, we found all of the verb phrases in corpus and divided them into different categories based on the Chinese characters which were consisted of them. At the same time we recorded their provenance which contained the index of the text and the sentence. An example is shown as follows.

eg1: 一百亿 元 人民币

TAGS:(VP(VP(NP-PRD(QP(CD)(CLP(M)))(NP(NN)))))

TAGS: (VP (NP-PRD(QP(CD)(CLP(M)))(NP(NN))))

TAGS: (VP(VP(NP-PRD(QP(CD)(CLP(M)))(NP(NN)))))

TAGS: (VP(NP-PRD(QP(CD)(CLP(M)))(NP(NN))))

Step2: Finding verb phrases that appear more than once.

Secondly, after dividing all of the verb phrases into different categories, we kept the categories that contain more than one verb phrases and removed the categories that contain only one verb phrase.

eg2: "公开 、 公平 、 公正 "

TAGS: (VP(PU)(VA)(PU)(VA)(PU)(VA)(PU))

TAGS: (VP(PU)(VA)(PU)(VA)(PU)(VA)(PU))

TAGS: (VP(PU)(VA)(PU)(VA)(PU)(VA)(PU))

TAGS: (VP(PU)(VA)(PU)(VA)(PU)(VA)(PU))

Step3: Finding categories appearing different.

Thirdly, after dividing all the verb phrases into different categories based on the Chinese characters which were consisted of them, we found out the categories in which there were different tagging of verb phrases.

eg3. " 抓大放小 "# 4#

TAGS: (VP(PP(-NONE-*T*-1))(VP(PU)(VV)(PU)))

TAGS: (VP(PU)(VV)(PU))

TAGS: (VP(PP(-NONE-*T*-1))(VP(PU)(VV)(PU)))

TAGS: (VP(PU)(VV)(PU))

Step4: Eliminating the Influence of Omitted Structure.

Fourthly, we eliminated the influence of omitted structure. In the results of step 3, we found some differences were only caused by the omitted structure. Omitted structure was related to parsing, and we didn't take care of this temporarily. So we eliminated the categories in which the differences were only caused by omitted structure.

eg4. " 抓大放小 "# 4#

TAGS: (VP(PP(-NONE-*T*-1))(VP(PU)(VV)(PU)))

TAGS: (VP(PU)(VV)(PU))

In the example above, the difference are only caused by omitted structure. So we should eliminate the category.

The operation of eliminating the influence of omitted structure was on the result of step 3. Firstly, we arranged a device to store verb phrase in a tree data structure. Secondly, we used these devices to prune the omitted structure. Thirdly, we restored the devices pruned to verb phrases. Fourthly, repeated step 3. If after the operation, the tags in a category are all the same, it means that, the differences in this category caused only by the omitted structure and it should be eliminated.

4.2 Experimental Results and Analysis.

In this paper, we mainly research the first 612 texts in Chinese Treebank 7.0 (CTB7.0). We find out a total of 37416 groups of verb phrases and 2430 groups contain more than one verb phrase. In these 2430 groups of verb phrases there are 688 groups in which we find the inconsistency. After eliminating the omitted structure there are only 245 groups. And the 245 groups are the finally result. We find the 245 groups can be divided into five categories.

The first kind of inconsistency of verb phrase is that the verb phrase mark appears more than once in a verb phrase. There is such a phenomenon in the TreeBank corpus that in the outer layer of a complete verb phrase a "VP" symbol was marked repeatedly. We see this phenomenon as the first kind of inconsistency.

In the statistics about verb phrases, we took "VP" as the signal of a verb phrase. Thus, if there is a repetition of a verb phrase marked symbol , we will find two verb phrases at least in the result which satisfy the condition that they share the same Chinese character while their verb phrase tagging are different and the cause of difference is only due to the additional "(VP)". According to the idea, we have found some categories in the results of classification of verb phrases which satisfy the condition that in each of these categories there are two different tagging at least and one of them is the substring of the other one and their difference is only due to the additional "(VP)".

The second kind of inconsistency is that the type of verb compounds annotated inconsistently. There is such a phenomenon in the TreeBank corpus that the verb compounds share the same tags of part of speech in different sentences while the type of verb compounds annotation is different. And this is the second kind of inconsistency.

There are six kinds of verb compounds, which include VCD, VCP, VNV, VPT, VRD and VSB. In a verb phrase, the relative position of verb compounds is steady. Thus, the relative position of tagging corresponding to the verb compounds is steady as well. According to the fact, we have created a table for each category of verb phrases with the row standing for the index of the verb phrase and the column standing for the relative position of the verb compounds to storing the entire symbol of verb compounds in it and compared the values in column. We have found the type of verb compounds annotated inconsistently in some categories.

The third kind of inconsistency is that the tagging of phrases are not complete. We can find such a phenomenon in the TreeBank corpus that some words share the same tags of part of speech in different sentences and some of them are marked the tags of phrase while some of them are not. This is the third one.

In a category of verb phrases, if each verb phrase is marked completely, the quantity of symbol belonging to every phrase will be the same. So, if a verb phrase isn't marked completely, its quantity of symbols will less than others'. According to the description, we have arranged a device to store each verb phrase in a category in a tree data structure. The number of nodes of a tree is equal to the number of symbols of the corresponding verb phrase. We have found some categories contain inconsistency due to the lack of the tags of phrase by comparing the number of nodes of every tree in the same category.

The fourth kind of inconsistency is similar to the third one. It is also caused by not complete annotation. But what is different is that the fourth one is caused by the lack of functional tags. In the TreeBank corpus some words share the same tags of part of speech in different sentences and some of them are marked the functional tags while some of them are not.

In a category of verb phrases, all of the verb phrases shared the same part-of-speech and each verb phrase is marked completely, but the length of catenation of symbols in each verb phrase is different. It means that some verb phrase is lack of functional tags.

The fifth kind of inconsistency is caused by the different tagging of part of speech. In the TreeBank corpus there are many conversion words and their tagging of part of speech in different context are different. As a result, the verb phrases which contain them will be marked with different tags of phrase. So, we class the fifth one as the category that is caused by the different tagging of part of speech.

In a category of verb phrases, the inconsistency may result from the different part-of-speech tagging. According to the fact, we have arranged a device to store each verb phrase in a tree data structure. In the tree data structure, the parent node of leaf node is the part-of-speech tagging of corresponding to the leaf node. So, we can get the part-of-speech tagging of each Chinese character in a verb phrase from the tree data structure easily. After getting the part-of-speech tagging, we catenate all of them which are from the same tree data structure as a string. We have found some categories that contain inconsistency because of the different part-of-speech tagging by comparing the strings that belong to the same category.

In the 245 groups of verb phrases there are 224 groups can be classed as the members of these five categories. It's about 91.43% and these five categories of inconsistency cover all kinds of inconsistency nearly. There are 63 groups belong to the first category, 9 groups belong to the second category, 26 groups belong to the third category, 51 groups belong to the fourth category, and 75 groups belong to the fifth category.

Index	Category	Example	Quantity	Percentage
1	VP repetition	(VP(VP(VV 失败))) (VP(VV 失败))	63	28.13%
2	verb compounds	(VP(VCD(VV 上市)(VV 交易))) (VP(VSB(VV 上市)(VV 交易)))	9	4.02%
3	tagging of phrase	(VP(ADVP(AD 共同))(VV 努力)) (VP(ADVP(AD 共同))(VP (VV 努力)))	26	11.61
4	functional tags	(VP(VC 为)(NP(NN 团长))) (VP(VC 为)(NP-PRD(NN 团长)))	51	22.77%
5	Different POS	(VP(VCD(VV 协调)(VV 发展))) (VP(VV 协调)(NP-OBJ(NN 发展)))	75	33.48%

Table 2. The distribution of inconsistency

5 Conclusions and Future Work

In this paper, we aim at find out the inconsistency in Chinese Treebank 7.0 (CTB7.0). Besides the method described before, we also have tried to solve this problem by to using other method which is based on the assumption that if we cluster the sentences in the corpus when we set the annotations as the conditions of similarity measurement, in the result, the small-scale clusters may represent the wrong annotations. But the result is not satisfied because of inappropriate grain size. What's more, what we have finished is inadequate. For the first method, we just consider the case that the verb phrases shared the same Chinese characters which were consisted of them while their tagging are different. We need to consider other cases in future. For the Second method, the grain sizes we have chosen is not enough.

The next jobs is to try to consider other situation to find the inconsistency in Chinese Treebank 7.0 (CTB7.0). For example, the verb phrase shared the same tags of part of speech while their tags are different. What's more, we should choose a proper grain size to remedy the method based on statistic.

Reference

Bo Liu, JiaHeng Zheng, Hu Zhang. 2008. Consistency check of segment using combination of rule and statistics. Computer Engineering and Design, 2008(29): 1814-1816

Hui Wang. 2003. A STUDY OF CHINESE WORD SENSE DISAMBIGUATION IN MT BASED ON GRAMMATICAL AND SEMANTIC KNOWLEDGE-BASES. JOURNAL OF GUANGXI NORMAL UNIVERSITY, 2003(21):86-93

Hu Zhang, Jiaheng Zheng. 2008. Consistency Check on POS Tagging of Chinese Corpus Based on Classification. Computer Engineering,2008(34):90-92

Jiang Liu, Jiaheng Zheng, Hu Zhang. 2005. Studies on the Consistency of Word Segmented Chinese Corpus. Application Research of Computers, 2005(9):52-54

Li Wei, Hongye Tan, Jiaheng Zheng, Jian Sun. 2012. Study of Keeping Consistency of Chinese Corpus of Complete Parsing. Journal of Guangxi Normal University:Natural Science Edition, 2012(28):139-142

Maosong Sun. 1999. On the consistency of word-segmented Chinese corpus. Applied Linguistics, 1999(2):87-90

Sichun Yang, Jiajun Chen. 2005. Research on Structur al Ambiguity in Chinese Automatic Syntactic Parsing. Journal of Kunming University of Science and Technology (Science and Technology), 2005(30):45-49

Xi Miao, Jiaheng Zheng. 2006. Classified Study On Inconsistency of Segment for Chinese Corpus. Journal of Shanxi University (N at. Sci. Ed.), 2006(1):22-25

Yongping Du, Jiaheng Zheng. 2001. Design and Reali zation of the Consistence Collation System in Segment and Property of Word Notation. Computer Development & Applications, 2001(10):16-18

Yin Liu. 2002. CHINESE-ENGLISH MACHINE TRANSLATION DISAMBIGUATING WITH RULE-BASED METHOD COMBINED WITH STATISTIC-BASED METHOD. Computer Applications, 2002(22):21-23

Yili Qian, Jiaheng Zheng. 2004. Research on the Method of Automatic Correction of Chinese Part-of-Speech Tagging. JOURNAL OF CHINESE INFORMATION PROCESSING, 2004(2):30-35

Yili Qian, Jiaheng Zheng. 2004. An Approach to Im proving the Quality of Part-of-Speech Tagging of Chinese Text. Itcc, vol. 2, pp.183, International Conference on Information Technology: Coding and Computing (ITCC'04) Volume 2, 2004

Local Phrase Reordering Model for Chinese-English Patent Machine Translation

Xiaodie Liu
Institute of Chinese Information Processing, Beijing Normal University, Beijing 100875, China
liuxiaodie2009@hotmail.com

Yun Zhu
Institute of Chinese Information Processing, Beijing Normal University, Beijing 100875, China
zhuyun@bnu.edu.com

Yaohong Jin
Institute of Chinese Information Processing, Beijing Normal University, Beijing 100875, China
jinyaohong@bnu.edu.cn

Abstract: We focused on when and how to reorder the Chinese NPs with two, three translation units for reordering in Chinese-English Machine Translation. By analyzing the features of translation units of the Chinese NPs, we built some formalized rules to recognize the boundaries of translation units using the boundary words to recognize what to reorder. By comparing the orders of Chinese and English NPs, we developed a strategy a local phrase reordering model on how to reorder the translation units. At last, we used a rule-based MT system to test our work, and the experimental results showed that our rule-based method and strategy were very efficient.

1 Introduction

Over the past decade, machine translation (MT) has seen many exciting developments, but phrase-based models, syntax-based models, dependency-based models cannot deal with the reordering at the sentence level very well, particularly the reordering in a hierarchical structure in which the reordering of Chinese NPs is dependent on. The Hierarchical Semantic-Category-Tree (HSCT) Model[1] used semantic features to handle the reordering at sentence level with a rule-based method. The system based on HSCT model could partition a sentence into a predicate and noun phases (NPs for short) and reorder them in sentence level, but this system did not reorder the inner orders in a NP. This paper aims to solve a type of the problem: reorder the inner components in a NP.

In Chinese-English MT, the structural difference in NPs between Chinese to English is a difficult problem, such as the different positions for the head of the NPs: the head of a Chinese NP is in the front; however that of an English NP is in the end. The language for patent usually was inclined to express complicated thought in long and complex words. Here is an example wherein the number of the translation units in a complicated Chinese NP happens to be three.

Example:

Chinese NP:所述图像传感器于红色、蓝色和绿色色彩通道的光谱灵敏度

English in Chinese order: the image sensor device in red, blue, and green color channels de the spectral sensitivities

Reference: the spectral sensitivities of the image sensor device in red, blue, and green color channels

Google: an image sensor means in said red, blue and green spectral sensitivity of color channel.

The Chinese NP "所述图像传感器于红色、蓝色和绿色色彩通道的光谱灵敏度"consists of a Chinese character "的" and a function word "于" and three translation units: A"所述图像传感器"、B"于红色、蓝色和绿色色彩通道" and C"光谱灵敏度", and the right English order of translation units was "C A B" according to the reference. However, the boundaries of "B and C" and the order of "A, B and C" in English of Google were wrong.

How to recognize the boundaries of the translation units "A, B, C" and how to reorder them were the main problems that to be solved in this paper.

The remainder of this paper is organized as follows. In Section 2, we at first the examined the features of translation units and sum boundary words for recognizing them, then analyzed differences in the orders of complicated Chinese-English NPs and summed a strategy on how to reorder the translation units when translate the complicated Chinese NPs to English. In Section 3, we used a rule-based method and designed a algorithm to recognize the translation units to solve what to reorder and how to reorder. In Section 4, we discussed the experiment results. Section 5 is the related work. Finally, a conclusion is given and the further work is expected in Section 6.

2 Analyses of the Chinese NPs

In this section, we intent to develop a strategy on reorder Chinese NP based on the translation units.

2.1 Translation units

This part focused on examining the features of the translation units and tried to sum some laws on the boundaries for recognizing the translation units.

A translation unit was a word or word-group of expressing the same meaning both in Chinese and English. Translation units were the equivalent in Chinese and English NPs, and it is certain that this study can only be based on contrasting Chinese and English NPs. The complicated Chinese NP consists of NP or prepositional phrases (PP for short), locative phrase (LP for short) etc. The translation unit may be as follows:

(1) NP, which was a smallest unit for reordering in Chinese-English machine translation;

(2)PP with a "preposition" and (1)

(3)LP with a "localizer" and (1)

(4)PP with a "preposition", (1) and a "localizer"

(5) PP with a "preposition", some (1) and a "localizer".

2.1.1 Outer Characteristics

In English, prepositions with flexible meanings are frequently used. They function as bonding agents in NPs. In English NPs, the translation units can be obtained by the prepositions, such as "the spectral sensitivities of the image sensor device in red, blue, and green color channels", the prepositions "of" and "in" can partition the NP into three translation units.

In Chinese NPs, the translation units can be obtained by the prepositions, localizers and the structural particle "的(de)".

- structural particle "的(de)"

Compare and analyze the difference as well as locations between English modifiers and Chinese auxiliary words so that the "的(de)" is especial, which servers two functions. First, "的(de)", marked as "de_1", was a boundary of two translation units and should be excluded from the two translation units, such as the "的" in the phrase "本发明的实施方式", which consist two translation units "本发明"and "实施方式". "的$_2$"; second,"的(de)", marked as "de_2" , is an inner conjunction of a translation unit, such as the "的" in the phrase "简明的装置".

Here we focuses on "de_1" and should distinguish it from "de_2". Based on the studying of the "的(de)",we discovered some language rules from authentic contexts: "de_2" were often behind of adjective, quantifier, verb and pronoun. In view of the cost and practicability, "de_2"can be eliminated more easily.

- prepositions

Preposition is one of Chinese functional words which have a complex function, involving various factors, such as "在(zai),根据(gen ju),作为(zuo wei)"etc. For example,

- localizers

There is a special grammatical method in Chinese language—the words of locality which represent pure directions, such as "上(on),中(in),外(outside)".

- others

Some time nouns, such as "时(when)"and some auxiliary words, such as "而言(er yan)".

Some prepositions and some localizers work hand in hand, such as "当……时", "在……中", "对……而言"etc.

The prepositions and localizers always worked with "de_1", for example, for Chinese NP "一种或多种作为湿润剂的醇类",the preposition "作为" and structural particle "de1" could partition it into three translation units, for Chinese NP "通常运转时的气体压力", the localizer "时"and structural particle "de1" could partition it into two translation units.

From the above analysis we could see structural particle "的(de)", prepositions, localizers and others could be outer boundaries words for recognize the translation units.

2.1.2 Inner Characteristics

In Chinese NPs, the NPs may modify the NPs without any prepositions, localizers and structural particle, but not in English NPs.

This section explores some laws at the beginning word and the end word of translation units in Chinese-English translation.

2.1.2.1 Left Characteristics

Chinese and English belong to two different

language families, in most cases, the source language cannot correspond to the target language well. However, the internal components of translation units shared some characters in common as the result of linguistic universality and identity of human thinking form.

By comparing the translation units, we can obtain some features of the beginning of translation units, which can be some implicit boundaries of two translation units.

- demonstrative pronoun

In English NPs, the translation units also can be obtained by the definite articles and demonstrative pronoun. In Chinese NPs, the translation units also can be obtained by demonstrative pronoun. For example, the word "这些(these)" is demonstrative pronoun in translation unit"这些业务(these services)"

- quantitative phrases

In Chinese NPs, the translation units could not obtained by indefinite articles and quantitative phrases. For example, the Chinese phases "一个,一种" and so on correspond to the English words "a, an, one" .

The Chinese words "第一, 第二, 第三, 第四" correspond to the English words "first, second, third, fourth".

- adjectives

An adjective usually modifies the noun.

The difference of Chinese and English exists in many ways such as morphological structure and word-formation which leads to the different words for a semantic feature between Chinese and English. Some adjectives, past participles, present participles in English were expressed in phase in Chinese.

- degree adverbs

The English adjective "notable" in translation unit "notable features" which are unique for English, thus appropriate version cannot find in Chinese vocabulary and expressed in phases "很显著" in translation unit "很显著的特点", wherein "很" is a degree adverb. There are many degree adverbs in Chinese, for example " 很(very), 非常(extremely), 十分(very much), 特别(specially), 极(too),(little), 更(more), 较(better),比较(better), 最(best)" etc.

- time adverbs

The past participle "coated" in translation unit "coated tank" which are unique for English, thus appropriate version cannot find in Chinese vocabulary and expressed in phases "已涂覆" in translation unit "已涂覆罐", wherein "已" is a time adverb. There are many time adverbs in Chinese, for example "已经(already), 曾经(once), 早已(already), 刚刚(just now), 正(be being),正在(be being),就(be going to),就要(be going to),将(be going to),将要(be going to),曾(once),刚(just now),才(already),在(be being)" etc.

- negative adverbs

The English adjective negative prefixes, such as "negative, opposite, and reverse" etc, corresponds to the negative adverbial words "不(un-),非(un-),没(dis-),没有(dis-),不用（un-）,未（dis-）"etc.

- others

The "resulting" in translation unit "resulting decoded" which are unique for English, thus appropriate version cannot find in Chinese vocabulary and expressed in phases "经解码" in translation unit "经解码语音".

The past participle "refrigerated" in translation unit "refrigerated substances" which are unique for English, thus appropriate version cannot find in Chinese vocabulary and expressed in phases "被制冷" in translation unit "被制冷物质", wherein "被" is an auxiliary word. There are many auxiliary words in Chinese, such as "所(suo)" etc.

The English adjective "movable" in translation unit "rotatable structure" which are unique for English, thus appropriate version cannot find in Chinese vocabulary and expressed in phases "可旋转" in translation unit "可旋转结构".

2.1.2.1 Right Characteristics

- Noun

In general, the end of a translation unit in Chinese patent was a noun.

- number words

The number words consist of the numbers from 0 to 9 and were labels related to the new inventions. Huge numbers of number words could not enter the knowledge base and were generated dynamically as NUM when knowledge base was loaded.

- letter words

The letter words consist of numbers from 0 to 9 and 26 English letters. As with the number words, Huge numbers of number words could not enter the knowledge base and were generated dynamically as SPN when knowledge base was loaded.

- auxiliary word "等(Deng)"

The auxiliary word "等(Deng)" Displays the enumeration entry.

As can be seen above, although Chinese does not have much overt morphology, it still distinguishes a translation unit from another by lexical devices.

When they were not outer boundary words in one continuous string, we used demonstrative pronoun, degree adverb, quantitative phrase, adjective, time adverbs, negative adverbs and others as the left boundary words to partition the string into two translation units utilizing contextual clues such as right characteristics. See table 1 for examples.

When they were not outer boundary words in one continuous string, we used number words, letter words, auxiliary word "等(Deng)" as the right boundary words to partition the string into two translation units.See table 2 for examples.

Table1.The left boundary words and examples

Left Boundary Words	Examples
demonstrative pronoun	(如权利要求 5)(所述的方法)->(the method) (according to claim 5)
degree adverb	(这项发明)(非常显著地一个特点)->(a very significant feature) of (this invention)
quantitative phrase	(这种丙烯酸树脂)(一个来源)->(one suitable source) of (these acrylic acrylate resins)
adjective	(支撑表面)(可能的总体压力)->(the possible total fluid pressure)of(a support surface)
time adverb	(该容器)(已经清洗的表面)-> (the cleaned surface) of (the containers)
negative adverb	(取向膜) (未拉伸的酰化纤维素膜)-> (unstretched cellulose acylate films) of (Orientation film)
others	(该工件)(被照射区)-> (the irradiated region) of (the work)

Table 2.The right boundary words and examples

Right Boundary Words	Examples
number words	(水箱 300)(底部组件 303) ->(a base assembly 303)(for the tank 300)
letter words	(主体部 400a)(膛)-> (the bore)of (the host section 400a)
等(deng)	(牵引电动机等) (负载装置)->(a load device)(such as the traction motor)

Taken together, the boundary words have two types: 1) The out boundary words ,such as "的(de)" , propositions and locatives; 2) The inner boundary words, which include left boundary words and right boundary words. The left boundary words lie in the first word or phrase in a translation unit and the right boundary words lie in the last word.

2.1 Reordering

Once the translation units had been recognized, a new process called reordering can be applied to them.

This part compared and analyzed the differences in the orders of Chinese-English NPs so as to find out the law and develop a strategy on how to translate the complicated Chinese NPs to English effectively.

According to the boundary words above, we found that there are three types of translation units:

- PPs

PPs with a preposition, such as "根据该形式" NP "根据该形式的模具", PPs with a preposition and a localizer, such as "在外模具部件 601 和管子 400 外表面之间" in NP "在外模具部件 601 和管子 400 外表面之间的界面"

- LPs

LPs are unique to Chinese, such as "主体上" in NP"主体上的主要压力",

- NPs

It could be one or more word, such as "/详视图/(a detailed view), /所述/局部/缩放/估算/器/(said local scale estimator)" and could include a "de_2" , such as 大部分常规的交通工具布线系统(most conventional vehicle wiring systems)" .

- NP_Bs

NP_Bs is unique to Chinese. It could be adjectives, pronouns, numerals and quantitative phrases in special position, such as "一些" which could occur in the NP "一些基于环保溶剂的清洗剂" which consist of three translation units "一些", "基于环保溶剂" and "清洗剂".

The Chinese NPs consist of NPs, PPs, LPs and NP_Bs; otherwise, the English NPs consist of NPs and PPs only.

The Chinese and English NPs share some characters in common:1) the NPs consist of PPs and NPs, 2) the PPs could not be head translation units, 3) the NPs must be the head translation units.

However, the position and order between the NPs and PPs in Chinese were different from English as the result of different culture and tradition, especially, the NP_Bs, LPS are unique for Chinese NPs. The primary dissimilarity is that the head translation unit must locate in the end and others translation units such as NPs, PPs and LPs must be modifiers to some extent, otherwise, in English, the beginning translation unit is the head translation unit and followed by other PPs as modifiers.

Based on aligned Chinese-English NP-pairs from 15 Patent documents, this paper compared the differences in orders of Chinese-English NPs and analyzed types of translation units so as to find out the laws in translating Chinese NPs to English.

For Chinese NPs, the PPs and LPs shared same function, so we use PPs for PPs and LPs.

2.1.1 Chinese NPs with two translation units

All combinations and the structure relations about two translation units can be listed in table 2, and we can see that in combinations of "NP1 NP2", the NP1 or NP2 were the NPs and the NP1 must modify NP2; in combinations of "PP NP", the NP must be the NPs and PP must modify the NP.

For the PPs and LPs, the prepositions were before the NPs and the locatives were behind the NPs, but the PPs or LPs could be moved as a whole. In table 2, we can see that there only one reordering way for the Chinese NPs with two translation units and b).

All structure relations between two translation units occur in Chinese, and we can find some examples to illustrate our reduction were right in table 3.

Table3: Chinese and English orders of NPs with two translation units

	Order in Chinese		Order in English
	Combinations	Structure Relations	
a)	NP1 NP2[1]	NP1 NP2	NP2 NP1
b)	PP[2] NP	PP NP	NP PP

Table4: examples of orders of Chinese and English NPs with two translation units

Chinese Orders -> English orders
NP1 NP2-> NP2 NP1 (模制工艺)的(操作参数)->the operating parameters of the molding process
PP NP -> NP PP (在前面实施方案中)(所述的相同类型的聚合材料)-> the same types of polymeric material in the earlier embodiment

2.1.2 Chinese NPs with three translation units

We can list all combinations and the structure relations about three translation units in the Chinese NPs. In table 4, we can see that: a) has three structure relations: (NP1 (NP2 NP3)) indicated that at first NP2 modified NP3, then they acted as a whole to be modified by NP1, ((NP1 NP2) NP3) indicated that at first NP1 modified NP2, then they acted as a whole to modify NP3,and ((NP1) (NP2) NP3) indicated that NP1 and NP2 respectively modify NP3.b) has three structure relations: ((PP NP1) NP2) indicated that at first NP1 modified NP2, then they acted as a whole to be modified by PP, ((PP NP1) NP2) indicated that at first PP modified NP1, then they acted as a whole to modify NP2,and ((PP1)(NP2) NP3) indicated that PP and NP1 respectively modify NP2, and c) has three structure relations:(PP1 (PP2 NP)) indicated that at first PP2 modified NP, then they acted as a whole to be modified by PP1, ((PP1 PP2) NP) indicated that PP1 and PP2 acted as a whole to modify NP, and ((PP1)(PP2) NP)

[1] The number behind NP or PP notes the order they appear in the linear sequence of Chinese NPs. The space among NP and PP is used to split the different translation units, and can stand for "的" in authentic Chinese NPs.

[2]

indicated that PP1 and PP2 respectively modify NP. d) has two structure relations: (NP1 (PP NP2)) indicated that at first PP modified NP2, then they acted as a whole to be modified by NP1, and ((NP1)(PP)NP2) indicated that NP1 and PP respectively modify NP2.e) has one structure relation (NP_B (PP NP)) which indicated at first PP modified NP, then they acted as a whole to be modified by NP_B.

Although, not all the structure relations among three translation units occur in Chinese, we can find some examples to illustrate our reduction were right in table 5.

Table5: Chinese and English orders of NPs with three translation units

	Order in Chinese		Order in English
	Combinations"	Structure Relations	
a)	NP1 NP2 NP3	(NP1(NP2 NP3))	NP3 NP2 NP1
		((NP1 NP2) NP3)	
		((NP1)(NP2) NP3)	
b)	PP NP1 NP2	(PP (NP1 NP2))	NP2 NP1 PP
		((PP NP1) NP2)	
		((PP)(NP1) NP2)	
c)	PP1 PP2 NP	(PP1 (PP2 NP))	NP PP2 PP1
		((PP1)(PP2) NP)	
		((PP1 PP2) NP)	NP PP1 PP2
d)	NP1 PP NP2	(NP1 (PP NP2))	NP2 PP NP1
		((NP1)(PP)NP2)	
e)	NP_B PP NP	(NP_B (PP NP))	NP_B NP PP

Table 6: Examples of orders of Chinese and English NPs with three translation units

Chinese Orders -> English Orders
1 NP1 NP2 NP3 -> NP3 NP2 NP1 1.1((材料)的(捏合度))的(调节范围)->the adjusting range for the kneading degree of the material =>(NP1 NP2) NP3 -> NP3 NP2 NP1 1.2(这些模具)的((一种形式)的(结构))-> the construction of one form of the moulds =>NP1 (NP2 NP3) -> NP3 NP2 NP1
2 PP1 PP2 NP-> NP PP2 PP1 (闸板部件接近于圆筒段时)的(材料间)的(捏合度)->the kneading degree between the material when the gate member is moved close to the cylindrical segment =>PP1 PP2 NP-> NP1 PP2 PP1
3 PP NP1 NP2-> NP2 NP1 PP 3.1 ((在内模具部件上)的(第一密封装置))的(优点)-> the high vapor pressure of the propellant in the MDI =>(PP NP1) NP2-> NP2 NP1 PP 3.2 (调节捏合度时)的((装置)的(操作性))->the operability of the apparatus at the time of adjusting the kneading degree =>PP (NP1 NP2)-> NP2 NP1 PP
4 NP1 PP NP2-> NP2 NP1 PP (上述旋转轴部)的((绕水平轴)的(旋转力))-> the rotation force around the horizontal axis of the rotation axis part =>NP1 PP+ +NP2-> NP2 NP1 PP
5 NP_B PP NP-> NP_B NP PP (一些) ((基于环保溶剂)的(清洗剂))-> some cleaner based on environment-friendly solvent =>NP_B PP NP-> NP_B NP PP

We all know that ambiguity can be caused by multiple and different semantic relations. So, how to reorder seems to be a big problem. However we could conclude some laws about how to reorder the English orders of Chinese NPs with three translation units as follows:

1) The reversed order is the only way for Chinese NPs "NP1 NP2 NP3" which had three modifications and three semantic relations;

2) The first NP and the reversed order for PP is the only way for Chinese NPs "PP PP NP". For the pattern "((PP1 PP2) NP)->NP PP1 PP2", it only occurs in a kind of special Chinese NPs, such as "从(from)……", "到/向(to)……";

3) The first NP2, second NP1 and third PP is the only way for Chinese NPs "PP NP1 NP2" which had three structure relations and for Chinese NPs "NP1 PP NP2". For the pattern is (NP1 PP NP2)->NP2 PP NP1, the PP in English has the front boundary, and there is ambiguity, too;

4) The first NP_E, second NP and third PP is the only way for Chinese NPs "NP_B PP NP" in e).

3 Method

In our existing MT system, the Chinese NPs were given, but how to recognize the two or three translation units in the Chinese NPs were unknown. They can be obtained by using boundary words, for an effective boundary word or a combination of boundary words could not be the end or beginning of a base NP in semantic and partition a language string into two translation units.

3.1 Recognitions

The boundary words have two types: 1) the out boundary word ,such as "的(de)" and propositions, 2) the inner boundary words, which include left boundary words and right boundary words. The left boundary words lie in the first word or phrase in a translation unit and the right boundary words lie in the last word.

The Chinese NPs are stored using a tree structure. Thus how to distinguish the "的(de)" into "de_1" and "de_2", how to recognize the front and rear boundaries and how to combine the words of a unit is important.

Using a rule-base method, we designed some tags and attributes for nodes to recognize the translation units:

1) Tag for Nodes

- MK

  It was a node for "de_1" and means there is a reordering operation.
- MK_Q

  It need to add a new node "de_1" before the left boundary words.
- MK_H

  It need to add a new node "de_1" after the right boundary words.
- L1

  L1s were the front boundaries of translation units.
- L1H

  L1Hs were the rear boundaries of translation units
- NP_Bng%

  NP_Bng% was the beginning position of an Chinese NP.
- NP_End%

  NP_END% was the end position of an Chinese NP.

2) Attributes for Node

- LEVEL

  It was used to put this attribute to "的(de)",if value=-1, recognize it as "de_1", if value=0 (default value), recognize it as "de_2".
- NOT_CHANGE

  It was used to keep a translation unit not moving.

We designed the algorithm as follows:

Step1: distinguishing the "的(de)" into"de_1" and "de_2"

- building 12 rules to rule out the "de_2" by putting a value "2"to the attribute "level" of "的(de)" when the words before "的(de)" were adjective, quantifier, verb and pronoun;
- building 1 rule to identify the "de_1" by putting the "de_1" with a tag "MK";

step2: recognizing the front and right boundaries

- recognizing the front boundaries L1 when the words were prepositions
- putting a tag "MK_Q" on the left boundary words when the words were nouns, NUM or SPN before the left boundary words;
- recognizing the rear boundaries L1H when the words were locatives etc;
- putting a tag "MK_H" on the right boundary words when the words behind the right boundary words were noun;

step3: Generating the PPs and NPs

- generating the PPs by combining the words by the combination pattern[3] of boundary: (L1,L1H) (L1,L1] ,

[3] Combination pattern (A,B) and [A,B] indicated combining the word from A to B, and "("indicate A or B was included, and A or B was excluded.

[L1H,L1H), (L1,MK], [MK,L1], (NP_Bng%,L1H), [MK,L1H) by programming.

- generating the NPs from some combinations of [L1H,NP_End%), (MK,MK) by programming.
- generating the NP_Bs from some combinations of (NP_Bng%,L1] by programming and put an attribute "NOT_CHANGE".

Through three steps above, we could obtain all the translation units "PPs, NPs and NP_Bs" for reordering.

3.2 Reordering

In reordering phase, we defined the head NP at the end as NP_E. Then, the NPs contained PPs, NP_Bs, DE1, NP and NP_E. The strategies for reordering the Chinese NPs are as follows:

Step1: building 1 reorder rule for the Chinese NPs "NP_B PP NP";

Step2: keeping the NP_Bs not moving and move the PPs behind the NP_Es in reverse;

Step3: moving the other NPs behind the NP_Es in reverse, delete the "的(de)" and add the English word "of".

4 Experiments and Results

In order to test the result of this rule-based method and the strategy of reordering, the experiments takes 500 authentic patent texts provide by SIPO as the training set. The evaluation will use the development data for the NTCIR-9 Patent Machine Translation Pilot Task, containing 2,000 bilingual Chinese-English sentence pairs. After integrating the method into an existing rule-based system (HSCTMT), we take a closed test on training set and an open text on evaluation set.

Table 7. Accuracy of Translation Units

System	Precision (%)
Closed test	99.26
Open test	98.77

In table 7, the accuracy of translation units using boundary words in our system was very high and the results illustrated our rule-based method was efficient.

Table 8. Accuracy of Reordering of Chinese NPs in our system and Google

System	Closed test Precision (%)	Open test Precision (%)
HSCTMT	97.26	89.77
Google	57.47	59.92

In table 8, the result of two test shows the strategy of reordering was efficient, the semantic analysis in a rule-based method has effectively improved the recognition result of units for reordering, and Google performs poorly in tests. There are two factors affecting the performance:

- Incorrect boundaries of the nested PPs and PPs with a boundary affected the results.
- The multi-category words affected the results.

5 Related Works

Many reordering methods or strategy have been proposed in recent years to address this problem from different aspects. Phrase-based models excel at capturing local reordering phenomena and memorizing multi-word translation [2], but they perform poorly in the long and nested sentences in Patent. Syntax-based models handle long-distance reordering better than phase-based models. Reference [3] introduced a set Syntax-based rules to decide if a DE construction should be reordered or not before translating to English. Reference [4] focused on a Chinese noun phrase [A DE B] and explored a log-linear DE classifier by using syntactic, semantic and discourse context to producing an English translation strategy. Reference [1] explored a Hierarchical Semantic-Category-Tree (HSCT) model, which present a sentence as a hierarchical structure based on the Hierarchical Network of Concepts theory(HNC theory) and handle the reordering in three levels: Sentence Level, Chunk Level and Word Level. Reference [5,6,7] designed a Chinese-English Patent Machine Translation system based on the HSCT model.

6 Conclusions and Future Work

Based on analysis of translation units, we used a rule-based method to recognize the boundaries of the translation units using boundary words. Based on the analysis Chinese-English orders of Chinese NPs with two or three translation units, we developed a strategy on how to reorder the Chinese NPs. The experimental results showed that our rule-based method and strategy were very efficient on the reordering the NPs.

In future, we will enrich and refine the rules to improve the performance and research on how translate Chinese NPs fluently.

Acknowledgement

The authors are grateful to Multi-level Kn owledge Representation of Mass Texts and C hinese Language Understanding System (Nat ional 863 Program, No.2012AA011104) and the Fundamental Research Funds of Central Universities for financial support.

Reference

[1]Zhu Xiaojian, Jin Yaohong,2010, Hierarchical Semantic-Category-Tree Model for Chinese-English Machine Translation, China Communications, Beijing,80-92

[2]KOEHN P,MARCU D. Statistical Phrase-based Translation [C]//Proceeding of the 2003 Conference of the North American Chapter of the A ssociation for Computational Linguistics on Human Language Technology, 48-54.

[3]Chao Wang, Michael Collins and Philipp Koehn. 2007 , Chinese syntactic reordering for statistical machine translation. In Proceeding of EMNLP-CoNLL, Prague, Czech Republic, June. Association for Computational Linguistics, 737-745.

[4]PiChuan Chang, Dan Jurafsky and Chrisstopher D. Manning.2009, Disambiguating "DE" for Chinese-English Machine Translation. In Proceeding fo the Fourth Workshop on Statistical Machine Translation, Athens, Greece, 30 March-31 March. Association for Computational Linguistics. 215-223.

[5]Yun Zhu, Yaohong Jin.: A Chinese-English Patent Machine Translation System Based on the Theory of Hierarchical Network of Concepts .J: The Journal of China Universities and Tele-communications, Beijing, 140 – 146. (2012)

Sentence Alignment of Historical Classics based on Mode Prediction and Term Translation Pairs

Chao Che **Xiaojun Zheng**
Key Laboratory of Advanced Design and Intelligent Computing
(Dalian University) , *Ministry of Education,*
Dalian, 116622, P. R. China
chechao101@163.com, zhengxiaojun@gmail.com

Abstract

Parallel corpora are essential resources for the construction of bilingual term dictionary of historical classics. To obtain large-scale parallel corpora, this paper proposes a sentence alignment method based on mode prediction and term translation pairs. On one hand, the method rebuilds the sentence alignment process according to characteristics of the translation of historical classics, and adds mode prediction into the sentence alignment. On the other hand, due to the lack of bilingual ancient Chinese dictionary, the method exploits the term translation pairs extracted from manually aligned sentence pairs to perform alignment. The method first predicts the alignment mode probability according to the character number, punctuation number and some characters of Chinese sentence, then performs sentence alignment using length alignment probability, term alignment probability and mode probability. Besides, the method selects anchor sentence pairs based on sentence length and predicted mode to prevent the spread of alignment errors. The experiment on "*Shi Ji*" demonstrates that mode prediction and term translation pair both enhance the performance of sentence alignment obviously.

1 Introduction

Translating the classics into English and introducing them to the world is an important way to spread Chinese culture. Because of the dynamic nature of historical development and huge differences between Chinese and Western languages, the translation of classics is very difficult. Bilingual term dictionary is very helpful for translation of historical classics. The term dictionary can be built by extracting term translation pairs from bilingual parallel corpora. Aiming at obtaining large-scale parallel corpora, we study the sentence alignment of historical classics. Currently the bilingual sentence alignment methods are mainly divided into following four types: (1) the method based on length(Gale and Church, 1993; Lu et al., 2003), which performs sentence alignment using the sentence length relation; (2) the method based on dictionary(Yu et al., 2010), which performs sentence alignment using the lexicon translation in bilingual dictionary; (3)the hybrid method(Moore, 2002; Chen and Lin, 2009; Tian et al., 2009), which makes use of many kinds of information including sentence length to improve the accuracy of alignment; (4) the method base on mode classification(Fattah et al., 2007); which regards sentence alignment as a mode classification problem and exploits classifier to align sentences.

Due to the various meanings of historical classics, the ratio of the sentence length between historical classics and its English translation is not uniform. Thus alignment method using sentence length alone does not have good performance. Owing to lack of ancient Chinese bilingual dictionary, we exploit the term translation pairs extracted from the sentence pairs aligned manually to do sentence alignment. Since the translator needs to explain the hiding meaning of historical classics when translating classics into English, the sentence alignment modes of classics are almost all "one-to-many". The sentence alignment of historical classics can be considered as finding corresponding English translation for every Chinese sentence. According to the above characteristics of historical classics, this paper proposed a sentence alignment method based on mode pre-

Proceedings of the Third CIPS-SIGHAN Joint Conference on Chinese Language Processing, pages 85–89,
Wuhan, China, 20-21 October 2014

diction and term translation pairs. The method first predicts the alignment mode probability based on the features of Chinese sentence, then run sentence alignment using sentence length and term translation pairs.

2 The Mathematical Model of Sentence Alignment Method

2.1 Sentence Alignment Probability

Given a Chinese text block $C=\{c_1,c_2,\cdots,c_m\}$ and the English translation $E=e_1,e_2,\cdots,e_n$, where c_i denotes a Chinese sentence and e_j is a English sentence. Sentence alignment aims at finding the alignment $\hat{A}$ with the maximum alignment probability among all alignments A, which can be denoted as following formula.

$$\hat{A}=\arg\max\left\{\prod_{M\in A}\begin{matrix}\Pr(<c,e>|M(c,e))\\ *\Pr(M(c,e))\end{matrix}\right\} \quad (1)$$

Wherein: $<c,e>$ is a pair of sentences, which is also called sentence bead. And e is the translation of c. $M(c,e)$ indicates the alignment mode. According to the sentence number in $<c,e>$, the alignment mode can be classified as: (1:0), (0:1), (1:1), (1:2), (2:1), (1:3), (3:1) etc. Due to the rich meaning of historical classics, every sentence of classics usually corresponds to more than one English sentence. On the contrary, there is hardly any English sentence corresponds to more than one Chinese sentence. Only 4 sentence pairs are aligned in "many-to-one" mode in the corpus containing 1233 pair of sentences. Since the alignment modes of most historical classics sentences are "one-to-many", sentence alignment can be regarded as finding the corresponding English sentences $e=e_je_{j+1}\cdots$ for each Chinese sentence c_i in $C=\{c_1,c_2,\cdots,c_m\}$. Given a Chinese sentence, formula (1) is turned into:

$$\hat{A}=\arg\max_{M\in A}\left\{\begin{matrix}\Pr(e|M(c,e),c)\\ *\Pr(M(c,e)|c)\end{matrix}\right\} \quad (2)$$

Wherein: $\Pr(M(c,e)|c)$ is the mode probability, which denotes the probability that the alignment mode is $M(c,e)$ given the sentence c. $\Pr(e|M(c,e),c)$ indicates the probability that sentence c align e given $M(c,e)$ and c. $\Pr(e|M(c,e),c)$ is the linear combination of length alignment probability and term alignment probability, and is defined as following:

$$\begin{aligned}\Pr(e|M(c,e),c)&=\lambda_1\Pr_{len}(e|M(c,e),c)\\ &+\lambda_2\Pr_{term}(e|M(c,e),c)\end{aligned} \quad (3)$$

Wherein: $\Pr_{len}(e|M(c,e),c)$ is the length alignment probability and $\Pr_{term}(e|M(c,e),c)$ denotes the term alignment probability. λ_1, λ_2 are the weight parameters and $\lambda_1+\lambda_2=1$.

2.2 The Length Alignment Probability

Since c is known, we can have the following formula not strictly.

$$\begin{aligned}&\Pr_{len}(e|M(c,e),c)\\ &=\Pr_{len}(<c,e>|M(c,e))\\ &=\Pr(\delta(L_c,L_e)|M(c,e))\end{aligned} \quad (4)$$

Wherein: L_c, L_e is the length of sentence c and e, respectively. Owing to the lack of mature ancient Chinese word segmentation algorithm, we take the character number as the length of Chinese sentence and take the word number as the length of English sentence. The punctuation in Chinese and English sentence is all taken into account. $\delta(L_c,L_e)$ indicates the length evaluation function, which obeys standard normal distribution, and is defined as follows.

$$\delta(L_c,L_e)=\frac{L_e-L_c\bullet c_p}{\sqrt{L_c\bullet s^2}} \quad (5)$$

Wherein: parameter c_p indicates the number of English words generated by one Chinese character in average, which can be obtained by calculating the length ratio between the paragraph P_e of English sentence e and the paragraph P_c of Chinese sentence c. The calculation formula is shown as formula (6). s^2 is the normalized factor guaranteeing $\delta(L_c,L_e)$ obey standard normal distribution, which can be obtained by calculating variance on bilingual corpus. It can be calculated as formula (7).

$$c_p=\frac{\sum_{e\in P_e}L_e}{\sum_{c\in P_c}L_c} \quad (6)$$

$$s^2=D\left(\frac{L_e-L_c\bullet c_p}{\sqrt{L_c}}\right) \quad (7)$$

Based on the 3σ principle of normal distribution, 99% values of $\delta(L_c,L_e)$ distribute in the range of [-3, 3]. To ensure the length probability is less than 1 and incremental, length probability is defined as following:

$$\begin{aligned}&\Pr_{len}(e \mid M(c,e),c)\\&= \Pr(\delta(L_c, L_e) \mid M(c,e))\\&= 1-\left|\frac{\delta(L_c, L_e)}{3}\right| = 1-\left|\frac{L_e - L_c \bullet c_p}{3\sqrt{L_c \bullet s^2}}\right|\end{aligned} \tag{8}$$

2.3 Term Alignment Probability

The "terms" in historical classics refer to the official title, posthumous, person name, location name and other titles. The terms appear frequently in historical classics. If a term occurs in a Chinese sentence, then its translation should occurs in the corresponding position of English sentence. Given that a pair of terms (t_c, t_e) occur in the sentence pair (c,e), the alignment function is defined as:

$$A(t_c, t_e) = \min_{i,j=1,2,\cdots}\left|\frac{pos_i(t_c)}{L_c} - \frac{pos_j(t_e)}{L_e}\right| \tag{9}$$

Wherein: $pos_i(t_c)$ and $pos_j(t_e)$ denote the positions where terms t_c and t_e appear in the sentence. If no term pair appears in the sentence pair, the term alignment probability is 0. If n pair of terms $(t_{c1}, t_{e1}), \cdots, (t_{cn}, t_{en})$ occur in the sentence pair, the term alignment probability can defined as:

$$\begin{aligned}&\Pr_{term}(e \mid M(c,e),c)\\&= 1 - A_{\min}(t_{cj}, t_{ej}) \prod_{i \neq j} (A(t_{ci}, t_{ei}) + 0.5)\end{aligned} \tag{10}$$

Wherein: $A_{\min}(t_{cj}, t_{ej})$ is the minimum value of all the alignment functions. (t_{cj}, t_{ej}) indicates the term pair when the alignment function is minimal.

2.4 Alignment Mode Probability

The historical classics are translated from Chinese to English. When translator sees a Chinese sentence, he almost determines how many English sentences should be used to translate the Chines sentence. Thus, the calculation of alignment mode probability can be considered as a classification problem of mode. We input a Chinese sentence to the classifier, and the classifier outputs the alignment probability. We take naïve Bayesian as the classifier, which is run by WEKA[1]. We employ the character number, punctuation number of Chinese sentence and the characters selected by feature selection function to predict the mode probability. We choose Information Gain (IG) as the feature function, which measures the number of bits of information obtained for category prediction by knowing the presence or absence of a character in a sentence.

3 The Framework of the Sentence Alignment Method

3.1 The steps of the sentence alignment method

Given a Chinese document D_c of historical classics and its English translation D_e, the sentence alignment is performed in the following steps.

(1) Divide the Chinese document into different paragraphs by paragraph mark, $D_c = \{C_1, C_2, \cdots, C_I\}$. The English document is also divided into different paragraphs, $D_e = \{E_1, E_2, \cdots, E_I\}$.

(2) Search anchor sentence pairs in in the paragraph pair (C_i, E_i). If anchors can be found, separate the Chinese and English paragraph into different text blocks, otherwise, regard the paragraph as a text block.

(3) Align the sentences in text blocks $c_1, c_2, \cdots, c_m$ and $e_1, e_2, \cdots, e_n$. For Chinese sentence c_i, calculate the probabilities of different alignment modes by formula (3). Select the English sentences $e_j \cdots e_{j+k}$ of the maximal alignment probability as its translation. Then find corresponding sentences for Chinese sentence c_{i+1} from English sentence e_{j+k+1}. Repeat the alignment until all the sentences in the text block are aligned.

(4) Align all the text blocks in paragraph pair (C_i, E_i). If $i+1 <= I$, $i = i+1$, goto step (2), otherwise, the sentence alignment is finished.

3.2 The selection of anchor sentence pairs

We make use of anchor sentence pairs to prevent the spread of alignment errors, which often occur in the alignment method utilizing the length information. To select anchor sentence pair, we first determines Chinese anchor sentence, then

[1] http://www.cs.waikato.ac.nz/ml/weka

find English anchor sentence according to Chinese anchor sentence. To ensure the anchor sentences is correct, Chinese anchor sentence must satisfy the following four conditions: (1) The anchor sentence is not the first sentence or the last sentence of the paragraph; (2) The alignment modes of the two sentences around the anchor sentence should be predicted as (1:1); (3) The length of anchor sentence should be less than the length threshold Th_l ; (4) Two sentences around anchor sentence should have Th_i more characters than anchor sentence. Condition (1) is defined because the anchor sentence has no function in alignment when it is first or last sentence. Conditions (2), (3) and (4) guarantee that corresponding sentence of anchor Chinese sentence has the smallest length in surrounding sentences. After the Chinese anchor sentence is determined, the English sentence of highest alignment probability is selected as English anchor. To enhance the computation efficiency, we do not search English anchor sentences in all sentences of the English paragraph. Instead, we find the anchor sentence in a window whose size is *wind* and whose center is at position pos_e. Position pos_e is the corresponding position of Chinese anchor sentence, calculated as formula (12).

$$pos_e = pos_c \frac{count(E)}{count(C)} \tag{11}$$

$$window = \begin{cases} 3, \text{if count(E)<=12} \\ 5, \text{if count(E)>12} \end{cases} \tag{12}$$

Wherein: count(*) denotes the sentence count of the paragraph *.

4 Experiment

4.1 Experimental setup

The bilingual corpora used in the experiment are composed of *Shi Ji* and its corresponding English translations drawn from *Records of the Grand Historian*, which is well-recognized authoritative translation by famous sinologist Burton Watson. We extract 1233 sentence pairs as test corpora from 7 hereditary houses, which are *The Hereditary House of King Yuan of Ch'u, The Hereditary Houses of Ching and Yen, The Hereditary House of King Tao-hui of Ch'I, The Hereditary House of Prime Minister Hsiao,* etc. We aligned manually 4144 sentence pairs to construct the parallel corpora as training corpora from five consecutive basic annals, which are *Basic Annals of Qin, Basic Annals of the First Emperor of the Qin, Basic Annals of Hsiang Yü, Basic Annals of Emperor Kao-tsu* and *Basic Annals of Empress Lü.* We extract 641 term translation pairs from the training corpora to calculate term alignment probability. The parameters of the proposed method are set as following: weigh parameters $\lambda_1 = 0.55$, $\lambda_2 = 0.45$, length threshold $Th_l = 12$, interval threshold $Th_i = 5$.

Since we find corresponding translation for Chinese sentence one by one, almost all the sentences can be aligned, the precision and recall of our method is nearly the same. We only employ precision p to test the method, which is as follows.

$$P = \frac{N_{correct}}{N_{align}} \times 100\% \tag{13}$$

Wherein: $N_{correct}$ denotes the number of correct sentence pairs acquired by the proposed method, N_{align} is the number of all the sentences acquired by the proposed method.

4.2 Experimental results and analysis

The method only using sentence length is employed as baseline method. To test the effect of mode prediction and anchors, we compare the performance the method not using mode prediction, the method not using anchors with the proposed method. The precision comparison of four methods is shown in table 1.

Method	Precision
Baseline	60.5%
Not using anchors	72.2%
Not using mode prediction	86.8%
The proposed method	92.5%

Table 1: The precision comparison of four methods

Table 1 shows that both the method not using mode prediction and the method not using anchor sentence pair, which all employ term alignment probability, outperform significantly baseline method. This confirms the effectiveness of term alignment probability. It can be also seen from table 1 that the use of the anchors significantly increases the precision about 20%. The experimental results demonstrate that the anchors can effectively prevent the error spread of the alignment method based on sentence length. The result also confirms the anchor sentence pairs we obtained are correct.

In table 1, we can see that the mode prediction increases precision by 6%. In the conventional method, all the aligned sentences whether long or short have the same mode probability. It is unreasonable since long sentences prefer "one-to-many" mode and short sentences tend to be "one-to-one" mode. The proposed method extracts the mode probability for the sentence with different features based on the training corpora, and employ different alignment probability according to features of the aligned sentence, so the precision of the proposed method is higher. However, since the model probability prediction is not very accurate, sometimes wrong mode probability leads to alignment errors. This is why the role of model prediction is not as significant as we expect.

5 Conclusion

To construct bilingual term dictionary of historical classics, this paper proposes a sentence alignment method based on mode prediction and term translation pairs. The method first obtains the mode alignment probability according to the features of Chinese sentence, then performs sentence alignment using length probability and term alignment probability. Furthermore, the method find anchor sentence pairs to prevent the spread of alignment errors. The sentence alignment experiment on "*Shi Ji*" confirms the effectiveness of the proposed method. In the future, we can further improve classification accuracy of model predictions and apply the sentence alignment in the term translation extraction of historical classics.

Acknowledgments

This work is funded the National Science Foundation of China (61402068, 61304206).

Reference

Chen, Xiang and Hong-fei Lin. 2009. Sentence Alignment of Bilingual Biomedical Abstract Based on Anchor Information. *Journal Of Chinese Information Processing*, 23(1): 58-62.

Fattah, Mohamed Abdel, David B. Bracewell, et al. 2007. Sentence alignment using P-NNT and GMM. *Computer Speech and Language*, 21: 594–608.

Gale, William A. and Kenneth W. Church. 1993. A program for aligning sentences in bilingual corpora. *Computational Linguistics*, 19(1): 75-102.

Lu, Xue-qiang, Qing-yin Li, et al. 2003. Sub-Sentence Alignment of Chinese-English Law Literature Based on Stat istical Approach. *Journal of Northeastern University*, 24(1): 23-26.

Moore, Robert C. 2002. Fast and Accurate Sentence Alignment of Bilingual Corpora. In *AMTA*, Springer.

Tian, Shengwei, Turgun Ibrahim, et al. 2009. Chinese-Uighur sentence alignment based on hybrid strategy with mistake spread suppression. In *International Conference on Environmental Science and Information Application Technology* Wuhan, China, IEEE.

Yu, Xin, Jian Wu, et al. 2010. Dictionary-based Chinese-Tibetan sentence alignment. In *International Conference on Intelligent Computing and Integrated Systems (ICISS)*, Guilin, China.

The CIPS-SIGHAN CLP 2014 Chinese Word Segmentation Bake-off

Huiming Duan
Key Laboratory of Computational Linguistics, Peking University, Beijing 100871, China
duenhm@water.pku.edu.cn

Zhifang Sui
Key Laboratory of Computational Linguistics, Peking University, Beijing 100871, China
szf@pku.edu.cn

Tao Ge
Key Laboratory of Computational Linguistics, Peking University, Beijing 100871, China
getao@pku.edu.cn

Abstract

This paper summarizes the SIGHAN 2014 Chinese Word Segmentation bake-off in several aspects such as dataset, evaluation results. In addition, we analyze errors of segmentation by instance and make a suggestion for improving segmentation systems.

1 Goal of the Chinese word segmentation bake-off

Chinese Word Segmentation is the preliminary step for Chinese information processing, which is extremely important and never neglected. Due to the properties of Chinese, the performance of Chinese word segmentation has an effect on the following analysis of Chinese text. As the organizer of the bake-off in Chinese word segmentation, not only do we show the performance of all participated systems, but also try to find out the weak point of these systems. In this way, participants are able to learn advantages of their systems and realize the problems which they did not pay attention to so that they could improve their system according to our feedbacks, which turns out to promote the study of Chinese word segmentation.

2 Dataset

2.1 Size of dataset

The dataset used in the SIGHAN2014 Chinese word segmentation bake-off is formed by sampling instances which are difficult to segment from approximately 1.3T Chinese corpus. This is a huge challenge for us. While sampling instances, we found that the distribution of sentences which are hard to segment does not depend on domains, in other words, these sentences appear in every domain.

2.2 Domains of dataset

Compared with the SIGHAN 2012 Chinese word segmentation bake-off which only focuses on the microblog domain, the dataset used in the shared task in SIGHAN2014 is formed by sampling sentences from a variety of domains. The dataset involves many subjects in both social sciences and natural sciences, and genres involved in the dataset are also taken into consideration. In this way, we can more clearly evaluate if current segmentation techniques can perform well in a wide range of domains.

2.3 Makeup of dataset

The SIGHAN2014 Chinese word segmentation bake-off mainly uses single sentences and paragraphs for evaluations. Additionally, discourses are also included.

As is known to all, there are two kinds of ambiguities in Chinese word segmentation – overlapping ambiguity and combinatorial ambiguity, which are difficult to deal with. In addition, OOV (out of vocabulary), which includes neologisms, abbreviations and uncommon terminology, is a challenge for Chinese word segmentation as well.

First, we show why the ambiguity of segmentation arises.

Segmentation ambiguity:

(1) Combinatorial ambiguity

It is not uncommon to see these words in Chinese: 树木、应对、根据地、正在、一道、一起、一块、一口气……

① 树木

树木自己要学会在土地里找水源，

——Here,树木 is a noun.

一年之计，莫如树谷；十年之计，莫如

Proceedings of the Third CIPS-SIGHAN Joint Conference on Chinese Language Processing, pages 90–95,
Wuhan, China, 20-21 October 2014

树木；终身之计，莫如树人。

——Here, 树木 is not a noun.树 is a verb rather than a noun.

② 应对

此时人们将无法正常地应对现实世界。

——Here,应对 is a verb.

在治疗前应对患者病变的部位(神经根定位)有明确的认识,

——Here, 应对 is two words。

③ 根据地

杨洁篪说，该报告毫无根据地攻击中国国防现代化，

——毫无根据地 should be segmented as 毫无 根据 地

(2) Overlapping ambiguity: 词语首尾的可成词性

There are many overlapping ambiguities in the dataset. For example:

塑造成：塑造+造成

心理学工作者：心理+理学+学工+工作+作者

司机会：司机 + 机会

心中立起：心中+中立+立起

正在家中看：正在+在家+家中+中看

在行军中：在行+行军+军中

以下划线：以下+下划线 (* All systems make a mistake segmenting this sequence)

在场论：在场+场论 (* "场论" is a word used in only a few domains)

享有的：享有+有的

We mainly test the performance of disambiguation of systems. Given that some ambiguous sequences of characters often appear in different context, we sometimes use multiple sentences to evaluate a sequence of characters. It is notable that some sentences' context can provide helpful information while some sentences do not have such information. We want to see the capability of systems to use context to solve overlapping ambiguities. For example：

"无数学"

因有**无数学**子从这里走出去

将有**无数学**子背负着青春的理想

自然会有**无数学**者谈论

无数学过的占卜、巫术

仍有**无数学**者在对其进行着不断的研究。

都有**无数学**生在学校里轮流读着已知的二战死难者名单

有**无数学**者分析过

不能以有**无数学**公式及其推导来衡量文章的水平高低。

动物有**无数学**头脑

诺贝尔奖有**无数学**奖

心中虽有**无数学**识

也有**无数学**不尽的知识

"在行"

由用户**在行**与行间选择要做这种计算的记录

尽管世行**在行**长提名权和任职条件上

其中结脉多因于气血凝滞，重**在行**气活血

并且**在行**文上有着程式性的规定

，**在行**业领先才能生存的前景下

在行唐县的推荐下，

应**在行**经前 3 天即开始服用

个个一专多能，吹、拉、弹、唱、舞样样**在行**，

不能担挑，拾柴却很在行，

As for names, we choose two lists of names as example:

Example 1：麦培东麦谢巧玲（女）麦耀堂严日初严建平严震铭苏开鹏苏西智苏丽珍（女）苏肖娟（女）苏泽光苏炤成苏晓鹏苏健康苏绮丽（女）苏耀华杜毅（女）杜耀明李乃尧李乃熺李大壮李子良李月华

Example 2：邓天生叶青纯田力普令狐安冯寿淼冯敏刚年福纯朱明国（黎族）朱保成刘玉亭刘亚洲刘建华（女）刘春良刘晓榕安立敏（女）许云昭许达哲孙忠同孙宝树孙思敬杜鹃（女）

3 Evaluation Results

Precision, recall and F-measure are used to evaluate participants' systems, just as previous bakeoffs did. Since the number of participants is not large (6 institutes and 7 systems), we can analyze the systems in detail for finding the weak points of the systems, which would promote the study of Chinese word segmentation.

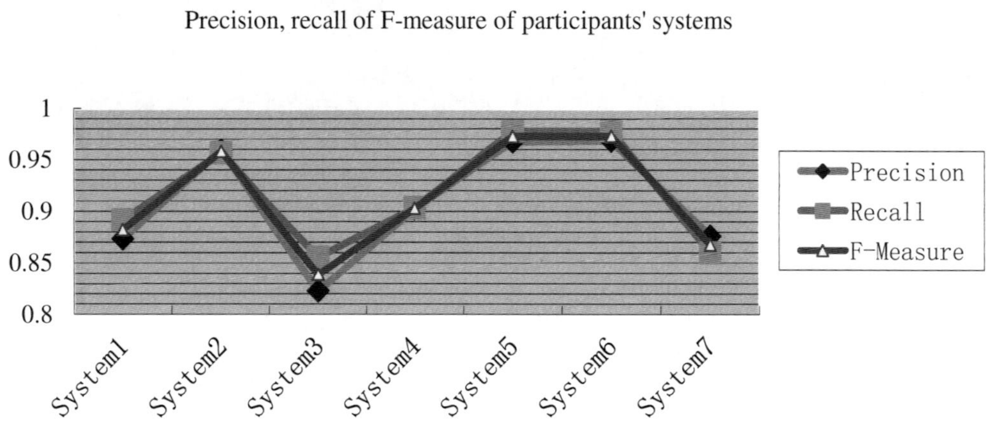

Table 1: Distribution of P,R,F of systems participating in this bake-off

3.1 Automatic Evaluation

For automatic evaluation, Precision, recall and F-measure are used to evaluate participants' systems.

The performance of 7 systems of 6 institutes participating in the bake-off is shown in Table1.

No.	Precision	Recall	F-Measure
System1	0.8734	0.8912	0.8822
System2	0.9592	0.9566	0.9579
System3	0.8226	0.8555	0.8387
System4	0.9025	0.9032	0.9029
System5	0.9673	0.9776	0.9724
System6	0.9681	0.9779	0.9730
System7	0.8760	0.8597	0.8678

Table 1: Precision, recall and F-measure of all systems participating in this bake-off

We compare the results in the bake-off with that in SIGHAN 2012

	Precision	Recall	F-Measure
2012	0.946	0.9496	0.9478
2014	0.9681	0.9779	0.9730

Table 2: The best systems in 2012 and 2014 bake-offs

	Precision	Recall	F-Measure
2012	0.9347	0.9316	0.9331
2014	0.9681	0.9779	0.9730

Table 3: Systems by the same institute in 2012 and 2014

	Precision	Recall	F-Measure
2012	0.1314	0.0845	0.1087
2014	0.1455	0.1224	0.1342

Table 4: Differences between the best system and the worst system in 2012 and 2014

3.2 Manual Inspection

3.2.1 Why manual inspection

In previous SIGHAN segmentation shared task, precision, recall and F-measure are only metric for evaluating systems. Although these metrics can reflect systems' performance to some extent, they cannot clearly show the specific weak point of the systems. It is likely that a system achieving high PRF does not deal with some details well and makes some silly mistakes. On the other hand, some systems whose PRF is not high can address some specific segmentation problems well. Of course, other factors such as the size of dictionary might also affect the results.

Since SIGHAN 2012 Chinese word segmentation bake-off, we have attempted to introduce evaluations for some specific cases, which could inform participants of the approximate accuracy range of each case and allow them to learn the weak points of their systems.

By manual inspection, we found some typical mistakes which should have been corrected but were not solved by most systems.

3.2.2 Methods of manual inspection

We use different types of lines (a single line, double line or dash line) to indicate how to segment a sequence of Chinese characters.

事实上 ， 在 互联网 地图 日益 得到 广泛 应用 之 时 ， 一些 互联网 地图 服务 质量 不 高 ， 内容 不准 的 问题 也 广受 网友 诟病 。 国家 测绘 地理 信息局 有关 负责人 表示 ， 互联网 地图 服务 基本 纳入 法制化 、 规范 化 管理 的 轨道 ， 对 提 高 互联网 地图 服务 质量 、 方 便 社会 各界 更 好 享受 互联网 地图 服务 、 保障 国家 地理 信息 安全 将 起 到 良好 作用 。 .
事实上 ， 在 互联网 地图 日益 得到 广泛 应用 之 时 ， 一些 互联网 地图 服务 质量 不 高 ， 内容 不 准 的 问题 也 广 受 网友 诟病 。 国家 测绘 地理 信息局 有关 负责人 表示 ，
事实上 ， 在 互联网 地图 日益 得到 广泛 应用 之 时 ， 一些 互联网 地图 服务 质量 不 高 ， 内容 不 准的 问题 也 广 受 网友 诟病 。 国家 测绘 地理 信息 局 有关 负责人 表示 ，
事实上 ， 在 互联网 地图 日益 得到 广泛 应用 之 时 ， 一些 互联网 地图 服务 质量 不 高 ， 内容 不 准 的 问题 也 广 受 网友 诟病 。 国家 测绘 地理 信息 局 有关 负责人 表示 ，
事实上 ， 在 互联网 地图 日益 得到 广泛 应用 之 时 ， 一些 互联网 地图 服务 质量 不 高 ， 内容 不准 的 问题 也 广 受 网友 诟病 。 国家 测绘 地理 信息 局 有关 负责人 表示 ，
事实上 ， 在 互联网 地图 日益 得到 广泛 应用 之 时 ， 一些 互联网 地图 服务 质量 不 高 ， 内容 不 准的 问题 也 广 受 网友 诟病 。 国家 测绘 地理 信息 局 有关 负责人 表示 ，
事实 上 ， 在 互联网 地图 日益 得到 广泛 应用 之时 ， 一些 互联网 地图 服务 质量 不 高 ， 内容 不准 的 问题 也 广 受 网友 诟病 。 国家 测绘 地理 信息 局 有关 负责人 表示 ，

Table 5: Using different types of lines as indicators to conduct human inspection

Example 3：Merge

这 其实 我 根本 也 没有 做 主权 嘛

a single line indicates that the sequence should be merged as 做主权

Example 4：Segment

充电 时间的确 太 长

a double line indicates that the sequence should be segmented as：时间 的确

Example 5: Re-combine

其中 的 解决 方 案之一 就 是 ：

a dash line indicates that the sequence should be re-combined as 方案 之一

By using different types of lines as indicators, one can easily learn the mistakes made by each system, as table 5 shows.

As shown in table 5, only one system segments the sequence without any mistake. In contrast, one of the systems makes many mistakes when segmenting simple terms, which may arise from the problem of word-collection or some further problems.

4 Analysis of Results

4.1 Excessive word-collection may have an adverse effect

In table 6, only one system segments ‘对方’.

It can be verified by table 7 that this system did not include ‘对方’ in its dictionary.

As shown in table 6 and table 7, a system which includes ‘对方’ in its dictionary segments ‘对方’ correctly while others make a mistake here. We hope that the system actually pays attention to the detail rather than happen to segment it well. There are many similar cases such as ‘平等’ and ‘杜鹃’.

Example 6: 公司派张世平等一批技术骨干和管理人员到国外学习。

“杜鹃” in example 7 is a noun while it is a person’s name in example 2. Therefore, 杜鹃 should be segmented in example 2.

在 庭审 中 ， 对 方 律师 竟 对 中 方 托收 银行 寄 送 托受 文件 的 事实 全盘 否认 。
在 庭 审 中 ， 对方 律师 竟 对 中方 托收 银行 寄送 托 受 文件 的 事实 全盘 否认 。
在 庭审 中 ， 对方 律师 竟 对 中 方 托收 银行 寄 送 托 受 文件 的 事实 全盘 否认 。
在 庭审 中 ， 对方 律师 竟 对 中方 托收 银行 寄送 托 受 文件 的 事实 全盘 否认 。
在 庭审 中 ， 对方 律师 竟 对 中方 托收 银行 寄送 托 受 文件 的 事实 全盘 否认 。
在 庭审 中 ， 对方 律师 竟 对 中 方 托收 银行 寄 送 托 受 文件 的 事实 全盘 否认 。
在 庭审 中 ， 对方 律师 竟 对 中方 托收 银行 寄送 托受 文件 的 事实 全盘 否认 。

Table 6: Segmentation results of all systems for a sentence

这 也 与 学生 请 愿书 中 对 方 艳华 的 评价 相同 。
这 也 与 学生 请愿书 中 对方 艳华 的 评价 相同 。
这 也 与 学生 请愿 书 中 对方 艳 华 的 评价 相同 。
这 也 与 学生 请愿书 中 对方 艳华 的 评价 相同 。
这 也 与 学生 请愿书 中 对方 艳华 的 评价 相同 。
这 也 与 学生 请愿 书 中 对方 艳 华 的 评价 相同 。
这 也 与 学生 请愿书 中 对 方 艳华 的 评价 相同 。

Table 7: Segmentation results of all systems for another sentence

Example 7：在位于羊西线的西部花卉市场里，一排排水仙、菊花、杜鹃、郁金香等争奇斗妍、姹紫嫣红，前来赏花、买花的市民络绎不绝。

We can also give many other examples: 长江[江 can be surname], 孙子[孙 can be surname], 王[王 can be surname]子, 行李[尉健行李铁印] etc. To address these problems, an effective personal name recognition method is necessary.

4.2 A lack of attention to details

Example 8：进攻者比防御者更容易包围对方的全部军队以及切断它们的退路,因为防御者处于驻止状态,而进攻者是针对防御者的这种状态进行运动的。

Example 8 is an instance in test set. In this sentence, 进攻者 appears three times and 防御者 appears twice. Nonetheless, some systems cannot deal with these terms consistently. The cause of the phenomenon is that the systems do not exploit the context well.

进攻 者 比 防御 者 更 容易 包围 对方 的 全部 军队 以及 切断 它们 的 退路 ， 因为 防御 者 处于 驻 止 状态 ， 而 进攻者 是 针对 防御者 的 这种 状态 进行 运动 的 。

Example 9：于廿七号晚上出发，

In example 9, seldom has 廿七号 been used in written language in recent years. However, a good system is supposed to take into consideration these cases. Incorrect segmentations are shown as follows.

于 廿七 号 晚上 出发 ，

于 廿 七 号 晚上 出发 ，

5 Conclusion

Although languages have many properties in common, their unique characters do not allow researchers to directly use techniques for processing other languages to process Chinese.

In addition, when devoted to language study, one can find that Chinese has significant uniqueness and flexibility, which should be paid much attention to. Only by carefully analyzing unique properties of Chinese can researchers come up with a better solution to improving their systems. Even though Chinese is so flexible that one cannot use a rule to describe the problems of Chinese word segmentation, researcher can try multiple rules to optimize their systems in multiple aspects and multiple levels, which requires them to be mindful of details.

As the organizers of this Chinese word segmentation bake-off, we may need to scrutinize details and make a standard which is detailed and easy to operate. For the bake-off, we are going to explore a better evaluation method which can show the results of systems more reasonably and objectively.

Acknowledgement: This paper is supported by National Key Basic Research Program of China 2014CB340504 and NSFC 61375074.

Reference

Shiwen Yu, Huiming Duan, Xuefeng Zhu, Bin Sun and Baobao Chang. 北大语料库加工规范：切分・词性标注・注音. 汉语语言与计算学报, 13(2), 121-158.

Hongmei Zhao and Qun Liu. The CIPS-SIGHAN CLP 2010 Chinese word segmentation bakeoff. In Proceedings of the First CPS-SIGHAN Joint Conference on Chinese Language Processing (pp. 199-209).

Duan, Huiming, Zhifang Sui, Ye Tian, and Wenjie Li. The CIPS-SIGHAN CLP 2012 Chinese Word Segmentation on Microblog Corpora Bakeoff. In Proceedings of the Second CIPS-SIGHAN Joint Conference on Chinese Language Processing, Tianjin, China, pp. 35-40. 2012.

Word Segmenter for Chinese Micro-blogging Text Segmentation — Report for CIPS-SIGHAN'2014 Bakeoff

Lu Xiang **Xiaoqing Li** **Yu Zhou**

Institute of Automation Chinese Academy of Sciences, Beijing, China
{lu.xiang, xqli, yzhou}@nlpr.ia.ac.cn

Abstract

This paper presents our system for the CIPS-SIGHAN-2014 bakeoff task of Chinese word segmentation. This system adopts a character-based joint approach, which combines a character-based generative model and a character-based discriminative model. To further improve the performance in cross-domain, an external dictionary is employed. In addition, pre-processing and post-processing rules are utilized to further improve the performance. The final performance on the test corpus shows that our system achieves comparable results with other state-of-the-art systems.

1 Introduction

Because Chinese text is written without natural delimiters, word segmentation is a prerequisite and fundamental task in Chinese natural language processing. And many approaches have been proposed for this task. Among these methods, the character-based tagging approach (Xue, 2003) has become the prevailing technique for Chinese word segmentation (CWS) due to its good performance. In recent years, within the framework of character-based, much efforts (Tseng et al., 2005; Zhang et al., 2006; Jiang et al., 2008) have been made to further improve word segmentation's performance.

The character-based joint model (Wang et al., 2010, Wang et al., 2012) achieves a good balance between in-vocabulary (IV) words recognition and out-of-vocabulary (OOV) words identification. So, in this evaluation task, following their work we adopt the character-based joint model as our basic system, which combines a character-based discriminative model and a character-based generative model. The generative module holds a robust performance on IV words, while the discriminative module can handle the extra features easily and enhance the OOV words segmentation.

Because the 2014 SIGHAN bakeoff task of Chinese Word Segmentation is an opened evaluation task and no training set is provided, the OOV problem will be more serious. Although the discriminative module can handle some cases of OOV, the performance is less preferable if no technique is utilized. So to further improve the performance of the basic system and minimize the OOV, we employ an external dictionary containing a large set of unknown words from different domains. Another notable problem is the Microblog text segmentation because Microblog has become a new Internet literary which is different from the genres of common text. To make our system more robust on Microblog text, we propose several simple but novel pre-processing and post-processing approaches in our system.

The final results show that our system performs well on test set and achieves comparable segmentation results with other participants.

2 System Description

2.1 Character-Based Joint Model

The character-based joint model in our system consists of two basic components:

- The character-based discriminative model.
- The character-based generative model.

The character-based discriminative model (Xue, 2003) is based on a Maximum Entropy (ME) framework (Ratnaparkhi, 1998) and can be formulated as follows:

$$P\left(t_1^n \mid c_1^n\right) \approx \prod_{k=1}^{n} P\left(t_k \mid t_{k-1}, c_{k-2}^{k+2}\right) \quad (1)$$

Where t_k is a member of {**B**, **M**, **E**, **S**}, in which **B**, **M** and **E** indicate the *Beginning*, *Middle* and *End* of character c_k in its associated word respectively, and **S** denotes that it's a *Single-character* word. For example, the word "北京市 (Beijing

Proceedings of the Third CIPS-SIGHAN Joint Conference on Chinese Language Processing, pages 96–100,
Wuhan, China, 20-21 October 2014

City)" will be assigned with the corresponding tags as: "北/B (North) 京/M (Capital) 市/E (City)".

This discriminative model can incorporate extra features easily and the Maximum Entropy Modeling Toolkit[1] given by Zhang Le is used to implement the module. In our experiments, this model is trained with Gaussian prior 1.0 and 600 iterations.

The character-based generative module is a character-tag-pair-based trigram model (Wang et al., 2009) and can be expressed as below:

$$P\left(\left[c,t\right]_1^n\right) \approx \prod_{i=1}^{n} P\left(\left[c,t\right]_i \mid \left[c,t\right]_{i-2}^{i-1}\right) \quad (2)$$

SRI Language Modeling Toolkit[2] (Stolcke, 2002) is used to train the generative trigram model with modified Kneser-Ney smoothing (Chen and Goodman, 1998) in our experiments.

The character-based joint model combines the above discriminative module and the generative module with log-linear interpolation as follows:

$$\begin{aligned} Score\left(t_k\right) &= \alpha \times \log\left(P\left(\left[c,t\right]_k \mid \left[c,t\right]_{k-2}^{k-1}\right)\right) \\ &\quad + \left(1-\alpha\right) \times \log\left(P\left(t_k \mid t_{k-1}, c_{k-2}^{k+2}\right)\right) \end{aligned} \quad (3)$$

Where the parameter $\alpha\left(0.0 \le \alpha \le 1.0\right)$ is the weight for the generative model and can be obtained from the development set. $Score\left(t_k\right)$ will be directly used to search for the best sequence. We set an empirical value 0.4 to α as there is no development-set for various domains.

2.2 Features

The feature templates used in the character-based discriminative model are listed below:

(a) $C_n\left(n=-2,-1,0,1,2\right)$;

(b) $C_nC_{n+1}\left(n=-2,-1,0,1\right)$;

(c) $C_{-1}C_1$;

(d) $T\left(C_{-2}\right)T\left(C_{-1}\right)T\left(C_0\right)T\left(C_1\right)T\left(C_2\right)$

In the above templates, C_n represents a Chinese character and the index n indicates the position. For example, when we consider the third character "奥" in the sequence "北京奥运会", template (a) results in the features as following: C_{-2}=北, C_{-1}=京, C_0=奥, C_1=运, C_2=会, and template (b) generates the features as: $C_{-2}C_{-1}$=北京, $C_{-1}C_0$=京奥, C_0C_1=奥运, C_1C_2=运会, and template (c) gives the feature $C_{-1}C_1$=京运.

Template (d) is the feature of character type and five type classes are defined: dates ("年", "月", "日", the Chinese character for "year", "month" and "day" respectively) represents class 0; foreign alphabets represent class 1; Arabic and Chinese numbers represent class 2; punctuation represents class 3 and other characters represent class 4. For example, when considering the character "，" in the sequence "八月，阿Q", the feature $T\left(C_{-2}\right)T\left(C_{-1}\right)T\left(C_0\right)T\left(C_1\right)T\left(C_2\right)$ will be set to "20341".

2.3 External Dictionary

OOV words is a main problem faced by a Chinese word segmenter and it will lead to lower accuracy if the sentence to be segmented contains many OOV words. To address the problem of OOV words, we use an external dictionary containing a large set of predefined words. We following the method presented in Low et al. (2005) to use the dictionary. In this method, some sequence of neighboring characters around C_0 will be looked up in a dictionary using maximum match strategy. And the longest matching word W will be chosen. Let t_0 be the boundary tag of C_0 in W, L the number of characters in W, and $C_1\left(C_{-1}\right)$ be the character immediately following (preceding) C_0 in the sentence. We then add the following features derived from the dictionary:

(e) Lt_0

(f) $C_nt_0\left(n=-1,0,1\right)$

For example, consider the sentence "北京奥运会...". When processing the current character C_0 "京", we will try to match the following candidates "京", "北京", "京奥", "北京奥", "京奥运", "北京奥运" and "京奥运会" against existing word in the external dictionary. Assuming that both "京奥" and "京奥运" are found in the dictionary, then the longest matching word "京奥运" will be chosen. And the value of W, t_0, L, C_{-1} and C_1 are "京奥运", **B**, 3, "北" and "奥" respectively.

In this work, we collect dictionaries from the Internet, including the title of Wikipedia[3], the title of Hudong Baike[4], Sogou word bank[5] and

[1] http://homepages.inf.ed.ac.uk/lzhang10/maxent_toolkit.html
[2] http://www.speech.sri.com/projects/srilm/

[3] http://zh.wikipedia.org
[4] http://www.baike.com/

some other internet dictionaries. Finally, we obtain a dictionary containing 5,893,038 words in our system.

2.4 Restrictions in Constructing Lattice

When considering a character in the sequence, we take the type information of both the previous and the next character into consideration and use some restrictions to obtain a better tag lattice (Wang et al., 2010). The restrictions are listed as follows:

- If the previous, the current and the next characters are all English or numbers, we would fix the current tag to be "M";
- If the previous and the next characters are both English or numbers, while the current character is a connective symbol such as "-", "/", "_", "\" etc., we would also fix the current tag to be "M";
- Otherwise, all four tags {B, E, M, S} would be given to the current character.

3 Rule-based Adaptation

The state-of-the-art Chinese word segmentation systems can achieve a quite high performance on well-formed text, while the performance of Microblog text segmentation is not satisfying due to the specificity of Microblog text. For example, there are lots of emotion symbols, URLs, abbreviations, consecutive and identical punctuations and special characters in Microblog text. In order to make our system more robust on segmenting Microblog data, we propose some heuristic pre-processing and post-processing rules to avoid some segmentation errors.

3.1 Pre-processing

As mentioned above, the Microblog texts contain much noise like special format words and characters. And such kind of noise will affect the segmentation performance. In order to remove these noise, we will pre-process the text before segmentation.

Since URL, email and consecutive punctuations should be treated as one word and these content types can be easily recognized using the regex expressions, we first replace all these content to special characters before segmentation, and then restore all the special characters to the original characters after the segmentation. Table 1 shows the content type we will process in the pre-processing stage.

[5] http://pinyin.sogou.com/dict/

Table 1: Content type of pre-processing

Type	Example
URL	http://t.cn/RPdBAPV
Email	hanhuahr@126.com
Consecutive punctuations	。。。 ！！！！

3.2 Post-processing

We use some heuristic rules to further post-process the results generated by the segmenter and the rules are described below:

1) **Numeral and Quantifier**: In our results, some numerals and quantifiers such as "两个" and "三张" are segmented as one unit. But in fact, the numeral and quantifier should be segmented into two words except some few words like "一个". So we use a simple rule to split these cases in which the previous word is a numeral and the next word is a quantifier.
2) **Continuous mimetic words**: There are many continuous mimetic words in Microblog, such as "哈哈哈哈哈", "呵呵呵". This kind of words should be treated as one unit. But our system splits each character into one word. Hence, we apply a rule to group the continuous mimetic words together.
3) **Emoticons**: some consecutive punctuations like ":-)" represent an emoticon and have some certain meanings. These emoticons should be grouped together. We have collected a list of emoticons from the web. For any consecutive punctuations, we join them together as a single word if they appear in the emoticon list.

4 Experiments

4.1 Data sets

Since the Chinese word segmentation task focuses on the performance of multi-domain, we use five datasets as our test data. Four of the five datasets are the test data of SIGHAN10 closed track and the rest one is the 500 Microblog messages released by SIGHAN12. Hence, our test data covers 5 domains: Literature (Testing-A, containing 671 sentences), Computer (Testing-B, containing 1,330 sentences), Medicine (Testing-C, containing 1,309 sentences), Finance (Testing-D, containing 561 sentences) and Microblog (Testing-E, containing 500 sentences). The training data of our segmenter consists of two parts: one is the Peking University Corpora (PKU) from January to June and the other is manually annotated Microblog data which contains nearly 7000 sentences.

4.2 Experimental Results

We first evaluate our approach on the five test datasets using different strategies. The results are shown in Table 2 and the evaluation criterion is F-score. The strategies we used are:

- **Joint**: represents the result of our model without dictionary.
- **+Dic**: represents the result of our model using the external dictionary.
- **+Rule**: represents the result of our model using the external dictionary and the pre-processing and post-processing rules.

Table 2: Evaluation results with different strategies

	Joint	+Dic	+Rule
Testing-A	0.9590	0.9622	0.9628
Testing-B	0.9589	0.9630	0.9634
Testing-C	0.9522	0.9557	0.9557
Testing-D	0.9670	0.9686	0.9696
Testing-E	0.9338	0.9381	0.9412

As Table 2 shows, our joint model performs well on all the five datasets even though the domain of the training data which is mainly composed of news data is different from the test sets. This shows that our character-based joint model is very robust and can achieve a good balance between in-vocabulary (IV) words recognition and OOV words identification

After the external dictionary added, the performance increased a lot, which shows the external dictionary is very useful and can help alleviate the OOV problem efficiently. Finally, we adopt the pre-processing and post-processing rules in our system, the performance can be further improved on all testing set except Testing-C.

Table 3: Final Result of the Test Set

	P	R	F
Final Test	0.9592	0.9566	0.9578

Since the final test data will be multi-domain, we add all the five datasets to the training data and retrain the segmentation model. Then we apply the retrained model to the final test data (containing 1,665 sentences) and the performance is shown in Table 3. Table 3 shows that our system can achieve an F-score of 0.9578.

5 Conclusion

Our system is based on a character-based joint model, which combines a generative module and a discriminative module. In addition, we employ an external dictionary and propose several pre-processing and post-processing rules to further improve the performance. Our system achieves comparable performance with other participants.

Acknowledgements

We would like to thank Mr. Zhilin Zhang for his great help in implementation and experiments of our system. This work is supported by the Hi-Tech Research and Development Program (863) of China under grant No. 2012AA011101 and High New Technology Research and Development Program of Xinjiang Uyghur Autonomous Region under grant No. 201312103.

References

Stanley F. Chen and Joshua Goodman, 1998. An empirical study of smoothing techniques for language modeling. *Technical Report TR-10-98, Harvard University Center for Research in Computing Technology*.

Wenbin Jiang, Liang Huang, Qun Liu and Yajuan Lu, 2008. A Cascaded Linear Model for Joint Chinese Word Segmentation and Part-of-Speech Tagging. In *Proceedings of ACL*, pages 897-904.

Adwait Ratnaparkhi, 1998. Maximum entropy models for natural language ambiguity resolution. University of Pennsylvania.

Andreas Stolcke, 2002. SRILM-an extensible language modeling toolkit. In *Proceedings of the International Conference on Spoken Language Processing*, pages 311-318.

Huihsin Tseng, Pichuan Chang, Galen Andrew, Daniel Jurafsky and Christopher Manning, 2005. A Conditional Random Field Word Segmenter for Sighan Bakeoff 2005. In *Proceedings of the Fourth SIGHAN Workshop on Chinese Language Processing*, pages 168-171.

Kun Wang, Chengqing Zong and Keh-Yih Su, 2009. Which is more suitable for Chinese word segmentation, the generative model or the discriminative one? In *Proceedings of the 23rd Pacific Asia Conference on Language, Information and Computation (PACLIC23)*, pages 827-834.

Kun Wang, Chengqing Zong and Keh-Yih Su, 2010. A Character-Based Joint Model for CIPS-SIGHAN Word Segmentation Bakeoff 2010. *Proceedings of CIPS-SIGHAN Joint Conference on Chinese Language Processing (CLP2010)*, pages 245-248.

Kun Wang, Chengqing Zong and Keh-Yih Su, 2010. A Character-Based Joint Model for Chinese Word Segmentation. In *Proceedings of the 23rd International Conference on Computational Linguistics (COLING)*, Beijing, China, August 23-27, 2010. Pages 1173-1181.

Kun Wang, Chengqing Zong and Keh-Yih Su, 2012. Integrating generative and discriminative character based models for Chinese word segmentation. *ACM Transactions on Asian Language Information Processing (TALIP).*

Low, Jin Kiat et al., 2005. A Maximum Entropy Approach to Chinese Word Segmentation. *Proceedings of the Fourth SIGHAN Workshop on Chinese Language Processing*, pages 161-164.

Nianwen Xue, 2003. Chinese Word Segmentation as Character Tagging. *Computational Linguistics and Chinese Language Processing*, 8 (1). pages 29-48.

Ruiqiang Zhang, Genichiro Kikui and Eiichiro Sumita, 2006. Subword-based Tagging for Confidence dependent Chinese Word Segmentation. In *Proceedings of the COLING/ACL*, pages 961-968.

Xiaojin Zhu, 2006. Semi-supervised learning literature survey. *Technical Report 1530*, Computer Sciences, University of Wisconsin-Madison.

Leveraging Rich Linguistic Features for Cross-domain Chinese Segmentation

Guohua Wu, Dezhu He, Keli Zhong, Xue Zhou and Caixia Yuan
School of Computer,
Beijing University of Posts and Telecommunications,
China, 100876
trustwugh@gmail.com, hedezhu@bupt.edu.cn, zhk@126.com
bupt.zhouxue@gmail.com, yuancx@bupt.edu.cn

Abstract

This paper describes the system that we use for Chinese segmentation task in the 3rd CIPS-SIGHAN bakeoff. We use character sequence labeling method for segmentation, and in order to improve segmentation accuracy over multi-domain, we present a CRF-based Chinese segmentation system integrating supervised, unsupervised and lexical features. We firstly preliminarily segment the target data using CRF model trained over three types of features mentioned above, from the result of which new words are detected and absorbed into the lexicon. To generalize across different domains, we then execute the second segment with the updated lexicon. The OOV recognition is further promoted with refined post processing. All the features we used share a unified feature template trained by CRF. Our system achieves a competitive F score of 0.9730 for this bakeoff.

1 Introduction

Word is the fundamental unit in natural language understanding. Since people do not retain the boundary information between words in practical use, Chinese Word Segmentation (CWS) is the very first step in Chinese information processing. A considerable amount of research has shown that using character sequence labeling is a simple but effective formulation of Chinese word segmentation task (Xue and others, 2003; Peng et al., 2004; Low et al., 2005; Zhao et al., 2006a), among which the method using sequence labeling based on CRF (Lafferty et al., 2001) is widely used with attractive performance. However, most of the existing segmentation systems greatly rely on data that the model was trained over. The segmentation performance tends to would reduce significantly when the test data differs greatly from the training data in phraseology and vocabulary. Exploiting corpora in multi-domain for model learning can solve the problem above directly, whereas labeling corpora manually costs a lot, so that it is unrealistic to label mass corpora.

So far there are two ways to improve the performance of cross-domain word segmentation system. The first way is proposed in (Zhao and Kit, 2007; Zhao and Kit, 2008; Zhao and Kit, 2011), in which they put forward a unified framework that integrated supervised and unsupervised segmentation together, where they could take full advantage of unsupervised segmentation to discover new word from untagged corpora and obtain the ability of supervised segmentation to recognize the known words at the same time. The segmentation system is generalized to some extent. The second way is to build a segmentation system with multi-layers. The first layer is a set of distinctive word segmentation subsystems, who might has an outstanding performance on specific domain. And the second layer combines all the outputs of these subsystems, determining the most possible segmentation boundaries on test dataset. Gao and Vogel (2010) used this method achieved top performance in three test domains out of the four during Bakeoff-2010 (Zhao and Liu, 2010). In this paper we follow the first method to improve the performance of cross-domain segmentation, meanwhile add some of the effective features that mentioned in method two. And the performance of handling OOV is improved by adding lexical feature and new words discovery.

In Section 2, we describe the features we adopted in our system. Section 3 represents how we discover new words from preliminary segmentation results and how we expand the lexicon to update lexical feature before we segment test data again to improve the segmentation performance.

Proceedings of the Third CIPS-SIGHAN Joint Conference on Chinese Language Processing, pages 101–107,
Wuhan, China, 20-21 October 2014

Word length	Tag sequence for a word
1	S
2	BE
3	BB_2E
4	BB_2B_3E
5	BB_2B_3ME
≥ 6	BB_2B_3M$\cdots$ME

Table 1: Illustration of character tagging

The experimental result that tested on Bakeoff dataset compared with the best official result is provided in Section 4. Section 5 leads to the conclusion.

2 System Description

We formulate Chinese word segmentation task into a sequence labeling problem and use CRF to train the segmentation model. Our implementation of CRF-based CWS system uses the CRF++[1] package by Taku Kudo. We regard “，”, “。”, “？”, “！”, “；” as the boundary of a sentence and both the training and testing corpora are segmented by these boundaries.

Zhao et al. (2006b) prove that CRF segmentation performance using 6-tag set for training is better than other tag set, so we adopt 6-tag (B, B_2, B_3, M, E, S) set labeling the characters in words. Table 1 explains how to label the characters in words with different length. We follow six n-gram character features that are used in (Zhao et al., 2006b; Zhao and Kit, 2008), as C_{-1}, C_0, C_1, $C_{-1}C_0$, C_0C_1 and $C_{-1}C_1$ respectively, in which C represents the character, subscript -1, 0 and 1 means the previous character, the current character and the next character. With respect to the other features in our system, the similar six n-gram feature template is also applied to them.

2.1 Character Type Features

We simply classify all the characters by its Unicode code point into 5 classes: Chinese character (C), English character (E), number[2] (N), punctuation (P) and others (O). Denote character type feature as CTF, and define the feature template as CTF_{-1}, CTF_0, CTF_1, $CTF_{-1}CTF_0$, CTF_0CTF_1 and $CTF_{-1}CTF_1$.

[1] `http://crfpp.googlecode.com/svn/trunk/doc/index.html`

[2] Numbers including Arabic numerals and its Chinese version accordingly.

2.2 Conditional Entropy Feature

Gao and Vogel (2010) improve the segmentation performance on 2010 Bakeoff (Zhao and Liu, 2010) dataset by using conditional entropy feature. The forward conditional entropy for specific character C is the entropy that combines all the entropy of characters which might appear in the following position after C throughout the corpora, recorded as $H_f(C)$, while the backward conditional entropy consists of all the entropy of characters that might appear in the next position after C throughout the corpora, denoted as $H_b(C)$. We could mix unlabeled corpora in multi-domain to calculate forward and backword conditional entropy, which makes this feature more domain adaptive. Forward and backward conditional entropy can be efficiently carried out with the aid of Statistical *bigram matrixes*.

Continuous values of conditional entropy can be mapped into discrete numeric values by means of the method proposed by Gao and Vogel (2010) as following: $[0, 1.0) \mapsto 0$, $[1.0, 2.0) \mapsto 1$, $[2.0, 3.5) \mapsto 2$, $[3.5, 5.0) \mapsto 4$, $[5.0, 7.0) \mapsto 5$, $[7.0, +\infty) \mapsto 6$. The template is similar to character feature template, and forward conditional entropy template is in accordance with the backward one. Here, the forward conditional entropy feature templates are given: $H_f(C_{-1})$, $H_f(C_0)$, $H_f(C_1)$, $H_f(C_{-1})H_f(C_0)$, $H_f(C_0)H_f(C_1)$, $H_f(C_{-1})H_f(C_1)$.

2.3 Lexical Feature

Appropriately using of lexical feature has shown some improvement in Segmentation, and hence we adopt the definition of lexical feature from (Gao and Vogel, 2010). Feature $L_{begin}(C)$ represents the maximum length of words begin with character C in the lexicon via forward maximum matching from character C in the current sentence, and $L_{end}(C)$ represents the maximum length of words end with character C in the lexicon via backward maximum matching from character C. When processing forward and backward maximum matching, we only deal with the word with length equal or greater than 2, furthermore, the lexical feature value will be 0 where matching failed. Especially when feature value is equal or greater than 6, we set these feature values to 6. We hope to increase the performance by using a large-scale cross-domain lexicon. Six feature templates are defined for

$L_{begin}(C)$: $L_{begin}(C_{-1})$, $L_{begin}(C_0)$, $L_{begin}(C_1)$, $L_{begin}(C_{-1})L_{begin}(C_0)$, $L_{begin}(C_0)L_{begin}(C_1)$ and $L_{begin}(C_{-1})L_{begin}(C_1)$. As six feature templates of $L_{end}(C)$ could be inferred from above.

2.4 Accessor variety feature

Accessor variety (AV) proposed by Feng et al. (2004) could be used to measure the possibility of whether a substring is a Chinese word. Zhao and Kit (2007) thought that the method above is agreed with the method proposed by Harris (1970), in which morpheme could be found in unfamiliar language. Zhao and Kit (2008)'s experiments proved that AV feature improves the performance of CRF segmentation model on dataset in Bakeoff-2003, Bakeoff-2005 and Bakeoff-2006 (Sproat and Emerson, 2003; Emerson, 2005; Levow, 2006) while achieved the best performance on close test in Bakeoff-2008 (Chen and Jin, 2008). Therefore in this paper, AV feature is employed and we make further improvement of the performance by making better use of AV feature method. As to substring s, AV feature is defined as follow:

$$AV(s) = \min\{L_{av}(s), R_{av}(s)\}$$

in which $L_{av}(s)$ and $R_{av}(s)$ represent the number of different characters before s and after s respectively, while the sign in the begin or the end of sentence would be double counted.

How we use AV is similar to (Zhao and Kit, 2008; Yang et al., 2011), considering the AV value of substrings with length is equal or less than 5 in sentence and designing several feature templates accordingly. We used the formula below to discrete AV value of substring s:

$$f(s) = t, \text{ if } 2^t \leq AV(s) < 2^{t+1}$$

Discrete value t is regarded as the feature value. The difference between our method and the method above is that for substring s, we marked the feature value of s on the first character of s, not on every character of s. Representation of lexical feature mentioned in Section 2.3 was used for reference because we believed labeling this way could highlight boundary information between words. Table 2 shows the differences in detail. For instance, consider all the substring consist of 4 characters. In this case, we have a substring "在我心中 (in the middle of my heart)" with AV feature value $t = 1$. So that we updated

In	Accessor Variety Feature Selection										T
	1 char		2 char		3 char		4 char		5 char		
而	9	9	5	5	2	2	0	0	0	0	S
在	10	10	5	5	2	1	1	1	1	1	S
我	9	9	5	3	2	2	1	0	1	0	S
心	8	8	5	5	2	2	1	0	1	0	B
中	9	9	8	8	2	0	1	0	1	0	E
，	11	11	8	0	2	0	0	0	1	0	S

Table 2: Comparison of how to use AV feature

feature values in "4 char" row. The left row indicates that for every character "在", "我", "心", "中", feature values should be set to 1 according to method (Zhao and Kit, 2008; Yang et al., 2011). The right row indicates the feature values in our method, in which only the first character "在" is given feature value of 1. We created 6 templates similar to character feature template for each row in Table 2.

In order to prove the effectivity of improved AV feature in our method, we continued to use the experiment setting of (Zhao and Kit, 2008; Yang et al., 2011) and and had experiment on the dataset of Bakeoff-2005 (Emerson, 2005) and the simplified Chinese dataset of Bakeoff-2010 (Zhao and Liu, 2010). OldAV stands for their AV feature while our feature named as NewAV. 6 n-gram character features and character type feature mentioned in Section 2.1 were used in each experiment. Evaluation indicator F score equals $F = 2RP/(R+P)$, in which R is the recall and P stands for precision. After combined corresponding training and test dataset of Bakeoff-2005 together without segmentation marks, statistical AV features were created. Then the training corpus, unlabeled corpus and test corpus of Bakeoff-2010 were combined together without segmentation marks to count AV features. The experiment results in Table 3 indicates that our improvement in AV feature is effective due to the performance is better than other old methods. These experiment results were not post-processed so as to compare segmentation performance easily.

2.5 Post-processing

Post-processing aimed at handling segmentation error in English word, Arabic numeric string and URL. Faced with this situation, these characters should be regarded as a whole segment unit, but out system might make segmentation errors. In

Bakeoff-2005		AS	CityU	MSRA	PKU
Baseline	F	0.954	0.955	0.971	0.950
	R_{OOV} [1]	0.700	0.798	0.772	0.778
OldAV	F	0.957	0.961	0.973	0.952
	R_{OOV}	0.688	0.807	0.747	0.770
NewAV	F	0.957	0.964	0.973	0.954
	R_{OOV}	0.688	0.822	0.743	0.773
Bakeoff-2010		A	B	C	D
Baseline	F	0.921	0.93	0.918	0.953
	R_{OOV}	0.629	0.773	0.72	0.853
OldAV	F	0.933	0.94	0.935	0.956
	R_{OOV}	0.656	0.784	0.77	0.848
NewAV	F	0.935	0.945	0.936	0.956
	R_{OOV}	0.659	0.807	0.763	0.843

[1] Recall of out-of-vocabulary (OOV) words.

Table 3: Comparion experiment on AV feature, n-gram feature and character type feature were used for each experiment

Table 4 we have an example of URL segmented incorrectly, and raw represents the original sentence; result shows the result after segmentation; final stands for the result after post-processing. To deal with this kind of problem, we have to make sure that when we take gaps away from the segmented sentence, it should be in correspondences with original characters in sentence. Here is a quick procedure of how we restored URL segmentation error. First, we put the original sentence in a string; then saved the segmented result in to a list. Every element in the list is a word with subscript starts from 0.

1. Use regular expression to find the start and the end position of the original sentence. In case `http://t.cn/aBPxzO`, the start and end index is 4 and 22 respectively.

2. Accumulating word length in the word list from left to right, we can get the start index of URL is 2 and end index is 3 according to word list.

3. Combine the 2nd and 3rd word in the word list as one word.

English word and Arabic numeric string can be handled in the same way.

raw	点击网址http://t.cn/aBPxzO
result	点击　网址　http://t.cn/aB　PxzO
final	点击　网址　http://t.cn/aBPxzO

Table 4: Post-processing of particular string (URL)

3 Improve The Segmentation Performance of New Words

The segmentation system that we described in Section 2 was not very stable when it comes to new words. New words with some sort of context can be segmented correctly while other context might lead to mistake. For example, the word "涅维拉济莫夫 (涅维拉济莫夫)" with context "文官涅维拉济 莫夫在起草一封贺信 (civil officer Nie Vilage is making a draft of congratulatory letter)" can be segmented correctly, but the sentence "于是涅维拉济莫夫开始绞尽脑汁 (hence Nie Vialge began to rack his brain)" was wrongly segmented. To solve this sort of problem, we tried to find these new words by rules, then added new words to the lexicon, re-calculated the lexical features of test corpora, segmented test corpora again in the end. Let 's mark the lexicon used for extracting lexical features when training segmentation model as $Lexicon_{train}$, and count the Bigram statistical information on segmented corpora of People's Daily 1998 and 2000 as PKU_{bigram} without smoothing. For the preliminary segmentation result, if word w meets the following conditions, we deemed w as a new word:

1. (w with length between 2 to 6) or (w with length greater than 6 and w is a foreign name at the same time (en dash • exists in w)),

2. w does not exist in $Lexicon_{train}$,

3. w is not a Chinese name,

4. w can not be the concatenation of w_{-1} and w_0 for $\forall(w_{-1}, w_0) \in PKU_{bigram}$.

We checked every word in result after segmentation so that we have a new version of new words list named $Lexicon_{test}$. If $Lexicon_{test}$ has two words with inclusion relation, we only reserved the word with longer length. Combine $Lexicon_{train}$ and $Lexicon_{test}$ together then we have a new word list named $Lexicon_{new}$. This new word list could be used for calculating lexical feature of the test corpora to update segmentation result.

Name	Features	Lexicon
Baseline	CF,CTF	None
Closed	CF,CTF,EF,AV	None
Open[1]	CF,CTF,EF,AV	Webdict
Refined[2]	CF,CTF,EF,AV	Webdict

[1] Webdict were used to calculate lexical feature for both testing and training.

[2] Webdict were used to calculate lexical feature for training, then the method mentioned in Section 3 was used for performance improvement.

Table 5: Feature combination: CF represents 6 n-gram features of character, CTF represents character type feature, EF represents conditional entropy feature and AV represents Accessor variety feature

Bakeoff-2005		AS	CityU	MSRA	PKU
Best closed	F	0.952	0.943	0.964	0.95
	R_{OOV}	0.696	0.698	0.717	0.636
Baseline	F	0.955	0.956	0.971	0.950
	R_{OOV}	0.708	0.806	0.772	0.779
Closed	F	0.957	0.963	0.974	0.954
	R_{OOV}	0.705	0.817	0.739	0.770
Open	F	0.958	0.965	0.977	**0.962**
	R_{OOV}	0.700	0.811	0.751	0.765
Refined	F	-	-	**0.976**	0.962
	R_{OOV}	-	-	0.751	0.766
Best open	F	0.956	0.962	0.972	0.969
	R_{OOV}	0.684	0.806	0.59	0.838

Table 6: Test result on Bakeoff-2005 dataset

4 Experiment

In order to prove the performance of our method, we considered four kinds of feature combination demonstrated in Table 5, in which *Closed* means closed test, *Open* means open test in which we used a cross-domain lexicon — Webdict[3]. *Refined* represents that we added new words' process proposed in Section 3 on the basis of *Open*. For *Refined*, we needed corpora to create statistical Bigram information and a lexicon for training. Because of the limited scale of labeled data and we have merely sufficient simplified Chinese training data and lexicon, we didn't process both the AS and CityU of Bakeoff-2005 for *Refined*. All the experiments in this section were linked to post-processing mentioned in Section 2.5. We tested our system on Bakeoff-2005 and Bakeoff-2010 dataset with major measure index F score.

Table 6 shows the experiment result on Bakeoff-2005. When computing conditional entropy feature and AV feature, corresponding test corpus and training corpus should be mixed together, wiping off of the segmentation boundaries before the feature extraction. "Best closed" indicates the best result on closed test of Bakeoff-2005 and "Best open" stands for the best open test of official outcome. Our closed test outcome fully exceeded the "Best closed", and open test outcome exist a slight achieves a slightly lower F scores compared with "Best open" only on PKU test set, which might due to the deficiency of corpora and might be improved only by enlarging the amount of training corpora.

Table 7 shows the test result on Bakeoff-2010 simplified Chinese dataset. When computing conditional entropy feature and AV feature, we needed to combine all of the simplified Chinese corpus together without segmentation boundaries of Bakeoff-2010 corpora to create the statistical feature values. "Best closed" and "Best open" shows the best result on official closed test and open test. Our closed test result on test set A differs greatly from "Best closed", yet the result is closer to "Best closed" on other test sets. The performance on *Closed* improves a lot comparing to the baseline. In addition, our method exceeded "Best open" on dataset C, D in open test, while slightly poorer results than the best on dataset A and B but the differences are not significant.

From the *Refined* results of both Table 6 and Table 7, we can observe that our strategy on detecting new words provide improvements over all the R_{OOV} compared to all the Open system in general. Meanwhile, our *Refined* model provide more balanced F scores among all the dataset.

It is proved on two Bakeoff datasets that our *Open* feature combination and *Refined* feature combination are effective. On account of lacking training corpus of this Bakeoff, Open data test is required. Hence we used *Open* and *Refined* feature combination in Table 5. With purpose of making model to be more cross-domain adaptive, we made use of a large number of unlabeled corpora to extract conditional entropy feature and AV feature. Web crawler was used to get totally 1.5G corpora in 5 domains, including finance, literature,

[3] `https://github.com/ling0322/webdict`

Bakeoff-2010		A	B	C	D
Best closed	F	0.946	0.951	0.939	0.959
	R_{OOV}	0.816	0.827	0.75	0.827
Baseline	F	0.921	0.933	0.918	0.954
	R_{OOV}	0.629	0.781	0.72	0.86
Closed	F	0.935	0.949	0.936	0.958
	R_{OOV}	0.658	0.819	0.763	0.853
Open	F	0.95	0.949	0.943	0.963
	R_{OOV}	0.509	0.766	0.571	0.879
Refined	F	0.95	0.949	0.943	0.963
	R_{OOV}	**0.519**	**0.768**	**0.572**	**0.883**
Best open	F	0.955	0.95	0.938	0.96
	R_{OOV}	0.655	0.82	0.768	0.847

Table 7: Test result on Bakeoff-2010 dataset

news, microblog and novel. The data we used is explained as followed:

- PKU-Corpus: labeled People's Daily corpus in year 1998 and 2000.
- PKU-Raw: PKU-Corpus without segmentation boundaries.
- Web-Corpus: combines all the unlabeled corpora from web crawler.
- Sample-Corpus: randomly select 15% from Web-Corpus.
- Entropy-Corpus: PKU-Raw together with Web-Corpus.
- AV-Corpus: PKU-Raw together with Sample-Corpus.

Finally we used PKU-Corpus as training data, and extracted from Entropy-Corpus to extract conditional entropy feature while making use of AV-Corpus to extract AV features, together with character feature and character type feature to train CRF word segmentation model. Our results on this bakeoff are showed in Table 8, which achieves a competitive F score of 0.9730. From this table, we can catch that *Refined* feature combination outperforms *Open*, which further confirms that the new word detection is critical for cross-domain Chinese segmentation.

5 Conclusion

In this paper we attempted to implement a word segmentation system with the ability to handle the situation of cross domain. We combined supervised and unsupervised global features together and improved the ability to recognize OOV through adding cross-domain lexical feature. Discovering new words from target test set then recomputing the lexical feature to refine the segmentation results makes the model more domain adaptive.

	Precision	Recall	F Score
Open	0.9673	0.9776	0.9724
Refined	0.9681	0.9779	0.9730

Table 8: Results on Bakeoff-2014 dataset

Yet our system still have many deficiencies which can be improved from three aspects. First of all, we only used one kind of unsupervised feature and there might be other unsupervised features or feature combination that could achieve better performance. Next, we coined all the feature into one set of template mainly due to its simplicity in practice. However, there might exist a more fitting feature template for different features. At last, our rule-based method to discover new words could be changed into automatic discovery.

Acknowledgments

This work was partially supported by National Natural Science Foundation of China Grant NO.61202248. Many thanks to our colleagues participating in this work. We also thank Huiming Duan and Zhifang Sui for their excellent organization.

References

Xiao Chen and Guangjin Jin. 2008. The fourth international chinese language processing bakeoff: Chinese word segmentation named entity recognition and chinese pos tagging. In *Proceedings of the Sixth SIGHAN Workshop on Chinese Language Processing*.

Thomas Emerson. 2005. The second international chinese word segmentation bakeoff. In *Proceedings of the Fourth SIGHAN Workshop on Chinese Language Processing*, volume 133.

Haodi Feng, Kang Chen, Xiaotie Deng, and Weimin Zheng. 2004. Accessor variety criteria for chinese word extraction. *Computational Linguistics*, 30(1):75–93.

Qin Gao and Stephan Vogel. 2010. A multi-layer chinese word segmentation system optimized for out-of-domain tasks. In *Proceedings of CIPS-SIGHAN*

Joint Conference on Chinese Language Processing (CLP2010), pages 210–215.

Zellig S Harris. 1970. *Morpheme boundaries within words: Report on a computer test*. Springer.

John Lafferty, Andrew McCallum, and Fernando CN Pereira. 2001. Conditional random fields: Probabilistic models for segmenting and labeling sequence data.

Gina-Anne Levow. 2006. The third international chinese language processing bakeoff: Word segmentation and named entity recognition. In *Proceedings of the Fifth SIGHAN Workshop on Chinese Language Processing*, pages 108–117, Sydney, Australia, July. Association for Computational Linguistics.

Jin Kiat Low, Hwee Tou Ng, and Wenyuan Guo. 2005. A maximum entropy approach to chinese word segmentation. In *Proceedings of the Fourth SIGHAN Workshop on Chinese Language Processing*, volume 1612164.

Fuchun Peng, Fangfang Feng, and Andrew McCallum. 2004. Chinese segmentation and new word detection using conditional random fields. In *Proceedings of the 20th international conference on Computational Linguistics*, page 562. Association for Computational Linguistics.

Richard Sproat and Thomas Emerson. 2003. The first international chinese word segmentation bakeoff. In *Proceedings of the Second SIGHAN Workshop on Chinese Language Processing*, pages 133–143, Sapporo, Japan, July. Association for Computational Linguistics.

Nianwen Xue et al. 2003. Chinese word segmentation as character tagging. *Computational Linguistics and Chinese Language Processing*, 8(1):29–48.

Ting-hao Yang, Tian-Jian Jiang, Chan-hung Kuo, Richard Tzong-han Tsai, and Wen-lian Hsu. 2011. Unsupervised overlapping feature selection for conditional random fields learning in chinese word segmentation. In *Proceedings of the 23rd Conference on Computational Linguistics and Speech Processing*, pages 109–122. Association for Computational Linguistics.

Hai Zhao and Chunyu Kit. 2007. Incorporating global information into supervised learning for chinese word segmentation. In *10th Conference of the Pacific Association for Computational Linguistics*, pages 66–74.

Hai Zhao and Chunyu Kit. 2008. Unsupervised segmentation helps supervised learning of character tagging for word segmentation and named entity recognition. In *The Sixth SIGHAN Workshop on Chinese Language Processing*, pages 106–111.

Hai Zhao and Chunyu Kit. 2011. Integrating unsupervised and supervised word segmentation: The role of goodness measures. *Information Sciences*, 181(1):163–183.

Hongmei Zhao and Qun Liu. 2010. The cips-sighan clp 2010 chinese word segmentation bakeoff. In *Proceedings of the First CPS-SIGHAN Joint Conference on Chinese Language Processing*, pages 199–209.

Hai Zhao, Chang-Ning Huang, and Mu Li. 2006a. An improved chinese word segmentation system with conditional random field. In *Proceedings of the Fifth SIGHAN Workshop on Chinese Language Processing*, volume 1082117. Sydney: July.

Hai Zhao, Chang-Ning Huang, Mu Li, and Bao-Liang Lu. 2006b. Effective tag set selection in chinese word segmentation via conditional random field modeling. In *Proceedings of PACLIC*, volume 20, pages 87–94.

Personal Attributes Extraction in Chinese Text Bakeoff in CLP 2014: Overview

Ruifeng Xu, Shuai Wang, Feng Shi
Key Laboratory of Network Oriented Intelligent Computation, Shenzhen Graduate School, Harbin Institute of Technology, China
xuruifeng@hitsz.edu.cn

Jian Xu
Department of Computing, The Hong Kong Polytechnic University, Hong Kong
csjxu@comp.polyu.edu.hk

Abstract

This paper presents the overview of Personal Attributes Extraction in Chinese Text Bakeoff in CLP 2014. Personal attribute extraction plays an important role in information extraction, event tracking, entity disambiguation and other related research areas. This task is designed to evaluate the techniques for extracting person specific attributes from unstructured Chinese texts, which is similar to slot filling, but focuses on person attributes. This task brings some challenges issues because Chinese language contains some common words and lacks of capital clues as in English. The task organizer manually constructs the query names and corresponding documents. The value/presence of the texts corresponding 25 pre-defined attributes are annotated to construct the training and testing dataset. The bakeoff results achieved by the participators show the good progress in this field.

1 Introduction

Personal Attributes Extraction in Chinese Text Task is designed to evaluate the techniques for extracting person specific attributes, such as birth date, spouse, children, education, and title etc. from unstructured Chinese texts. These techniques play an important role in information extraction, event tracking, entity disambiguation and other related research areas.

Slot filling task has been proposed as one of shared tasks in the TAC KBP workshop since 2009 [1]. Generally speaking, the mainstream techniques for slot filling and person attributes extraction may be camped into two major approaches, namely: Rule-based approach and statistics-based ones [2,3,4]. Rule-based approach normally defines the extraction rules manually or learns the rules automatically. The rules play the key role in this approach. As long as finding the constraint information which matches the rules in the text, the system may extract the target extraction information. As for the statistics-based approach, it has good portability to this extraction problem. Several statistics machine learning models such as Hidden Markov Model (HMM) and Condition Random Fields (CRFs) are employed. The shortcoming for this approach is that it requires large amount of training data which is always unavailable.

Currently, there are limited existing works on personal attributes extraction in Chinese text. Comparing to the works on English, the characteristics of Chinese language including the Chinese word segmentation, the confusion of named entity with common words, lack of capital clues bring more difficulties for person attributes extraction in Chinese.

The task of person attributes extraction in Chinese text in CLP 2014 bakeoff is designed on the basis of the slot filling task in the TAC KBP workshop [1]. The task organizer provides a collection of documents corresponding to a target person and a knowledge base which contains partial list of attributes for the person. Participants are required to extract additional attributes from the collections of documents. The task is similar to the slot filling, but it focuses on person attributes extraction. Furthermore, the collection of documents is not limited to the news corpus.

Proceedings of the Third CIPS-SIGHAN Joint Conference on Chinese Language Processing, pages 108–113,
Wuhan, China, 20-21 October 2014

2 Task Definition

2.1 Task description

The Personal Attributes Extraction in Chinese Text Task is motivated by a component of a full slot filling (SF) system. This task focuses on the refinement of output from Chinese slot filling systems. Especially, personal attributes extracted from the unstructured text is useful for the construction of Chinese knowledge graph.

In this task, the participants are provided a set of document collection in several person name folders. In each folder, source documents named as XXX_Ti.xml and Wikipedia knowledge base named as XXX 维基百科记录.xml are given. The Wikipedia knowledge base for each person is an XML document, in which attributes are located in the tags of Facts. In addition, unstructured text for that person is also provided with the wiki_text tag. Example 1 gives a sample record in Wikipedia knowledge base.

```
<entity wiki_title="周强" type="PER" id=""
name="周强">
  <facts class="Infobox">
    <fact name="nationality">中国</fact>
    <fact name="birthdate">1960年4月</fact>
    <fact name="education">西南政法大学
</fact>
  </facts>
  <wiki_text>周强（1960年4月一），湖北黄
梅人，西南政法大学民法专业毕业，法学硕士。
  </wiki_text>
</entity>
```

Example 1: A Sample Wikipedia knowledge base.

The extraction task focused on extracting values for a set of pre-defined attributes ("slots") for target person entity from given source documents. Given an entity, the system is required to extract the correct value(s) for that pre-defined attribute from source documents and return the slot filler together with its provenance, which is a set of text spans from source document that justify the correctness of the slot filler. The extraction system need not extract the attribute values given in the Wikipedia knowledge base.

2.2 Dataset preparation

The person names are manually selected from the web, in which 10 person names are used in training dataset and 90 person names, including 48 names for Chinese person and 42 names for foreign person are used in testing dataset. The corresponding knowledge base is constructed from Wikipedia person entity while the source documents in each folder are constructed based on search engine output with manually selection.

The personal attributes are categorized as being Person (PER) slots based on the type of entities about which they seek to extract information. The attributes are also categorized by the content and quantity of their fillers [5].

2.2.1 Attribute slot content

Attribute slot content are divided into three categorizations, namely Name, Value, or String.

Name slots are required to be filled by the name of a person. Name slots including the alternative name, spouse name, city of birth, country of death and so on. The detailed slot descriptions are given in the Personal Attributes Extraction in Chinese Text Task website.

Value slots are required to be filled by either a numerical value or a date such as age and birth date. The numbers and dates in these fillers can be spelled out (forty-two; December 7, 1941) or written as numbers (42; 12/7/1941).

String slots are basically a "catch all", meaning that their fillers cannot be neatly classified as names or values. The text excerpts (or "strings") that make up these fillers can sometimes be just a name, but are often expected to be more than a name. The typical string slots including cause of death and religion.

2.2.2 Attribute slot quantity

Slots are labeled as Single-value or List-value based on the number of fillers they can take. Since one slot may have different representations, participant is required to extract all of these representations.

Single-value slots can have only single filler. While most single-value slots are obvious (e.g., a person can only have one date of birth), some may be less apparent.

List-value slots can take multiple fillers as they are likely to have more than one correct answer in the source data. For example, people may have multiple children, employers, or alternate names.

2.2.3 Attribute Table

The following table of all 25 pre-defined attribute slots and their categorizations is given below.

Slot name	Content	Quantity
Alternate Names	Name	List
Children	Name	List
Cities of Residence	Name	List
City of Birth	Name	Single
City of Death	Name	Single
Countries of Residence	Name	List
Country of Birth	Name	Single
Country of Death	Name	Single
Other Family	Name	List
Parents	Name	List
Schools Attended	Name	List
Siblings	Name	List
Spouses	Name	List
Stateorprovince of Birth	Name	Single
Stateorprovince of Death	Name	Single
Statesorprovinces of Residence	Name	List
Age	Value	Single
Date of Birth	Value	Single
Date of Death	Value	Single
Cause of Death	String	Single
Charges	String	List
Religion	String	List
Title	Name	List
Member of	Name	List
Employee of	Name	List

Table 1. Attribute slots

In this task, the organizer collects the source documents under each person name by using the search engine. Using the person name and the related attribute names as the query to search on the Internet, the top N high quality web pages are manually selected as the source documents. During the set construction, the organizer avoids to the attribute slots overlapping between different source documents. Table 2 gives the statistical information for source document.

Sets	Max	Min	Average	Total
Train set	4	1	2	24
Test set	5	1	2	235

Table 2. Statistical information of source documents

The instance means one person's attribute slot appears in one source document. Table 3 lists the detail information about the instance number of one related person attribute in one source document.

attributes	Max	Min	Average
Single	6	0	1
List	47	0	1

Table 3. Instances in source documents

As mentioned above, the person attributes are divided into two categorizations: Single and List. The total instance numbers for the two categorizations in the training set and testing set are shown as follows.

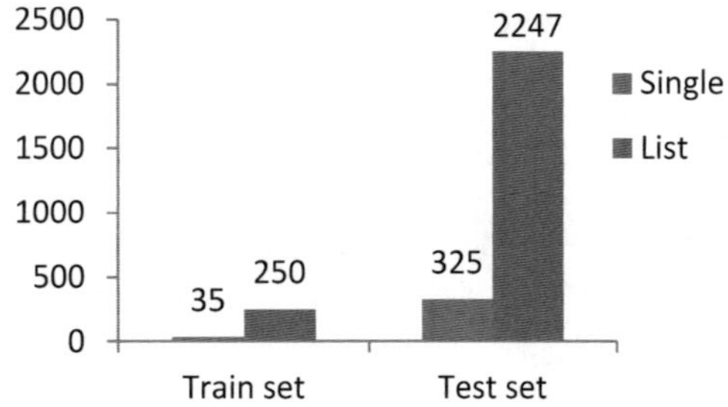

Figure 1. The instance numbers in the training set and testing set.

3 Evaluation Metrics

In the evaluation, both the lenient evaluation and strict evaluation are performed. In the strict evaluation, all instance attributes are compared to the answers while in the lenient evaluation, the offset string_begin and string_end are ignored. The detail evaluation metrics are shown as follows.

3.1 Single Attributes Evaluation Metric

$$\text{Score}_{\text{single}} = \frac{\text{NumCorrect}}{\text{NumSingleSlot}} \quad (1)$$

When numCorrect is zero, the numCorrect is set to 1.0;

3.2 List Attributes Evaluation Metric

$$ListSlotValue = \frac{(F_\beta{}^2+1)*IP*IR}{F_\beta{}^2*(IP+IR)} \quad (2)$$

$$Score_{list} = \frac{\sum ListSlotValue}{NumListSlots} \quad (3)$$

When IP is the instance precision and IR is the instance recall, in the evaluation we set the weight $F_\beta = 2$, and when both IP and IR are zero, we set the ListSlotValue to zero;

3.3 Overall Evaluation Metric

$$SF_{value} = \frac{1}{2}(Score_{single} + Score_{list}) \quad (4)$$

The overall evaluation metric is the average of single attributes evaluation score and list attributes evaluation score. The participant systems are ranked according to SF_{value}.

4 Performance of the Participants

In this bakeoff, 6 teams submitted 6 valid results. The team ID and the corresponding participants are listed in Table 4.

Team ID	Organization
CIST-BUPT	北京邮电大学
ICTNET_002	中国科学院计算所
WZ_v4	法国 INALCO
BLCU-yudong	北京语言大学
Result-BUPT	北京邮电大学
CASIA_CUC_PAES	中国科学院自动化所

Table 4. The Bakeoff Participants

The achieved performances of these systems under lenient and strict evaluations, are shown in Figure 2 and Figure 3, respectively. the performances of Personal Attributes Extraction in Chinese Text (the SF_Value) are uniformly lower than 0.5. Especially the ListScore lower than 0.4.

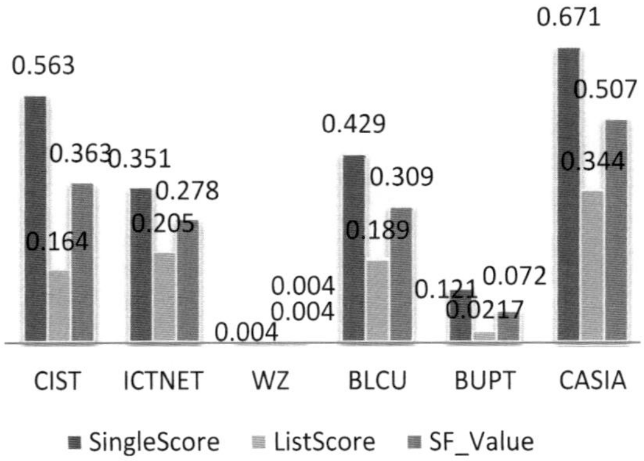

Figure 2. The lenient evaluation results

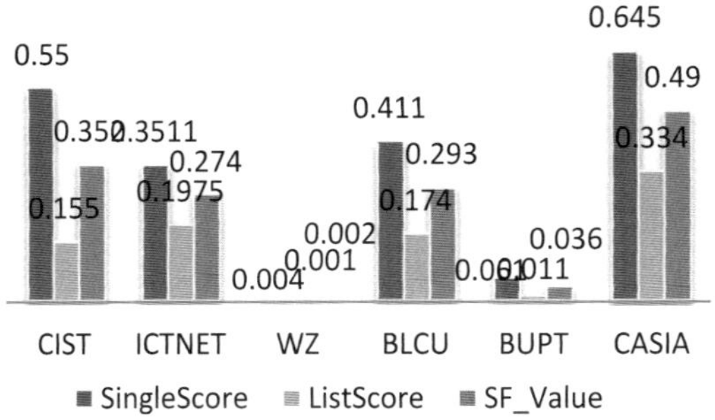

Figure 3. The strict evaluation results

Three participants submit the technical reports for this task.

Dong YU et al. [6] use a mixture framework consists of supervised learning and rule based extractor and human knowledge database. Firstly, they divide 25 attributes into several groups. A specific combination of methods for extracting the values for each group is developed. The CRF model and regular expression are employed to extract the instances, and the protagonist dependency relationship based filter and attribute keywords based filter are employed to post-process the answers extract. This system achieves the SF_Value of 0.309 under lenient evaluation and 0.293 under strict evaluation.

Kailun Zhang et al. [7] propose a method based on the combination of trigger words, dictionary and rules. This system narrow down the extraction scope by building attributes trigger words. The attributes such as state, province, and school, the cause of death and some similar fixed attributes are extracted by dictionary lookup directly through building the attributes dictionary. Some attributes extraction rules are developed to extract other instances. This system achieves the SF_Value of 0.363 under lenient evaluation and 0.352 under the strict evaluation.

Zhen Wang et al. [8] use a dependency patterns matching technique to extract the attribute instances. In order to get the ontology, they use some patterns to match dependency relations and save the extracted information into RDF format file. An alignment process is used to group same classes and remove duplicates in RDF files. Finally, they align their ontology to CLP's. The performance of this system may be limited to some language process problems. It achieves SF_Value of 0.0043 under lenient evaluation and 0.0025 under strict evaluation.

The top performance system, CASIA_CUC_PAES did not provide the technical report. This system achieves SF_Value of 0.507 under lenient evaluation and 0.490 under strict evaluation.

5 Analysis

The SF_Value performances of Personal Attributes Extraction in Chinese Text systems are lower than 0.5 while the Single Score is lower than 0.7 and the ListScore is lower than 0.4. In this section, we analyze the factors influence the extraction performance.

(1) One object sometimes have different expressions in Chinese language, for example, the capital of China 北京 can be expressed as 北京市 or 京，and even the date 1990 年 5 月 6 日 can be expressed as May 6, 1941, or 1990-5-6, or 5/6/1990 and so on. The extraction system has the difficulty to extract all of these instances.

(2) In this evaluation, most system distinguish the titles and the alternate names hardly. Generally, alternate names refer to the assigned persons that are distinct from the "official" name. Alternate names may include aliases, stage names, alternate transliterations, abbreviations, alternate spellings, nicknames, or birth names. Compared with other slots, more inference should be used for selecting appropriate fillers for Alternate Names because the canonical names of entities often absent from source documents. As for the Titles or other extraneous information added to a name do not justify an alternate name. Generally, a given name alone is not a correct alternate name unless the person is unambiguously known that way.

(3) The administrative region divisions in different countries are not the same. Thus, most systems distinguish the city and the state or province hardly. For example, the 福冈县 in Japan is divided as state or province level, but the 浮山县 in China should be divided as city level. In the bakeoff, the geopolitical entities are divided to three levels (city, town, or village). Thus, these attributes are hardly distinguished, especially for the statistical-based system.

(4) Another problem is that attributes of string value are not be extracted exactly. For example, a mention of a serious illness is not an acceptable filler of cause of death unless it is explicitly linked to the death of the assigned person in the document. Assessors should be lenient in their judgment of the fullness of selected strings for cause of death. These types of attributes are basically a "catch all", meaning that their fillers cannot be neatly classified as names or values. The text excerpts (or "strings") that make up these fillers can sometimes be just a name, but are often expected to be more than a name.

Due to various factors and complication of the evaluations, the organizer may only ensure the relative fairness for each system. Meanwhile, it is observed that some errors in the submitted results are come at very small points. The carefully development will be helpful.

Furthermore, to make the evaluation results comparable, the organizer should use a uniform standard in te evaluation (besides the SingleScore, ListScore, and the SF_Value).

6 Conclusion

The Personal Attributes Extraction in Chinese Text task for CLP2014 has raised the problem in Chinese personal attributes extraction. Besides the basic difficulty of Chinese nature language processing and information extraction, there are other difficulties like common words detection, co-reference resolution. 6 teams have submitted their results. Most teams use rule-based methods or matching techniques while other team utilizes the statistical-based technique. Some proposed techniques are shown effective in person attribute extraction. The organizer expects this bakeoff is helpful to the research on person attribute extraction in Chinese text.

Acknowledgements

This study was supported by the National Natural Science Foundation of China No. 61370165, Natural Science Foundation of Guangdong Province S2013010014475, MOE Specialized Research Fund for the Doctoral Program of Higher Education 20122302120070, Open Projects Program of National Laboratory of Pattern Recognition, Shenzhen International Co-operation Research Funding GJHZ20120613 110641217, Shenzhen Foundational Research Funding JCYJ20120613152557576.

Reference

[1] Heng Ji and Raslfph Grishman. 2011. Knowledge Base Population: Successful Approaches and Challenges. Proc. 49th Annual Meeting Assn. Computational Linguistics.

[2] Zheng Chen, Suzanne Tamang, Adam Lee, Xiang Li, Wen-Pin Lin, Matthew Snover, Javier Artiles, MarissaPassantino and Heng Ji. 2010. CUNYBLENDER TAC-KBP2010 Entity Linking and Slot Filling System Description. Proc. TAC 2010 Workshop.

[3] Guillermo Garrido, Anselmo Peñas and Bernardo, Cabaleiro. 2013. UNED Slot Filling and Temporal Slot Filling systems at TAC KBP 2013. System description. Proc.

TAC 2013 Workshop.

[4] Bryan Kisiel, Justin Betteridge, Matt Gardner, Jayant Krishnamurthy, Ndapa Nakashole, Mehdi Samadi, Partha Talukdar, Derry Wijaya, Tom Mitchell. 2013. CMUML System for KBP 2013 Slot Filling. Proc. TAC 2013 Workshop.

[5] Joe Ellis, Heather Simpson, Kira Griffitt, Hoa Trang Dang etc, TAC KBP Slot. http://projects.ldc.upenn.edu/kbp/.

[6] Dong YU, Cheng YU, Gongbo TANG, Qin QU, Chunhua LIU, Yue TIAN, Jing YI. 2014. An Introduction to BLCU Personal Attributes Extraction System. Proc. Third SIGHAN Workshop on Chinese Language Processing.

[7] Kailun Zhang, Mingyin Wang, Xiaoyue Cong, Fang Huang, Hongfa Xue, Lei Li. 2014. Personal Attributes Extraction Based on the Combination Trigger Words, Dictionary and Rules. Proc. Third SIGHAN Workshop on Chinese Language Processing.

[8] Zhen Wang. 2014. Extraction system for Personal Attributes Extraction of CLP2014. Proc. The Third SIGHAN Workshop on Chinese Language Processing.

Personal Attributes Extraction Based on the Combination of Trigger Words, Dictionary and Rules

Kailun Zhang, Mingyin Wang, Xiaoyue Cong, Fang Huang, Hongfa Xue, Lei Li,Zhiqiao Gao

Beijing University of Posts and Telecommunications,
China，100876
kailun0315@qq.com, wmy512@qq.com, cxy0105@bupt.edu.cn

xprince.hf@gmail.com, xuehongfa@vip.qq.com, leili@bupt.edu.cn, 526804113@qq.com

Abstract

Personal Attributes Extraction in Unstructured Chinese Text Task is a subtask of The 3rd CIPS-SIGHAN Joint Conference on Chinese Language Processing (CLP-2014). In this report, we propose a method based on the combination of trigger words, dictionary and rules to realize the personal attributes extraction. We introduce the extraction process and show the result of this bakeoff, which can show that our method is feasible and has achieved good effect.

Keywords: Unstructured Chinese Text, Personal Attributes Extraction, Trigger Words, Dictionary, Rules

1 Introduction

In recent years, with the development of Internet, masses of information provide the majority of Internet users with a lot of convenience. However, with the increase of amount of information, screening redundant information and seeking for the knowledge which users really want from a lot of unstructured texts is getting more and more difficult. For example, when we search for the details of someone, general search engines usually return a number of pages, and we must identify these pages one by one even if we just need a little of them. Therefore, extracting personal attributes from unstructured texts has become a very important task. Personal attributes extraction in unstructured Chinese text task is designed to extract person specific attributes, such as date of birth, spouse, husband, children, education, or title etc. from unstructured Chinese texts. The corresponding techniques play an important role in information extraction, event tracking, entity disambiguation and other related research areas.

In our report, a method based on the combination of trigger words, dictionary and rules to realize the personal attributes extraction is introduced. We build a basic framework including trigger words, dictionaries and rules that relative to the task to extract personal specific attributes. In Section 2, we introduce two basic methods about information extraction and several recent researches on this theme while the detailed description of the task is represented in Section 3. In Section 4, we give the step to build our basic model of extraction. We talk the main framework in Section 4.1. Then from Section 4.2 to Section 4.4, we describe the process to build trigger word table, attribute dictionaries and personal attribute rules one by one in a detailed way. We show the evaluation metrics and the final experiment results in Section 5 to prove the feasibility of our method. In Section 6, we point out the shortage of our system and propose some suggestions to improve our model and then make a conclusion.

2 Related Works

Rule-based methods and statistics-based ones are two main ways of information extraction at present. Information extraction based on the rules is a two phase process consists of learning and applying, including the study of rules and the application of using rules for target information extraction. Information extraction rules mainly come from the target context in constraint environment. As long as finding the constraint information which can meet the rules in the text, we could also find the target extraction information. Thus, learning and extracting the rules themselves becomes the key point to the rule-based information extraction. As for the method of statistics-based, its accuracy is generally low, but it has good portability to this extraction problem. Some statistics models have strong statistical theory basis and wholesome training algorithms such as HMM and CRFs and so on. However, statistics-based information extraction requires a large amount of labeled training data.

Currently, there are not many references about the personal attributes extraction and there is no more mature system to solve this problem. However, personal attributes extraction has a very close relation to the information extraction, and personal entities also belong to the category of the entity. So, to a certain extent, the entity relation extraction method can also be applied to personal attribute extraction. Ye [1] and some other researchers treated the personal attribute extraction as a specific application in the entity relationship extraction. They use the "Hownet" to acquire the trigger words which can describe the personal attributes, then change the relationship between trigger words and names into a classification problem. Their solution needs manual

Proceedings of the Third CIPS-SIGHAN Joint Conference on Chinese Language Processing, pages 114–119,
Wuhan, China, 20-21 October 2014

labeled data during classifier training and is under the help of semantic resource. Wang [2] and some other researchers put forward a relationship judgment algorithm which is based on the semantic similarity between the current tuples and the relationship set to filter and classify the relational tuples that are extracted according to the pattern, using Wikipedia as a knowledge database. This is under the foundation of extraction model of sentence groups such as blocks and named entity recognition marker. Wang [3] and others tried to use the method of knowledge engineering to extract personal attributes. They sum up some rules manually under the foundation of mass analysis about web texts and researches in natural language processing and then built a pattern repository to do the match. Yu [4] adopted the way of using trigger words and classifier to exact personal basic information, and carried out a character search engine based on the stored exaction information.

3 Task Descriptions

In this task, there are 25 predefined personal attributes to be extracted, including alternate_names, date_of_birth, age, country_of_birth, stateorprovince_of_birth, city_of_birth, date_of_death, country_of_death, stateorprovince_of_death, city_of_death, coutriea_of_residence, stateorprovince_of_residence, cities_of_residence, title, member_of, employee_of, religion, spouse, children, parents, siblings, other_family, charges, cause_of_death and schools_attended. The testing data are provided by a series of folders which are named after people whose attributes need to be extracted. In each folder, a XML document of Wikipedia and some unstructured Chinese texts about the person are included. Except for the actual attribute values, the extraction results should also contain the source documents that the values come from and their positions in the documents. For the attributes that are already located in the tags of "Facts" in the document of Wikipedia, we do not need to extract them repeatedly. For those attributes whose values are not unique, such as parents, children and the residence of cities, it is responsible for us to extract all probable attribute values.

4 Methods

Before the selection of methods to extract, we've analyzed the attributes to be extracted, the sample data and also the testing data provided by the conference carefully. Because we don't have enough data as the training data, and it requires quantities of work to collect and label the training data artificially, we gave up the extraction method based on statistics. While, through the observation of a large number of Wikipedia pages and personal information, we found that most of the attributes have a great similarity in the expression and discipline. Therefore, what we use is a method that combines the trigger words, dictionaries and rules together to achieve the task of personal attributes extraction.

4.1 Basic Framework

As shown in Figure 1, the architecture includes several parts:

1. The test corpus is provided by the conference. The corpus includes several XML files about persons whose personal attributes are to be extracted, containing the persons' Wikipedia records, and a number of unstructured documents relating to the persons.

2. Build attributes trigger words. The trigger words are aimed to narrow down the extraction scope, such as birth date and place of birth appears in sentences containing "出生" (birth) or "生于" (born).

3. Build attributes dictionary. The dictionary is in the view of the state, province, and school, the cause of death and some similar fixed attributes or some attributes which could be extracted by dictionary lookup directly.

4. Build attributes extraction rules. We sum up the general characteristics of the attributes from the corpus using the combination features of word segmentation, part-of-speech (POS) tagging, named entity recognition (NER) and sentence parsing. Then we formulate the rules of grammar corresponding to these characteristics respectively. As a result, we can use these rules in the process of personal attributes extraction respectively.

5. Extract the attributes information. Extract attributes from the input unstructured documents according to the rules and structure of the dictionary.

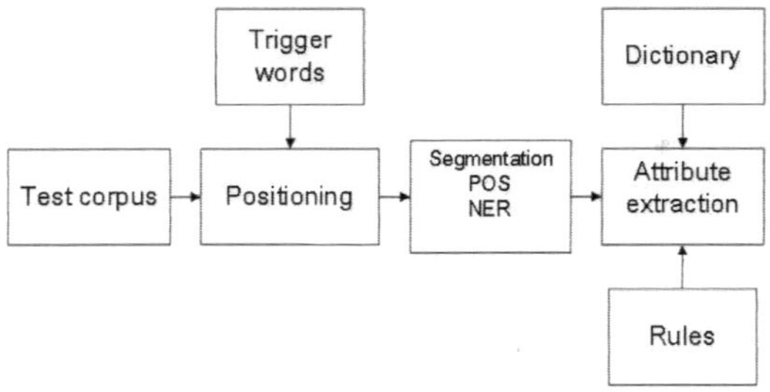

Figure 1 System Framework

4.2 Build Trigger word Table

So-called trigger word refers to a particular attribute extraction having the effect of location and identification that can activate the extraction task. When a sentence contains trigger words in a certain document, it could trigger the corresponding attribute extraction task in the sentence, so that the scope of the attribute extraction would be greatly narrowed. In this work, by analyzing the text characteristic and the description of the Chinese language style, we built trigger word sets for part of the corresponding attributes, while the attributes without trigger words require full range extraction in document. Trigger word table is shown in Table 1.

Table 1 Trigger word Table of Personal Attributes Extraction

Name of Attributes	Trigger word Set
alternate_names	本名（autonym），原名(primitive name），曾用名(used name)，中文名(Chinese name)，英文名(English name)，日文名(Japanese name)，全名(full name)，谥(posthumous title), 号称(known), 字(styled)，尊名(name being), etc.
date_of_birth, country_of_birth, city_of_birth, stateorprovince_of_birth	出生 (birth), 生于(born)
age	岁(age)
date_of_death, country_of_death, city_of_death, stateorprovince_of_death, cause_of_death	逝世 (die), 去世(pass away)，死于 (die of), 卒于(die in)，殉命于(to perish)，病死 (die in one's bed), 病故 (die of illness), and the year and date extracted from the record in the <date_of_death> tag.
schools_attended, countries_of_residence, citis_of_residence, statesorprovince_of_residence,	就读 (attend), 受教育(educated by)，选修(elective course)，学习(study), 毕业(graduate), 转读(transfer)，读书(read), 硕士(master)，博士 (PhD), 学士(bachelor)，本科(undergraduate), 迁居(move), 流亡 (exile), 移居(migrate)，定居(settle), 故居(hometown), 长大(grow up), 多年 (many years), 几年(several years), 居住(live)，任(appoint)，创作出(create)，从事(be occupied in)，工作(work)
title	担任(take charge of), 历任(successively held the posts of), 成为 (become), 任(appoint)，为(as), 当(work as), 封(confer), etc.
member_of, employee_of	进入 (enter into), 签约(sign a contrast), 打工 (work part-time)，任教(work as a teacher)，旗下(subordinate), 受聘(offered appointment)，晋升 (promote), 任命(nominate), 升(promote)，聘(employ)
religion	信奉 (believe in), 信仰(belief), 信 (believe)，徒(follower)
spouse	配偶(spouse)，妻(wife)，结婚 (marriage)，丈夫(husband)，完婚 (get married)，太太 (Mrs.), 夫人(madam)，遗孀(widow)，嫁，娶(take to wife), 结为伉俪(married couple)，奉子成婚(shotgun marriage), 王后(Queen), 皇后(King), etc.
parents	父亲(father), 母亲(mother), 其父 (one's father), 其母(one's mother)，庶母(concubine of one's father), 妈妈(Mama)，随父(following one's father)，随母(following one's mother), etc.
children	儿子(son), 女儿(daughter), 子女(children)，之子(one's son)，之女(one's daughter)，幼女(infantile daughter)，幼子(infantile son)，长子(eldest son), 长女(eldest daughter), 次子 (second son), 次女(second daughter), 二子(second son), 三子(third son), 四子(fourth son), etc.
siblings	哥哥(older brother)，弟弟(younger brother), 姐姐(older sister)，妹妹(younger sister), 长兄(eldest brother), 姊姊(sister)，大妹 (eldest sister), 小妹(youngest sister), 二哥(second elder brother)，兄弟(brother), etc.
other_family	祖父 (grandfather), 祖母(grandmother)，叔叔(uncle), 表兄(elder male cousin), 表姐(elder female cousin)，妹夫(brother-in-law)，同族兄弟(Cousins), 岳父(father-in-law), 侄 (nephew), 甥 (nephew), 舅 (mother's brother)，堂姐(elder female cousin), 堂兄 (elder male cousin), 内兄(brother-in-law), etc.
charges	Words containing "罪"(crime)

4.3 Build Attribute Dictionary

We built attribute dictionary aiming at national, provincial or state, city, school, etc. for those attributes, which can be extracted directly by dictionary lookup. Compared to the rules, dictionary extraction is more convenient and with higher accuracy. For part of attributes, we built 8 dictionaries referring to the country, school, religion etc., as shown in Table 2.

Table 2 Dictionary of Personal Attributes Extraction

Name of Attributes	Content of Dictionary
country_of_birth, country_of_death, countries_of_residence	The full names and abbreviations of all the countries
city_of_birth, city_of_death, citis_of_residence	The cities of all countries and the towns or areas of China
stateorprovince_of_birth, stateorprovince_of_death, statesorprovince_of_residence	The states or provinces of all countries
schools_attended	All schools and colleges throughout the world
religion	All religions
cause_of_death	Common cause of death, such as "自杀"(suicide), "枪决"(execute by shooting), etc
charges	Common crime, such as drug trafficking, debt, etc.
title	Words about job, rank, field position and ancient official position, and the title attribute from the sample data

4.4 Build Personal Attribute Rules

Rules are very important for the proposed personal attributes information extraction. Its quality directly decides the effect of information extraction. While we were studying the personal attributes, we found that the expression of same attributes have a lot of similarities. Based on the similarity, in combination with word segmentation, part-of-speech tagging, and named entity recognition, we built rules for each corresponding attribute. Rule sets are shown in Table 3.

Table 3 Rules of Personal Attributes Extraction

Name of Attributes	Rules
alternate_names	The words after the trigger words connected with punctuation marks; The recent word tagged by "NN" after the trigger words; The quoted words after the trigger words
date_of_birth	Generated in advance all the regular time format templates, and match the time format in the first sentence containing trigger words as the result
country_of_birth, city_of_birth, stateorprovince_of_birth	Match the corresponding dictionary in the first sentence containing the trigger words
age	extract numbers followed by the "岁", taking the maximum as a result; Add specific rules to extract, For the Chinese digital age, such as "六十岁"
date_of_death	Match time format in the sentence containing the trigger words as a result when the content of <date_of_death> tag is empty.
country_of_death, city_of_death, stateorprovince_of_death	Match the corresponding dictionary in the sentence containing the trigger words
cause_of_death	Match the corresponding dictionary in the sentences containing trigger words; Search for the string with a tag sequence of NN or NN + NN + VV or NN + NN or NN + VV or NN + VA after the "由于" or "因" whose tag is "P" with a distance less than five words until meeting punctuation.
schools_attended, countries_of_residence, citis_of_residence, statesorprovince_of_residence,	Match the corresponding dictionary in the sentence containing the trigger words
title	Match the title dictionary backward in the phrase containing trigger words or the character name; The recent word tagged by "NN" after the phrase with the structure of the trigger words or character name + "是"; match the title dictionary in all the sentences containing the character name when the query failed.
member_of, employee_of	The chunks tagged by "ORG" after named entity recognition in the sentences containing the

	trigger words or title attribute; Search for the recent chunk tagged by "NP" in phrase containing trigger words, bidirectionally; Mark the results containg " 会 ", " 军 ", " 队 " as member_of atrribute value, the rest as employee_of attribute values
religion	Match the religion dictionary in the sentences containing trigger words
spouse, parents, children, siblings	The chunks tagged by "PER" after named entity recognition in the sentences containing the trigger words, rejecting the character name
other_family	The chunks tagged by "PER" after named entity recognition in the sentences containing the trigger words, rejecting the character name or the name marked by other attributes.
charges	match the corresponding dictionary in sentences containing the character name; Search for the string with a tag sequence of VV or AD+VV before the trigger word. The string between the phrase and the trigger word is the value.

5 Experiments

This work is designed to extract person specific attributes from unstructured Chinese texts. The testing date contains 323 documents about 90 persons, including 233 documents to extract attributes and 90 documents from Wikipedia records. The organizer of Personal Attributes Extraction in Unstructured Chinese Text Subtask of The 3rd CIPS-SIGHAN Joint Conference on Chinese Language Processing (CLP-2014) takes the same evaluation metrics adopted in the slot filling of TAC KBP. Deails of the result is presented in [5].

Single attributes evaluation metric

$$Score_{single} = \frac{NumCorrect}{NumSingleSlot}$$

When NumCorrect is zero, we set NumCorrect to 1.0;

List attributes evaluation metric

$$ListSlotValue = \frac{({F_\beta}^2 + 1) * IP * IR}{{F_\beta}^2 * (IP + IR)}$$

$$F_\beta = 2 \; to \; weight \; precision \; over \; recall$$

$$IP = Instance \; precision$$

$$IR = Instance \; recall$$

$$Score_{list} = \frac{\sum ListSlotValue}{NumListSlots}$$

When both IP and IR are zero, we set ListSlotValue to 0.0;

Overall evaluation metric

$$SF_{value} = \frac{1}{2}(Score_{single} + Score_{list})$$

We use the average of single attributes evaluation score and list attributes evaluation score as the final evaluation score. In the evaluation, both the lenient evaluation and strict evaluation are performed. In the strict evaluation, all instance attributes are compared to the answers while in the lenient evaluation, the offsets of the string from the beginning word to the ending word are ignored. Table 4 and Table 5 give the results for lenient evaluation and strict evaluation, respectively. Note that there are 6 teams participated in this bakeoff, as shown in the first column of Table 4 and Table 5, in which our team is called CIST-BUPT.

Table 4 the Lenient Evaluation Results

Team	Single Score	List Score	SF_Value
CIST-BUPT(Ours)	0.562770563	0.163700429	0.363235496
ICTNET_002	0.350649351	0.204901063	0.277775207
WZ_v4	0.004329004	0.004293061	0.004311033
BLCU-yudong	0.428571429	0.188841894	0.308706661
Result-BUPT	0.121212121	0.021722095	0.071467108
CASIA_CUC_PAES	0.670995670	0.343781890	0.507388780

Table 5 the Strict Evaluation Results

Team	Single Score	List Score	SF_Value
CIST-BUPT(Ours)	0.549783550	0.154629430	0.352206490
ICTNET_002	0.350649351	0.197119695	0.273884523
WZ_v4	0.004329004	0.000653766	0.002491385
BLCU-yudong	0.411255411	0.173962498	0.292608955
Result-BUPT	0.060606061	0.01135351	0.035979785
CASIA_CUC_PAES	0.645021650	0.33398837	0.489505010

We can see that our method has achieved good results, ranking the second place in the six teams. The results fully show that the method based on the combination of trigger words, dictionary and rules is feasible to some extent, and the trigger words and rules we formulated have performed well.

But there are still some problems in our method. The list attributes evaluation score is far lower than the single attributes evaluation score, which shows that we possibly have missed a lot of instances. And when considering the offsets of the extracted string, both the single attribute and list attributes evaluation score declined. This indicates that there are some errors, for example, the attribute value is correct but the source or object is wrong. In future work, we need to develop special improved strategies to extract more accurate results.

6 Conclusions and Future Work

In this report, we proposed a method based on the combination of trigger words, dictionary and rules to extract person specific attributes from unstructured Chinese texts. The trigger words can narrow the scope of extraction and then they are combined with specific dictionary lookup and extraction rules to implement the extraction of 25 person specific attributes.

Given the limited time and the first try in this kind of bakeoff, our system still has some shortages to be improved. For example, in the case of "Missing Words", we can specify the rules or collect and tag data artificially in order to get more training data and then use the method of machine learning to extract person attributes. On the other hand, to improve the case of "Incorrect Words", we plan to increase the judgment of the subject in one sentence so that we can avoid the situation that the attributes we extract belong to other people. Otherwise, we can also try to make more specific rules for the place names which occurs in schools or organizations to reduce their effects to those related attributes about place.

We believe that if we do some improvements to our system as above, we can get a more accurate extraction result. And we are also looking forward to developing more formal and more relatively complete machine learning algorithms and rules to realize the extraction of person specific attributes in unstructured Chinese with less human labor in the loop.

Acknowledgements

This work was supported by the National Natural Science Foundation of China under Grant 61202247, 71231002, 61202248 and 61472046; EU FP7 IRSES MobileCloud Project (Grant No. 612212); the 111 Project of China under Grant B08004; Engineering Research Center of Information Networks, Ministry of Education; the Fundamental Research Funds for the Central Universities under Grant2013RC0304; the project of Beijing Institute of Science and Technology Information.

References

[1] Zheng Ye, Hongfei Lin, Sui Su, Jingjing Liu, Person Attribute Extracting Based on SVM, Journal of Computer Research and Development[J], 2007, 44:271-275

[2] Quanjian Wang, Fang Wang. Wikipedia Based Name and Resume Information Extraction[J]. Computer Applications and Software, 2011, 27(7):170-174.

[3] Ying Wang. Research on Web Information Extraction Applied to Chinese Name Search Engine. Lanzhou University. Thesis, 2006.

[4] Manquan Yu. Research on Knowledge Mining in Person Tracking. Institute of Computing Technology, Chinese Academy of Science. Dissertation, 2006.

[5] CLP 2014 Shared Task: Personal Attributes Extraction in Chinese Text. Evaluation Report for The 3rd CIPS-SIGHAN Joint Conference on Chinese Language Processing (CLP-2014), 2014.

An Introduction to BLCU Personal Attributes Extraction System

Dong YU, Cheng YU, Gongbo TANG, Qin QU, Chunhua LIU, Yue TIAN, Jing YI
College of Information Science, Beijing Language and Cultural University
Beijing 10083, China
yudong_blcu@126.com

Abstract

We describe our methods for share task of personal attributes extraction. We divide all 25 attributes into several categories and propose 4 kinds of pipelines to carry out value extraction. There are two stages in the process. The first stage uses CRF model or regular expression based extractor to produce initial answers. In the second stage, we propose two methods to filter out mistake answers: protagonist dependency relationship based filter and attribute keywords based filter.

1 Introduction

In this paper, we describe the BLCU-PAE system for CIPS-SIGHAN 2014 bakeoffs. The Personal Attributes Extraction (PAE) in Chinese Text Task is designed to extract person specific attributes, like date of birth and death, family relationships, education, title etc. from unstructured Chinese texts. The corresponding techniques play an important role in information extraction, event tracking, entity disambiguation and other related research areas.

In the task, the incomplete attributes of a target person are defined as Slots, i.e. the extracted attribute value need to be filled into these slots. There are 3 kinds of slots, name slots, value slots and string slots, in which only entity name, number/time and string can be filled in. Single-value slots have only one correct answer while list-value slots have a set of answers. There are totally 25 attributes need to be extracted, as shown in Table 1.

Slot filling task has been one of shared tasks in the TAC KBP workshop [Ji and Grishman, 2011] science 2009. In this area, earlier systems generally use one main pipeline that contains 3 stages: document retrieval, answer extraction, and answer combination. Supervised learning normally leads to a reasonably good performance. Both bootstrapping and rule based pattern matching with trigger words are used in [Li, et al., 2013]. Active learning techniques are also used in the task [Chen, et al, 2010]. UNED system introduces a graph structure to solve the problem [Garrido, et al., 2013]. CMUML uses distant supervision and CRF-based structured prediction for producing the final answers [Kisiel, et al., 2013]. Up to now, slot filling remains a very challenging task; most of the shortfall reflects inadequacies in the answer extraction stage.

Type	Attribute
Single slots	city_of _birth, city_of_death, country_of_birth, country_of_death, State_or_province_of_birth, State_or_province_of_death, date_of_birth, date_of_death, cause_of_death, age
List slots	alternative_name, children, cities_of_residence, countries_of_residence , parents, other_family, member_of, siblings, employee_of, spouses, school_attended, religion, charges, titles, state_or_province_of_residence

Table 1: List of all attributes

Our system uses a mixture framework consists of supervised learning and rule based extractor and human knowledge database. We divide 25 attributes into several groups. Each group uses a specific combination of methods for value extraction. Protagonist dependency relationship and key words of attribute are used to filter out suspicious values.

The rest of the paper is organized as follows. Section 2 gives an overview of our system. Section 3 describes models and methods used in the system in detail. Section 4 gives evaluation results and analysis.

Proceedings of the Third CIPS-SIGHAN Joint Conference on Chinese Language Processing, pages 120–125,
Wuhan, China, 20-21 October 2014

2 Overview

At a high level, our PAE system takes a document *d* as input, and produces a set of attributes, each of which contains a specific type *t* and a value *v*. The whole process makes use of a large count of annotated biography corpus collected from BaiduBaike[1] and Chinese Wikipedia[2]. Both supervised machine learning and human designed rules are used for attributes extraction, describes in subsection 2.1.

2.1 The framework

In order to explore various knowledge of person attribute, a large number of biography web pages are collected and divided into sentences. For each attribute, we select a certain number of sentences that contain attribute value, label the position of each value as training data. Meanwhile, attribute value context words are used as keywords for attribute extraction. Figure 1 is the overall framework of our system.

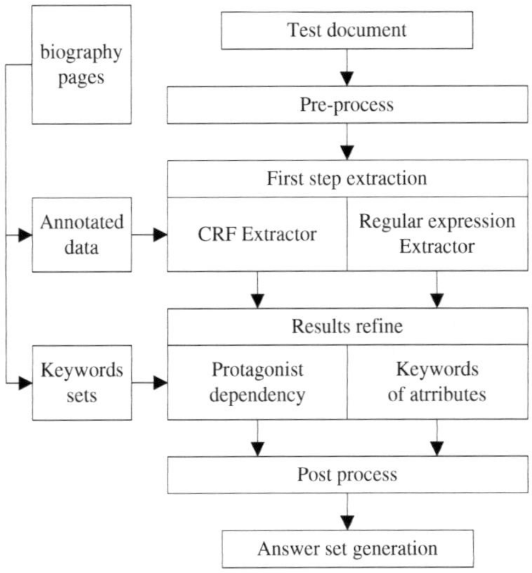

Figure 1: Framework of the system

As shown in Figure 1, the PAE process contains 4 stages:

- Pre-process stage,
- First step extraction,
- Results refine stage,
- Post-process stage.

In the pre-process stage, we divide a test document into sentences, and then carry out a NLP-pipeline on each sentence. Conversely, the post-process stage needs to combine all values extracted from these sentences and produce a final answer set. We will describe both stages in detail in Section 3.

In the first step of extraction, two kinds of extractors are proposed. The first one is CRF extractor. For an attribute, if its context features are obviously difference from others and it has a number of labeled sentences, then attribute extraction can be seen as a sequence labeling problem and CRF model can be used to solve it.

Otherwise, if two or more attributes have similar context, they will have similar features, so CRF cannot distinguish one from another. For example, attributes of *Data of birth* and *Date of death* often appear together in biographies. Data sparse is another obstacle of using CRF, as attribute of "*Religion*" only has dozens of samples. In this situation, regular expression is a better and more direct way for attribute extraction.

Both CRF and regular expression make mistakes during extraction. In our test, there are mainly two kinds of errors:

- Protagonist mismatch,
- Error values caused by models.

So results refine stage is required. In our system, dependency parser is used to filter out values that not related to the protagonist of test document. Keywords of attributes are collected and used to filter out error values. We will describe these methods in detail in section 3.

2.2 Categories of Attributes

The task needs to extract 25 attributes and some of them vary widely from others. Build a model for each attribute can be very consume. So we classify all attributes into several categories, and adopt different extraction pipelines. There are 4 kinds of extraction pipelines in our system. Attribute categories and their extraction pipeline are shown in Table 2.

We train CRF models for attributes related to name entities, such as places, organizations, names. Attributes of *city_of_birth*, *country_of_birth*, and *state_or_province_of_birth* are all place extraction problem, so we train a same CRF model for these attributes. So do place of death and residence.

For attributes that are considered unsuitable for CRF, we use rule based regular expression to extract answers in the first step extraction, including date of birth and death and religion.

For attributes that highly related to person, protagonist dependency between person and values can effectively find out error answers. For

[1] http://www.baike.baidu.com/
[2] http://zh.wikipedia.org

other attributes, for instance *titles*, *member_of*, *cause_of_death*. Other attributes use key words concluded from the training data to refine the answers.

Extraction pipelines	Attribute Categories
CRF only	alternate_names
CRF + protagonist dependency	age, cause_of_death, charges, employee_of, member_of, titles, places of death, places of birth, places of residence
Regular expression only	religion
Regular expression + keywords	date_of_birth, date_of_death, schools_attended, family relationships

Table 2: Attribute Categories

2.3 Resource and toolkits used

We collected more than 40k biographies pages from BaiduBaike and about 6k biographies pages from WikiPedia. The original webpage is very noisy, so we did not use all data for training but select good samples as training data.

We mainly used two toolkits for NLP pipeline, including Chinese word segmentation, POS tagging, NER and dependency parsing: SWJTU Yebol[3] Chinese word segmentation toolkit and LTP-Cloud[4][Che, et al., 2010]. The segmentation accuracy of Yebol can achieve 99.8% and it also used to label time string, place, person name etc. . LTP-Cloud is a cloud based Chinese analysis system that provides dependency parsing, POS tagging and semantic parsing services.

We use CRF++[5] toolkit to train CRF based extractor.

2.4 Data annotation

We annotate start and end of attribute values in sentence level according to the task guideline. Here is an example for *employee_of*: "08年7月4日离职【新浪】加入【盛大文学】，任CEO。" We annotate each category a data set individually. As we used rule-based methods for extraction, such as children, parents, religion, etc, we just summarized their samples and features from training data, and did not annotate them one by one. Finally, we annotate about 25K of positive examples and equal number of negative examples for CRF based extractors.

3 Methods and models

3.1 Pre-process

We adopt a NLP pipeline for each document. Workflow is shown in Figure 2.

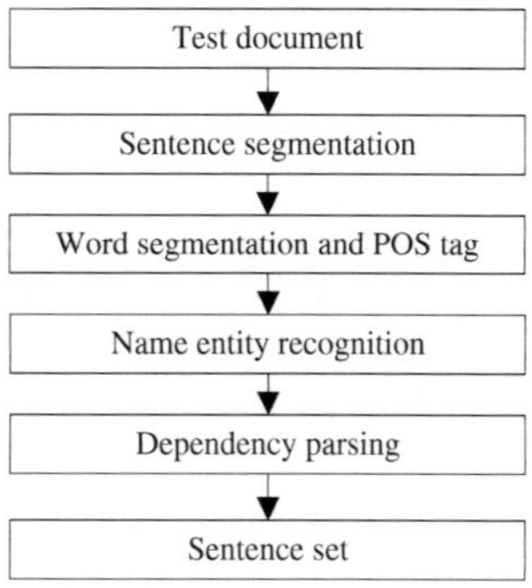

Figure 2: Workflow of pre-process

Pre-process stage is carried out on both train biographies and test documents. We use punctuation to split a document into sentences. Name entity recognition includes time string, person name, place and organization. Dependency parsing is used to find connections between any two words. Pre-process produces a set of sentences all related to document protagonist.

3.2 CRF models training

As mentioned in 2.2, we totally train 10 CRF models. For each model, we use corresponding set of annotated sentences as positive samples, where all values of specific attribute are labeled. Additionally, in order to enhance the model, we also select equal number of negative samples without the attribute. Both positive and negative samples are used for training CRF model.

We use general feature template during training process, mainly include context words and POS tags of context words. The number of training samples for each model is listed in Table 3.

At prediction time, sentences of test document are segmented into word, and tokenized into CRF format, and then the model can tag out all predicted values for the attribute.

[3] http://ics.swjtu.edu.cn/
[4] http://www.ltp-cloud.com/
[5] http://sourceforge.jp/projects/sfnet_crfpp/

Model	Positive Examples	Negative Examples
alternate_names	1230	692
age	513	464
places of birth	10717	1533
places of death	733	1216
places of residence	2194	705
cause_of_death	2122	184
charges	353	939
employee_of	1678	2383
member_of	2330	396
titles	2626	281

Table 3: The statistic of annotations

3.3 Protagonist dependency based filter

CRF based attribute extractor can effectively recognize the existence of attributes in a test sentence and can label out value positions. However, in PAE task, we only need to extract attributes belongs to the protagonist of a test document. For sentences that refers to more than one person, match extracted values with the protagonist can be very difficult. For example, in sentence “他的妹妹 Isobel 因肺炎去世，卡罗瑟斯与妻子 Helen 前往……”,“肺炎(pneumonia)” is not *Cause_of_death* of protagonist “卡罗瑟斯” but his sister, while CRF always recognize it as a value.

Dependence relationship can help filter out mismatch values. For a test sentence, dependency parsing can convert it into a tree, in which nodes are words. Relationship between any two words can be described by a connected path in the tree. The method is described as follows.

In our test, for each attribute value extracted by CRF or regular expression, we find its head verb and the closest person name in a same sub tree, if the person is protagonist, then we believe that the value is valid. Otherwise, we filter out the value. If test sentence does not have any person or reference, we keep all extracted results by default. Figure X shows an instance of the idea.

Sentence “何雨春，著名画家，1957 年出生于大连。” involves a *title* “画家” and a *place_of_birth* “大连” and a person “何雨春”. As shown in Figure 3, two values are dominated by the same verb “出生”, the person also in the same sub tree, so both values are available.

On the contrary, in the last instance, the value “肺炎” is dominated by verb “去世”, the closest person dominated by the same verb is “Isobel”, while protagonist “卡罗瑟斯” is dominated by verb “前往”, so the value is filtered out. As shown in Figure 4.

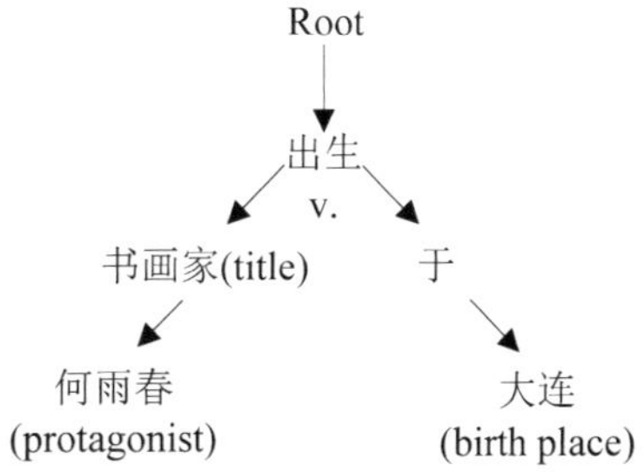

Figure 3: A positive example

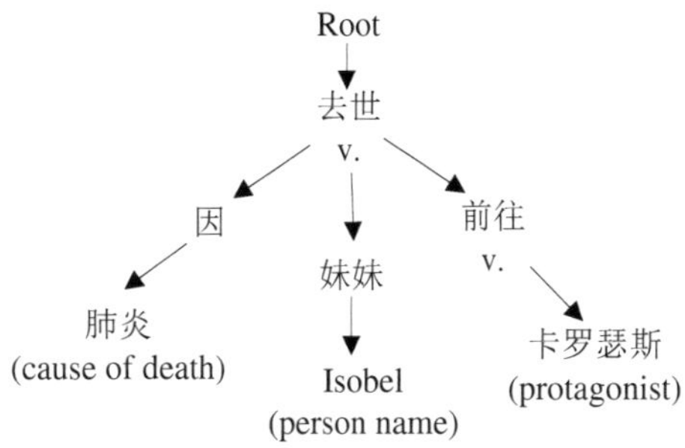

Figure 4: A negative example

In the third instance, “真德秀是南宋后期与魏了翁齐名的理学家。”, there are two persons “真德秀” and “魏了翁”, and a *title* “理学家”. Literally, 魏了翁 is closer to the title than 真德秀, but in dependency tree, 真德秀 and 理学家 are dominated by same verb “是” while 魏了翁 is dominated by verb “齐名”, so we think the value “理学家” refers to 真德秀.

3.4 Keywords based filter

Another type of mistakes in our system is caused by defect of models, for example, in “2005.11-2006.1 双流县中和镇人民政府工作，……”, the system incorrectly labels “2005.11” as *date_of_birth* in the first step. We find that contexts of this kind of error values are obviously different from right ones. So high frequency context words of attributes can help filter out error values.

The method firstly collects all context words of positive samples of a specific attribute, select a set of words with high frequency as keywords. At test time, we require that there is at least one keyword in context of extracted value. Otherwise, the extracted value will be abandoned.

Key words based filter can effectively improve accuracy of CRF model. However, it has influence on recall rate. In our system, we collect keywords and used for extracting 5 kinds of familial relationships, schools attended, alternate names, date of death and birth. Table 4 gives some of keywords we used in our system.

Attribute	Keywords
Schools_attended	毕业; 读; 学习; 培训; 肄业; 考 入; 深造; 获得; 学位
siblings	兄; 哥; 姐; 妹; 弟
spouse	妻; 老婆; 媳妇; 爱人; 未婚夫; 老公; 丈夫;
Date_of_death	逝; 牺牲; 卒; 身亡; 去世; 薨; 死; 辞世; 病故; 歿

Tabel 4: Examples of attribute keywords

3.5 Rule and knowledge based methods

Rule based extractor is designed by using regular expression. We use this method in the first step of extraction in *date_of_birth*, *date_of_death*, and *religion*. The first two have very similar contexts so we cannot use CRF to distinguish between them. For the last one, the number of training samples is too small to train a CRF model.

In addition to above methods, human knowledge is also involved in the system, including:

- Country-state/province database,
- Family relationship database,
- Religion database.

As mentioned in 2.2, we train 3 CRF models that can label out birth place, death place and residence place in a test document, regardless level of places. However the PAE task needs to recognize city, state/province and country of places in detail. So we collect a database that contains all countries and most of states/provinces, and divide extracted place sting into different levels, place that is not in database is regarded as city.

Similarly, all family relationships and all religions are also collected. Both databases are used for designing regular expressions and results refine to produce more accurate values.

3.6 Post-process and answer generation

The whole PAE process is done in sentence level and it produces a collect of labeled sentences, one sentence has only one kind of attribute.

In the post-process stage, we need to combine all extracted values together and compute offset of position for each value in original document to generate final XML format answer set. In which all values are written as a record that contain name of protagonist, original document file name, attribute name, attribute values and attribute value offset in the document.

4 Evaluation

4.1 Evaluation matrices

The PAE task takes the same evaluation metrics adopted in the slot filling of TAC KBP. For single attributes, system score is computed by (1), where we set *NumCorrect* to 1.0 when it is zero.

$$Score_{\text{single}} = \frac{NumCorrect}{NumSingleSlot} \quad (1)$$

$$Score_{\text{list}} = \frac{\sum ListSlotValue}{NumListSlots} \quad (2)$$

For list attributes, system score is computed by (2), in which *ListSlotValue* is defined by (3),

$$ListSlotValue = \frac{(F_\beta^2 + 1) * IP * IR}{F_\beta^2 * (IP + IR)} \quad (3)$$

Where F_β = 2 (to weight precision over recall), IP = instance precision and IR = instance recall . Also we set *ListSlotValue* to 0.0, when both IP and IR are zero. System performance is finally evaluated by (4), that is the average of single attributes evaluation score and list attributes evaluation score.

$$SF_{value} = \frac{1}{2}\left(Score_{\text{single}} + Score_{\text{list}}\right) \quad (4)$$

In the evaluation, both the lenient evaluation and strict evaluation are performed. In the strict evaluation, all instance attributes are compared to the answers while in the lenient evaluation, the offset *string_begin* and *string_end* are ignored.

4.2 Evaluation results

In evaluation, there are totally 90 test persons and 233 test documents. Table 5 shows the evaluation results of our system and the best performance system.

In general, there is still a big gap between our system and the best one. In our system, performances of lenient and strict results are similar. Single score is obviously better than list score, shows that multi-value attributes is more difficult to extract.

Evaluation	Single Score	List Score	SF Value
Lenient (best)	0.6710	0.3438	0.5074
Lenient (ours)	0.4286	0.1888	0.3087
Strict (best)	0.6450	0.3340	0.4895
Strict (ours)	0.4113	0.1739	0.2926

Table5: The evaluation results

4.3 Analysis

Our system still has a lot room for improvements. The first one is to make better use of context in phase level other than sentence level. In our own test, we get more than 0.7 IP score in sentence attributes extraction. However, when it comes to document level, relevance between sentences are more important. In this situation, anaphora resolution and entity link can help to improve the performance of system.

In our system, most of values are extracted based on supervised learning. It is a great challenge for data pre-process and annotation. Bootstrapping style methods can help mining more samples, and active learning framework can be a more effective method to obtain a higher knowledge coverage rate.

Acknowledgements

The research work is partially funded by the Natural Science Foundation of China (No. 61300081, 61170162), and the Fundamental Research Funds for the Central Universities in BLCU (No. 14YJ03005).

Reference

Heng Ji and Raslfph Grishman. 2011. Knowledge Base Population: Successful Approaches and Challenges. *Proc. 49th Annual Meeting Assn. Computational Linguistics.*

Yan Li, Yichang Zhang, Doyu Li, Xin Tong, Jianlong Wang, Naiche Zuo, Ying Wang, Weiran Xu, Guang Chen, Jun Guo. 2013. PRIS at Knowledge Base Population 2013. *Proc. TAC 2013 Workshop.*

Zheng Chen, Suzanne Tamang, Adam Lee, Xiang Li, Wen-Pin Lin, Matthew Snover, Javier Artiles, Marissa Passantino and Heng Ji. 2010. CUNYBLENDER TAC-KBP2010 Entity Linking and Slot Filling System Description. *Proc. TAC 2010 Workshop.*

Guillermo Garrido, Anselmo Peñas and Bernardo Cabaleiro. 2013. UNED Slot Filling and Temporal Slot Filling systems at TAC KBP 2013. System description. *Proc. TAC 2013 Workshop.*

Bryan Kisiel, Justin Betteridge, Matt Gardner, Jayant Krishnamurthy, Ndapa Nakashole, Mehdi Samadi, Partha Talukdar, Derry Wijaya, Tom Mitchell. 2013. CMUML System for KBP 2013 Slot Filling. *Proc. TAC 2013 Workshop.*

Wanxiang Che, Zhenghua Li, Ting Liu. LTP: A Chinese Language Technology Platform. *In Proceedings of the Coling 2010:Demonstrations.* 2010, pp13-16, Beijing, China.

Overview of SIGHAN 2014 Bake-off for Chinese Spelling Check

Liang-Chih Yu[1,2], Lung-Hao Lee[3,4], Yuen-Hsien Tseng[3], Hsin-Hsi Chen[4]
[1]Dept. of Information Management, Yuen-Ze University
[2]Innovation Center for Big Data and Digital Convergence, Yuen-Ze University
[3]Information Technology Center, National Taiwan Normal University
[4]Dept. of Computer Science and Information Engineering, National Taiwan University
lcyu@saturn.yzu.edu.tw, lhlee@ntnu.edu.tw,
samtseng@ntnu.edu.tw, hhchen@ntu.edu.tw

Abstract

This paper introduces a Chinese Spelling Check campaign organized for the SIGHAN 2014 bake-off, including task description, data preparation, performance metrics, and evaluation results based on essays written by Chinese as a foreign language learners. The hope is that such evaluations can produce more advanced Chinese spelling check techniques.

1 Introduction

Chinese spelling errors frequently arise from confusion between multiple Chinese characters which are phonologically and visually similar, but semantically distinct (Liu et al., 2011). The SIGHAN 2013 Chinese Spelling Check Bake-off was the first campaign to provide data sets as benchmarks for the objective performance evaluation of Chinese spelling checkers (Wu et al. 2013). The collected data set is publicly available at http://ir.itc.ntnu.edu.tw/lre/sighan7csc.htm. The competition resulted in the integration of effective NLP techniques in the development of Chinese spelling checkers. Language modeling was used to glean extra semantic clues and collect web resources together to identify and correct spelling errors (Chen et al., 2013). A hybrid model was proposed to combine language models and statistical machine translation for spelling error correction (Liu et al. 2013). A linear regression model was trained using phonological and orthographic similarities to correct misspelled characters (Chang et al. 2013). Web-based measures were adopted to score candidates for Chinese spelling error correction (Yu et al., 2013). A graph model was used to represent the sentence, using the single source shortest path algorithm for correcting spelling errors (Jia et al. 2013)

SIGHAN 2014 Bake-off, again features a Chinese Spelling Check task, providing an evaluation platform for the development and implementation of automatic Chinese spelling checkers. Given a passage composed of several sentences, the checker should identify all possible spelling errors, highlight their locations and suggest possible corrections. While previous tasks were based on essays written by native Chinese speakers, the current task is based on essays written by learners of Chinese as a Foreign Language (CFL), which should provide a greater challenge

The rest of this article is organized as follows. Section 2 provides an overview of the SIGHAN 2014 Bake-off Chinese Spelling Check task. Section 3 introduces the data sets used for evaluation. Section 4 proposes evaluation metrics. Section 5 compares results for the various contestants. Finally, we conclude this with findings and future research directions in Section 6.

2 Task Description

This task evaluates Chinese spelling checker performance based on Chinese text passages consisting of several sentences with and without spelling errors. The checker should identify incorrect characters in the passage and suggest corrections. Each character or punctuation mark occupies 1 spot for counting location. The input instance is given a unique passage number *PID*. If the sentence contains no spelling errors, the checker should return "PID, 0". If an input passage contains at least one spelling error, the output format is "PID [, location, correction]+", where the symbol "+" indicates there is one or more instance of the predicting element "[, location, correction]". "Location" and "correction"

Proceedings of the Third CIPS-SIGHAN Joint Conference on Chinese Language Processing, pages 126–132,
Wuhan, China, 20-21 October 2014

respectively denote the location of incorrect character and its correct version. Table 1 presents some examples. In Ex. 1, the 15th character "無" is wrong, and should be "舞". There are 3 wrong characters in Ex. 2, and correct characters "生," "直," and "關" should be used in locations 3, 26, and 35, respectively. Location "0" denotes that there is no spelling error in Ex. 3

Example 1	
Input	(pid= A2-1051-1) 後天是小明的生日，我要開一個無會。
Output	A2-1051-1, 15, 舞
Example 2	
Input	(pid=B1-0201-1) 我一身中的貴人就是我姨媽，從我回來台灣的時候，她一只都很照顧我，也很觀心我。
Output	B1-0201-1, 3, 生, 26, 直, 35, 關
Example 3	
Input	(pid=C1-1849-1) 聯合國報告指出，至二零五零年，全球人口將達九十二億，新增人口幾乎全來自開發中國家。
Output	C1-1849-1, 0

Table 1. Some examples used in our task

3 Data Preparation

The learner corpus used in our task was collected from the essay section of the computer-based Test of Chinese as a Foreign Language (TOCFL), administered in Taiwan. The writing test is designed according to the six proficiency levels of the Common European Framework of Reference (CEFR). A total of 1714 essays were typed online (i.e., not hand-written), and then spelling errors were manually annotated by trained native Chinese speakers who also provided corrections corresponding to each error. The essays were then split into three sets as follows

- Training Set

This set included 1,301 selected essays with a total of 5,284 spelling errors. Each essay is represented in SGML format shown in Fig. 1. The title attribute is used to describe the essay topic. Each passage is composed of several sentences, and each passage contains at least one spelling error, and the data indicates both the error's location and corresponding correction. All essays in this set are used to train the developed spelling checker.

```
<ESSAY title= "寫給即將初次見面的筆友的一封信">
<TEXT>
<PASSAGE id="B1-0112-1">那一天我會穿牛仔褲和紅色的外套；頭會帶著藍色的帽子。如果你找不到我，可以打我的手機。
</PASSAGE>
<PASSAGE id="B1-0112-2">我記得你說你想試試看越南菜是有什麼味覺，午餐我會帶你去吃。我也想試試看那一家的越南菜；網路站說很多人喜歡那一家餐廳。</PASSAGE>
</TEXT>
<MISTAKE id="B1-0112-1" location="19">
<WRONG>帶著</WRONG>
<CORRECTION>戴著</CORRECTION>
</MISTAKE>
<MISTAKE id="B1-0112-2" location="46">
<WRONG>網路站</WRONG>
<CORRECTION>網路上</CORRECTION>
</MISTAKE>
</ESSAY>
```

Figure 1. An essay represented in SGML format

- Dryrun Set

A total of 20 passages were given to participants to familiarize themselves with the final testing process. Each participant can submit several runs generated using different models with different parameter settings. In addition to make sure the submitted results can be correctly evaluated, participants can fine-tune their developed models in the dryrun phase. The purpose of dryrun is output format validation only, and no dryrun outcomes were considered in the official evaluation

- Test Set

Table 2 shows a statistical summary of the prepared test set. The set consists of 1,062 testing passages, each with an average of 50 characters. Half of these passages contained no spelling errors, while the other half included at least one spelling error each for a total of 792 spelling errors used to evaluate the spelling checkers. The evaluation was conducted as an open test. In addition to the data sets provided, registered research teams were allowed to employ any linguistic and computational resources to detect and correct spelling errors. Besides, passages written by CFL learners may suffer from grammatical errors, missing or redundant words, poor word selection, or word ordering problems. The task in question focuses exclusively on spelling error correction.

Test Set	Stat.
Number of essays	413
Number of passages	1,062
Number of characters	53,114
Average number of characters in all passages	50.01
Number of passages *with* errors	531
Total number of characters in the passages *with* errors	26,609
Number of erroneous characters	792
Average number of characters in passages *with* errors	50.11
Average number of spelling errors in passages *with* errors	1.49
Number of passages *without* errors	531
Total number of characters in the passages *without* errors	26,505
Average number of characters in passages *without* errors	49.92

Table 2. Descriptive statistics of the test set.

4 Performance Metrics

Table 3 shows the confusion matrix used for performance evaluation. In the matrix, TP (True Positive) is the number of passages with spelling errors that are correctly identified by the spelling checker; FP (False Positive) is the number of passages in which non-existent errors are identified; TN (True Negative) is the number of passages without spelling errors which are correctly identified as such; FN (False Negative) is the number of passages with spelling errors for which no errors are detected.

Correctness is determined at two levels. (1) Detection level: all locations of incorrect characters in a given passage should be completely identical with the gold standard. (2) Correction level: all locations and corresponding corrections of incorrect characters should be completely identical with the gold standard. The following metrics are measured at both levels with the help of the confusion matrix.

- False Positive Rate (FPR) = FP / (FP+TN)
- Accuracy = (TP+TN) / (TP+FP+TN+FN)
- Precision = TP / (TP+FP)
- Recall = TP / (TP+FN)
- F1= 2 *Precision*Recall/(Precision+Recall)

Confusion Matrix		System Result	
		Positive (Erroneous)	Negative (Correct)
Gold Standard	Positive	**TP**	**FN**
	Negative	**FP**	**TN**

Table 3. Confusion matrix for evaluation.

Take for example, 5 testing inputs with gold standards shown as "C1-1765-2, 0", "C1-1833-2, 3, 再, 47, 反", "B1-0176-3, 15, 棄, 22, 身", "B1-0206-5, 0", and "B1-2707-4, 48, 現". The system may output the result shown as "C1-1765-2, 0", "C1-1833-2, 3, 再, 47, 返", "B1-0176-3, 7, 氣, 22, 身, 35, 德", "B1-0206-5, 13, 的", and "B1-2707-4, 48, 現". The evaluation tool will yield the following performance.

- False Positive Rate (FPR) = 0.5 (=1/2) Notes: {"B1-0206-5, 13, 的"}/{"C1-1765-2, 0", "B1-0206-5, 0"}
- Detection-level
  - Acc.=0.6 (=3/5). Notes: {"C1-1765-2, 0", "C1-1833-2, 3, 47", "B1-2707-4, 48"} / {"C1-1765-2, 0", "C1-1833-2, 3, 47", "B1-0176-3, 15, 22", "B1-0206-5, 0", "B1-2707-4, 48"}
  - Pre.= 0.5 (=2/4). Notes: {"C1-1833-2, 3, 47", "B1-2707-4, 48"} / {"C1-1833-2, 3, 47", "B1-0176-3, 7, 22, 35", "B1-0206-5, 13", "B1-2707-4, 48"}
  - Rec.= 0.67 (=2/3). Notes: {"C1-1833-2, 3, 47", "B1-2707-4, 48"} / {"C1-1833-2, 3, 47", "B1-0176-3, 15, 22", "B1-2707-4, 48"}
  - F1=0.57 (=2*0.5*0.67/(0.5+0.67))

- Correction-level
  - Acc.=0.4 (=2/5). Notes: {"C1-1765-2, 0", "B1-2707-4, 48, 現"} / {"C1-1765-2, 0", "C1-1833-2, 3, 再, 47, 反", "B1-0176-3, 15, 棄, 22, 身", "B1-0206-5, 0", "B1-2707-4, 48, 現"}
  - Pre.= 0.25 (=1/4). Notes: { "B1-2707-4, 48, 現"} / {"C1-1833-2, 3, 再, 47, 返", "B1-0176-3, 7, 氣, 22, 身, 35, 德", "B1-0206-5, 13, 的", and "B1-2707-4, 48, 現"}
  - Rec.= 0.33 (=1/3). Notes: {"B1-2707-4, 48, 現"} / {"C1-1833-2, 3, 再, 47, 反", "B1-0176-3, 15, 棄, 22, 身", "B1-2707-4, 48, 現"}
  - F1=0.28 (=2*0.25*0.33/(0.25+0.33))

5 Evaluation Results

Table 4 summarizes the submission statistics for 19 participant teams including 10 from universities and research institutions in China (BIT, CAS, CAU, LYFYU, NJUPT, PKU, SCAU, SJTU, SUDA, and ZJOU), 8 from Taiwan (ITRI, KUAS, NCTU & NTUT, NCYU, NTHU, NTOU, SinicaCKIP, and SinicaSLMP) and one private firm (Lingage). Among 19 registered teams, 13 teams submitted their testing results. In formal testing phase, each participant can submit at most three runs that adopt different models or parameter settings. In total, we had received 34 runs.

Table 5 summarizes the participants' developed approaches and the usage of linguistic resources for this bake-off evaluation. Among 13 teams that participated the official testing, KUAS and PKU did not submit their reports of developed models. We can observe that most of participants adopt statistical approaches such as n-gram model, language model, and machine-learning model. In addition to the Bakeoff 2013 CSC Datasets, some linguistic resources are used popularly for this bake-off evaluation such as Sinica Corpus, Web as Corpus, Google Web 1T N-gram, and Chinese Gigaword Corpus.

Participant (Ordered by abbreviations of names)	**#Runs**
Beijing Institute of Technology (**BIT**)	2
Chinese Academy of Sciences (**CAS**)	2
China Agriculture University (**CAU**)	0
Industrial Technology Research Institute (**ITRI**)	0
National Kaohsiung University of Applied Sciences (**KUAS**)	3
Lingage Inc. (**Lingage**)	0
Luoyang Foreign Language University (**LYFYU**)	0
National Chiao Tung University & National Taipei University of Technology (**NCTU & NTUT**)	2
National Chiayi University (**NCYU**)	3
Nanjing University of Posts and Telecommunications (**NJUPT**)	3
National Tsing Hua University (**NTHU**)	3
National Taiwan Ocean University (**NTOU**)	2
Peking University (**PKU**)	3
South China Agriculture University (**SCAU**)	3
Chinese Knowledge and Information Processing Group, IIS, Academia Sinica (**SinicaCKIP**)	3
Speech, Language and Music Processing Lab, IIS, Academia Sinica (**SinicaSLMP**)	0
Shanghai Jiao Tong University (**SJTU**)	3
Soochow University (**SUDA**)	2
Zhejiang Ocean University (**ZJOU**)	0
Total	**34**

Table 4. Submission statistics for all participants

Participant	Approach	Linguistic Resources
BIT	• N-gram Model • Heuristic Rules • Layer-Based Chinese Parsing	• Bakeoff 2013 CSC Datasets • Chinese Penn Treebank • HIT-CIR TongyiciCilin (Extended) • OpenCC • Sinica Corpus • Tsai's list of Chinese Words
CAS	• Decision-Making Model	• Bakeoff 2013 CSC Datasets, • Web as Corpus
NCTU & NTUT	• CRF-based Word Segmentation • Part-of-Speech Tagger • Tri-gram Language Model	• Chinese Gigaword Corpus • Chinese Information Retrieval Benchmark • Sinica Corpus • Taiwan Panorama Magazine • Wikipedia (zh-tw version)
NCYU	• Rule Induction	• Bakeoff 2013 CSC Datasets • E-HowNet
NJUPT	• 2-Chars & 3-Chars Model • CRF Model	• Bakeoff 2013 CSC Datasets • Web as Corpus
NTHU	• Noisy Channel Model	• Bakeoff 2013 CSC Datasets • Google Web 1T N-gram • Sinica Corpus
NTOU	• N-gram Model • Language Model • Rule-based Classifier • SVM-based Classifier	• Bakeoff 2013 CSC Datasets • Sinica Corpus
SCAU	• N-gram Model • Language Model	• Web as Corpus
SinicaCKIP	• Error Template Rule • Tri-gram Language Model	• Bakeoff 2013 CSC Datasets • Google Web 1T N-gram
SJTU	• Graph Model • CRF Model • Rule-Based System	• Bakeoff 2013 CSC Datasets • OpenCC • Sinica Corpus • Sogou Chinese Dictionary
SUDA	• 5-gram Language Model	• Chinese Gigaword Corpus

Table 5. A summary of participants' developed systems

Table 6 shows the task testing results. In addition to accurate error detection and correction, another key performance criteria is reducing the rate of false positives, *i.e.*, the mistaken identification of errors where none exist. The research teams, KUAS, NCTU&NTUT, NCYU and SUDA, achieved very low false positive rates, *i.e.*, less than 0.05.

Detection-level evaluations are designed to identify spelling errors and highlight their locations in the input passages. Accuracy is a key performance criterion, but accuracy can be affected by the distribution of testing instances. A neutral baseline can be easily achieved by always reporting all testing errors are correct without errors. According to the test data distribution, the baseline system can achieve an accuracy level of 0.5. Some systems (*i.e.*, CAS, KUAS, and NCYU) achieved promising results exceeding 0.6. Each participating team was allowed submit up to three iterative runs based on the same input, and several teams sent different runs aimed at optimizing either recall or precision rates. We thus used the F1 score to reflect the tradeoff between precision and recall. In the testing results, KUAS provided the best error detection results, providing a high F1 score of 0.633.

For correction-level evaluations, the systems need to locate errors in the passages and indicate the corresponding correct characters. The correction accuracy provided by the KUAS submission (0.7081) significantly outperformed the other teams. However, in terms of correction precision, the spelling checker developed by KUAS and

NCYU outperforms the others at 0.8. Most systems were unable to effectively correct spelling errors, with the better systems (CAS, and KUAS) achieving a correction recall rate of slightly above 0.3. The system developed by KUAS provided the highest F1 score of 0.6125 for spelling error correction. It is difficult to correct all spelling errors found in the input passages, since some sentences contain multiple errors and only correcting some of them are regarded as a wrong case. In summary, none of the submitted systems provided superior performance in all metrics, though those submitted by KUAS, NCYU, and CAS provided best overall performance.

Submission	FPR	Detection-Level				Correction-Level			
		Acc.	Pre.	Rec.	F1	Acc.	Pre.	Rec.	F1
BIT-Run1	0.3352	0.4313	0.371	0.1977	0.258	0.4115	0.3206	0.1582	0.2119
BIT-Run2	0.3277	0.4482	0.4061	0.2241	0.2888	0.4303	0.365	0.1883	0.2484
CAS-Run1	0.1525	0.6149	0.7148	0.3823	0.4982	0.5829	0.676	0.3183	0.4328
CAS-Run2	0.1563	0.613	0.7098	0.3823	0.4969	0.581	0.6706	0.3183	0.4317
KUAS-Run1	0.1073	0.6008	0.7421	0.3089	0.4362	0.5951	0.7349	0.2976	0.4236
KUAS-Run2	0.0452	0.7194	0.9146	0.484	0.633	0.7081	0.9108	0.4614	0.6125
KUAS-Run3	0.0452	0.6525	0.8857	0.3503	0.502	0.6488	0.8835	0.3427	0.4939
NCTU&NTUT-Run1	0.0377	0.5132	0.6296	0.064	0.1162	0.5094	0.6	0.0565	0.1033
NCTU&NTUT-Run2	0.0998	0.5028	0.5138	0.1055	0.175	0.4925	0.4592	0.0847	0.1431
NCYU-Run1	0.1827	0.4831	0.4489	0.1488	0.2235	0.467	0.3899	0.1168	0.1797
NCYU-Run2	0.0414	0.6008	0.8543	0.2429	0.3783	0.5885	0.8406	0.2185	0.3468
NCYU-Run3	0.0414	0.5913	0.844	0.2241	0.3542	0.5791	0.8281	0.1996	0.3217
NJUPT-Run1	0.3898	0.403	0.3344	0.1959	0.247	0.3964	0.3191	0.1827	0.2323
NJUPT-Run2	0.6026	0.275	0.202	0.1525	0.1738	0.258	0.1645	0.1186	0.1379
NJUPT-Run3	0.5593	0.2853	0.1885	0.1299	0.1538	0.2665	0.1416	0.0923	0.1117
NTHU-Run1	0.0829	0.5235	0.6106	0.1299	0.2143	0.5113	0.56	0.1055	0.1775
NTHU-Run2	0.1507	0.5047	0.5152	0.1601	0.2443	0.484	0.4406	0.1186	0.1869
NTHU-Run3	0.3691	0.4228	0.3677	0.2147	0.2711	0.3823	0.2659	0.1337	0.1779
NTOU-Run1	0.258	0.4652	0.4219	0.1883	0.2604	0.4557	0.3965	0.1695	0.2375
NTOU-Run2	0.9925	0.1045	0.1688	0.2015	0.1837	0.0678	0.1143	0.1281	0.1208
PKU-Run1	0.9454	0.0367	0.0195	0.0188	0.0192	0.0348	0.0157	0.0151	0.0154
PKU-Run2	0.1168	0.4915	0.4609	0.0998	0.1641	0.4783	0.3861	0.0734	0.1234
PKU-Run3	0.4087	0.3616	0.2439	0.1318	0.1711	0.3418	0.1842	0.0923	0.123
SCAU-Run1	0.2034	0.4821	0.4518	0.1676	0.2445	0.4774	0.4375	0.1582	0.2324
SCAU-Run2	0.6441	0.275	0.2315	0.194	0.2111	0.2627	0.2083	0.1695	0.1869
SCAU-Run3	0.5009	0.3522	0.2907	0.2053	0.2406	0.3427	0.2712	0.1864	0.221
SinicaCKIP-Run1	0.1149	0.5169	0.5643	0.1488	0.2355	0.516	0.5612	0.1469	0.2328
SinicaCKIP-Run2	0.1827	0.564	0.6298	0.3107	0.4161	0.5395	0.589	0.2618	0.3625
SinicaCKIP-Run3	0.2655	0.5367	0.5607	0.339	0.4225	0.5104	0.5188	0.2863	0.3689
SJTU-Run1	0.5951	0.3117	0.2685	0.2185	0.2409	0.2938	0.2349	0.1827	0.2055
SJTU-Run2	0.2279	0.5471	0.5856	0.322	0.4156	0.5377	0.5709	0.3032	0.3961
SJTU-Run3	0.1921	0.5367	0.5802	0.2655	0.3643	0.5311	0.5696	0.2542	0.3516
SUDA-Run1	0.2524	0.4539	0.3881	0.1601	0.2267	0.4426	0.3527	0.1375	0.1978
SUDA-Run2	0.032	0.5292	0.7385	0.0904	0.1611	0.5235	0.7119	0.0791	0.1424

Table 6. Testing results of our Chinese spelling check task.

6 Conclusions and Future Work

This paper provides an overview of SIGHAN 2014 Bake-off Chinese spelling check, including task design, data preparation, evaluation metrics, and performance evaluation results. The task also encourages the proposal of unorthodox and innovative approaches which could lead to a breakthrough. Regardless of actual performance, all submissions contribute to the common effort to produce an effective Chinese spell checker, and the individual reports in the Bake-off proceedings provide useful insight into Chinese language processing.

We hope the data sets collected for this Bake-off can facilitate and expedite the development of effective Chinese spelling checkers. All data sets with gold standards and evaluation tool are publicly available for research purposes at http://ir.itc.ntnu.edu.tw/lre/clp14csc.htm.

Based on the results of this Bake-off, we plan to build new language resources to improve existing and develop new techniques for computer-aided Chinese language learning. In addition, new data sets obtained from CFL learners will be investigated for the future enrichment of this research topic.

Acknowledgments

Associate research fellow Dr. Li-Ping Chang, the Vice Director of Mandarin Training Center in National Taiwan Normal University (NTNU), is appreciated for supporting the NTNU learner corpus used in our evaluation. We would like to thank Kuei-Ching Lee for developing the evaluation tool. Finally, we thank all the participants for taking part in our task.

This research was partially support by Ministry of Science and Technology, Taiwan, under the grant MOST 102-2221-E-002-103-MY3, MOST 102-2221-E-155-029-MY3, and MOST 103-2221-E-003-013-MY3, and the "Aim for the Top University Project" of National Taiwan Normal University, sponsored by the Ministry of Education, Taiwan.

Reference

Tao-Hsing Chang, Hsueh-Chih Chen, Yuen-Hsien Tseng, and Jian-Liang Zheng. 2013. Automatic detection and correction for Chinese misspelled words using phonological and orthographic similarities. *Proceedings of the 7th SIGHAN Workshop on Chinese Language Processing (SIGHAN-13)*, pages 97-101.

Kuan-Yu Chen, Hung-Shin Lee, Chung-Han Lee, Hsin-Min Wang, and Hsin-Hsi Chen. 2013. A study of language modeling for Chinese spelling check. *Proceedings of the 7th SIGHAN Workshop on Chinese Language Processing (SIGHAN-13)*, pages 79-83.

Zongye Jia, Peilu Wang, and Hai Zhao. 2013. Graph model for Chinese spelling checking. *Proceedings of the 7th SIGHAN Workshop on Chinese Language Processing (SIGHAN-13)*, pages 88-92.

Xiaodong Liu, Fei Cheng, Yanyan Luo, Kevin Duh, and Yuji Matsumoto. 2013. A hybrid Chinese spelling correction using language and statistical machine translation with reranking. *Proceedings of the 7th SIGHAN Workshop on Chinese Language Processing (SIGHAN-13)*, pages 54-58.

Chao-Lin Liu, Min-Hua Lai, Kan-Wen Tien, Yi-Hsuan Chuang, Shih-Hung Wu, and Chia-Ying Lee. 2011. Visually and phonologically similar characters in incorrect Chinese words: Analyses, identification, and applications. *ACM Transaction on Asian Language Information Processing*, 10(2), Article 10, 39 pages.

Shih-Hung Wu, Chao-Lin Liu, and Lung-Hao Lee. 2013. Chinese spelling check evaluation at SIGHAN bake-off 2013. *Proceedings of the 7th SIGHAN Workshop on Chinese Language Processing (SIGHAN-13)*, pages 35-42.

Liang-Chih Yu, Chao-Hong Liu, and Chung-Hsien Wu. 2013. Candidate scoring using web-based measure for Chinese spelling error correction. *Proceedings of the 7th SIGHAN Workshop on Chinese Language Processing (SIGHAN-13)*, pages 108-112.

Extended HMM and Ranking models for Chinese Spelling Correction

Jinhua Xiong, Qiao Zhao, Jianpeng Hou,
Qianbo Wang, Yuanzhuo Wang and Xueqi Cheng
CAS Key Laboratory of Network Data Science and Technology
Institute of Computing Technology, Chinese Academy of Sciences
University of Chinese Academy of Sciences
xjh@ic.ac.cn, zhangqiao@software.ict.ac.cn

Abstract

Spelling correction has been studied for many decades, which can be classified into two categories: (1) regular text spelling correction, (2) query spelling correction. Although the two tasks share many common techniques, they have different concerns. This paper presents our work on the CLP-2014 bake-off. The task focuses on spelling checking on foreigner Chinese essays. Compared to online search query spelling checking task, more complicated techniques can be applied for better performance. Therefore, we proposed a unified framework for Chinese essays spelling correction based on extended HMM and ranker-based models, together with a rule-based model for further polishing. Our system showed better performance on the test dataset.

1 Introduction

The number of people learning Chinese as a Foreign Language (CFL) is booming in recent decades, and the number is expected to become even larger for the years to come[1]. Therefore spelling correction tool to support such learners to correct and polish their essays becomes very valuable. Spelling correction has been studied for many years on regular text and web search query. Although the two tasks share many common techniques, they have different concerns. Compared to web search query spelling correction which normally need to give corrections instantly, complicated techniques can be applied to spelling correction on essays, in order to improve the performance. Spelling correction on Chinese essays of CFL learners faces the following challenges:

(1) There is no word boundary between Chinese word, which may result in the error on splitting, and the error may accumulate.

(2) The number of error type is more than other case, because CFL learners are prone to different kinds of error which we can not imagine as a native speaker. Meanwhile, more errors can be caused by various Chinese input methods. As illustrated in Table 1, some errors can be found only in the essays of CFL learners, e.g. the 3rd and the last errors.

Error Types	Misspelled	Corrections
Homophone	聯合國公布	聯合國公佈
Near-homophone	好碼差不多一樣	號碼差不多一樣
Similar-shape	列如：家庭會變冷漠	例如：家庭會變冷漠
Others errors	每個禮拜1、3、5	每個禮拜一、三、五
	受了都少苦	受了多少苦

Table 1. Examples of spelling error

(3) Chinese language is continuously evolving, for example, traditional Chinese and simple Chinese may have different choices for the same word. In some cases, it is very difficult to distinguish them. Therefore, online high quality corpus is needed for decision-making.

To address the above challenges, we present a unified framework, named HANSpeller, to combine different methods for Chinese essays spelling detecting and correction. The contribu-

[1] http://www.cipsc.org.cn/clp2014/webpage/en/four_bakeoffs/Bakeoff2014cfp_ChtSpellingCheck_en.htm

Proceedings of the Third CIPS-SIGHAN Joint Conference on Chinese Language Processing, pages 133–138,
Wuhan, China, 20-21 October 2014

tion of our approach is as follows: (1) A HMM-based approach is used to segment sentences and generate candidates for sentences spelling correction. (2) Under this framework, all kinds of error types can be easily integrated for candidates generating. We collected some error types which only may be found in CFL learner essays, and add them into candidates generating process. And then ranking-based approach is used for choosing candidates for correction. (3) In order to address the evolving feature of Chinese, we not only collect high quality Taiwan web pages and also use search engine results to help decision-making on candidates.

The rest of the paper is organized as follow. In Section 2, we introduce related work on spelling checking. Then our unified framework approach is discussed in detail in Section 3. Section 4 presents the detailed experiment on the task. Section 5 concludes the paper and discusses future work.

2 Related work

Chinese essays spelling correction as a special kind of spelling correction research effort has been promoted by efforts such as the SIGHAN bake-offs (Wu et al., 2013).

Spelling correction was first proposed for English (Peterson, 1980). And it can be mainly divided into single word and context-sensitive spelling correction technology.

For the single word spelling error, it commonly uses dictionary-based method. It matches the original word with all the words in dictionaries to determine whether the word has spelling errors.

For the context-sensitive spelling errors, there are two major kinds of processing methods: Rule-based methods and Statistics-based methods. Rule-based methods use some rules generated fromrelevant grammars, the collocation of words, syntactic knowledge, etc, for spelling correction. Mangu and Bill (1997) proposed a transition-based learning method for spelling correction. Their methods generated three types of rules from training data, which constructs a high performance and concise system for English. A statistics-based method first finds related candidates, and then ranks the candidates based on the statistical model. Atwell and Elliott (1987) used n-gram and part-of-speech language models for spelling correction. Cucerzan and Brill (2004) presented an iterative process for query spelling check, using a query log and trust dictionary. And the noisy channel mode is used to select the best correction. Ahmad and Kondrak (2005) also learned a spelling error model from search query logs to improve the quality of query spelling check. Li et al. (2006) applied distributional similarity based models for query spelling correction. Gao et al. (2010) presented a large scale ranker-based system for search query spelling correction, the ranker uses web scale language models and many kinds of features for better performance, including: surface-form similarity, phonetic-form similarity, entity, dictionary, and frequency features. Microsoft (2010) provides Microsoft web n-gram services. Google (2010) has developed a Java API for Google spelling check service.

As for Chinese spelling correction, an early work was by (Chang, 1995), which used a character dictionary of similar shape, pronunciation, meaning, and input-method-code to deal with the spelling correction task. The system replaced each character in the sentence with the similar character in dictionary and calculated the probability of all modified sentences based on language model.

Zhang et al. (2000) introduced a method that can handle not only Chinese character substitution, but also insertion and deletion errors. They distinguished the way of matching between the Chinese and English, thus largely improved the performance over the work of (Chang 1995).

Huang et al. (2007) used a word segmentation tool (CKIP) to generate correction candidates, and then to detect Chinese spelling errors.

Hung et al. (2008) introduced a method which used the manually edited error templates to correct errors.

Zheng et al. (2011) found the fact that when people typed Chinese Pinyins, there are several wrong types. Then they introduced a method based on a generative model and the typed wrong types to correct spelling errors.

Liu et al. (2011) pointed out visually and phonologically similar characters are major factors for errors in Chinese text. And by defining appropriate similarity measures that consider extended Cangjie codes, visually similar characters can be quickly identified.

Note that all spelling correction methods require lexicons and/or language corpora. And Chinese essays spelling correction has some different concerns with query spelling correction. In our approach, we adopt the method based on statistics combining with lexicon and rule-based methods.

3 The Unified Framework for Chinese Spelling Correction

In this section we present a unified framework, named HANSpeller, for Chinese spelling correction based on extended HMM and ranking models. The major idea of our approach is to model the spelling correction process as a ranking and decision-making problem. Generally speaking, our approach has four major steps: Firstly the spelling correction process generates lots of candidates for sentences being checked; and then a ranking algorithm is applied to rank top-k correction candidates for later decision; the third step conducts rule-based analysis for specific correction task, e.g. the correction rule of the usage of three confusable words "的", "地" and "得". Finally, the system makes decision whether to output the correction or not based on the previous output and global constrains.

The system architecture is illustrated in Figure 1. This framework provides a unified approach for spelling correction tasks, which can tailored to different scenarios and can be regarded as a language independent framework. To move to another language scenario, you only need to collect some language related corpus, but you don't need to be a language expert.

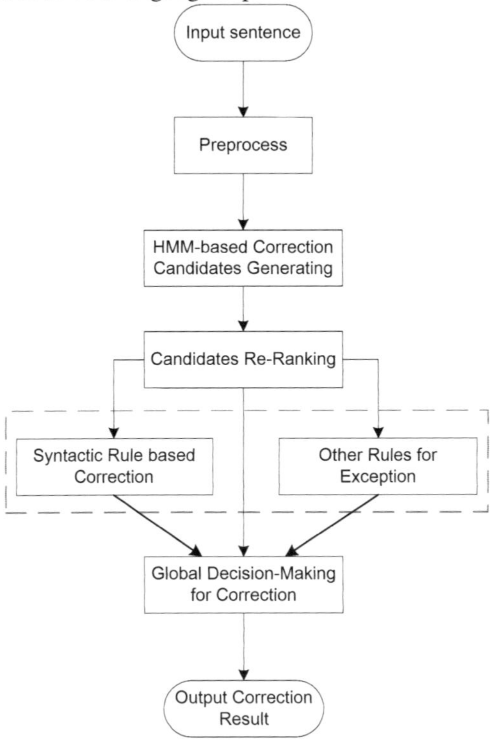

Figure1. The Unified Framework (HANSpeller) for Chinese Spelling Correction

3.1 Generating Candidates

Generating candidates of spelling correction task is the basic part for the whole task, because it determines the upper bound of precision and recall rate of the approach. The spelling correction problem can be typically formulated under the framework of noisy channel model. According to such a model, the spelling correction task is to find the correction with the highest probability of yielding the misspelled input sentence. Formally, given an "observed" sentence S which might contain error characters, we need to find the corrected sentence $\hat{C}$ with the highest probability of different replacement C. Symbolically, it is represented by:

$$\hat{C} = arg\,max_c\, p(C|S) \qquad (1)$$

By applying Bayes' Rule, we can rewrite Formula 1 as:

$$\hat{C} = arg\,max \frac{p(S|C)p(C)}{p(S)}$$
$$\approx arg\,max\,(p(S|C)p(C) \qquad (2)$$

where $p(S|C)$, called the "error model", represents the chance that a correct Chinese character could be written to the wrong one, while $p(C)$ is the n-gram language model which evaluates the quality of the corrected Chinese sentence.

To solve the above problem, the HMM approach can be used. And the spelling correction can then be ranked by multiplying the error model and language model.

The above one step method for Chinese essays spelling correction faces the following challenges: (1) For high quality spelling correction, the training of HMM is not a trivial task. (2) The long-span dependency in sentences makes first-order hidden Markov model not enough to catch context information. (3) Too many candidates make the algorithm not efficient enough, and right corrections may be concealed by the wrong corrections.

To address the above issues, some extensions have been made on HMM-based spelling correction approach. Firstly, the HMM-based method is used only for candidates generating, not for finally output correction generating. And all kinds of possible error transformations can be integrated into the framework of HMM approach, so as to get high recall rate. Secondly, higher-order hidden Markov model is used to capture long-span context dependency. Thirdly, a pruning dynamic programming algorithm is adopted to dynamically select the best correction candidates for each round of sentence segmentation and correction.

3.2 Ranking Candidates

In the candidates generation phase, top-k best candidates for a sentence are generated, but the HMM-based framework does not have the flexibility to incorporate a wide variety of features useful for spelling correction, such as the online search results and CKIP Parser results, which can significantly improve the precision of spelling correction.

Given the original sentence, our system first creates a list of candidate sentences. The candidates in the list will be re-ranked at this stage based on the confidence score generated by a ranker, herein by a SVM classifier. We choose the top-2 candidates in the re-ranked candidate list to make the final decision.

We use a lot of features in the re-ranking phase. The features can be grouped into the following categories:

1) **Language model features**, which calculate the n-gram probability of a candidate sentence.
2) **Dictionary features**, which check whether parts of a candidate sentence can match to one or more words or idioms in the dictionaries.
3) **Edit Distance features**, which compute the edit number and its weight, from the original sentence to the candidate sentence.
4) **Segmentation features**, which use the results of the maximum matching segmentation algorithm and that of CKIP Parser segmentation.
5) **Online Resources features**, which use Bing or other search engine's search results, when submitting the spelling correction part and the corresponding part of the original sentence to the search engine.

3.3 Rule-based Correction for Errors

As illustrated in Figure 1, the third step conducts rule-based analysis for specific correction task. One of most common errors is the usage of three confusable words "的", "地" and "得". To correct such common errors, syntactic analysis is needed. For other errors, some other specific rules can be developed for them.

The following sentence contains an error of Chinese syntax:

今天/我/穿著/剛/買/地/新/衣服。

Here the character "地" should be corrected to another character "的". To deal with such kind of errors, sentence parsing must be done before the syntactic rules are applied to check and correct such errors. We have summarized three rules according to Chinese grammar as follows:

1) The Chinese character "的" is the tag of attributes, generally used in front of subjects and objects. Words in front of "的" are generally used to modify, restrict things behind "的".
2) The Chinese character "地" is adverbial marker, usually used in front of predicates(verbs, adjectives). Words in front of "地" are generally used to describe actions behind "地".
3) The Chinese character "得" marks the complement, generally used behind predicates. The part follows "得" is generally used to supplement the previous action.

3.4 Decision-making on Corrections

Through the above processing steps, top candidates for each sub-sentence have been generated. To make the final decision on spelling correction, global constrains should be considered, including the whole error rate of the corpus, which error type should be paid more weight than others, which sub-sentence corrects should be output, etc. Combining the above constrains together, the system determines the final decision for spelling corrections.

4 Experiment and Evaluation

4.1 Experimental Setting

The following corpora are used to train our model, including Taiwan Web as Corpus, SogouW dictionary, a traditional Chinese dictionary of words and idioms, a pinyin mapping table and a cangjie code table of common words. The details of them are described below.

1) Taiwan Web Pages as Corpus

As we known, Taiwan web pages contain high quality traditional Chinese text, so we gathered pages from the Web under .tw domain to build the corpus, containing around 3.2 million web pages. And then the content extracted from these pages is used to build traditional Chinese n-gram model, where n is from 2 to 4.

2) SogouW Dictionary

SougoW dictionary[2] is built from the statistical analysis of Chinese Internet corpus by Sogou Search Engine. It contains about 150,000 high-frequency words of the Chinese Internet. But words in the corpus are simple Chinese characters; it is then translated into traditional Chinese by Google translating service.

3) Chinese Words and Idioms Dictionary
As introduced in [Chiu *et al.* 2013], we also obtained the Chinese words [3]and Chinese idioms[4] published by Ministry of Education of Taiwan, which are built from the dictionaries and related books. There are 64,326 distinct Chinese words and 48,030 distinct Chinese idioms. And we combine these two dictionaries with SogouW dictionary to build our trie tree dictionary.

4) Pinyin and Canjie Code Tables
We collected more than 10000 pinyins of words commonly used in Taiwan to build the homophone and near-homophone words table, which will be used in candidate generation phase. In addition, cangjie code can be used to measure the form/shape similarity between Chinese characters. Therefore, we collected cangjie codes to build the table of Similar-form characters.

5) Segmentation Resources
Besides using the Maximum Matching Method for Chinese word segmentation, we also use the CKIP Parser results to help ranking the candidates. For example, the segmentation of "特續下滑" is "特/續/下滑" while "持續下滑" is "持續/下滑". Thus the segmentation results of wrong candidate sentence will have more words than the correct one.

6) Online Resource
In addition to the above, we use the Bing search results as one feature in candidates ranking phase, which improve the performance obviously. For example, the sentence "根據聯合國公布的數字" has several candidate sentences, one of them may be "根據聯合國公佈的數字". If we use Bing to search the error correction part and the corresponding part of the original sentence "聯合國公佈" and "聯合國公布", the search results will be obviously enough to identify the correct candidate sentence, because the first one is more popular than the second one on the web corpus.

4.2 Evaluation Results

At the CLP-2014 bake-off, the evaluation task is to correct errors in sentences. It is divided into two related subtasks. One is error detection and the other is error correction. There are 1062 sentences with/without spelling errors. The evaluation metrics, including false positive rate, accuracy rate, precision rate, recall rate and F1-score, is provided by the Chinese Spelling Check Task group. The confusion matrix as follow is to help to calculate the related indicators.

Confusion Matrix		System Results	
		Positive (Error)	Negative (No Error)
Gold Standard	Positive	TF	FN
	Negative	FP	TN

Table 2. Confusion Matrix

Each index calculation is as follows:
False Positive Rate (FPR) = FP / (FP + TN)
Accuracy (A) =
(TP + TN) / (TP + TN + FP + FN)
Precision (P) = TP / (TP + FP)
Recall (R) = TP / (TP + FN)
F1-score = 2 * P * R / (P + R)

Our system showed good performance on the evaluation test. Among all 13 teams, our performance ranks second place. The two submitted test results are illustrated in Table 3. Meanwhile, since such an open test is an extremely challenging task, there is still much room for further improvement.

	RUN1		RUN2	
	Detection Level	Correction Level	Detection Level	Correction Level
FPR	0.1525		0.1563	
A	0.6149	0.5829	0.613	0.581
P	0.7148	0.676	0.7098	0.6706
R	0.3823	0.3183	0.3823	0.3183
F1	0.4982	0.4328	0.4969	0.4317

Table 3. Evaluation at CLP-2014 Bake-off

5 Conclusion and Future Work

This paper proposed a unified framework (HANSpeller) for Chinese essays spelling correction based on extended HMM and ranker-

[2] http://www.sogou.com/labs/dl/w.html
[3]http://www.edu.tw/files/site_content/m0001/pin/yu7.htm?open
[4] http://dict.idioms.moe.edu.tw/cydic/index.htm

based models. The rule-based strategy is used for further correction polishing, and for final decision on whether outputs the correction or not. Our approach has been evaluated at CLP-2014 bake-off on Chinese spelling correction task, and made good performance with ranking second among 13 teams.

Some interesting future works on Chinese spelling correction include: (1) collecting and considering more error types in the candidates generating process, (2) how to better dealing with the difference between traditional and simple Chinese.

Acknowledgments

This work was supported by the National Basic Research Program of China (Grant No. 2014CB340406), the National High Technology Research and Development Program of China (Grant No. 2014AA015204) and the NSFC for the Youth (Grant No. 61402442).

Reference

Shih-Hung Wu, Chao-Lin Liu, and Lung-Hao Lee (2013). Chinese Spelling Check Evaluation at SIGHAN Bake-off 2013. Proceedings of the 7th SIGHAN Workshop on Chinese Language Processing (SIGHAN'13), Nagoya, Japan, 14 October, 2013, pp. 35-42.

Chao-Lin Liu, Min-Hua Lai, Kan-Wen Tien, Yi-Hsuan Chuang, Shih-Hung Wu, and Chia-Ying Lee. 2011. Visually and Phonologically similar characters in incorrect Chinese Words: analyses, Identification, and Applications. ACM Transactions on Asian Language Information Processing, 10(2), 10:1-39.

James L. Pterson. 1980. Computers programs for detecting and correcting spelling errors. Communications of the ACM, pp 23: 676-687

Lidia Mangu and Eric Bill. 1997. Automatic rule acquisition for spelling correction. In Proceeding of the 14th International Conference on Machine Learning, pp 187-194, San Francisco, CA

Eric Atwell and Stephen Elliott. 1987. Dealing with ill-formed English text. In the Computational Analysis of English: A Corpus-Based Approach, London.

Ahmad, F., and Kondrak, G. 2005. Learning a spelling error model from search query logs. In HLT_EMNLP, pp 955-962.

Li, M., Zhu, M., Zhang, Y. and Zhou, M. 2006. Exploring distributional similarity based models for query spelling correction. Proceedings of ACL 2006, pp 2025-1032.

Jianfeng Gao, Xiaolong Li, Daniel Micol, Chris Quirk, and Xu Sun. 2010. A large scale ranker-based system for search query spelling correction. The 23rd International Conference on Computational Linguistics 2010 (COLING 2010). pp 358-366.

Microsoft Microsoft web n-gram services. 2010. http://research.microsoft.com/web-ngram

Google. 2010. A Java API for Google spelling check service. http//code.google.com/p/google-api-spellingjava/

Chang-Huang Chang. 1995. A new approach for automatic Chinese spelling correction, Proceedings of Natural Language Processing Pacific Rim Symposium. pp 278-283

Lei Zhang, Ming Zhou, Chang-Ning Huang, and Hui-Hua Pan. 2000b. Automatic detecting/correcting errors in Chinese text by an approximate word-matching algorithm. In Proceedings of the 38the Annual Meeting on Association for Computational Linguistics, pp 248-254, Morristwon NJ.

S. Cucerzan and E. Brill. 2004. Spelling correction as an iterative process that exploits the collective knowledge of web users. In Proceedings of EMNLP, volume 4, pp 293-300.

Huang, Chuen-Min and Wu, Mei-Chen and Chang, Ching-Che. 2007, Error detection and correction based on Chinese phonemic alphabet in Chinese text. Modeling Decisions for Artificial Intelligence. pp. 463-476.

Hung, Ta-Hung and Wu, Shih-Hung. 2008. Chinese Essay Error Detection and Suggestion System. Taiwan E-Learning Forum.

Y. Zheng, C. Li, and M. Sun. 2011. Chime: An efficient error-tolerant Chinese pinyin input method. In Proceedings of the 22nd International Joint Conference on Artificial Intelligence.

Chinese Word Spelling Correction Based on Rule Induction

Jui-Feng Yeh, Yun-Yun Lu, Chen-Hsien Lee, Yu-Hsiang Yu, Yong-Ting Chen
Department of Computer Science and Information Engineering, National Chiayi University
No.300 Syuefu Rd., Chiayi City 60004, Taiwan (R.O.C.)
`{ralph, s1020447, s1020443, s1002967, s1003008}@mail.ncyu.edu.tw`

Abstract

The importance of learning Chinese is increasing in the latest decades. However, the learning of Chinese is not easy for foreigners as a second language learning. Sometimes they write some text or document, but there always have many error words. So, how to detect the error word in document is becoming more then more important. This issue is very extensive, not only can help foreigners to learning Chinese but also can detect the error word. This paper had proposed method can divide five sections of structure: First sections are input sentence; second sections are parsing and word segmentation; third sections are fine the wrong word; forth sections are remove duplicate; fifth sections are final output. In this paper we use language model to detect Chinese spelling. It is had four part, E-Hownet, CKIP, similar pronunciation and shape dictionary, use the preset word to compare the word correction which in database. We use the bi-gram to promote our performance.

1 Introduction

Learning Chinese is very important in this era, because the Chinese is main market customers. Since the trend of the times, there have many of foreigners beginning to learn Chinese. But Chinese is not easy to learn, because sometime the same word has many pronouns, or same pronounce has different word, even the much the words have similar glyph. Chinese unlike English, there have thousands of words in Chinese, different combinations have different meaning. Although pronounce the same, but there will be different words with different meaning, sometimes there were having some misunderstanding because using the wrong word. So how to learn Chinese is very import research. This topic is extensive, not only for foreigners to learn Chinese, but also can help to detect the wrong word in the document.

In recent years, there has a lot of paper to research about Chinese learning. Chinese learning in today not only face to face teaching, but also can learn in a mobile system. There have many type smartphone applications about learning Chinese, sometimes there also has another country's language. Michael B. Syson et al. (2012) propose a system ABKD which is learning the game in multimodal, this system has two languages for learning, one is Chinese the other is Japanese. This system is learning about the Chinese Hanzi and Japanese Kanji by the game. Vincent Tam et al. (2012) use iOS-Base devices to propose an e-learning software, this device is extendible and ubiquitous, this paper proposes different learning type like it can learn the characters in correct stroke sequences of Chinese, it also has some mini-game to help learning Chinese. This author also proposes another paper is main on writing Chinese, and not only focus on iOS-base, but also for other smart phone (ex: android). Xiangyu Qiu et al. (2012) propose a method about learning Chinese font style and transferring, it's based on strokes and structure, they propose a new glyph decryption method, it divides the Chinese characters two parts, one is the stable side call structure, the other side is mutable called style. Mei-Jen Audrey Shih et al. (2011) propose an online system to learn Chinese, online learning system is convenience for user, it is assembled to abound environment and had a broad content search opportunity, this paper is focused on how to learn Chinese language effectively in an online learning environment. Lee Jo Kim et al. (2011) propose a tool which supports Chinese language teaching and learning system based on ICT-Base, this tool can help peer assisted

Proceedings of the Third CIPS-SIGHAN Joint Conference on Chinese Language Processing, pages 139–145,
Wuhan, China, 20-21 October 2014

learning environment. Lung-Hsiang et al. (2012) propose a mobile assisted system about learning vocabulary, they use the Mobile-Assisted language learning (MALL), they present two case studies in the Mobile-Assisted Language Learning, this system is main on two languages, one is English, the other is Chinese, specially it is not learning the word, it is learning about the "idioms" and learning how to construct sentences. Shang-Jen Chuanget al. (2011) propose a new recognition of Traditional Chinese handwriting by neural networks, their recognition of Traditional Chinese handwriting by PNN and SVM, their database is 20 people's Traditional Chinese handwriting, and use different quantization methods for everyone. Yingfei Wu (2011) proposes a learning system of "Chinese calligraphy" on mobile systems, Calligraphy is good for learning Traditional Chinese font, because it needs step by step to write the Chinese word, but calligraphy is not easy, even a word usually has many different font styles, the calligraphy need ink and paper, so they propose a new mobile system which can easy to learning Calligraphy without use paper and ink. David Tawei Ku et al. (2012) proposes the Chinese learning in situated learning, it is trend a ubiquitous learning environment, and the feature focuses on real life learning situation, and problem solving practice, this learning system divides two parts, one is integrating situated learning strategy and the other is context awareness technology. Yanwei Wang et al. (2011) proposes a discriminative learning method of MQDF (Modified quadratic discriminant function), MQDF is based on sample importance weights, this method is investigated and compared other discriminative learning methods about MQDF. DA-Han Wang (2012) propose a handwriting recognition system, this system commonly combines character classification confidence scores, they propose two regularized classes-dependent confidence transformation (CT) methods. Yunxue Shao (2011) propose a similar handwritten Chinese characters method base on multiple instance learning, they solved the problem by Asaboost framework, the method is found week classifiers to select some self-adapting critical regions. Lung-Hsiang Wong (2010) propose a Mobile-Assisted language learning (MALL), their have two case studies, and focus on "creative learner outputs", student in two studies language by one-to-one mobile devices, and capture the picture of the real life.Shih-hung Wu et al. (2013) propose a paper for Chinese Spelling Check task which at SIGHAN bake-off 2013, in this paper, thay describe all detail of the task for Chinese spelling check, include the task descripition, data preparation, performance metrics, and evaluation results.

This paper proposes five steps to find the wrong words in a document: First is input the sentence; the second uses the CKIP to word segment; the third is finding the wrong word. In the third step, the main method in this paper divides the words in document for three parts, The first is the single word, sometimes the single words mean there does not have any match word before or after this single word, in other words, is there maybe had word error, so we compose the word which before or after this single word, this word most be the single word too. After composing two of single words, it can generate a new word than regarded as a suspicious error word. The second is about idioms, most of the idioms are composed of four words, so we take the four words to pronounce and glyph to compare with the E-Hownet. The other words (ex: two words, three words), we also compare with the E-Hownet, if it can find the same word in E-Hownet, it means this word is correct, use it as a suspicious error word. Forth is remove duplicate, this step is remove the duplicate wrong word. Finally opput the file.

2 Method

In this section, our proposed method is to check out the foreigners will get the word wrong and then correct for the right word. The sentences written by people learning Chinese as a foreign language (CFL) may contain a variety of grammatical errors, such as word choice, missing words, and so on. It focuses on spelling errors in this bake-off. We will introduce the framework of the proposed system and method, which is divided into two parts: training phase and test phase that will describe in section 2.1 and section 2.2.

2.1 Training phase

As shown in figure 1, training phase is to construct the dictionary which is used in test phase, there are including the similar pronunciation & shape dictionary and training data dictionary. E-Hownet is used to find the wrong word and correct the wrong word, it also can use to construct the rule induction. And

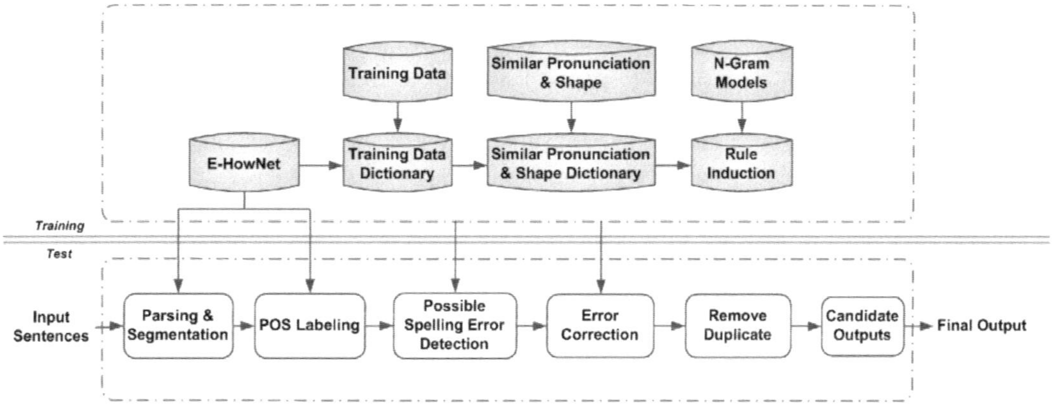

Figure 1: the framework of the proposed system.

n-gram models is also used to be the ranking score construct the rule induction. Finally, the candidate outputs are generated according to our rule induction. We will describe more detail in the follows.

First, we go to pre-process the data from the bake-off organizer. Step 1, we removed unnecessary portions of each sentence in the input file, such as PID number. The results will feed into the tool which is the CKIP Autotag, then it will do word segmentation and part-of-speech tagging based on E-Hownet. The corresponding part-of-speech (POS) of each word is obtained in the sentences. Each word has a part of speech at the end of a word in parentheses. Step 2, we are going to remove unessential blank spaces and parentheses. This step allows us to be more convenient for the implementation of our program. These processes are also used in the test phase.

Next, we introduce our rule induction in the following.

- Let A_i $(i = 1 \sim n)$ mean incorrect word, $A_{ak}(k = 1 \sim m,\ m \leq 4)$ mean k-th incorrect word, $Sim(A_{ak})$ mean the similar word with A_{ak}.
- Let $\mathrm{E-HN}(A_{a1}, A_{a2}, \dots \dots A_{am})$ mean that A_{a1} to A_{am} can combine into a word which can be find in E-Hownet, $\mathrm{LOC}(B_i)$ mean location of the word.
- $a_j = LOC\left(E - HN\left(A_{ap}, Sim(A_{aq})\right)\right)$, $b_r = LOC(E - HN\left(Sim(A_{ap}), Sim(A_{aq})\right))$, when $p = 1, q = 2 \sim m$ or $q = 1, p = 2 \sim m$. a_j $(j = 1 \sim m)$ mean that $A_{ap}, Sim(A_{aq})$ combine into a word which can find in E-Hownet, b_r $(r = 1 \sim n)$ mean that $\mathrm{Sim}(A_{ap}), Sim(A_{aq})$ combine into a word which can find in E-Hownet.
- $Min((a_1, a_2, \dots, a_m), (b_1, b_2, \dots, b_n)$ mean that output the minimum, this indicates the position of the front in the E-Hownet which is the more correct word.

2.2 Test phase

In the previous section, the rule induction is built in training phase. We will describe the test phase of the framework in this section. The word segmentation and part of speech (POS) labeling are the same as training phase. Then, we begin the processes with the third step, we have to detect the wrong word. There are some proposed method to find the wrong word in the following.

- In the previous step, we have the word segmentation, we choose the words more than two characters, then compared the words with E-Hownet or training data dictionary. If there is not the same words in E-Hownet or training data dictionary, we determine it as incorrect words.
- For the judge idioms, we choose all word with four characters, and compared the word with E-Hownet and the similar pronunciation & shape dictionary. If there is not the same words in the training data dictionary, E-Hownet or similar pronunciation & shape dictionary, we determine it as incorrect words.
- To the judge the sentences written by CFL, we focus on "的 (De)", "地 (De)", "得 (De)". Behind the "的 (De)" must connect the verb, behind the "地 (De)"

must be a noun. Further, behind the "得 (De)" must be a verb, fornt the "得 (De)" can be an adverb, Nv or Nh. If the characters do not comply with the POS of the above, we determine it as incorrect words.
- Finally, we strengthen the judgment of single character. Behind or found the single character is the same as single characters, we combine the character to the word which contain two characters. And we determine it as incorrect words.

According the above, we begin the processes which is comparing the wrong words with similar pronunciation & shape dictionary, that is in order to find the similar words, then if the similar words can be found in E-Hownet or training data dictionary, we saved the incorrect words in a text file named wrong, and saved the similar words in a text file named correct, this focuses on two characters of the word in the case of one character wrong. The proposed method also aim the two characters of the word in the case of all characters wrong, eg., 勞刀 (嘮叨). The processes as is same as above, but the incorrect words saved in a text file named double_wrong, and the similar saved in a text file named double_correct. The fifth step, we are going to remove duplicates. First, If the words in the text named wrong can be found in the text named double_wrong, we will remove the words in wrong. Second, if identify the words appear more than twice, we will remove the unnecessary words. It is helping us to reduce the process time. We will output the result in the final step. The processes will find the words and find the corresponding sentence, then save the position and correct word in the file named output. Finally, according the PID to sort the sentence and output to the specified format. For example, input: "(pid= A2-1051-1) 後天是小明的生日，我要開一個無會。", output: "A2-1051-1, 15, 舞", If the input contains no spelling errors, the system should return "pid, 0".

3 Experiments

According to the Chinese spelling check task in SIGHAN, this paper is dedicated to the detection and correction of errors in sentences. The evaluate is divided into two parts: Subtask 1 is detection level that is to find out the location of incorrect spelling characters in the sentences, then the subtask 2 is correction level, which is to find out the location of spelling error in subtask 1 and then correct the error. In section 3.1, we will describe the data sets, performance metrics, then we will show our evalution in section 3.2.

3.1 Data sets

```
<ESSAY title="少子化現象">
<TEXT>
<PASSAGE id="C1-1792-1">在日本行成「少子化」現象的可能原因有一些。其中一個是「晚婚化」。</PASSAGE>
</TEXT>
<MISTAKE id="C1-1792-1" location="4">
<WRONG>行成</WRONG>
<CORRECTION>形成</CORRECTION>
</MISTAKE>
</ESSAY>
```

Figure 2: an example of the training data.

In this bake-off, the evaluation is an open test. Participants can employ any linguistic and computational resources to develop the spelling checker, and provide passages of CFL's essays from the NTNU learner corpus for training purpose. The corpus was released in SGML format which is shown in figure 2. Moreover, there are at least 1000 different degrees of difficulty of testing passages for testing. In this paper, we use C++ to develop our proposed method.

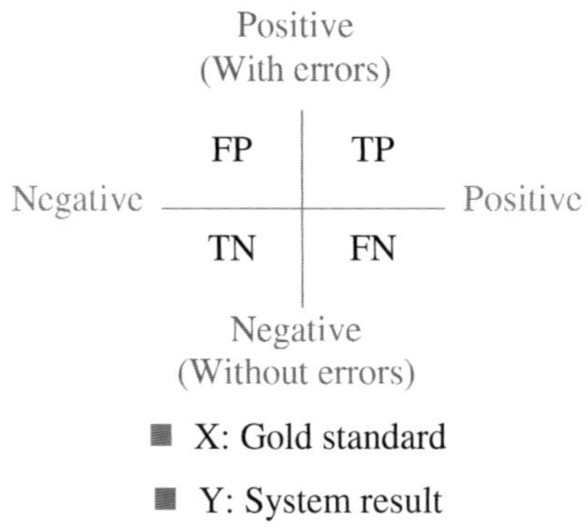

Figure 3: A quadrant map of performance metrics.

The judging correctness are divided into two parts: detection level and correction level. The following are showing some performance metrics and quadrant map shown in figure 3 that is measured in both levels of indicators:

- **TP**: System determines the character for errors related to the actual error, and the judgments the system is correct.
- **FP**: System determines the character for errors is not related to the actual error, and the judgments of the system is incorrect.
- **FN**: System determines the character for errors is related to the actual error, and the judgments of the system is incorrect.
- **TN**: System determines the character for errors is not related to the actual error, and the judgments of the system is correct.

The following is the performance metrics in this

- **False Positive Rate** $= \frac{FP}{(FP+TN)}$
- **Accuracy** $= \frac{(TP+TN)}{(TP+TN+FP+FN)}$
- **Precision** $= \frac{TP}{(TP+FP)}$
- **Recall** $= \frac{TP}{(TP+FN)}$
- **F1 − Score** $= \frac{2 \times Precision \times Recall}{(Precision+Recall)}$

3.2 Evaluation

Figure 4 is our data of evaluation, which the largest difference between the first and the second. The proposed method is only aimed to the training data in run1, then we make changes for run2 in the data which is provided by run1.

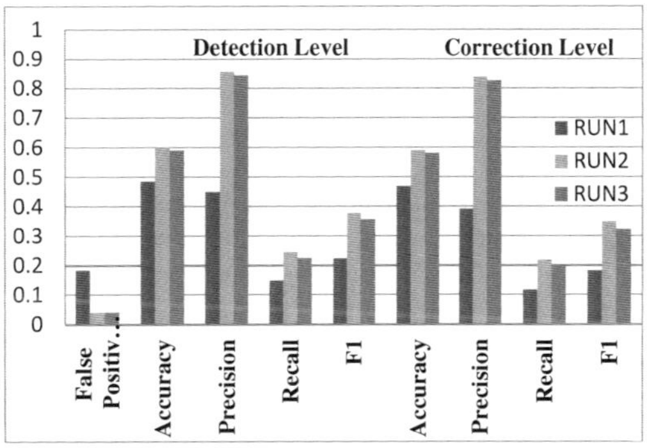

Figure 4: Performance evaluation.

According to the table 1, our false positive rate is the third in this bake-off, which means that our proposed method is feasible, but there is room for improvement. There are two parts of performance evaluation: detection level and correction level which is shown in table 2 and table 3.In the accuracy and precision, we can see that our proposed method can be the top three, but our method in recall is relatively weaker than another. This performance evaluation shows that our method is viable, but our method may be overly strict cause our relatively low

Table 1: Top five of the false positive rate.

Participating teams	False Positive Rate
NCYU*	0.0414
NCTU&NTUT	0.0377
SUDA	0.032
KUAS	0.0452
NTHU	0.0829

Table 2: Top four of performance evaluation in Detection Level.

Participating teams	Accuracy	Precision	Recall	F1
NCYU*	0.6008	0.8543	0.2429	0.3783
KUAS	0.7194	0.9146	0.484	0.633
CAS	0.6149	0.7148	0.3823	0.4982
SJTU	0.5471	0.5856	0.322	0.4156

Table 3: Top four of performance evaluation in Correction Level.

Participating teams	Accuracy	Precision	Recall	F1
NCYU*	0.5885	0.8406	0.2185	0.3468
KUAS	0.7081	0.9108	0.4614	0.6125
CAS	0.5829	0.676	0.3183	0.4328
SJTU	0.5377	0.5709	0.3032	0.3961

4 Conclusions

This study proposes a method for Chinese text detect spelling error. The method in our study is focus on word classify to easy detect Chinese spelling error. The word is classifying three class, single word, idioms and other words (two words, three words et.)The experimental result shows the performance it good, and we also apply this method in "SIGHAN 8 Chinese spelling check task", and the final result pretty good. In the feature, we hope can raise the performance and find the other word classifies. More word class can helpful to find the Chinese spelling error. After the Chinese spelling error, we will start to study the relationship between grammar and spelling errors, because in this paper we only care about the word pronouns and glyph, but in recent years some spelling error has been regularization, it most to understanding the context then detect it is right or wrong, so the issue about the relationship between grammar and spelling errors is need to study, if we can fine the relationship then the Chinese spelling detect correct rate must can raise higher.

Acknowledgments

This work is supported in part by the National Science Council, Taiwan, R.O.C., under the project grant numbers NSC 102-2221-E-415-006-MY3.

Reference

Qiu, X., Jia, W., and Li, H. 2012. A Font Style Learning and Transferring Method Based on Strokes and Structure of Chinese Characters. In Computer Science and Service System (CSSS), pp. 1836-1839.

Syson, M. B., Estuar, M. R. E., and See, K. T. 2012. ABKD: Multimodal Mobile Language Game for Collaborative Learning of Chinese Hanzi and Japanese Kanji Characters. In Proceedings of the The 2012 IEEE/WIC/ACM International Joint Conferences on Web Intelligence and Intelligent Agent Technology-Volume 03 pp. 311-315.

Tam, V., and Cheung, R. L. 2012. An Extendible and Ubiquitious E-learning Software for Foreigners to Learn Chinese on iOS-Based Devices. InAdvanced Learning Technologies (ICALT), 2012 IEEE 12th International Conference on pp. 46-48.

Tam, V., and Huang, C. 2011. An Extendible Software for Learning to Write Chinese Characters in Correct Stroke Sequences on Smartphones. InAdvanced Learning Technologies (ICALT), 2011 11th IEEE International Conference on pp. 118-119.

Li, K. H., Cheng, T. F., Lou, S. J., and Tsai, H. Y. 2012. Application of Game-based Learning (GBL) on Chinese language learning in elementary school. In Digital Game and Intelligent Toy Enhanced Learning (DIGITEL), 2012 IEEE Fourth International Conference on pp. 226-230.

Ku, D. T., and Chang, C. C. 2012. Development of context awareness learning system for elementary Chinese language learning. In Proceedings of the 2012 Sixth International Conference on Genetic and Evolutionary Computing on pp. 538-541.

Tam, V., and Luo, N. 2012. Exploring Chinese through learning objects and interactive interface on mobile devices. In Teaching, Assessment and Learning for Engineering (TALE), 2012 IEEE International Conference on pp. H3C-7.

Shih, M. J., and Yang, J. C. 2011. How to Learn Chinese through Online Tools? From the Perspective of Informal Learning to Culture Immersion. InAdvanced Learning Technologies (ICALT), 2011 11th IEEE International Conference on pp. 305-306.

Kim, L. J., Lim, S. H., and Ying, L. T. 2011. ICT-based peer assisted learning environment: Using online feedback tools for Chinese Language writing tasks. In Electrical and Control Engineering (ICECE), 2011 International Conference on pp. 6612-6614.

Wong, L. H., and Looi, C. K. (2010, April). Mobile-assisted vocabulary learning in real-life setting for primary school students: Two case studies. In Wireless, Mobile and Ubiquitous Technologies in Education (WMUTE), 2010 6th IEEE International Conference on pp. 88-95.

Chuang, S. J., Zeng, S. R., and Chou, Y. L. 2011. Neural Networks for the Recognition of Traditional Chinese Handwriting. In Computational Science and Engineering (CSE), 2011 IEEE 14th International Conference on pp. 645-648

Wu, Y., Yuan, Z., Zhou, D., and Cai, Y. 2013. Research of virtual Chinese calligraphic learning. In Multimedia and Expo (ICME), 2013 IEEE International Conference on pp. 1-5.

Ku, D. T., and Chang, C. C. 2012. Development of context awareness learning system for elementary Chinese language learning. In Proceedings of the 2012 Sixth International Conference on Genetic and Evolutionary Computing on pp. 538-541.

Zhao, Z., and Ma, X. 2012. Prediction of Prosodic Word Boundaries in Chinese TTS Based on Maximum Entropy Markov Model and Transformation Based Learning. In Computational Intelligence and Security (CIS), 2012 Eighth International Conference on pp. 258-261.

Lin, C. C., and Tsai, R. H. 2012. A Generative Data Augmentation Model for Enhancing Chinese Dialect Pronunciation Prediction. Audio, Speech, and Language Processing, Transactions on, 20(4), 1109-1117.

Wang, Y., Ding, X., and Liu, C. 2011. MQDF discriminative learning based offline handwritten Chinese character recognition. In Document Analysis and Recognition (ICDAR), 2011 International Conference on pp. 1100-1104.

Shao, Y., Wang, C., Xiao, B., Zhang, R., and Zhang, Y. 2011. Multiple instance learning based method for similar handwritten Chinese characters discrimination. In Document Analysis and Recognition (ICDAR), 2011 International Conference on pp. 1002-1006.

Wu, S. H., Liu, C. L., & Lee, L. H (2013). Chinese Spelling Check Evaluation at SIGHAN Bake-off 2013. Proceedings of the 7th SIGHAN Workshop on Chinese Language Processing (SIGHAN'13), Nagoya, Japan, 14 October, 2013, pp. 35-42

Academia Sinica CKIP. http://ckipsvr.iis.sinica.edu.tw/

Academia Sinica E-Hownet. http://ehownet.iis.sinica.edu.tw/

Evaluation Report of the fourth Chinese Parsing Evaluation: CIPS-SIGHAN-ParsEval-2014

Qiang Zhou
Center for Speech and Language Technology
Research Institute of Information Technology
Tsinghua National Laboratory for Information Science and Technology
Tsinghua University, Beijing 100084, China.
zq-lxd@mail.tsinghua.edu.cn

Abstract

This paper gives the overview of the fourth Chinese parsing evaluation: CIPS-SIGHAN-ParsEval-2014, including its parsing, evaluation metrics, training and test data. The detailed evaluation results and simple discussions will be given to show the difficulties in Chinese syntactic parsing.

1 Introduction

For Chinese parsing evaluations, we have successfully held three times in 2009, 2010 and 2012. They are the CIPS-ParsEval-2009 (Zhou and Li, 2009), CIPS-SIGHAN-ParsEval-2010 (Zhou and Zhu, 2010) and CIPS-SIGHan-ParsEval-2012 (Zhou, 2012) respectively. Each evaluation has its different theme and goal.

The first ParsEval-2009 focused on Chinese chunk parsing. Three kinds of chunking tasks were designed for the Chinese chunks with different descriptive complexities. The evaluation results showed that as the increasing of the word number and descriptive complexity of the chunks from base chunks (BC) to functional chunks (FC) and event descriptive chunks (EDC), the final F1-value will also decrease about 6 points from 92% to 86% and 80%.

The second ParsEval-2010 and third ParsEval-2012 focused on Chinese syntactic parsing. They had different points of emphasis for parse tree evaluation.

In ParsEval-2010, we compared the parsing performance differences in two kinds of Chinese sentences. One is the EDC clauses with about 10 words averagely. The other is the complete sentences with about 23 words averagely. Evaluation results showed that there were about 8% drops for the complete sentence in the labelled F1-score measure.

In ParsEval-2012, we compared the parsing performance differences in two kinds of syntactic constituent in Chinese complete sentences. One is the syntactic constituents with complex internal compound relationships, including event combination and concept composition relations. The other is the syntactic constituents with ordinary internal relations, such as subject-predicate, predicate-object, modifier-head, etc. Evaluation results showed that there were 20% drops for the syntactic constituents with complex internal relations in the labelled F1-score measure.

The above evaluation results in the Chinese clause and sentence levels show that the complex sentence parsing is still a big challenge for the Chinese language.

This time we will focus on the deeper parsing evaluation in the Predicate-Argument Structure (PAS) level to test whether the parser can deal with different syntactic alternatives with same event contents. We will introduce a new lexicon-based Combinatory Categorical Grammar (CCG) (Steedman 1996, 2000) annotation scheme in the evaluation, and propose a new implicit predicate argument (IPA) relation annotation method to build a large scale CCG bank with detailed PAS annotations. The special lexical dependency pairs automatically extracted from the CCG bank will be used as the final gold-standard data for evaluating parsers' IPA recognition capacity.

Same with previous ParsEval-2010 and ParsEval-2014, we also set two tracks in the ParsEval-2014. One is the Close track in which model parameter estimation is conducted solely on the train data. The other is the Open track in which

Proceedings of the Third CIPS-SIGHAN Joint Conference on Chinese Language Processing, pages 146–152,
Wuhan, China, 20-21 October 2014

any datasets other than the given training data can be used to estimate model parameters. We will set separated evaluation ranks for these two tracks.

In addition, we will evaluate following two kinds of methods separately in each track.

1) Single system: parsers that use a single parsing model to finish the parsing task.

2) System combination: participants are allowed to combine multiple models to improve the performance. Collaborative decoding methods will be regarded as a combination method.

2 Evaluation Task and Metrics

2.1 Parsing Evaluation Task

Input: A Chinese sentence with correct word segmentations. The following is an example:

小型(small) 木材(wood) 加工场(factory) 在(is) 忙(busy) 着(-modality) 制作(build) 各(several) 种(-classifier) 木制品(woodwork) 。(period) (A small wood factory is busy to build several woodworks.)

Parsing goal: Assign appropriate CCG category tags to the words in the sentence and generate CCG derivation tree for the sentence.

Output: The CCG derivation tree with CCG category tags and feature annotations.

- (S{decl} (S (NP (NP/NP 小型) (NP (NP/NP 木材) (NP 加工场))) (S\NP ([S\NP]/[S\NP] 在) (S{Cmb=LW}\NP (S\NP (S\NP 忙) ([S\NP]\[S\NP] 着)) (S\NP ([S\NP]/NP 制作) (NP (NP/NP ([NP/NP]/M 各) (M 种)) (NP 木制品)))))) (wE 。))

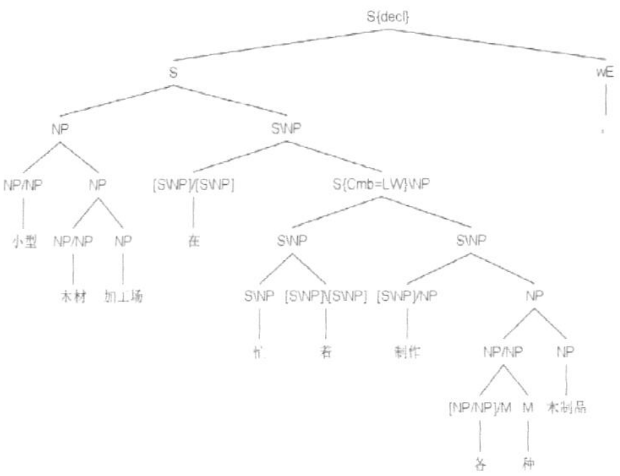

(1)

2.2 Parsing Evaluation Metrics

There are two parsing stages for the CCG parsers. One is the syntactic category (CCG category) assignment stage. The other is the parse tree (CCG derivation tree) generation stage. So we design two different sets of metrics for them.

For the syntactic category (SC) parsing stage, basic metrics are SC tagging precision (SC_P), recall (SC_R) and F1-score(SC_F1).

- SC_P= (# of correctly tagged words) / (# of automatically tagged words) * 100%
- SC_R= (# of correctly tagged words) / (# of gold-standard words) * 100%
- SC_F1= 2*SC_P*SC_R / (SC_P + SC_R)

The correctly tagged words must have the same syntactic categories with the gold-standard ones.

To obtain detailed evaluation results for different syntactic categories, we will classify all tagged words into different sets and compute different SC_P, SC_R and SC_F1 for them. The classification condition is as follows.

If (SC_Token_Ratio >=10%), then the syntactic tag will be one class with its SC tag, otherwise all other low-frequency SC-tagged words will be classified with a special class with Oth_SC tag. Where, SC_Token_Ratio= (word token # of one special SC in the test set) / (word token # in the test set) * 100%.

For the CCG derivation tree generation stage, the lexical dependency pairs (LDPs) automatically extracted from the CCG derivation trees will be used as the basic evaluation units. Basic metrics for them are LDP precision (LDP_P), recall (LDP_R) and F1-score (LDP_F1).

- LDP_P = (# of correctly labeled LDPs) / (# of automatically parsed LDPs) * 100%
- LDP_R= (# of correctly labeled LDPs) / (# of gold-standard LDPs) * 100%
- LDP_F1= 2*LDP_P*LDP_R / (LDP_P+LDP_R)

The correctly labeled LDPs must have the same annotation information with the gold-standard ones.

To obtain detailed evaluation results for different LDPs, we can classify them into 5 sets and compute different LDP_P, LDP_R and LDP_F1 for them respectively.

(1) LDPs with complex event relations in the sentence levels;

(2) LDPs with concept compound relations in the chunk levels;

(3) LDPs with predicate-argument relations in the clause levels, including head-complement and adjunct-head relations.

(4) LDPs with other non-PA relations in the chunk and clause levels, including modifier-head and operator-complement relations.

(5) All other LDPs.

We compute the weighted average of the F1-scores of the first four sets (Tot4_F1) to obtain the final ranked scores for different proposed parser systems. The computation formula is as follows: Tot5_F1=$\sum LDP\_F1_i * LDP\_Ratio_i$，$i \in [1,4]$.

LDP_Ratio_i is the distributional ratio for the ith LDP set in the test set. It computation formula is: LDP_Ratio_i= (# of LDPs in i^{th} set) / (# of all LDPs) * 100%

For comparison analysis, we also compute the weighted average of F1-scores of all five sets for ranking reference.

3 Evaluation data

We used the annotated sentences in the TCT version 1.0 (Zhou, 2004) as the basic resources and designed the following transformation and annotation procedures to obtain the final training and test data for the parsing evaluation task.

Firstly, we automatically transformed all the TCT parse trees into CCG derivation trees by using the TCT2CCG tool (Zhou, 2011), and built a CCG bank version 1.0 for the TCT data. In the bank, most of clauses can be obtained correct CCG derivation trees due to the direct application of the syntax-semantics linking (SSL) principles among the basic syntactic constructions in Chinese sentences. The above CCG derivation tree (1) in section 2.1 is a good example. But there are still many syntactic constructions consist of implicit predicate-argument (IPA) relations, such as the topicalization and relative clause constructions. They can't be automatically transformed into correct CCG derivation trees through the explicit SSL mapping rules. To deal with the problem, we proposed to manually annotate the IPA relations in these special constructions and restructure the corresponding CCG derivation sub-trees according to these annotated PA tags.

The key for IPA annotation is to find the suitable construction examples that carry the IPA relations in Chinese sentences. So we classify all the event constructions (ECs) in the Chinese sentences into the following three sets:

1) Basic event constructions (BEC)

They are the typical subject-predicate-object constructions in Chinese clause level. The direct SSL can be found in the constructions. So the current TCT2CCG tool is OK for them. A simple example is as follows:

- 我(I) 读过(have read) 这本书(the book). (I have read the book.)

2) Derived event constructions (DEC)

They are the derived constructions in Chinese clause level due to some special pragmatics purposes or contexts. Most of them are the topicalization or argument-ellipsis constructions. The following is a topicalization example:

- 这本书(the book) 我(I) 读过(have read). (The book, I have read.)

The topicalized deep object “这本书(the book)” should be given special IPA tags to show the detailed SSL relations.

3) Transformed event constructions (TEC)

Most of them are the relative sub-clauses to describe the special event backgrounds for an ongoing main event predicate. The structural particle 的(*de*) is used as the relative marker for them. The following is a relative sub-clause example (underlined) in a complete clause:

- <u>我(I) 读过(have read) 的(*de*) 这本书(the book)</u> 很有趣(very interesting). (<u>The book that I have read</u> is very interesting.)

It is a big challenge to identify whether the relative noun phrases are the real extracted arguments in TECs or not.

Based on the above event construction classification, we proposed an EC-based IPA annotation scheme. For each DEC or TEC example extracted from Chinese real sentences, two or three independent annotators were asked to select the suitable corresponding BEC menu for them on an IPA annotation platform. Some detailed information about the IPA annotation procedure can be found in (Qiu, 2014).

After manual IPA annotation, we can obtain the following ECs with IPA tags for the above two DEC and TEC examples:

- [T-np-Arg2 这本书(the book)] [S-np-Arg1 我(I)] [P-vp-Pred 读过(have read)][1]
- [S-np-Arg1 我(I)] [P-vp-Pred 读过(have read)] 的(*de*) [H-np-Arg2 这本书(the book)]

So, they show the same event contents with the following corresponding BEC annotation:

[1] Each event chunk will be given the following tag combinations: <Functional tag>-<Constituent tag>-<PA tag>. Some tags used in these examples are listed as follows: T-topic, S-subject, P-predicate, O-object, H-head; np-noun phrase, vp-verb phrase; ArgX-different argument position, Pred-predicate position

- [S-np-Arg1 我(I)] [P-vp-Pred 读过(have read)] [O-np-Arg2 这本书(the book)]

These detailed IPA tags provided us with enough indicators for further CCG derivation tree rebuilding. Some main CCG rebuilding principles are as follows:

1) The same CCG tags should be assigned to the event target predicates (ETP) in the corresponding BEC, DEC and TEC examples. So in the above three ECs, the ETP "读(read)" should be assigned the same CCG tag: (S\NP)/NP.
2) The deep arguments with same IPA tags should be linked to the same argument positions in the corresponding ETP's CCG tags. For example, the argument chunk with IPA tag "Arg1" should be linked to the first NP argument position in the corresponding ETP-读(read): $(S\backslash NP_1)/NP_2$.

Based on the above principles, we proposed a CCG derivation tree rebuilding algorithm. Please refer (Qiu, 2014) for more details about the algorithm. Here, we will give some figures to show the key idea of rebuilding procedure for the DEC and TEC examples.

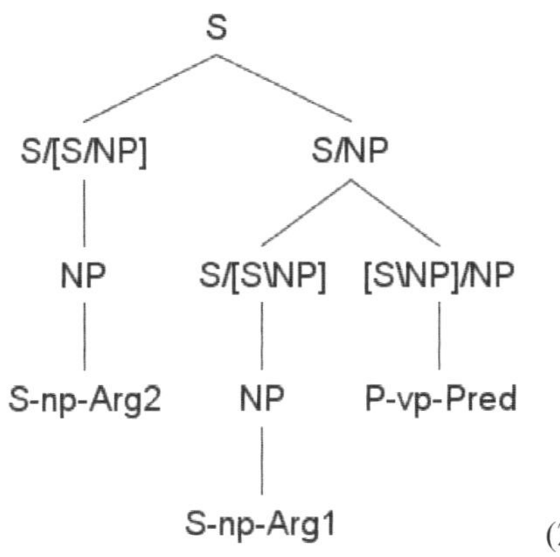

(2)

Figure (2) shows the rebuilt CCG derivation tree for a topicalized DEC. Two CCG type raising (TR) rules are used for locating two deep arguments:

- For deep subject: NP → S/(S\NP)
- For deep object: NP → S/(S/NP)

The CCG forward composition rule: S/(S\NP) (S\NP)/NP $\rightarrow_B$ S/NP, is used for the SSL of the deep subject. The special CCG forward application rule: S/(S\NP) S\NP → S, is used for the SSL of the topicalized deep object.

Figure (3) shows the rebuilt CCG derivation tree for a relative sub-clause TEC. The SSL of the deep subject is same with the above figure (2). The CCG co-indexing (CI) scheme is used for the SSL of the extracted deep object. It is assigned as a special feature in the CCG tag of the structure particle 的 (*de*): $(NP_1/NP_2)\backslash(S/NP_3)$ [CI:2=3], which means that the modified head (NP_2) of the relative clause is co-index with reduced deep object (NP_3) in the relative clause.

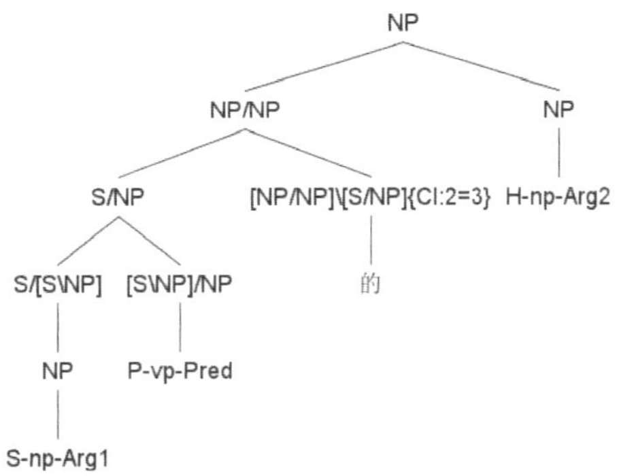

(3)

The rebuilt CCG derivation trees can provide consistent representations for different shallow syntactic alternatives with the same deep PA relations. Therefore, the same lexical dependency pairs for describing the PA relations in the above three different BEC, DEC and TEC examples can be automatically extracted (Hockenmaier et al., 2007) from the corresponding rebuilt CCG derivation trees:

- 读(read), (S\NP)/NP, 1, 我(I)
- 读(read), (S\NP)/NP, 2, 书(book)

They describe the same event contents consist in the above three EC examples. So we used these LDPs as the benchmark data for CCG parse tree evaluation.

4 Evaluation Results

4.1 Training and Test data

All the news and academic articles annotated in the TCT version 1.0 (Zhou, 2004) are selected as the basic training data for the evaluation. It consists of about 480,000 Chinese words. 1000 sentences extracted from the TCT-2010 version are used as the basic test data. After the TCT2CCG transformation, EC-based IPA annotation and CCG derivation tree rebuilding, all the training and test data have been annotated with suitable CCG format tags and derivation trees.

Table 1 Basic statistics of the training and test data: Average Sentence Length (ASL)= Word Sum/ Sent. Sum

	Sent. Sum	Word Sum	Char. Sum	ASL
Training Set	17558	473587	762866	26.97
Test Set	1000	24108	34079	24.11

Table 1 shows the basic statistics of the training and test set. Figure 1 and Figure 2 list the distribution curve of the annotated sentences with different lengths (word sums) in the training and test set. They show very similar statistical characteristics. Their peaks are located in the region of 14 to 23. More than 75% annotated sentences have 15 or more Chinese words. The average sentence length is about 25. All these data show the complexity of the syntactic parsing task in the Chinese real world texts.

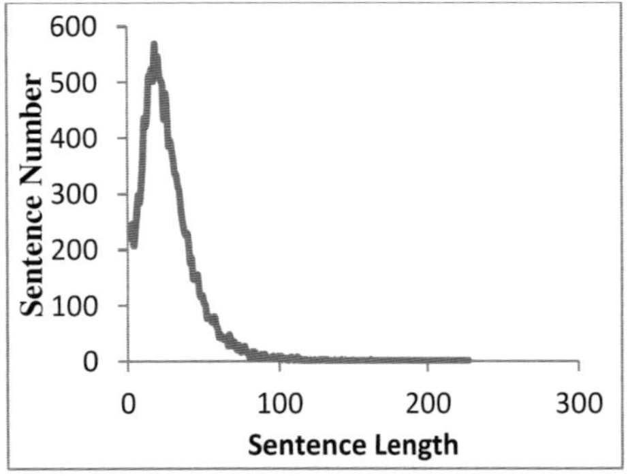

Figure 1 Sentence Length Distribution of the Training Set

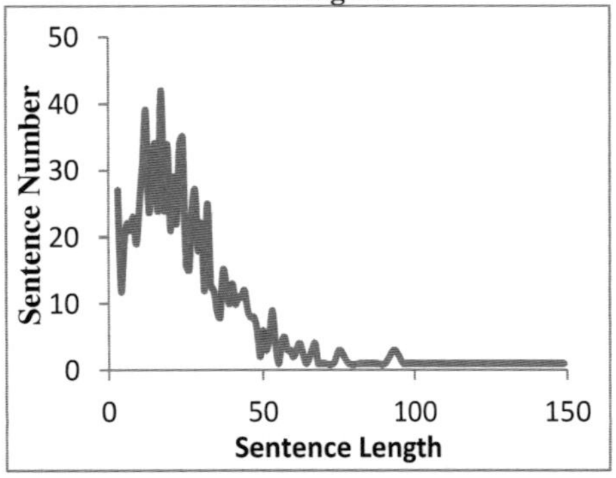

Figure 2 Sentence Length Distribution of the Test Set

4.2 General results

9 participants proposed the registration forms. Among them, only 1 participant proposed the final evaluation result. Table 2 lists the basic information of these participants.

错误!未找到引用源。 shows the ranked results of the proposed systems in the only Open track. Due to the difficulty of Chinese CCG parsing, the proposed system didn't show good parsing performance: SC_F1=71.81%, Tot5_LDP_F1=41.95%. Compared with the state-of-the-art English CCG parsers (Clark et al., 2004), the syntactic category tagging (supertagging) performance has about 20% drops in the Chinese CCG parser. It may indicate that the unknown word supertagging may be a big challenge for the Chinese language.

Table 4 lists the parsing performances of the LDPs with different internal dependency relations. As we have expected, the parsing performances of the LDPs with other non-PA relations (class 4) are the highest ones among them. The LDP-F1 score of them is about 5% better than the overall Tot4-LDP-F1 score. The second ones are the LDPs with PA relations. They show about 6% drops compared with the LDP with non-PA relations. It indicates that some outside lexical semantic resources may need for efficient PAS analysis. The parsing performances of the LDPs with complex event relations (class 1) and concept compound relations (class 2) are much lower than the overall LDP-F1 score with about 10-30% drops. Between them, the F1 score of the LDPs in class 1 is about 19% lower than that of class 2. A possible reason is that they may need more long-distance dependency features that are very difficult to be extracted through current statistical parsing model. These performance changing trends are very similar with that were found in ParsEval-2012.

Table 2 Participant information for ParsEval-2014

ID	Participants	Systems (Open/Close)
1	NLP Labortory, Zhengzhou University	/
2	Brandeis University, USA	/
3	Beijing University of Posts and Telecommunications	/
4	Institute of Automation, CAS	1/0
5	Harbin Institute of Technology	/
6	Singapore Univ. of Technology and Design	/
7	Institut national des langues et civilisation Orientales(INALCO)	/
8	Zhejian Institute of Marine	/
9	Yahoo Corp.	/

Table 3 Ranked results in the Open Track of the CCG parsing task

ID	Models	SC_F1	LDP_P	LDP_R	LDP_F1	Tot4_LDP_P	Tot4_LDP_R	Tot4_LDP_F1	Rank
4	Single	71.81%	42.32%	42.27%	42.29%	41.83%	42.07%	41.95%	1

Table 4 Evaluation results of the different classes of LDPs in the Open Track

	Class 1			Class 2			Class 3			Class 4			Class 5		
ID	P	R	F1	P	R	F1	P	R	F1	P	R	F1	P	R	F1
4	12.99%	11.92%	12.43%	26.80%	36.87%	31.04%	40.69%	40.47%	40.58%	47.60%	46.71%	47.15%	45.81%	43.62%	44.69%

5 Conclusions

Combinatory categorical grammar can provide strong platform for describing the deep PAS of different shallow syntactic alternatives with same event contents. So we introduced CCG into the 4th Chinese parsing evaluation (ParsEval-2014) and proposed an EC-based IPA annotation method to build a new CCG-based evaluation benchmark data. Although the number of the proposed systems was not enough to show the real application potential of CCG parsing for the Chinese language, we still think CCG parsing is a good direction need to be explored in the future.

Acknowledgments

The research was supported by National Basic Research Program of China (Grant No.: 2013CB329304) and National Science Foundation of China (Grant No.: 61373075). Thanks Mr. Zhou Xiaocong to develop the LDP evaluation tools for the evaluation task.

References

Clark, S., Copestake, A., Curran, J.R., Zhang, Y., Herbelot, A., Haggerty, J., Ahn, B.G., Wyk, C.V., Roesner, J., Kummerfeld, J., Dawborn, T.: 2009 Large-scale syntactic processing: Parsing the web. *Final Report of the 2009 JHU CLSP Workshop*

Clark, Stephen and James R. Curran. Parsing the WSJ using CCG and log-linear models. 2004. In *Proceedings of the 42nd Annual Meeting of the Association for Computational Linguistics*, pages 103–110, Barcelona, Spain.

Hockenmaier, J., Steedman, M.: 2007. CCGbank: A Corpus of CCG Derivations and Dependency Structures Extracted from the Penn Treebank. *Computational Linguistics* 33(3), 355--396

Han Qiu. 2014. Research on Chinese Predicate-Argument Structure Analysis and Annotation. Master thesis. Dept. of computer science and technology, Tsinghua University.

Mark Steedman. 1996. *Surface Structure and Interpretation*. MIT Press, Cambridge, MA.

Mark Steedman. 2000. *The Syntactic Process*. MIT Press, Cambridge, MA.

Qiang Zhou. 2004. Chinese Treebank Annotation Scheme. *Journal of Chinese Information*, 18(4), p1-8.

Qiang Zhou, Yuemei Li. 2009. Evaluation report of CIPS-ParsEval-2009. In Proc. of First Workshop on Chinese Syntactic Parsing Evaluation, Beijing China, Nov. 2009. pIII—XIII.

Qiang Zhou, Jingbo Zhu. 2010. Chinese Syntactic Parsing Evaluation. *Proc. of CIPS-SIGHAN Joint Conference on Chinese Language Processing* (CLP-2010), Beijing, August 2010, pp 286-295.

Qiang Zhou. 2011. Automatically transform the TCT data into a CCG bank: designation specification Ver 3.0. Technical Report CSLT-20110512, Center for speech and language technology, Research Institute of Information Technology, Tsinghua University.

Qiang Zhou. 2012. Evaluation Report of the third Chinese Parsing Evaluation: CIPS-SIGHAN-ParsEval-2012. Proc. of *CIPS-SIGHAN Joint Conference on Chinese Language Processing* (CLP-2012), Tianjin.

Generative CCG Parsing with OOV Prediction

Huijia Wu
Institute of Automation, Chinese Academy of Science
huijia.wu1@ia.ac.cn

Abstract

This paper presents our system for the CIPS-SIGHAN-2014 bakeoff task of Simplified Chinese Parsing (Task 3). The system adopts a generative model with OOV prediction model. The former has a PCFG form while the latter uses a three-layer hierarchical Bayesian model. The final performance on the test corpus is reported together with the performance of the OOV model.

1 Introduction

Statistical parsing is the process of discovering the syntactic relations in a sentence, according to the rules of a formal grammar. There exist a body of parsers based on various linguistic formalisms, such as LFG, HPSG, TAG and CCG. (Riezler et al., 2002; Sarkar and Joshi, 2003; Cahill et al., 2004; Miyao and Tsujii, 2005; Clark and Curran, 2007). The parsing techniques also vary from the generative model to the discriminative model. The former uses a joint probability distribution including both the observations and the targets, while the latter only models the conditional probability measure to describe the randomness of the targets based on the observations (Hockenmaier, 2003a, 2003b; Clark and Curran, 2007).

The out-of-vocabulary (OOV) problem is far-from solved in statistical parsing, especially in CCG. There are lots of categories such that a computer would be less likely to remember a word. Clark proposed a supertagger to assignment several possible categories to a word which provides highly accurate and efficient results (Clark, 2002).

In this task we propose a three layer hierarchical Bayesian model to predict the OOV, using the POS tag as the hidden layer. Further, we estimate a OOV's category through integrating all possible POS tags, which means that we need to find relations between OOV and POS. To achieve this goal, we create a mapping between a CCG tree and a TCT tree, which is another kind of syntactic tree according the Tsinghua Chinese Treebank (TCT).

Leaf nodes	Unary trees	Head left:	Head right:
(S\NP)/NP | 喜欢	S/(S\NP) | NP	S\NP (S\NP)/NP NP	S NP S\NP

Table 1: The four different kinds of expansion

The final report has two parts, one is the evaluation performance based on the test corpus, the other is the performance on OOV prediction.

2 Our System

Our system combines a generative model for parsing with a OOV prediction model. The former follows heavily from (Hockenmaier, 2003a) with slightly modification, which includes the definition of head nodes, using Dirichlet prior as the smoothing technique. The latter is a three-layer hierarchical Bayesian model: the input and the output layer corresponds to a OOV and its category, respectively, composed with a POS tag as the hidden layer.

2.1 Generative Model for Parsing

In this evaluation task, we adopt a generative model as the CCG parsing algorithm. One advantage of the generative model is it needs less human intervention than the discriminative model, which means that, if we have enough data, together with the proper generative model, the algorithm can learn from the data, of the data and for the data with a competitive performance, while the discriminative model needs a lot of manual feature templates, which sounds like cheating since the features are designed by human, rather than the computer itself.

Our generative model bases on (Hockenmaier

Proceedings of the Third CIPS-SIGHAN Joint Conference on Chinese Language Processing, pages 153–156,
Wuhan, China, 20-21 October 2014

, 2003a), which defines a generative model over CCG derivation trees. This model acts like a PCFG form, which does not incorporate the notion of combinatory trees. Instead, it is a generative model over sub-trees. By contrast to Hockenmaier, we use a different approach of defining head node, which is a functor categories (categories that accept arguments). Since from a modelling point of view, isolating a head node from a non-head one just make a generative process more hierarchical, there is no statistically significant differences between a head node and a non-head node.

The derivations of a CCG tree can be represented by top-down expansions. As mentioned in (Hockenmaier, 2003a), there are four kinds of leaf nodes in a CCG tree, which corresponds to four kinds of expansion (Table 1). Follow this convention, we have the following generating process:

1. **Expansion probabiltiy**: Start from a root, choose a type of expansion N by $P(\text{exp}|C)$ with exp $\in$ {left, right, unary, leaf} and $C \in \mathcal{C}$.

2. **Lexical probability**: If it meets a leaf node, a word w is generated with probability $P(w|C, \text{exp} = \text{leaf})$, stop.

3. **Head probability**: Otherwise, choose a head node with probability $P(H|C, \text{exp})$.

4. **Non-head probability**: Finally, generate a non-head node w.p. $P(D|C, \text{exp}, H)$.

2.2 Inference and Learning

The parameter estimation step is similar to a PCFG parser based on the maximum likelihood estimation (MLE), but the estimator may become sparsity due to the huge number of parameters. This may cause the problem of overestimation. To avoid this, we can use a regularization term or a prior as the smoothing technique.

In this task, we prefer a Dirichlet distribution as the prior to other smoothing methods. Since it is easy to implement and forms a conjugate prior to a multinomial distribution. We put a Dirichlet prior $\text{Dir}(\alpha)$ on a lexical distribution $P(w|C, \text{exp} = \text{leaf})$. In the experiment we set the $\alpha = (1, 1, \ldots, 1)$ as a uniform distribution.

The learning or decoding algorithm is the well-known CKY algorithm. But efficiency is still a problem, since the number of categories is large, for a long sentence more computing steps will be needed to compose two adjacent cells in a chart than other lexicon-based parsers. Fortunately, Clark and Curran proposed an log-likelihood CCG parser which is efficient enough to large-scale NLP tasks (Clark and Curran, 2007).

2.3 Estimating the OOV

The supertagger proposed by Clark uses a maximum entropy model to predict a word's categories, based on the idea that given a set of manual features, we need to find a category distribution restricted on the set acts an uniform predictor to unknown words. This maximum entropy principle may not apply to OOV estimating, for the reasons that the OOV is rare, statistically insignificant and unable to catch by a statistical model.

Manual rules can get a more accurate prediction than the statistical model, but these rules are also non-flexible, time-confusing and heavy-lifting. To overcome this problem, we propose a mapping between a CCG tree and a TCT tree with the same terminal nodes.

To make this mapping possible we first need to verify the existence, uniqueness and reversibility of such a mapping. Luckily such a mapping is exist since the CCG tree is generated by a TCT tree. To make it simpler we omit the condition of the uniqueness and reversibility. Now the problem is: Can we find a such a mapping to help us to predict the OOV?

Obviously, the mapping is the relation between the syntactic symbols (POS) and the semantic symbols (category). If we can find the estimator of $P(\text{cat}|\text{pos})$ our problem is easily solved by:

$$P(O|C) = \frac{P(C|O)P(O)}{\sum_{O\in\{OOV\}} P(C|O)P(O)} \tag{1}$$

$$= \frac{P(O)\sum_{S\in\{POS\}} P(C|S)P(S|O)}{\sum_{O\in\{OOV\}}\left\{P(O)\sum_{S\in\{POS\}} P(C|S)P(S|O)\right\}} \tag{2}$$

In the above equations, O stands for the OOV, which is a random variable assigned values from all possible OOV. C indicates the category and S stands for POS tag.

How to create such a mapping matrix? We start from the root node, using a depth-first search algorithm to find the correspondence between nodes in each tree. Notice that the CCG tree is binary, while the TCT tree is not. To find the correct map, we first need to binarize the TCT tree. But the set of all possible binary trees may become huge when there are many children of a node. Fortunately we just need to expand all binary nodes through one direction.

This model acts like the maximum entropy model, since they all use the context features, but the difference is the former focuses on a more restricted conditions based on the tree structure, while the features in the latter is at the sentence level.

3 Experiment

3.1 Datesets

The data uses in the system composed of two parts, one is for the parser, the other is for the OOV prediction model. The data used by the former comes from the sponsor (CCG bank) with 17558 parsed sentences, 984 categories, while the latter uses data from both the CCG bank and the TCT bank with 9034 sentences. To find the mapping tree with the same leaf nodes, we extract such tree pairs from the two data sets. Finally we get a data set for the OOV prediction model with 5360 tree pairs.

3.2 Experimental Results

There are two kinds of metrics to be evaluated, one is the syntactic category evaluation metrics, the other is the parsing tree evaluation metrics. We report both of these metrics, together with the performance of the OOV prediction model.

Table 2 and 3 gives the performance of the parser on the test set, based on the syntactic category evaluation metrics and the parsing tree evaluation metrics, respectively.

The notations in Table 3 are explained as follows (Qiang Zhou, 2014):

- LDP_CE stands for the lexical dependency pairs (LDPs) with complex event relations in the sentence levels.
- LDP_CC stands for the LDPs with concept compound relations in the chunk levels.
- LDP_PA stands for the LDPs with predicate-argument relations in the clause levels, including head-complement and adjunct-head relations.
- LDP_MO stands for the LDPs with other non-PA relations in the chunk and clause levels, including modifier-head and operator-complement relations.

Category	Precision	Recall	F1
NP	79.71	89.07	84.13
NP/NP	63.31	67.63	65.4
Others	70.57	67.47	68.99
All	71.80	71.81	71.81

Table 2: The performance based on the syntactic category evaluation metrics

Relation	Precision	Recall	F1
LDP_CE	12.98	11.92	12.43
LDP_CC	26.80	36.87	31.04
LDP_PA	40.69	40.47	40.58
LDP_MO	45.99	45.33	45.66
Others	45.81	43.62	44.69
All	42.31	42.27	42.29

Table 3: The performance based on the parsing tree evaluation metrics

Table 4 shows the performance of the OOV estimation model, OOV-POS is the baseline model, which means that a node's category is taken exactly on the corresponding POS tag, +head means such a category is not just on its POS tag, but also with its parent's node's POS tag. +sister has the similar meaning.

Model	Precision	Recall	F1
OOV-POS	60.02	72.10	65.46
+parent	83.15	88.12	85.56
+sister	76.2	82.41	79.18
+parent, sister	86.67	90.2	88.39

Table 4: The results of OOV prediction model

4 Conclusion

This report has shown a generative CCG parser with a OOV prediction model. One contribution of this report is the development of a Bayesian model to predict the OOV with high accuracy. The techniques we use is easy to extend to a more complicated system.

Acknowledge

We would like to thank Qiang Zhou for helpful discussion.

References

Clark, Stephen. 2002. *A maximum-entropy-inspired parser* . In Proceedings of the 1st Meeting of the NAACL, pages 132–139, Seattle, WA.

Clark, Stephen and James R. Curran. 2003. *Log-linear models for wide-coverage CCG parsing.*. In Proceedings of the EMNLP Conference, pages 97–104, Sapporo, Japan.

Clark, Stephen and James R. Curran. 2004b. *Parsing the WSJ using CCG and log-linear models.* In Proceedings of the 42nd Meeting of the ACL, pages 104–111, Barcelona, Spain.

Clark, Stephen, Julia Hockenmaier, and Mark Steedman. 2002. *Building deep dependency structures with a wide-coverage CCG parser.* In Proceedings of the 40th Meeting of the ACL, pages 327–334, Philadelphia, PA.

Geman, Stuart and Mark Johnson. 2002. *Dynamic programming for parsing and estimation of stochastic unification-based grammars.* In Proceedings of the 40th Meeting of the ACL, pages 279–286, Philadelphia, PA.

Collins, Michael. 1996. *A new statistical parser based on bigram lexical dependencies.* In Proceedings of the 34th Meeting of the ACL, pages 184–191, Santa Cruz, CA.

Collins, Michael. 1999. *Head-driven statistical models for natural language parsing.* PhD thesis, University of Pennsylvania.

Collins, Michael. 2003. *Head-driven statistical models for natural language parsing.* Computational Linguistics, 29(4):589–637.

Hockenmaier, Julia and Mark Steedman. 2002a *Acquiring compact lexicalized grammars from a cleaner treebank.* In Proceedings of the Third LREC Conference, pages 1974–1981, Las Palmas, Spain.

Hockenmaier, Julia and Mark Steedman. 2002b *Generative models for statistical parsing with Combinatory Categorial Grammar.* In Proceedings of the 40th Meeting of the ACL, pages 335–342, Philadelphia, PA.

Hockenmaier, Julia. 2003a *Data and Models for Statistical Parsing with Combinatory Categorial Grammar.* Ph.D. thesis, University of Edinburgh.

Hockenmaier, Julia. 2003b *Parsing with generative models of predicate-argument structure.* In Proceedings of the 41st Meeting of the ACL, pages 359–366, Sapporo, Japan.

Lari, K. and S. J. Young. 1990. *The estimation of stochastic context-free grammars using the inside-outside algorithm.* Computer Speech and Language, 4(1):35–56.

Mark Johnson, Thomas L. Griffiths and Sharon Goldwater. 2007. *Inference for PCFGs via Markov Chain Monte Carlo.* Human Language Technologies 2007: The Conference of the North American Chapter of the Association for Computational Linguistics; Proceedings of the Main Confer- ence, pages 139-146.

Percy Liang, Slav Petrov, Michael I. Jordan, Dan Klein. 2007. *The infinite PCFG using hierarchical Dirichlet processes.* Empirical Methods in Natural Language Processing and Computational Natural Language Learning(EMNLP/CoNLL).

Qiang Zhou. 2004. *Chinese Treebank Annotation Scheme.* Journal of Chinese Information, 18(4), p1-8.

Qiang Zhou. 2011. *Automatically transform the TCT data into a CCG bank: designation specification Ver 3.0.* Technical Report CSLT-20110512, Center for speech and language technology, Research Institute of Information Technology, Tsinghua University.

Ratnaparkhi, Adwait, Salim Roukos, and Todd Ward. 1994. *A maximum entropy model for parsing.* In Proceedings of the International Conference on Spoken Language Processing, pages 803–806, Yokohama, Japan.

Sarkar, A. and Joshi, A. 2003. *Tree-adjoining grammars and its application to statistical parsing.* In Bod, R., Scha, R., and Sima'an, K., editors, Data-oriented parsing. CSLI.

Steedman, Mark. 1996. *Surface Structure and Interpretation.* MIT Press, Cambridge, MA.

Steedman, Mark. 2000. *The Syntactic Process.* The MIT Press, Cambridge, MA.

Steedman, Mark, Steven Baker, Stephen Clark, Jeremiah Crim, Julia Hockenmaier, Rebecca Hwa, Miles Osborne, Paul Ruhlen, and Anoop Sarkar. 2002. *Semi-supervised training for statistical parsing: Final report.* Technical report, Center for Language and Speech Processing, Johns Hopkins University, Baltimore, MD.

Yonatan Bisk and Julia Hockenmaier. 2013. *An HDP Model for Inducing Com- binatory Categorial Grammars.* Transactions of the Association for Compu- tational Linguistics Vol 1.

An Improved Graph Model for Chinese Spell Checking*

Yang Xin[1,2], **Hai Zhao**[1,2,†], **Yuzhu Wang**[1,2] **and Zhongye Jia**[1,2]
[1]Center for Brain-Like Computing and Machine Intelligence,
Department of Computer Science and Engineering,
Shanghai Jiao Tong University, Shanghai 200240, China
[2]Key Laboratory of Shanghai Education Commission for Intelligent Interaction
and Cognitive Engineering, Shanghai Jiao Tong University, Shanghai, 200240, China
xuechen.xy@gmail.com, zhaohai@cs.sjtu.edu.cn,
hfut0830@sjtu.edu.cn, jia.zhongye@gmail.com

Abstract

In this paper, we propose an improved graph model for Chinese spell checking. The model is based on a graph model for generic errors and two independently-trained models for specific errors. First, a graph model represents a Chinese sentence and a modified single source shortest path algorithm is performed on the graph to detect and correct generic spelling errors. Then, we utilize conditional random fields to solve two specific kinds of common errors: the confusion of "在" (at) (pinyin is 'zai' in Chinese), "再" (again, more, then) (pinyin: zai) and "的" (of) (pinyin: de), "地" (-ly, adverb-forming particle) (pinyin: de), "得" (so that, have to) (pinyin: de). Finally, a rule based system is exploited to solve the pronoun usage confusions: "她" (she) (pinyin: ta), "他" (he) (pinyin: ta) and some others fixed collocation errors. The proposed model is evaluated on the standard data set released by the SIGHAN Bake-off 2014 shared task, and gives competitive result.

*This work was partially supported by the National Natural Science Foundation of China (No. 60903119, No. 61170114, and No. 61272248), the National Basic Research Program of China (No. 2013CB329401), the Science and Technology Commission of Shanghai Municipality (No. 13511500200), the European Union Seventh Framework Program (No. 247619), the Cai Yuanpei Program (CSC fund 201304490199 and 201304490171), and the art and science interdiscipline funds of Shanghai Jiao Tong University (A study on mobilization mechanism and alerting threshold setting for online community, and media image and psychology evaluation: a computational intelligence approach).

†Corresponding author.

1 Introduction

Spell checking is a routine processing task for every written language, which is an automatic mechanism to detect and correct human spelling errors. Given sentences, the goal of the task is to return the locations of incorrect words and suggest the correct words. However, Chinese spell checking (CSC) is very different from that in English or other alphabetical languages from the following ways.

Usually, the object of spell checking is words, but "word" is not a natural concept in Chinese, since there are no word delimiters between words in Chinese writing. An English "word" consists of Latin letters. While a Chinese "word" consists of characters, which also known as "漢字" (Chinese character) (pinyin[1] is 'han zi' in Chinese). Thus, essentially, the object of CSC is misused characters in a sentence. Meanwhile, sentences for CSC task are meant to computer-typed but not those handwritten Chinese. In handwritten Chinese, there exist varies of spelling errors including non-character errors which are probably caused by stroke errors. While in computer-typed Chinese, a non-character spelling error is impossible, because any illegal Chinese characters will be filtered by Chinese input method engine so that CSC never encounters "out-of-character (OOC)" problem. Thus, the Chinese spelling errors come from the misuse of characters, not characters themselves.

Spelling errors in alphabetical languages, such as English, are always typically divided into two categories:

- The misspelled word is a non-word, for example "come" is misspelled into "cmoe";

[1]Pinyin is the official phonetic system for transcribing the sound of Chinese characters into Latin script.

Proceedings of the Third CIPS-SIGHAN Joint Conference on Chinese Language Processing, pages 157–166,
Wuhan, China, 20-21 October 2014

- The misspelled word is still a legal word, for example "come" is misspelled into "cone".

While in Chinese, if the misspelled word is a non-word, the word segmenter will not recognize it as a word, but split it into two or more words with fewer characters. For example, if "你好世界" in Example 1 of Table 1 is misspelled into "你好世節", the word segmenter will segment it into "你好/世/節" instead of "你好/世節". For non-word spelling error, the misspelled word will be mis-segmented.

Name	Example 1	Example 2
Golden	你好/世界	好好/地/出去/玩
Misspelled	你好/世/節	好好/的/出去/玩
Pinyin	ni hao shi jie	hao hao de chu qu wan
Translation	hello the world	enjoy yourself outside

Table 1: Two examples for Chinese spelling error. Both examples have the same pinyin.

Thus CSC cannot be directly applied those edit distance based methods which are commonly used for alphabetical languages. CSC task has to deal with word segmentation problem first, since misspelled sentence could not be segmented properly by word segmenter.

There also exist Chinese spelling errors which are unrelated with word segmentation. For example, "好好地出去玩" in Example 2 of Table 1 is misspelled into "好好的出去玩", but both of them have the same segmentation. So it is necessary to perform further specific process.

In this paper, based on our previous work (Jia et al., 2013b) in SIGHAN Bake-off 2013, we describe an improved graph model to handle the CSC task. The improved model includes a graph model for generic spelling errors, conditional random fields (CRF) for two special errors and a rule based system for some collocation errors.

2 Related Work

Over the past few years, there were many methods proposed for CSC task. (Sun et al., 2010) developed a phrase-based spelling error model from the clickthrough data by means of measuring the edit distance between an input query and the optimal spelling correction. (Gao et al., 2010) explored the ranker-based approach which included visual similarity, phonological similarity, dictionary, and frequency features for large scale web search. (Ahmad and Kondrak, 2005) proposed a spelling error model from search query logs to improve the quality of query. (Han and Chang, 2013) employed maximum entropy models for CSC. They trained a maximum entropy model for each Chinese character based on a large raw corpus and used the model to detect the spelling errors.

Two key techniques, word segmentation (Zhao et al., 2006a; Zhao and Kit, 2008b; Zhao et al., 2006b; Zhao and Kit, 2008a; Zhao and Kit, 2007; Zhao and Kit, 2011; Zhao et al., 2010) and language model (LM), are also popularly used for C-SC. Most of those approaches can fall into four categories. The first category consists of the methods that all the characters in a sentence are assumed to be errors and an LM is used for correction (Chang, 1995; Yu et al., 2013). (Chang, 1995) proposed a method that replaced each character in the sentence based on a confusion set and computed the probability of the original sentence and all modified sentences according to a bigram language model generated from a newspaper corpus. The method based on the motivation that all the typos were caused by either visual similarity or phonological similarity. So they manually built a confusion set as a key factor in their system. Although the method can detect misspelled words well, it was very time consuming for detection, generated too much false positive results and was not able to refer to an entire paragraph. (Yu et al., 2013) developed a joint error detection and correction system. The method assumed that all characters in the sentence may be errors and replaced every character using a confusion set. Then they segmented all new generated sentences and gave a score of the segmentation using LM for every sentence. In fact, this method did not always perform well according to (Yu et al., 2013).

The second category includes the methods that all single-character words are supposed to be errors and an LM is used for correction, for example (Lin and Chu, 2013) . They developed a system which supposed that all single-character words may be typos. They replaced all single-character words by similar characters using a confusion set and segmented the newly created sentences again. If a new sentence resulted in a better word segmentation, spelling error was reported. Their system gave good detection recall but low false-alarm rate.

The third category utilizes more than one approaches for detection and an LM for correction. (Hsieh et al., 2013) used two different systems for error detection. The first system detected error characters based on unknown word detection and LM verification. The second one solved error detection based on a suggestion dictionary generated from a confusion set. Finally, two systems were combined to obtain the final detection result. (He and Fu, 2013) divided typos into three categories which were character-level errors (CLEs), word-level errors (WLEs) and context-level errors (CLEs), and three different methods were used to detect the different errors respectively. In addition to using the result of word segmentation for detection, (Yeh et al., 2013) also proposed a dictionary-based method to detect spelling errors. The dictionary contained similar pronunciation and shape information for each Chinese character. (Yang et al., 2013) proposed another method to improve the candidate detections. They employed high confidence pattern matching to strengthen the candidate errors after word segmentation.

The last category is formed by the methods which use word segmentation for detection and different models for correction (Liu et al., 2013; Chen et al., 2013; Chiu et al., 2013). (Liu et al., 2013) used support vector machine (SVM) to select the most probable sentence from multiple candidates. They used word segmentation and machine translation model to generate the candidates respectively. The SVM was used to rerank the candidates. (Chen et al., 2013) not only applied LM, but also used various topic models to cover the shortage of LM. (Chiu et al., 2013) explored statistical machine translation model to translate the sentences containing typos into correct ones. In their model, the sentence with the highest translation probability which indicated how likely a typo was translated into its candidate correct word was chosen as the final correction sentence.

3 The Revised Graph Model

The graph model (Jia et al., 2013b) of SIGHAN Bake-off 2013 is inspired by the idea of shortest path word segmentation algorithm which is based on the following assumption: a reasonable segmentation should maximize the lengths of all segments or minimize the total number of segments (Casey and Lecolinet, 1996). A directed acyclic graph (DAG) is thus built from the input sentence similar. The spelling error detection and correction problem is transformed to a single source shortest path (SSSP) problem on the DAG.

Given a dictionary $\mathbb{D}$ and a similar characters $\mathbb{C}$, for a sentence S of m characters $\{c_1, c_2, \ldots, c_m\}$, the original vertices V of the DAG in (Jia et al., 2013b) are:

$$\begin{aligned} V = &\{w_{i,j} | w_{i,j} = c_i \ldots c_j \in \mathbb{D}\} \\ &\cup \{w^k_{i,j} | w^k_{i,j} = c_i \ldots c'_k \ldots c_j \in \mathbb{D}, \\ &\qquad \tau \leq j - i \leq T, \\ &\qquad c'_k \in \mathbb{C}[c_k], k = i, i+1, \ldots, j\} \\ &\cup \{w_{-,0}, w_{n+1,-}\}. \end{aligned}$$

where $w_{-,0}$ = "<S>" and $w_{n+1,-}$ = "</S>" are two special vertices represent the start and end of the sentence.

However, the graph model cannot be applied to continuous word errors. Take the following sentence as an example, "健康" (health) (pinyin: jian kang) is misspelled into "建缸" (pinyin: jian gang). Because the substitution strategy does not simultaneously substitute two continuous characters.

- 然後，我是計劃我們到我家一個附近的‘建缸’ (pinyin: jian gang) 中心去游泳。

  Translation after correction: And then, we plan to go swimming near my house.

For example, the substitution of "建缸" (pinyin: jian gang) may be "碱缸" (pinyin: jian gang), "建鋼" (pinyin: jian gang), "建行" (pinyin: jian hang) and so on, none of which is the desired correction. So we revise the construction method of the graph model. Considering efficiency, we only deal with the continuous errors with 2 characters. The revised V are:

$$\begin{aligned} V = &\{w_{i,j} | w_{i,j} = c_i \ldots c_j \in \mathbb{D}\} \\ &\cup \{w^k_{i,j} | w^k_{i,j} = c_i \ldots c'_k \ldots c_j \in \mathbb{D}, \\ &\qquad \tau \leq j - i \leq T, \\ &\qquad c'_k \in \mathbb{C}[c_k], k = i, i+1, \ldots, j\} \\ &\cup \{w^l | w^l = c'_l c'_{l+1} \in \mathbb{D}, \\ &\qquad c'_l, c'_{l+1} \in \mathbb{C}\} \\ &\cup \{w_{-,0}, w_{n+1,-}\}. \end{aligned}$$

With the modified DAG G, the "建缸" (pinyin: jian gang) is substituted as "健康" (health) (pinyin: jian kang), "峴港" (Danang) (pinyin: xian gang), "潛航" (submerge) (pinyin: qian hang) and so on, which have already contained the desired correction.

4 The Improved Graph Model

The graph model based on word segmentation in (Jia et al., 2013b) includes the revised graph model in section 3 still has its limitations. For a sentence, in the graph construction stage, the substitution is only applied to the situation that the number of words after segmenting has to be decreased, which means there exists new longer word after segmentation. In addition, if the segmentation result of a sentence is a single character, the graph model does not work, because a single character will not be substituted. For example in the following two sentences, the "他" (he) (pinyin: ta) in the first sentence should be corrected into "她" (she) (pinyin: ta) and the "的" (of)(pinyin: de) in the second sentence should be corrected into "地" (-ly, adverb-forming particle) (pinyin: de), however, the graph model does not work for this case.

- 雖然我不在我的國家，不能見到媽媽，可是我要給'他' (him) (pinyin: ta)打電話！

  Translation after correction: Though I'm not in my country so that I cannot see my mum, I would like to call her!

- 我們也不要想太多；我們來好好'的' (of) (pinyin: de)出去玩吧！

  Translation after correction: We would not worry too much, just enjoy ourselves outside now!

The graph model is also powerless for the error situation that the wrong character was segmented into a legal word. Take the following sentence as an example, the word "心裡" (in mind, at heart) (pinyin: xin li) will be not separated after the building the graph, so "裡" (pinyin: li) could not be corrected into "理" (pinyin: li).

- 我對心'裡' (pinyin: li)研究有興趣。

  Translation after correction: I'm interested in psychological research.

For the sake of alleviating the above limitations of the graph model, we utilize CRF model to deal with two kinds of errors, and a rule based system is established to cope with the pronoun errors: "她" (she) (pinyin: ta), "他" (he) (pinyin: ta) and collocation errors.

4.1 CRF Model

Two classifiers using CRF model are respectively trained to tackle the common character usage confusions: 在" (at) (pinyin: zai), 再" (again, more, then) (pinyin: zai) and "的" (of)(pinyin: de), "地" (-ly, adverb-forming particle) (pinyin: de), "得"(so that, have to) (pinyin: de). We assume that the correct character selection is related with its neighboring two words and part-of-speech (POS) tags. The classifiers are trained on a large five-gram token set which is extracted from a large POS tagged corpus. The feature selection algorithm is according to (Zhao et al., 2013; Wang et al., 2014; Jia et al., 2013a). The feature set for CRF model is as follows:

$$w_{j,-2}, pos_{j,-2}, w_{j,-1}, pos_{j,-1}, w_{j,0}, pos_{j,0}, \\ w_{j,1}, pos_{j,1}, w_{j,2}, pos_{j,2}$$

where j is the token index to indicate its position, $w_{j,0}$ is the current candidate character and $pos_{j,0}$ is its POS tag. ICTCLAS (Zhang et al., 2003) is adopted for POS tagging.

A set of feature strings that we used are presented in Table 2. The labels for "的" (of) (pinyin: de), "地" (-ly, adverb-forming particle) (pinyin: de), "得"(so that, have to) (pinyin: de) are 1, 2, 3 and "在" (at) (pinyin: zai), "再" (again, more, then) (pinyin: zai) are 1, 2.

4.2 The Rule Based System

To effectively handle pronoun usage errors for "她" (she) (pinyin: ta), and "他" (he) (pinyin: ta) and other collocation errors, we design a rule based system extracted from the development set.

The Table 3 is the rules we set for solving the pronoun usage errors, where the $prefix[i]$ is the current word $w[i]$'s prefix in a sentence. For the others rules, we divide them into five categories, which are presented in Table 4 – Table 8. In Table 4, we only present several typical rules in Rule 3. The negation symbol "¬" in the Table 6 and Table 7 means that the word in corresponding position is not the one in the brackets. Each rule in the tables is verified by the Baidu[2] search engine. If the error situation is legally emerged in the search result, we will not correct the error any more.

[2]http://www.baidu.com/

Feature	Example1	Example2
$w_{j,-2}$	“來”	“和”
$w_{j,-1}$	“好好”	“你”
$w_{j,1}$	“出”	“一起”
$w_{j,-2}$,$w_{j,-1}$	“來”,“好好”	“和”,“你”
$w_{j,-2}$,$w_{j,-1}$,$w_{j,1}$	“來”,“好好”,“出”	“和”,“你”,“一起”
$w_{j,1}$,$w_{j,2}$	“出”,“去”	“一起”,“。”
$pos_{j,-2}$	*v*	*p*
$pos_{j,-1}$	*z*	*r*
$pos_{j,1}$	*v*	*s*
$pos_{j,-2}$,$pos_{j,-1}$	*v,z*	*p,r*
$pos_{j,-1}$,$pos_{j,1}$	*z,v*	*r,s*
$pos_{j,1}$,$pos_{j,2}$	*v,v* o	*s,w*
$pos_{j,-2}$,$pos_{j,-1}$,$pos_{j,1}$	*v,z,v*	*p,r,s*
$w_{j,-1}$,$pos_{j,1}$	“好好”,*v*	“你”,*s*
$pos_{j,-1}$,$w_{j,1}$	*z*,“出”	*r*,“一起”
$pos_{j,-2}$,$pos_{j,-1}$,$w_{j,1}$	*v,z*,“出”	*p,r*,“一起”

Table 2: Feature strings for sentences “我們來好好地出去玩吧！” and “我只要和你在一起。”.

$prefix[i]$ does not contain	$prefix[i]$ contains	$w[i]$	corrected $w[i]$
(媽 and 爸) or (她 and 他) or (母 and 父) or (女 and 男) or (太太 and 先生)	她 or 媽 or 母 or 女 or 妹 or 姊 or 姐 or 婆 or 阿姨 or 太太	他	她
她 or 媽 or 母 or 女 or 妹 or 姊 or 姐 or 婆 or 阿姨 or 太太	他 or 爸 or 父 or 男 or 哥 or 先生	她	他

Table 3: Specific rules for the pronouns “她、他” confusion.

$w[i]$	$pos[i+1]$	corrected $w[i]$
阿	w	啊
馬 or 碼	w	嗎
門	r, n	們
把	r, n	吧

Table 4: Rule 1. The correction related with right neighbored POS tag.

5 Experiments

5.1 Data Sets and Resources

The proposed method is evaluated on the data sets of SIGHAN Bake-off shared tasks in 2013 and 2014. In Bake-off 2013, the sentences were collected from 13 to 14-year-old students' essays in formal written tests (Wu et al., 2013). In Bake-off 2014, the sentences were collected from Chinese as a foreign language (CFL) learners' essays selected from the National Taiwan Normal University (NTNU) learner corpus[3]. All the data sets are in traditional Chinese.

In Bake-off 2013, the essays were manually annotated with different labels (see Figure 1). There is at most one error in each sentence. However, the development set in Bake-off 2014 is enlarged and the error types (see Figure 2) are more diverse. More than one error might be in each sentence. And there exists continuous errors as in Figure 2.

```
<DOC Nid="00001">
<P>我看過許多勇敢的人，不怕措折地奮鬥，這種精神值得我們學習。</P>
<TEXT>
<MISTAKE wrong_position=13>
<WRONG>措折</WRONG>
<CORRECT>挫折</CORRECT>
</MISTAKE>
</TEXT>
</DOC>
```

Figure 1: A sample of annotated essay in Bake-off 2013.

```
<ESSAY title="寫給即將初次見面的筆友的一封信">
<TEXT>
<PASSAGE id="B1-0118-3">然後，我是計畫我們到我家一個附近的建缸
中心去游泳。我程經跟我講過你很會游泳。</PASSAGE>
</TEXT>
<MISTAKE id="B1-0118-3" location="18">
<WRONG>建缸中心</WRONG>
<CORRECTION>健康中心</CORRECTION>
</MISTAKE>
<MISTAKE id="B1-0118-3" location="19">
<WRONG>建缸中心</WRONG>
<CORRECTION>健康中心</CORRECTION>
</MISTAKE>
<MISTAKE id="B1-0118-3" location="27">
<WRONG>程經</WRONG>
<CORRECTION>曾經</CORRECTION>
</MISTAKE>
</ESSAY>
```

Figure 2: A sample of annotated essay in Bake-off 2014.

Statistical information on data sets is shown in Table 9. Three development sets are named as

[3] http://www.cipsc.org.cn/clp2014/webpage/en/four_bakeoffs/Bakeoff2014cfp_ChtSpellingCheck_en.htm

$w[i]$	$suffix[i]$ contains	corrected $w[i]$
帶	帽，眼鏡，皮帶，手環	戴
負，府	費，錢，經濟，薪水	付
做，座	車，巴士，飛機，捷運，船，高鐵	坐

Table 5: Rule 2. The correction related with the current word's suffix.

$w[i-1]$	$w[i]$	$w[i+1]$	corrected $w[i]$
知	到	–	道
¬(內，肝，腎)	臟	–	髒
–	總	於	終
–	俄	¬(羅)	餓
改	以	改	一
¬(很)	多	很	都
心	理	¬(学，研)	裡
¬(一，二，這，兩，幾，草，壓)	根	¬(部，本，據，源，基，治，除	跟

Table 6: Rule 3. The correction related with neighbored words.

$w[i-2]$	$w[i-1]$	$w[i]$	$w[i+1]$	$w[i+2]$	corrected $w[i]$
林	依	神	–	–	晨
鋼	鐵	依	–	–	衣
游	泳	世	–	–	池
星	期	路	–	–	六
西	門	丁	–	–	町
–	–	很	不	得	恨
–	–	仍	在	了	扔
–	–	打	出	租	搭
–	–	機	程	車	計
–	–	¬(少)	子	化	少

Table 7: Rule 4. The correction related with two neighbored words.

$w[i-1]$	$w[i]$	$w[i+1]$	$w[i+2]$	$w[i+3]$	corrected $w[i]$ and $w[i+1]$
–	自	到	–	–	知道
–	式	式	–	–	試試
–	蘭	滿	–	–	浪漫
–	令	令	–	–	冷冷
–	排	排	–	–	拜拜
–	柏	柏	–	–	伯伯
–	莎	增	–	–	沙僧
–	旅	管	–	–	旅館
–	棒	組	–	–	幫助
–	想	心	–	–	相信
–	名	性	–	–	明星
–	頂	頂	大，有	名	鼎鼎
–	白	花	商	店	百貨
為	是	嗎	–	–	什麼

Table 8: Rule 5. Two words are simultaneously corrected.

DEV13, DEV14C and DEV14B and the test set is named as TEST14 respectively. In the DEV14B, there are 4624 errors, in which the statistics information of the three common character usage confusions in section 4 is shown in Table 10, so it is necessary to deal with them respectively.

The dictionary $\mathbb{D}$ used in SSSP algorithm is *SogouW*[4] dictionary from *Sogou inc.*, which is in simplified Chinese. The *OpenCC*[5] converter is used for simplified-to-traditional Chinese converting. Similar character set $\mathbb{C}$ provided by (Liu et al., 2010) is used to substitute the original words in the graph construction stage. The LM is built on the Academia Sinica corpus (Emerson, 2005) with IRSTLM toolkit (Federico et al., 2008). The CRF model is achieved by training and tuning on the Academia Sinica corpus with the toolkit *CRF++ 0.58*[6]. For Chinese word segmentation, the *ICTCLAS2011*[7] is exploited.

[4]http://www.sogou.com/labs/dl/w.html

[5]http://code.google.com/p/opencc/

[6]https://code.google.com/p/crfpp/downloads/list

[7]http://www.ictclas.org/ictclas_download.aspx

Name			Data Size (lines)	Character number (k)
Development set	Bake-off 2013		700	29
	Bake-off 2014	C1	342	16
		B1	3004	149
Test set			1062	53

Table 9: Statistical information of data sets.

Error Type	Number	Percent (%)
在，再	101	2.18
的，地，得	398	8.61
她，他	101	3.98

Table 10: Three common character usage confusions in the DEV14B.

5.2 The Improved Graph Model

We treat the graph model without filters in Bake-off 2013 as our baseline in Bake-off 2014. The edge function is the linear combination of similarity and log conditional probability:

$$\omega^L = \omega_s - \beta \log P$$

where $\omega_0 \equiv 0$ which is omitted in the equation, and ω_s for different kinds of characters are shown in Table 11. The LM is set to bigram according to (Yang et al., 2012). Improved Kneser-Ney method is used for LM smoothing (Chen and Goodman, 1999).

Type	ω_s
same pronunciation same tone	1
same pronunciation different tone	1
similar pronunciation same tone	2
similar pronunciation different tone	2
similar shape	2

Table 11: ω_s used in ω^L.

We utilize the correction precision ($\mathcal{P}$), correction recall ($\mathcal{R}$) and F1 score ($\mathcal{F}$) as the metrics. The computational formulas are as follows:

- Correction precision:

$$\mathcal{P} = \frac{\text{number of correctly corrected characters}}{\text{number of all corrected characters}};$$

- Correction recall:

$$\mathcal{R} = \frac{\text{number of correctly corrected characters}}{\text{number of wrong characters of gold data}};$$

- F1 macro:

$$\mathcal{F} = \frac{2\mathcal{P}\mathcal{R}}{\mathcal{P} + \mathcal{R}}.$$

We firstly use the revised graph model in section 3 to tackle the continuous word errors. The results achieved by the graph model and its revision on DEV14B with different β are shown in Figure 3 respectively. We can see that the result with the revised graph model is not improved, and even worse than the baseline. Therefore, for the improved graph model in Bake-off 2014, we remain use the graph model in Bake-off 2013 without any modification.

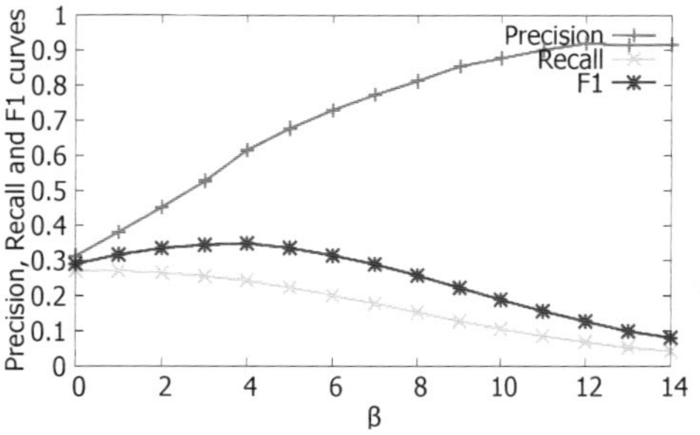

(a) The graph model.

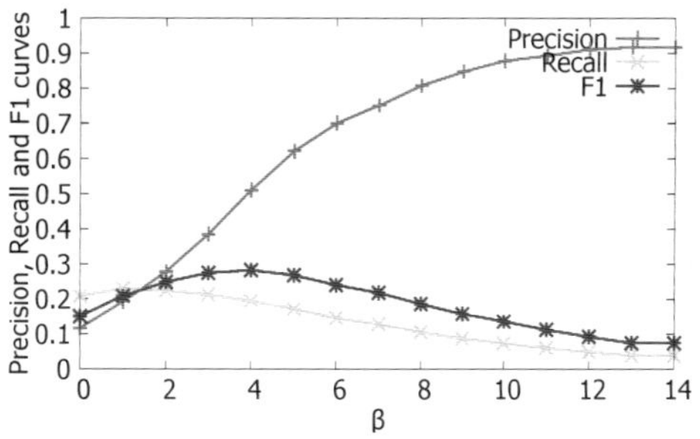

(b) The revised graph model.

Figure 3: The results of the graph model and its revision on DEV14B.

To observe the performance of the improved graph model in detail, on the three development sets: DEV13, DEV14C, DEV14B, we report the results from the following settings:

1. *CRF*. We use the CRF model to process the common character usage confusions: “在” (at) (pinyin: zai), “再” (again, more, then) (pinyin: zai) and “的” (of) (pinyin: de),

	Dev13			Dev14C			Dev14B		
Model	$\mathcal{P}$	$\mathcal{R}$	$\mathcal{F}$	$\mathcal{P}$	$\mathcal{R}$	$\mathcal{F}$	$\mathcal{P}$	$\mathcal{R}$	$\mathcal{F}$
Graph (baseline)	0.802	0.6	0.686	0.790	0.238	0.366	0.729	0.2	0.314
+CRF	0.623	0.6	0.611	0.75	0.38	0.504	0.631	0.282	0.389
+CRF+Rule_Post	0.512	0.614	0.558	0.723	0.421	0.532	0.699	0.461	0.555
+CRF+Rule_Pre	0.526	0.614	0.567	0.75	0.38	0.504	0.706	0.479	0.571
+CRF+Rule_Pre+Rule_Post	0.51	0.611	0.556	0.723	0.421	**0.532**	0.706	0.484	**0.574**

Table 14: The results with different models.

"地" (-ly, adverb-forming particle) (pinyin: de), "得"(have to, get, obtain) (pinyin: de) on all development sets. The results achieved by the CRF model are shown in Table 12.

Development set	$\mathcal{P}$	$\mathcal{R}$	$\mathcal{F}$
Dev13	0.060	0.014	0.023
Dev14C	0.718	0.162	0.264
Dev14B	0.549	0.072	0.128

Table 12: The results of CRF model.

2. *Rule*. The rule based system is carried out on the development sets to solve the fixed collocation errors. The results achieved by the rule based system are shown in Table 13.

Development set	$\mathcal{P}$	$\mathcal{R}$	$\mathcal{F}$
Dev13	0.111	0.034	0.052
Dev14C	0.583	0.076	0.135
Dev14B	0.766	0.253	0.380

Table 13: The results of the rule based system.

3. *Graph+CRF*. In this setting, the graph model with different β in ω^L is performed on the *CRF* results. For each development set, an optimal β could be found to obtain the optimal performance.

4. *CRF+Graph+Rule_Post*. Based on the results of the *Graph+CRF* model, we add the rule based system. Similarly, the optimal β could be found.

5. *CRF+Rule_Pre+Graph*. Different from the third setting, we firstly utilize the rule based system on the development sets, and then use the graph model with different β in ω^L.

6. *CRF+Rule_Pre+Graph+Rule_Post*. Based on the results of *CRF+Rule_Pre+Graph* model, we add the rule based system at last.

In Table 14, we compare different improved graph models on the development sets, in which we set β as 6 in ω^L. We could find that though the results of the improved graph model on Dev13 are relatively declined, the results both on the Dev14C and Dev14B are improved. The results in Table 14 prove that CRF model and the rule based system are effective to cover the shortage of the graph model.

5.3 Results

In Bake-off 2014, we submit 3 runs, using the *CRF+Rule_Pre+Graph* model and the weight function ω^L, of which the β is set as 0, 6, and 10, respectively. The results on Test14 are listed in Table 15.

Metric	Run1	Run2	Run3
False Positive Rate	0.5951	0.2279	0.1921
Detection Accuracy	0.3117	0.5471	0.5367
Detection Precision	0.2685	0.5856	0.5802
Detection Recall	0.2185	0.322	0.2655
Detection F1-Score	0.2409	0.4156	0.3643
Correction Accuracy	0.2938	0.5377	0.5311
Correction Precision	0.2349	0.5709	0.5696
Correction Recall	0.1827	0.3032	0.2542
Correction F1-Score	0.2055	0.3961	0.3516

Table 15: Official results of Bake-off 2014.

6 Conclusion

In this paper we present an improved graph model to deal with Chinese spell checking problem. The model includes a graph model and two independently-trained models. To begin with, the graph model is utilized to solve generic spell checking problem and SSSP algorithm is adopted as the model implementation. Furthermore, a CRF model and a rule based system are used to cover the shortage of the graph model. The effectiveness of the proposed model is verified on the data released by the SIGHAN Bake-off 2014 shared task and our system gives competitive results according to official evaluation..

References

Farooq Ahmad and Grzegorz Kondrak. 2005. Learning a spelling error model from search query logs. In *Proceedings of Human Language Technology Conference and Conference on Empirical Methods in Natural Language Processing*, pages pp. 955–962, Vancouver, British Columbia, Canada, October.

Richard G Casey and Eric Lecolinet. 1996. A survey of methods and strategies in character segmentation. *IEEE Transactions on Pattern Analysis and Machine Intelligence*, 18(7):690–706.

Chaohuang Chang. 1995. A new approach for automatic Chinese spelling correction. In *Proceedings of Natural Language Processing Pacific Rim Symposium*, pages pp. 278–283, Seoul, Korea.

Stanley F Chen and Joshua Goodman. 1999. An empirical study of smoothing techniques for language modeling. *Computer Speech & Language*, 13(4):359–393.

Kuanyu Chen, Hungshin Lee, Chunghan Lee, Hsinmin Wang, and Hsinhsi Chen. 2013. A study of language modeling for Chinese spelling check. In *Proceedings of the Seventh SIGHAN Workshop on Chinese Language Processing*, pages pp. 79–83, Nagoya, Japan, October.

Hsunwen Chiu, Jiancheng Wu, and Jason S. Chang. 2013. Chinese spelling checker based on statistical machine translation. In *Proceedings of the Seventh SIGHAN Workshop on Chinese Language Processing*, pages pp. 49–53, Nagoya, Japan, October.

Thomas Emerson. 2005. The second international Chinese word segmentation Bakeoff. In *Proceedings of the Fourth SIGHAN Workshop on Chinese Language Processing*, pages pp. 123–133, Jeju Island, Korea.

Marcello Federico, Nicola Bertoldi, and Mauro Cettolo. 2008. IRSTLM: an open source toolkit for handling large scale language models. In *Proceedings of 9th Annual Conference of the International Speech Communication Association*, pages pp. 1618–1621, Brisbane, Australia.

Jianfeng Gao, Xiaolong Li, Daniel Micol, Chris Quirk, and Xu Sun. 2010. A large scale ranker-based system for search query spelling correction. In *Proceedings of the 23rd International Conference on Computational Linguistics*, pages pp. 358–366, Beijing, China, August.

Dongxu Han and Baobao Chang. 2013. A maximum entropy approach to Chinese spelling check. In *Proceedings of the Seventh SIGHAN Workshop on Chinese Language Processing*, pages pp. 74–78, Nagoya, Japan, October.

Yu He and Guohong Fu. 2013. Description of HLJU Chinese spelling checker for SIGHAN Bakeoff 2013. In *Proceedings of the Seventh SIGHAN Workshop on Chinese Language Processing*, pages pp. 84–87, Nagoya, Japan, October.

Yuming Hsieh, Minghong Bai, and Kehjiann Chen. 2013. Introduction to CKIP Chinese spelling check system for SIGHAN Bakeoff 2013 evaluation. In *Proceedings of the Seventh SIGHAN Workshop on Chinese Language Processing*, pages pp. 59–63, Nagoya, Japan, October.

Zhongye Jia, Peilu Wang, and Hai Zhao. 2013a. Grammatical error correction as multiclass classification with single model. In *Proceedings of the Seventeenth Conference on Computational Natural Language Learning: Shared Task*, pages pp. 74–81, Sofia, Bulgaria, August.

Zhongye Jia, Peilu Wang, and Hai Zhao. 2013b. Graph model for Chinese spell checking. In *Proceedings of the Seventh SIGHAN Workshop on Chinese Language Processing*, pages pp. 88–92, Nagoya, Japan, October.

Chuanjie Lin and Weicheng Chu. 2013. NTOU Chinese spelling check system in SIGHAN Bakeoff 2013. In *Proceedings of the Seventh SIGHAN Workshop on Chinese Language Processing*, pages pp. 102–107, Nagoya, Japan, October.

Chaolin Liu, Minhua Lai, Yihsuan Chuang, and Chiaying Lee. 2010. Visually and phonologically similar characters in incorrect simplified Chinese words. In *Proceedings of the 23rd International Conference on Computational Linguistics: Posters*, pages pp. 739–747, Beijing, China, August.

Xiaodong Liu, Kevin Cheng, Yanyan Luo, Kevin Duh, and Yuji Matsumoto. 2013. A hybrid Chinese spelling correction using language model and statistical machine translation with reranking. In *Proceedings of the Seventh SIGHAN Workshop on Chinese Language Processing*, pages pp.54–58, Nagoya, Japan, October.

Xu Sun, Jianfeng Gao, Daniel Micol, and Chris Quirk. 2010. Learning phrase-based spelling error models from clickthrough data. In *Proceedings of the 48th Annual Meeting of the Association for Computational Linguistics*, pages pp. 266–274, Uppsala, Sweden, July.

Peilu Wang, Zhongye Jia, and Hai Zhao. 2014. Grammatical error detection and correction using a single maximum entropy model. In *Proceedings of the Eighteenth Conference on Computational Natural Language Learning: Shared Task*, pages pp. 74–82, Baltimore, Maryland, June.

Shihhung Wu, Chaolin Liu, and Lunghao Lee. 2013. Chinese spelling check evaluation at SIGHAN Bakeoff 2013. In *Proceedings of the Seventh SIGHAN Workshop on Chinese Language Processing*, pages pp. 35–42, Nagoya, Japan, October.

Shaohua Yang, Hai Zhao, Xiaolin Wang, and Baoliang Lu. 2012. Spell checking for Chinese. In *International Conference on Language Resources and Evaluation*, pages pp. 730–736, Istanbul, Turkey, May.

Tinghao Yang, Yulun Hsieh, Yuhsuan Chen, Michael Tsang, Chengwei Shih, and Wenlian Hsu. 2013. Sinica-IASL Chinese spelling check system at SIGHAN-7. In *Proceedings of the Seventh SIGHAN Workshop on Chinese Language Processing*, pages pp. 93–96, Nagoya, Japan, October.

Juifeng Yeh, Shengfeng Li, Meirong Wu, Wenyi Chen, and Maochuan Su. 2013. Chinese word spelling correction based on N-gram ranked inverted index list. In *Proceedings of the Seventh SIGHAN Workshop on Chinese Language Processing*, pages pp. 43–48, Nagoya, Japan, October.

Liangchih Yu, Chaohong Liu, and Chunghsien Wu. 2013. Candidate scoring using web-based measure for Chinese spelling error correction. In *Proceedings of the Seventh SIGHAN Workshop on Chinese Language Processing*, pages pp. 108–112, Nagoya, Japan, October.

Huaping Zhang, Hongkui Yu, Deyi Xiong, and Qun Liu. 2003. HHMM-based Chinese lexical analyzer ICTCLAS. In *Proceedings of the second SIGHAN workshop on Chinese language processing*, pages pp. 184–187, Sapporo,Japan.

Hai Zhao and Chunyu Kit. 2007. Incorporating global information into supervised learning for Chinese word segmentation. In *Proceedings of the 10th Conference of the Pacific Association for Computational Linguistics*, pages pp. 66–74, Melbourne, Australia.

Hai Zhao and Chunyu Kit. 2008a. An empirical comparison of goodness measures for unsupervised Chinese word segmentation with a unified framework. In *Proceedings of the Third International Joint Conference on Natural Language Processing*, pages pp. 9–16, Hyderabad, India.

Hai Zhao and Chunyu Kit. 2008b. Unsupervised segmentation helps supervised learning of character tagging for word segmentation and named entity recognition. In *Proceedings of the Third International Joint Conference on Natural Language Processing*, pages pp. 106–111, Hyderabad, India.

Hai Zhao and Chunyu Kit. 2011. Integrating unsupervised and supervised word segmentation: The role of goodness measures. *Information Sciences*, 181(1):163–183.

Hai Zhao, Chang-Ning Huang, and Mu Li. 2006a. An improved Chinese word segmentation system with conditional random field. In *Proceedings of the Fifth SIGHAN Workshop on Chinese Language Processing*, volume 1082117, pages pp. 162–165, Sydney, Australia, July.

Hai Zhao, Chang-Ning Huang, Mu Li, and Bao-Liang Lu. 2006b. Effective tag set selection in Chinese word segmentation via conditional random field modeling. In *Proceedings of the 20th Pacific Asia Conference on Language, Information and Computation*, volume 20, pages pp. 87–94, Wuhan, China.

Hai Zhao, Chang-Ning Huang, Mu Li, and Bao-Liang Lu. 2010. A unified character-based tagging framework for Chinese word segmentation. *ACM Transactions on Asian Language Information Processing*, 9(2):1–32.

Hai Zhao, Xiaotian Zhang, and Chunyu Kit. 2013. Integrative semantic dependency parsing via efficient large-scale feature selection. *Journal of Artificial Intelligence Research*, 46:203–233.

Introduction to NJUPT Chinese Spelling Check Systems in CLP-2014 Bakeoff

Lei Gu, Yong Wang, Xitao Liang
Nanjing University of Posts and Telecommunications, China
gulei@njupt.edu.cn, 13041127@njupt.edu.cn, centaolang@163.com

Abstract

Chinese spelling check (CSC) is an essential issue in the research field of Chinese language processing (CLP). This paper describes the details of two CSC systems we developed to solve this problem. The first system was built based on CRF model, and the modules of such system include word segmentation, error detection and error correction. Another system was based on 2-Chars&&3-Chars model, and its modules include bigram segmentation, error detection and error correction. Using the final test data set provided by CLP2014, the final experimental result of the system based on 2-Chars&&3-Chars model was better, which achieved 0.403 detection accuracy with 0.3344 detection precision and 0.3964 correction accuracy with 0.3191 correction precision.

1 Introduction

Language Spelling check is an important subject in the field of language processing both in Chinese and English. Compared with English, how to detect and correct spelling errors in Chinese sentences automatically is more difficult. In English, there are two classes of spelling errors: non-word spelling errors and real-word spelling errors. Non-word spelling errors generally refer to the wrong spelling words that not exist in a dictionary, such as a sentence 'buu some apples' where 'buu' is an error word which can't be found in a dictionary. Real-word spelling errors usually refer to the wrong words which are misused in sentences but exist in a dictionary, for example, in the sentence 'bye some apples', 'bye' is misused in such sentence but can be found in a dictionary.

Chinese spelling check is different. Firstly, for Chinese electronic documents, there are not non-word spelling errors, because each misspelled character is exist in reality, such as "產玲婦女 chan ling fu nv", "玲(齡) ling" is a character misused but exists in reality. Secondly, in English sentences, each word is separated by a space, so it's easier to detect misspelled words. But there are no word delimiters between words in Chinese sentences, and a Chinese word may consist of a single-character or more, so it's hard to decide whether a single-character is wrong or it's a part of a misspelled word.

Generally, phonologically similar or visually similar characters result in the misspelled words in Chinese sentences. For instance, "嬰兒個紓 ying er ge shu", "數 shu" is misspelled as "紓 shu" because both are pronounced as "shu". In the sentence "不斷曾加 bu duan ceng jia", "增 zeng" is misspelled as "曾 ceng" because "曾" is similar with "增" in visual. For most CSC systems, to correct the misspelled words, it's necessary to build a module to replace the wrong characters by similar characters extracted from the character confusion sets which are edited based on phonologically and visually similarity between characters. In our experiment, the confusion sets provided by SIGHAN Bake-off 2013 are used in both CSC systems (Wu et al., 2013).

Lots of colleges and research institutions have made efforts to solve such CSC problems in recent years. There have been two types of methods of spelling check: rule-based methods and statistical methods. Data driven, the statistical spelling check approaches appear to be more robust and performs better than simple rule-based methods (Chiu et al., 2013). Wang et al. (2013) built a system and its main idea is to exchange potential error character with its confusable ones and rescore the modified sentence using a conditional random field (CRF)-based word segmentation/part of speech (POS) tagger and a tri-gram language model (LM) to detect and correct possible spelling errors. Lin and Chu (2013) also proposed a system and the modules in their system include word segmentation, N-gram model probability estimation, similar character replacement, and filtering rules. In this paper, we build two CSC systems based on CRF model and 2-Chars&&3-Chars model. The rest of this paper will introduce the two CSC systems in detail, and it's organized as follows. We will introduce the first system based on CRF model in section 2, in section 3 we'll describe the second system based on 2-Chars&&3-Chars model, at last we'll make conclusions in section 4.

2 System Based On CRF Model

As is shown in Figure 1, our system gets the input sentences firstly, then the sentences will be segmented by word which is based on CRF model, after the step of word segmentation, error words in the sentences segmented will be picked out by some rules and be dealed with the module of error correction. Details of the models will be discussed in the following subsections.

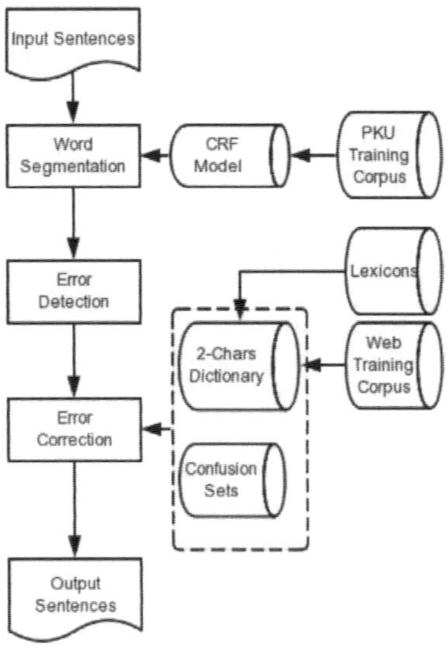

Figure 1. Framework of CSC system based on CRF model

2.1 Word Segmentation

Chinese word segmentation (CWS) is the first step for Chinese language processing. In recent years, Chinese spelling checkers have incorporated word segmentation (Chiu et al., 2013) and many word segmentation methods have been proposed. Such as support vector machine (SVM), conditional random field (CRF) and maximum entropy Markov models (MEMMs), among them, CRF-based approach has been shown to be effective with very low computational complexity (Wang et al., 2013).

The module word segmentation of our first CSC system uses condition random fields (CRF) approach. CRFs are a class of undirected graphical models with exponent distribution (Lafferty et al., 2001). A common used special case of CRFs is linear chain, which has a distribution of:

$$P_{\wedge}(\bar{y} \mid \bar{x}) = \frac{1}{Z_{\bar{x}}} \exp(\sum_{t=1}^{T} \sum_{k} \lambda_k f_k(y_{t-1}, y_t, \bar{x}, t))$$

where $f_k(y_{t-1}, y_t, \bar{x}, t)$ is a function which is usually an indicator function; λ_k is the learned weight of feature f_k; and $Z_{\bar{x}}$ is the normalization factor. The feature function actually consists of two kinds of features, that is, the feature of single state and the feature of transferring between states.

In this system, we use a public tool CRF++ (Li et al., 2009) for CRF implementation and regard the PKU (Emerson, 2005) corpus as the training corpus.

The process of word segmentation using CRF++ is as follows:

a. Convert the simplified Chinese sentences in the PKU training corpus to traditional Chinese;

b. Train the CRF++ tool;

c. Segment the sentences inputted into this system.

2.2 Error Detection

If there're no misspelled words in a sentence, the sentence could be divided into serial correct words after ideal word segmentation. But if a sentence contains misspelled words, the segmentation could separate words containing misspelled character by serial single characters (Chang et al., 2013). For instance, the sentence "儘管婦女的數量不斷增加 jin guan fu nv de shu liang bu duan zeng jia" which has no misspelled words will be segmented into "儘管/婦女/的/數量/不斷/增加". However, the sentence "儘管婦女的數量不斷正加 jin guan fu nv de shu liang bu duan zheng jia" with an error word "正加" ("增 zeng" is misspelled as

"正 zheng") will be segmented into "儘管/婦女/的/數量/不斷/正/加". In this sentence "正加" is an error word, so it is segmented into serial two single characters "正" and "加".

In the error detection module of our first CSC system , we make a rule that error occurs in the serial single characters generated by word segmentation. Like the serial characters "正" and "加", one of these serial characters should be an error.

2.3 Error Correction

In this system, we build a 2-Chars dictionary extracted from a large number of lexicons and a web training corpus which is collected from lots of news reports, compositions and other data on the web.

The way to build a 2-Chars dictionary is as follows:

a. Segment the sentences in web training corpus by bigram. For example, "邁向充滿希望的新世紀 mai xiang chong man xi wang de xin shi ji" will be segmented as "邁向/向充/充滿/滿希/希望/望的/的新/新世/世紀";

b. Count the frequency (indicates how many times a word presents in the web training corpus) of each word;

c. Add each word and its frequency into the 2-Chars dictionary.

The format of words in the 2-Chars dictionary is [Word:Frequency]. For example:

邁向:23 向充:3 充滿:75 滿希:7
希望:322 望的:16 的新:195 新世:25
世紀:230 ...

In our system, we just deal with the error words consist of two characters. We take the serial single characters " 正 " and " 加 " for example. Firstly, " 正 " will be replaced by its similar character lists one by one, then the similar character will be combined with "加" to a new word "?加". If the new word "?加" do exist in the 2-Chars dictionary, the similar character will be added into the candidates list. After the treatment of all similar characters of "正", "加" will be replaced by its similar character lists like the processing of " 正 ". At last, if the length of candidates list is more than one, we will choose the new word with the highest frequency in the 2-Chars dictionary.

Table 1 and table 2 show the processing of "正" and "加", from these two table, we can find that the frequency of new word "增加" consist of "增" and "加" is higher than "正下" and "正夾", so "增" should be the correct character of "正".

Confusion Sets	New Word	Exist In 2-Chars Dic?, Frequency
陣	陣加	False
禎	禎加	False
增	增加	True, 248
鴆	鴆加	False
...		

Table 1. The processing of "正"

Confusion Sets	New Word	Exist In 2-Chars Dic?, Frequency
家	正家	False
下	正下	True, 1
茄	正茄	False
夾	正夾	True, 1
...		

Table 2. The processing of "加"

2.4 Analysis Of The Result

We submitted two experimental results using two different number of lexicons. As shown in table 3 and table 4, the final results of the first CSC system are not so good.

The defect of word segmentation and the limit of 2-Chars dictionary may result in the bad result. Besides the future work of improving the performance of this CSC system, we propose another CSC system without word segmentation in section 3.

Run-2	Accuracy	Precision	Recall	F1
Detection Level	0.275	0.202	0.1525	0.1738
Correctio n Level	0.258	0.1645	0.1186	0.1379
False Positive Rate	0.6026			

Table 3. Run-2 result of system based on CRF model

Run-3	Accuracy	Precision	Recall	F1
Detection Level	0.2853	0.1885	0.1299	0.1538
Correction Level	0.2665	0.1416	0.0923	0.1117
False Positive Rate	0.5593			

Table 4. Run-3 result of system based on CRF model

3 System Based On 2-Chars&&3-Chars Model

Although the first module of most Chinese spelling checkers are word segmentation, there still exist many problems which may have bad influences on the next modules of the spelling checkers. Such as "但是 嬰兒出生率不正加反而減少 dan shi ying er chu sheng lv bu zheng jia fan er jian shao" ("增 zeng" is misspelled as "正 zheng"), the result of word segmentation is "但是/嬰兒/出生率/不正/加/反而/減少" where "不正" is regarded as a word which results in the neglect of wrong word "正加".

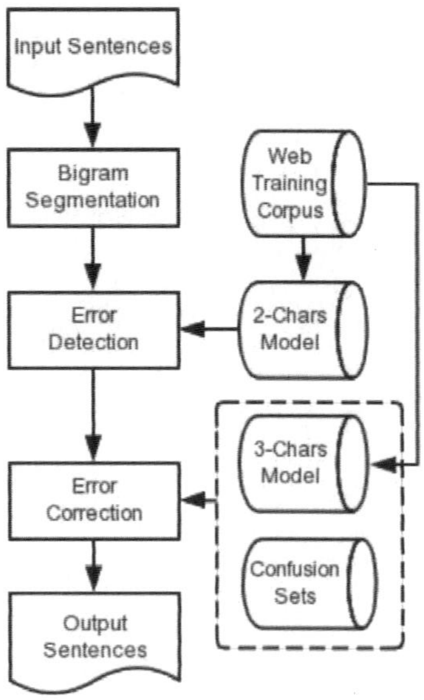

Figure 2. Framework of CSC system based on 2-Chars&&3-Chars model

According to the reasons above, we propose a system without word segmentation. Figure 2 shows the framework of our second system based on 2-Chars&&3-Chars model. After getting input sentences, system will segment them by bigram, then the next module based on 2-Chars model will detect errors in these segmented sentences. After error detection, a 3-Chars model is used to correct errors by some rules. Details of this system will be described in the following subsections.

3.1 Bigram Segmentation

A significant difference between the bigram segmentation and the word segmentation is: words in the sentences are non overlapping, but bigrams are overlapping.

With respect to the sentence "全球的婦女人口正加 quan qiu de fu nv ren kou zheng jia", the segmentation results of different methods are as follows:

By word: 全球/的/婦女/人口/正/加

By bigram: 全球/球的/的婦/婦女/女人/人口/口正/正加

Compared with word segmentation, it's easier to segment sentences by bigram, because it don't need any segmentation tools. In this CSC system, all sentences will be segmented by bigram. After segmentation, this system will detect errors in these bigrams.

3.2 Error Detection

In this system, we build a 2-Chars Model and a 2-Chars dictionary extracted from a web training corpus which is collected from lots of news reports, compositions and other data on the web. The format of words in this 2-Chars dictionary is the same as the dictionary in the first CSC system.

In the sentence "全球的婦女人口正加 quan qiu de fu nv ren kou zheng jia", "增 zeng" is misspelled as "正 zheng" so the result of bigram segmentation is: 全球/球的/的婦/婦女/女人/人口/口正/正加.

The module of error detection gets a string array consist of the results of segmentation. Take the first word "全球" as an example, we call it "Current-Word (C-Word)" and its next word "球的" is called "Next-Word (N-Word)". We make a rule that if C-Word ("全球") or N-Word ("球的") don't exist in the 2-Chars dictionary, the second character of C-Word "球" would be an error.

Using the rule above, the system will find "口正" isn't exist in the 2-Chars dictionary, then "正" is regraded as an error.

3.3 Error Correction

Like 2-Chars model, we also build a 3-Chars model. And we edited a 3-Chars dictionary just like 2-Chars dictionary but ignore the frequency of a word.

The method of building a 3-Chars dictionary is segmenting the sentences in web training corpus by trigram. For example, "邁向充滿希望的新世紀 mai xiang chong man xi wang de xin shi ji" will be segmented as "邁向充/向充滿/充滿希/滿希望/希望的/望的新/的新世/新世紀";

Compared with the format of words in 2-Chars dictionary, the format of 3-Chars words in the dictionary is as follows:

邁向充 向充滿 充滿希 滿希望
希望的 望的新 的新世 新世紀
. . .

As shown in the module of error detection, "正" is an error character in the word "口正" (C-Word). We combine "口正" with its next word "正加" (N-Word) into a new 3-Chars word "口正加", then the error "正" will be replaced by the characters extracted from its confusion sets. If a new 3-Chars word "口?加" can be found in the 3-Chars dictionary, the similar character will be regarded as the correct one.

Table 5 shows the method of determining whether a new word is correct or not. As shown in this table, "口增加" do exist in the 3-Chars dictionary, and "增" should be the correct one.

Confusion Sets	New Word	Exist In 3-Chars Dic?
陣	口陣加	False
禎	口禎加	False
增	口增加	True
鴆	口鴆加	False
...		

Table 5. The processing of "正"

3.4 Analysis Of The Result

Table 6 shows the result of system based on 2-Chars&&3-Chars model. We found that all the performances of this system is better than the system based on CRF model.

Run-1	Accuracy	Precision	Recall	F1
Detection Level	0.403	0.3344	0.1959	0.247
Correction Level	0.3964	0.3191	0.1827	0.2323
False Positive Rate	0.3898			

Table 6. The Result Of System Based On 2-Chars&&3-Chars Model

4 Conclusion

In this paper, we introduce two Chinese spelling check systems and the experimental results show that the CSC system without word segmentation do better than the system incorporated with word segmentation. The work to improve the performance of the system with word segmentation is still continued. And in the future, we'll do more research and work on the system based on 2-Chars&&3-Chars.

References

Tao-Hsing Chang, Hsueh-Chih Chen, Yuen-Hsien Tseng, and Jian-Liang Zheng. 2013. Automatic Detection and Correction for Chinese Misspelled Words Using Phonological and Orthographic Similarities. Proceedings of SIGHAN-7, 97-101.

Hsun-wen Chiu, Jian-cheng Wu, and Jason S. Chang. 2013. Chinese Spelling Checker Based on Statistical Machine Translation. Proceedings of SIGHAN-7, 49-53.

Thomas Emerson. 2005. The Second International Chinese Word Segmentation Bakeoff. Proceeding of the Fourth SIGHAN Workshop on Chinese Language Processing, 123-133.

Yu He and Guohong Fu. 2013. Description of HLJU Chinese Spelling Checker for SIGHAN Bakeoff 2013. Proceedings of SIGHAN-7, 84-87.

Yu-Ming Hsieh, Ming-Hong Bai, and Keh-Jiann Chen. 2013. Introduction to CKIP Chinese Spelling Check System for SIGHAN Bakeoff 2013 Evaluation. Proceedings of SIGHAN-7, 59-63.

Zhongye Jia, Peilu Wang, and Hai Zhao. 2013. Graph Model for Chinese Spell Checking. Proceedings of SIGHAN-7, 88-92.

John Lafferty, Andrew McCallum, and Fernando Pereira. 2001. Conditional random fields: probabilistic models for segmenting and labeling sequence data. Proceedings of International Conference of Machine Learning, 591-598.

Shoushan Li and Chu-Ren Huang. 2009. Word Boundary Decision with CRF for Chinese Word Segmentation. 23rd Pacific Asia Conference on Language, Information and Computation, 726-732.

Chuan-Jie Lin and Wei-Cheng Chu. 2013. NTOU Chinese Spelling Check System in SIGHAN Bake-off 2013. Proceedings of SIGHAN-7, 102-107.

Yih-Ru Wang, Yuan-Fu Liao, Yeh-Kuang Wu, and Liang-Chun Chang. 2013. Conditional Random Field-based Parser and Language Model for Traditional Chinese Spelling Checker. Proceedings of SIGHAN-7, 69-73.

Shih-Hung Wu, Chao-Lin Liu, and Lung-Hao Lee. 2013. Chinese Spelling Check Evaluation at SIGHAN Bake-off 2013. Proceedings of SIGHAN-7, 35-42.

Zhiting Xu, Xian Qian, Yuejie Zhang, and Yaqian Zhou. 2007. CRF-based Hybrid Model for Word Segmentation, NER and even POS Tagging. Proceedings of Sixth SIGHAN Workshop on Chinese Language Processing, 167-170.

Chinese Spelling Check System Based on Tri-gram Model

Qiang Huang, Peijie Huang*, Xinrui Zhang, Weijian Xie, Kaiduo Hong, Bingzhou Chen, Lei Huang
College of Informatics, South China Agricultural University,
Guangzhou 510642, Guangdong, China
kasim0079@qq.com, pjhuang@scau.edu.cn,
nealrichardrui@gmail.com, tsewkviko@gmail.com,
HKDNZ@hotmail.com, cbtpkzm@163.com, hl_mark@163.com

Abstract

This paper describes our system in the Chinese spelling check (CSC) task of CLP-SIGHAN Bake-Off 2014. CSC is still an open problem today. To the best of our knowledge, n-gram language modeling (LM) is widely used in CSC because of its simplicity and fair predictive power. Our work in this paper continues this general line of research by using a tri-gram LM to detect and correct possible spelling errors. In addition, we use dynamic programming to improve the efficiency of the algorithm, and additive smoothing to solve the data sparseness problem in training set. Empirical evaluation results demonstrate the utility of our CSC system.

1 Introduction

Spelling check is a common task in every written language, which is an automatic mechanism to detect and correct human errors (Wu et al., 2013). The problem of devising algorithms and techniques for automatically correcting words in text began as early as the 1960s on computer techniques for automatic spelling correction and automatic text recognition (Kukich, 1992), and it has continued up to the present. A spelling checker should have both capabilities consisting of error detection and error correction. Spelling error detection is to indicate the various types of spelling errors in the text. Spelling error correction is further to suggest the correct characters of detected errors.

Chinese as a foreign language (CFL) have attracted more and more attention, and this trend is continuing. For this purpose, at the SIGHAN Bake-offs, Chinese spelling check (CSC) task are organized to provide an evaluation platform for developing and implementing automatic Chinese spelling checkers. However, spelling check in Chinese is very different from that in English or other alphabetic languages. There are no word delimiters between words and the length of each word is very short. A Chinese "word" usually comprises two or more characters. The difficulty of Chinese processing is that many Chinese characters have similar shapes or similar (or same) pronunciations. Some characters are even similar in both shape and pronunciation (Wu et al., 2010; Liu et al., 2011).

There are many research effort developed for CSC recently, including rule-based model (Jiang et al., 2012; Chiu et al., 2013), n-gram model (Wu et al., 2010; Wang et al., 2013b; Chen et al., 2013), graph theory (Bao et al., 2011; Jia et al., 2013), statistical learning method (Han and Chang, 2013), etc. Some of them are hybrid model.

Language modeling (LM) is widely used in CSC, and the most widely-used and well-practiced language model, by far, is the n-gram LM (Jelinek, 1999), because of its simplicity and fair predictive power. Our work in this paper continues this general line of research by using a tri-gram LM to detect and correct possible spelling errors. In addition, in order to solve the high complexity in the computation process of the tri-gram based CSC, dynamic programming is used to improve the efficiency of the algorithm. Moreover, additive smoothing to solve the data sparseness problem in training set.

The rest of this paper is organized as follows. In Section 2, we briefly present the proposed

* Corresponding author

Proceedings of the Third CIPS-SIGHAN Joint Conference on Chinese Language Processing, pages 173–178,
Wuhan, China, 20-21 October 2014

CSC system, confusion sets and the choice of n-gram order. Section 3 details our Chinese tri-gram model. Evaluation results are presented in Section 4. Finally, the last section summarizes this paper and describes our future work.

2 The Proposed System

2.1 System Overview

Figure 1 shows the flowchart of our CSC system.

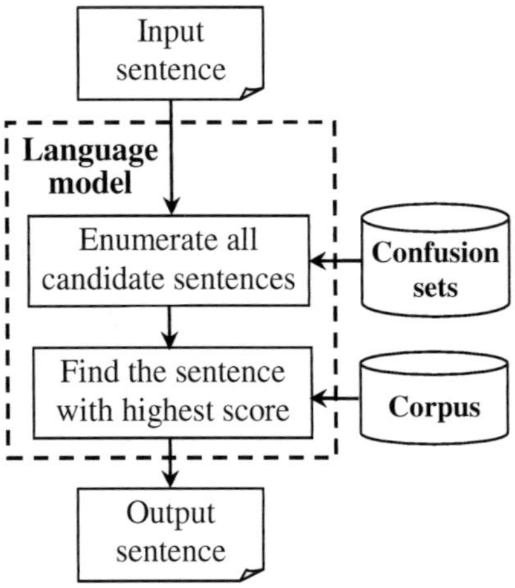

Figure 1. The flowchart of the CSC system.

The system is mainly composed by three components: confusion sets, corpus and language model. It performs CSC in the following steps:

1. Given a test sentence, the CSC system gets the confusion sets of each character in the sentence.

2. For each character in this sentence, the system will enumerate every character of its confusion set to replace the original character. We will get a candidate sentence set after this step.

3. The system will calculate the score of every candidate sentence by using the n-gram model. We use the corpus of CCL [1] and sogou [2] to generate the frequency of n-gram. Finally, the sentence with highest score will be chosen as the final output.

Due to the high complexity of step 2 and step 3, we optimize the algorithm by using dynamic programming.

2.2 Confusion Set

Confusion set is a ready set of commonly confused characters plays an important role in spelling error detection and correction in texts (Wang et al., 2013a). Most Chinese characters have other characters similar to them in either shape or pronunciation. Since pinyin input method is currently the most popular Chinese input method, the confusion sets used in our system is constructed from a homophone dictionary of *qingsongcha* website [3]. Some Chinese characters with similar pronunciation, such as the nasal and the lateral consonants, retroflex and non-retroflex, etc., are also added to the confusion sets in our system.

2.3 Language Modeling

Language modeling can be used to quantify the quality of a given word string, and most previous researches have adopted it as a method to predict which word might be a correct word to replace the possible erroneous word (Chen et al., 2009; Liu et al., 2011; Wu et al., 2010). The most widely-used and well-practiced language model, by far, is the n-gram language model (Jelinek, 1999), because of its simplicity and fair predictive power.

In n-gram modeling, choosing a proper order of the n-gram is important. On the one hand, higher order n-gram models along with larger corpora tend to increase their quality, and thus will yield lower perplexity for human-generated text. On the other hand, the higher order n-gram models, such as four-gram or five-gram, usually suffer from the data sparseness problem, which leads to some zero conditional probabilities (Chen et al., 2013). For these reasons, we have developed a Chinese character tri-gram model to determine the best character sequence as the answers for detection and correction.

3 Chinese Tri-gram Model

3.1 Tri-gram Model

Given a Chinese character string $C = c_1, c_2, \ldots, c_L$, the probability of the character string in tri-gram model is approximated by the product of a series of conditional probabilities as follows (Jelinek, 1999),

$$P(C) = \prod_{l=3}^{L} P(c_l | C^{l-1}) \approx \prod_{l=3}^{L} P(c_l | c_{l-2}, c_{l-1}). \quad (1)$$

In the above tri-gram model, we make the approximation that the probability of a character depends only on the two immediately preceding

[1] ccl.pku.edu.cn:8080/ccl_corpus/index.jsp?dir=xiandai

[2] www.sogou.com/labs/dl/c.html

[3] www.qingsongcha.com/

words.

The easiest way to estimate the conditional probability in Eq. (1) is to use the maximum likelihood (ML) estimation as follows,

$$P(c_l | c_{l-2}, c_{l-1}) = \frac{N(c_{l-2}, c_{l-1}, c_l)}{N(c_{l-2}, c_{l-1})} \quad , \qquad (2)$$

where $N(c_{l-2}, c_{l-1}, c_l)$ and $N(c_{l-2}, c_{l-1})$ denote the number of times the character strings "c_{l-2}, c_{l-1}, c_l" and "c_{l-2}, c_{l-1}" occur in a given training corpus, respectively.

3.2 Getscore Function Definition

We define the candidate sentence as $C' = c'_1, c'_2, ..., c'_L$, which is the character string derived from the original sentence C by replacing some characters using their confusion sets. The *getscore* function is used to select the most suitable candidate sentence. Figure 2 shows the pseudo-code of the *getscore* function by using tri-gram model.

function getscore(c'_{i-2}, c'_{i-1}, c'_i)
begin
  $ret \leftarrow \dfrac{N(c'_{i-2}, c'_{i-1}, c'_i)}{N(c'_{i-2}, c'_{i-1})}$
  if $c'_i = c_i$ then
  begin
    $ret \leftarrow ret \times \lambda$
  end
end

Figure 2. Pseudo-code of *getscore* function.

Now we add a rule if $c'_i = c_i$, it will get an extra score λ. In the future work, we will add other rules or algorithms to improve the *getscore* function.

For example, in "一心一{億,意}", in comparing with other string candidates as shown in Figure 3, we found the string of the highest score "一心一意". So we detect the error spot and select '意' as the corrected character.

3.3 Dynamic Programming

Due to the high complexity of enumerating candidate sentences, we use the dynamic programming (DP) to optimize the tri-gram model.

The confusion set of c_i is defined as $V[i]$, and each element in the confusion set is label by

$$getscore(\text{"一心一"}) = \frac{N(\text{"一心一"})}{N(\text{"一心"})} \times \lambda = 0.00248$$

$$getscore(\text{"心一億"}) = \frac{N(\text{"心一億"})}{N(\text{"心一"})} \times \lambda = 0$$

$$getscore(\text{"一心一"}) = \frac{N(\text{"一心一"})}{N(\text{"一心"})} \times \lambda = 0.00248$$

$$getscore(\text{"心一意"}) = \frac{N(\text{"心一意"})}{N(\text{"心一"})} = 0.01574$$

Figure 3. *Getscore* function calculating example.

$0,1,2,3...$, so the jth element in $V[i]$ will be represented as $V[i][j]$. The score of the candidate sentence with the maximum score is defined as $dp[i][j][k]$, where i is the length, $V[i-1][j]$ is the i-1th character, and $V[i][k]$ is the ith character. Because tri-gram model depends only on last three characters, we can deduce the state transition equation of the DP algorithm as follow:

$$strtmp = V[i-1][j], V[i][k], V[i+1][l] \quad , \qquad (3)$$

$$dp[i+1][k][l] = \max(dp[i+1][k][l], dp[i][j][k] * getscore(strtmp)). \qquad (4)$$

Pseudo-code of dynamic programming is shown in Figure 4. The complexity of the algorithm is reduced to acceptable level as $O(MN^3)$, where M is the length of the input sentence, and N is the size of a confusion set.

3.4 Additive Smoothing

In statistics, additive smoothing, which also called Laplace smoothing, or Lidstone smoothing, is a technique used to smooth categorical data. Given an observation $x = (x_1, x_2, ..., x_d)$ from a multinomial distribution with N trials and parameter vector $\theta = (\theta_1, \theta_2, ..., \theta_d)$, a "smoothed" version of the data gives the estimator:

$$\hat{\theta} = \frac{x_i + \alpha}{N + \alpha d} \qquad i = 1,2,..., d \, , \qquad (5)$$

where $\alpha > 0$ is the smoothing parameter ($\alpha = 0$ corresponds to no smoothing). Additive smoothing is a type of shrinkage estimator, as the resulting estimate will be between the empirical estimate x_i / N, and the uniform probability $1/d$. Using Laplace's rule of succession, some authors have argued that α should be 1 (in which case the term add-one smoothing is also used), although in practice a smaller value is typically chosen.

In a tri-gram model, the data consists of the number of occurrences of each string in corpus.

```
Procedure DP()
begin
  for i ← 3 to str.length do
    for j ← 0 to V[i - 1].size do
      for k ← 0 to V[i].size do
        for l ← 0 to V[i + 1].size do
        begin
            strtmp ← V[i − 1][j], V[i][k], V[i + 1][l]
            dp[i + 1][k][l] ← max(dp[i + 1][k][l], dp[i][j][k] * getscore(strtmp))
        end
end
```

Figure 4. Pseudo-code of dynamic programming.

Additive smoothing allows the assignment of non-zero probabilities to Chinese characters which do not occur in the training set. So we use additive smoothing to process the data sparse problem.

We redefine the new *getscore* function as Figure 5.

function getscore(c'_{i-2}, c'_{i-1}, c'_i)

begin

  $ret \leftarrow \dfrac{N(c_{i-2}, c_{i-1}, c_i) + \alpha}{N(c_{i-2}, c_{i-1}) + \alpha d}$

  if $c'_i = c_i$ then

  begin

    $ret \leftarrow ret \times \lambda$

  end

end

Figure 5. Pseudo-code of *getscore* function with additive smoothing.

4 Empirical Evaluation

4.1 Task

The goal of this shared task, i.e. the Chinese spelling check (CSC) task, in CLP-SIGHAN Bake-Off 2014 is developing the computer assisted tools to detect (combining error checking and correction) several kinds of grammatical errors, i.e., redundant word, missing word, word disorder, and word selection. The system should return the locations of the improper characters and must point out the correct characters. Passages of CFL (Chinese as a Foreign Language) learners' essays selected from the National Taiwan Normal University (NTNU) learner corpus are used for training purpose. Two training datas (one consisting of 461 spelling errors and another having 4823 spelling errors) are provided as practice. The final test data set for the evaluation consists of 1062 passages cover different complexities.

4.2 Metrics

The criteria for judging correctness are: (1) Detection level: binary classification of a given sentence, i.e., correct or incorrect should be completely identical with the gold standard. All error types will be regarded as incorrect. (2) Identification level: this level could be considered as a multi-class categorization problem. In addition to correct instances, all error types should be clearly identified.

In CSC task of CLP-SIGHAN Bake-Off 2014, ninth metrics are measured in both levels to score the performance of a CSC system. They are False Positive Rate (FPR), Detection Accuracy (DA), Detection Precision (DP), Detection Recall (DR), Detection F-score (DF), Correction Accuracy (CA), Correction Precision (CP), Correction Recall (CR) and Correction F-score (CF).

4.3 Evaluation Results

The CSC task of CLP-SIGHAN Bake-Off 2014 attracted 19 research teams. Among 19 registered research teams, 13 participants submitted their testing results. For formal testing, each participant can submit at most three runs that use different models or parameter settings. Finally, there are 34 runs submitted in total.

Table 1 shows the evaluation results of the final test. Run1, run2 and run3 are the three runs of our system with different λ in *getscore* function mentioned in Subsection 3.2. We have

	FPR	DA	DP	DR	DF	CA	CP	CR	CF
Run1	0.2034	0.4821	0.4518	0.1676	0.2445	0.4774	0.4375	0.1582	0.2324
Run2	0.6441	0.275	0.2315	0.194	0.2111	0.2627	0.2083	0.1695	0.1869
Run3	0.5009	0.3522	0.2907	0.2053	0.2406	0.3427	0.2712	0.1864	0.221
Average	0.2841	0.4633	0.4958	0.2106	0.2836	0.4485	0.4616	0.1811	0.2498
Best	0.032	0.7194	0.9146	0.484	0.633	0.7081	0.9108	0.4614	0.6125

Table 1. Evaluation results of final test.

chosen three runs with different estimated recall levels as submissions. The "Best" indicates the high score of each metric achieved in CSC task. The "Average" represents the average of the 34 runs.

As we can see from Table 1, we achieve a result close to the average level. The major weakness of our system is its low recall rate, which might be the result of not applying a separate error detection module.

It is our first attempt on Chinese spelling check. The potential of the n-gram method is far from fully exploited. Some typical errors of our current system will be presented in the next subsection, and the corresponding improvements are summarized in the last section.

4.4 Error Analysis

Figure 6 shows some typical error examples of our system ("O" original, "M" modified):

Case1:

O: 我 **戴**著 藍色 的 帽子

M: 我 **帶**著 藍色 的 帽子

Case 2:

O: 我們 在 健**缸** 中心 門口 等

M: 我們 在 健**缸** 中心 門口 等

Case 3:

O: 我們 **十**一點半 在 南門 碰頭

M:我們 **是** 一點半 在 南門 碰頭

Figure 6. Error examples.

The first case is an overkill error that belongs to long distance error correction problem. Our system didn't recognize the dependencies of "戴" and "帽子", and "我帶著" get a highest score in tri-gram model. So our system select "帶" to replace "戴", and leads to error at the same time.

In the second case, because "康" is not in the confusion set of "缸", we can't correct the error of "健缸" to "健康".

The third case is also an overkill error which is due to the out of vocabulary (OOV) problem. In this case, the original sentence is in fact correct but unfortunately, the our system didn't recognize "十一點半" and gave it high penalty.

5 Conclusions and Future Work

This paper presents the development and preliminary evaluation of the system from team of South China Agricultural University (SCAU) that participated in the Bake-Off 2014 task. We have developed a Chinese character tri-gram language model to determine the best character sequence as the answers for detection and correction. It is our first attempt on Chinese spelling check, and tentative experiment shows we achieve a not bad result. However, we still have a long way from the state-of-arts results.

There are many possible and promising research directions for the near future. A separate module for possible spelling error detection will be added to the system to improve the detection accuracy. In addition, although language modeling has been widely used in CSC, the n-gram language models only aim at capturing the local contextual information or the lexical regularity of a language. Future work will explore long-span semantic information for language modeling to further improve the CSC. Moreover, characters of similar shapes are not as frequent, but still exist with a significant proportion (Liu et al., 2011). Orthographically similar characters will be added to the confusion sets of our CSC system.

Acknowledgments

This work was partially supported by the Innovation Training Project for College Students of Guangdong Province under Grant No.1056413096 and No.201410564290.

References

Zhuowei Bao, Benny Kimelfeld, Yunyao Li. 2011. A Graph Approach to Spelling Correction in Domain-Centric Search. *In Proceedings of the 49th*

Annual Meeting of the Association for Computational Linguistics (ACL 2011), pp. 905–914.

Berlin Chen. 2009. Word Topic Models for Spoken Document Retrieval and Transcription. *ACM Transactions on Asian Language Information Processing*, Vol. 8, No. 1, pp. 2:1-2:27.

Hsun-wen Chiu, Jian-cheng Wu and Jason S. Chang. 2013. Chinese Spelling Checker Based on Statistical Machine Translation. *In Proceedings of the 7th SIGHAN Workshop on Chinese Language Processing (SIGHAN'13)*, Nagoya, Japan, 14 October, 2013, pp. 49-53.

Kuan-Yu Chen, Hung-Shin Lee, Chung-Han Lee , et al.. 2013. A Study of Language Modeling for Chinese Spelling Check. *In Proceedings of the 7th SIGHAN Workshop on Chinese Language Processing (SIGHAN'13)*, Nagoya, Japan, 14 October, 2013, pp. 79-83.

Dongxu Han, Baobao Chang. 2013. A Maximum Entropy Approach to Chinese Spelling Check. *In Proceedings of the 7th SIGHAN Workshop on Chinese Language Processing (SIGHAN'13)*, Nagoya, Japan, 14 October, 2013, pp. 74-78.

Frederick Jelinek. 1999. *Statistical Methods for Speech Recognition*. The MIT Press.

Zhongye Jia, Peilu Wang and Hai Zhao. 2013. Graph Model for Chinese Spell Checking. *In Proceedings of the 7th SIGHAN Workshop on Chinese Language Processing (SIGHAN'13)*, Nagoya, Japan, 14 October, 2013, pp. 88-92.

Ying Jiang, Tong Wang, Tao Lin, et al. 2012. A rule based Chinese spelling and grammar detection system utility. *In Proceedings of the 2012 International Conference on System Science and Engineering (ICSSE)*, pp. 437-440.

Karen Kukich. 1992. Techniques for Automatically Correcting Words in Text. *ACM Computing Surveys*, Vol. 24, No.4, pp. 377-439.

Chao-Lin Liu, Min-Hua Lai, Kan-Wen Tien, et al.. 2011. Visually and Phonologically Similar Characters in Incorrect Chinese Words: Analyses, Identification, and Applications. *ACM Transactions on Asian Language Information Processing*, Vol. 10, No. 2, pp. 1-39.

Yih-Ru Wang, Jason S. Chang, Jian-Cheng Wu, et al.. 2013a. Automatic Chinese Confusion Words Extraction Using Conditional Random Fields and the Web. *In Proceedings of the 7th SIGHAN Workshop on Chinese Language Processing (SIGHAN'13)*, Nagoya, Japan, 14 October, 2013, pp. 64-68.

Yih-Ru Wang, Yuan-Fu Liao, Yeh-Kuang Wu, et al.. 2013b. Conditional Random Field-based Parser and Language Model for Traditional Chinese Spelling Checker. *In Proceedings of the 7th SIGHAN Workshop on Chinese Language Processing (SIGHAN'13)*, Nagoya, Japan, 14 October, 2013, pp. 69-73.

Shih-Hung Wu, Yong-Zhi Chen, Ping-Che Yang, et al.. 2010. Reducing the False Alarm Rate of Chinese Character Error Detection and Correction. *In Proceeding of CIPSSIGHAN Joint Conference on Chinese Language Processing (CLP 2010)*, Beijing, 28-29 Aug., 2010, pp. 54-61.

Shih-Hung Wu, Chao-Lin Liu, and Lung-Hao Lee. 2013. Chinese Spelling Check Evaluation at SIGHAN Bake-off 2013. *In Proceedings of the 7th SIGHAN Workshop on Chinese Language Processing (SIGHAN'13)*, Nagoya, Japan, 14 October, 2013, pp. 35-42.

Introduction to BIT Chinese Spelling Correction System at CLP 2014 Bake-off

Min Liu
School of Computer Science and Technology, Beijing Institute of Technology
luis328@foxmail.com

Ping Jian
School of Computer Science and Technology, Beijing Institute of Technology
pjian@bit.edu.cn

Heyan Huang
School of Computer Science and Technology, Beijing Institute of Technology
hhy63@bit.edu.cn

Abstract

This paper describes the Chinese spelling correction system submitted by BIT at CLP Bake-off 2014 task 2. The system mainly includes two parts: 1) N-gram model is adopted to retrieve the non-words which are wrongly separated by word segmentation. The non-words are then corrected in terms of word frequency, pronunciation similarity, shape similarity and POS (part of speech) tag. 2) For wrong words, abnormal POS tag is used to indicate their location and dependency relation matching is employed to correct them. Experiment results demonstrate the effectiveness of our system.

1. Introduction

Spelling check, which is an automatic mechanism to detect and correct human spelling errors, is a common task in every written language. The number of people learning Chinese as a Foreign Language (CFL) is booming in recent decades and this number is expected to become even larger for the years to come. However, unlike English learning environment where many learning techniques have been developed, tools to support CFL learners are relatively rare, especially those that could automatically detect and correct Chinese spelling and grammatical errors. For example, Microsoft Word® has not yet supported these functions for Chinese, although it supports English for years. In CLP Bake-off 2014, essays written by CFL learners were collected for developing automatic spelling checkers. The aims are that through such evaluation campaigns, more innovative computer assisted techniques will be developed, more effective Chinese learning resources will be built, and the state-of-art NLP techniques will be advanced for the educational applications.

By analyzing the training data released by the CLP 2014 Bake-off task2[1] and the test data used in SIGHAN Bake-off 2013[2], we find that the main errors focus on two types: One is wrong characters which result in "**non-words**" that are similar to OOV (out-of-vocabulary). For example, the writer may misspell "身邊" as "生邊", and "根據" as "根處" (The former appears because of the words' similar pronunciation and the latter comes up due to their similar shape). These are even not words and of course do not exist in the vocabulary. The other type is words which are correct in the dictionary but incorrect in the sentence. Some of them may be misspelled, like "情愛" in phrase "情愛的王宜家", which is a misspelling of word "親愛". But we can find "情愛" in the dictionary and it is not a non-word. Others are words which are not used correctly. This usually happens when the writer does not understand their meaning clearly. For example, writers often confuse "在" and "再", such as "高雄是再台灣南部一個現代化城市". Here, it is "在" but not "再" the right one. Different from non-words, we call these words "**wrong words**". According to the statistics obtained from the training data of CLP 2014 Back-off, there are nearly 3,400 wrong words which are about twice more than non-words, 1,800 ones.

Spelling check and correction is a traditional task in natural language processing. Pollock and Zamora (1984) built a misspelling dictionary for spelling check. Chang (1995) adopted a bi-gram language model to substitute the confusing character. Zhang et al. (2000) proposed an approximate word matching method to detect and correct spelling errors. Liu et al. (2011)

[1] http://www.cipsc.org.cn/clp2014/webpage/cn/four_bakeoffs/Bakeoff2014cfp_ChtSpellingCheck_cn.htm

[2] http://tm.itc.ntnu.edu.tw/CNLP/?q=node/27

Proceedings of the Third CIPS-SIGHAN Joint Conference on Chinese Language Processing, pages 179–185,
Wuhan, China, 20-21 October 2014

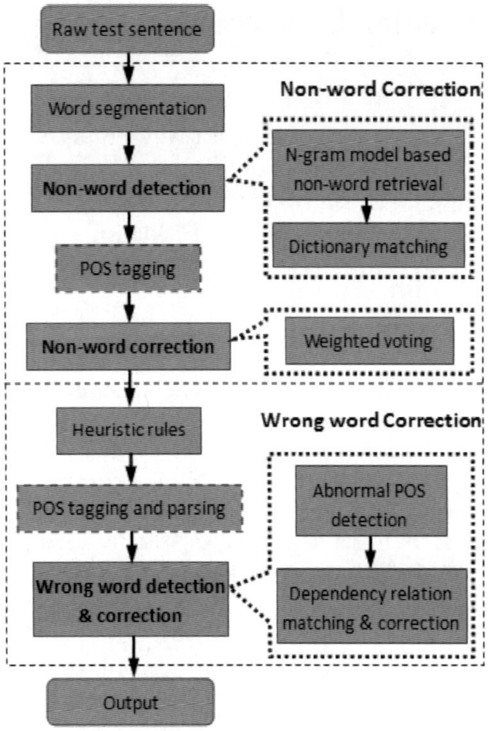

Figure 1: System architecture

extended the principles of decomposing Chinese characters with the Cangjie codes to judge the visual similarity between Chinese characters. SIGHAN Bake-off 2013 for Chinese spelling check inspired a variety of spelling check and correction techniques (Wu et al., 2013). Typical statistical approaches such as maximum entropy model and machine translation model performed well assisted by rule based model and other language analysis techniques.

Compared with the test data in SIGHAN Bake-off 2013, there are more wrong words and the text is more colloquial in the current Bake-off, which make the correction task more challenging.

2. System Architecture

In terms of the error types of the task, our system is mainly composed by two stages: non-word correction and wrong word correction. In detail, stage one consists of several parts: word segmentation, non-word detection, POS (part of speech) tagging and non-word correction. The second stage is conducted by heuristic rules correction, POS tagging & parsing, and wrong word detection & correction. The figure 1 shows the architecture of our system.

2.1 Preparations

To cater to the need of error correction system for linguistic resources, three dictionaries/bases are constructed: a dictionary, a word-POS base and a dependency relation base.

We use Tsai's list of Chinese words[3] collected by Chih-Hao Tsai as a basic dictionary and make use of Sinica Corpus[4] to add frequency for each word in it. Considering that Pinyin[5] can be useful in pronunciation similarity spelling error detection and correction, we add it to each word in the dictionary with the help of TagPinyin[6] developed by International R&D Center for Chinese Education. Since this tool can only tag Pinyin for simplified Chinese, we use OpenCC[7] to make the conversion between traditional Chinese and simplified Chinese. By this way, we obtain the dictionary like the example below:

```
胛 胛 jia 1      胛骨 jia gu 1
慚 慚 can 3     慚色 can se 1  慚愧 can kui   58
```

There are more than 239,000 words totally in the dictionary. The words have the same first character are put in one line and they are indexed by their first character to boost the efficiency of searching. Each item consists of three parts: the word ("慚愧"), the Pinyin ("can kui"), and the frequency ("58").

Penn Chinese Treebank7.0 (CTB7.0) (Xue et al., 2005) is employed to build the word-POS base and the dependency relation base. In this way, the word category information and candidates for correct words are provided. Taking domain and area stuff into consideration, we extract the mz (news magazine from Sinorama), bc (broadcast conversation from New Tang Dynasty TV etc.) and wb (weblogs) parts of CTB7.0, which form a dependency corpus including 30,861 sentences. The simplified characters in the corpus are also converted by OpenCC. We get about 42,000 items in the word-POS base and the format is as following:

```
揭露      JJ   1    NN  1    VV  16
揮        VV   4
揮之不去  VV   2
```

---

[3] http://technology.chtsai.org/wordlist/

[4] http://app.sinica.edu.tw/kiwi/mkiwi/

[5] Pinyin is the standard system of romanized spelling for transliterating Chinese.

[6] http://nlp.blcu.edu.cn/downloads/download-tools/

[7] http://code.google.com/p/opencc/

In the example above, the first column is the word and the following are all the POSes and their frequencies by counting the corpus.

The dependency relation base is made up of dependency relations extracted from the CTB corpus. It includes one word with all its head words and the corresponding frequencies in each line. The following is an example:

抗議	ROOT 4	事件 3	以示 1	...

Here, "抗議" is headed by "ROOT" which means that it is the root word in the sentence. By this way, more than 300,000 dependency relations were extracted from the corpus.

Originally, we considered Sinica Treebank[8], which is a traditional Chinese corpus in nature, as the more proper one to generate the POS and dependency base. However, the POS category and the dependency relation type of the bank are too trivial. In addition, the parsing unit in Sinica Treebank is not a natural sentence but segments divided by punctuations, which results in lack of dependency types. Many relations between segments degenerate to "ROOT" in the Treebank.

2.2 Non-word Correction

This stage mainly includes non-word detection & correction stage and it starts from the segmentation of raw error sentences. When segmentation is done for the input file, we find that the words involving misspelled character might be separated into serial characters. For example, sentence "這個學期已經過了兩個裡拜了。" will be segmented into "這 個 學期 已經 過了 兩個 裡 拜 了 。" and potential non-word "裡拜" is impossible to be found as a word. Dictionary based non-word detection would not work in this case. We utilize a simple n-gram model here to retrieve the missing words. The method in detail is described as following: The uncommon co-occurrence of adjacent characters after segmentation can be found by pre-trained character n-gram model. The retrieving begins at the first single-character word with low probability, and combines it with one single-character word before or after it. To further confirm whether the combination is reasonable or not, we traverse the dictionary to find if there is a "dependable" candidate word which can make sure that the retrieved non-word can be substituted by a real word in the dictionary. For simplicity, we only consider words who have the same Pinyin form with the retrieved word as the "dependable" words.

After the non-word retrieval, a dictionary matching is competent to detect the non-words in the sentences. In the step of non-word correction, the word which cannot be matched from the dictionary completely will be substituted by a word in the dictionary. A weighted voting approach is employed here to select the most possible candidate word.

$$\hat{w}(w_{\text{non}}) = \arg\max_{w_i \in \text{Dic}} Score(w_i, w_{\text{non}}), \quad (1)$$

$$Score(w, w_{\text{non}}) = logFr_w + Sim(w, w_{\text{non}}), \quad (2)$$

$$Sim(w, w_{\text{non}}) = \alpha_1 Sim_{\text{pro}} + \alpha_2 Sim_{\text{shap}} + \alpha_3 Sim_{\text{POS}}, \quad (3)$$

$$Sim_{\text{pro}} = \begin{cases} 1 & \text{same pronunciation} \\ 0 & \text{otherwise} \end{cases}, \quad (4)$$

$$Sim_{\text{shap}} = \begin{cases} 1 & \text{same shape} \\ 0 & \text{otherwise} \end{cases}, \quad (5)$$

$$Sim_{\text{POS}} = \begin{cases} 1 & \text{same category} \\ 0 & \text{otherwise} \end{cases}, \quad (6)$$

where, w_{non} represents the non-word to be substituted while w is the candidate word. *Fr* in the formulation indicates the frequency of the word in the dictionary. Besides the frequency, three types of similarity measures are considered in our system: the pronunciation similarity, the shape similarity and the lexical category similarity. If the candidate word in the dictionary has the same or similar pronunciation with the target word, Sim_{pro} is set 1, else it is set 0. The setting of Sim_{shap} is the same. Because characters of similar pronunciations are the most common source of errors in the training set, the weight coefficient α_1 is set 2 and α_2 and α_3 are both set 1 in our system. The similar pronunciation and similar shape character set offered by SIGHAN Bake-off 2013 are employed to scope the candidates.

As for the category similarity, it is known that there is no lexical category for an out-of-dictionary word. To predict the probable class of the target non-word (more precisely, it's the class of the location where the non-word locates), a sequential labeling POS tagger is applied. We believe that the tagger will label a known word depending more on the word itself but label an unknown word relying more on its context. Experiments and analyses on the training data show that about 80% non-words are

[8] http://rocling.iis.sinica.edu.tw/CKIP/engversion/treebank.htm

specified with the category which is valid for the corresponding correct words. For instance, sentence "我 已經 *其待 了 很久" is tagged as following:

我_PN　已經_AD　*其待_VV　了_AS　很久_NN

For the non-word "*其待", tag "VV" is marked, which indicates that it needs a verb there in accordance with the context. "VV" is also one of the possible categories of the word "期待", which is the word that there was supposed to be. In the weighted voting module, candidates who own the same POS tag with the target word are preferred to be selected.

In consideration of all the measures, candidate word with the highest score will be chosen as the correction result.

2.3 Wrong Word Correction

After all the non-words are substituted by in dictionary words, several heuristic rules are utilized to deal with some phenomena with strong regularity. These rules include:

- Replace "門" by "們": if there is any word in a predefined set or its first-class similar words in HIT-CIR TongyiciCilin (Extended)[9] (Che et al., 2010) appearing before "門", it should be "們". The set used in the task is:
  {我, 你, 妳, 他, 她, 人, 同學, 兄弟, 親人, 客人, 對手, 成員, 公司, 工廠, 企業}.
- Correction of interjections: if "阿", "把", "巴", "拉" and "麻" etc. locate before a dot mark (。？！，、；：) and segmented as a single character word, it should be "啊", "吧", "啦" or "嘛".
- The gender related correction: correct "他", "她", "你", "妳" into the one appears more frequently in the context (within the sentences owning the same Pid). Here is an example: "妳" will be corrected by "你" in sentence "我希望，你會妳自己發現怎麼做。可是我覺得你得問朋友怎麼辦。所以我覺得你上課的時候不應該喝酒。而且喝酒對你的身體不好，害你很容易感冒。"
- Correction of "De" ("De" refers to one of the word "的", "地" and "得"): which "De" will be used depends on the category of its head word located after it in the sentence.
  If the category of the head word is adjective or adverb, it should be "得".
  If the one is noun or punctuation, it should be "的".
  If the one is verb, it should be "地".
  To make use of the dependency structure this rule should be carried out after the POS tagging and parsing step.

[9] http://www.ltp-cloud.com/

For common errors, a novel method comprising abnormal POS detection and dependency relation matching is designed.

It is found that the POS tag of some words in a sentence may look strange when there is a wrong word in the sentence. Two examples are as following:

他_PN 過失_VV 已經_AD 三_CD 年_M 多_AD 了_SP
再_AD 台灣_VV 生活_NN 怎麼樣_VA

The existence of wrong word "過失" and "再" confuses the sequential POS tagger and abnormal labeling comes up. Sometimes it happens on the wrong words themselves, such as "過失" being labeled with an impossible class "VV" (verb); sometimes other words around are affected by the wrong word, such as "台灣" being tagged as a verb due to the wrongly used word "再" before it.

To locate and correct these wrong words, a dependency parsing is carried out following the POS retagging and all the dependency pairs involving the abnormal word are extracted to be examined. The left side in Figure 2 shows the dependency pairs related with "過失". Distinct with the first one, POS tagging at this stage is conducted on the sentence where the non-words has been replaced by in-dictionary ones. This is hoped to achieve a higher tagging precision.

By traversing the dependency base, if there is no exact matching of these dependencies but similar ones (by pronunciation or by shape) in the base, we have reason to believe that the matched similar pairs imply the answer we expect. The right side of Figure 2 exhibits the matched pairs in the dependency base. In the example, the wrong word "過失" is to be changed with "過世". In the same way, "再 台灣" will be corrected by "在 台灣" since the latter is frequent in the base.

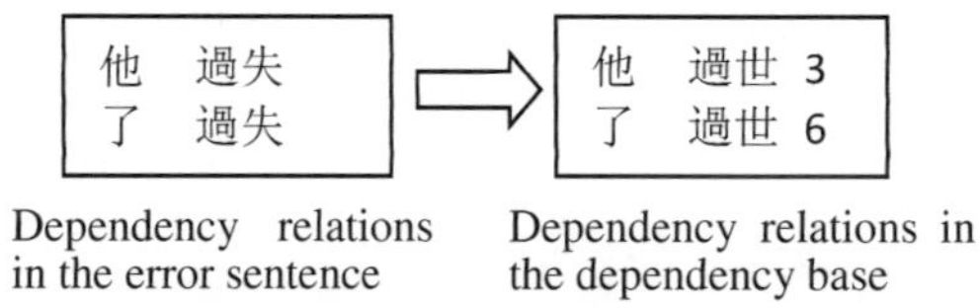

Figure 2: Wrong word correction via dependency relation matching

3. Experiments

In this section, several experiments are conducted to verify the proposed methods described in Section 2. The final official provided test dataset consists of 1,062 sentences with or without spelling errors in traditional Chinese. Since the released training data are hardly employed to train models in our system, we regard it as a development set where some parameters are settled.

3.1 Training N-gram, Word Segmentation, POS Tagging and Parsing Models

Sinica Corpus was used to train the CRF based word segmentation model implemented by CRF++[10], while the final test sets released by SIGHAN Bake-off 2013 were used to train the single character word n-gram model. The POS tagger and parser were trained at the extracted part of CTB7.0 (the same part where the dependency base is built). The texts were converted into tradition Chinese by OpenCC. Like word segmentation, CRF based sequential labeling model is utilized for the POS tagging. It can achieve an accuracy more than 93% when trained and tested at CTB. Dependency trees of the test sentences were obtained by a fast parser, the Layer-based dependency parser[11], which considers hierarchical parsing as sequence labeling (Jian and Zong, 2009).

3.2 Metrics

The criteria for judging correctness are:

(1) **Detection level**: all **locations** of incorrect characters in a given passage should be completely identical with the gold standard. (2) **Correction level:** all **locations** and corresponding **corrections** of incorrect characters should be completely identical with the gold standard. The following metrics are measured in both levels with the help of the confusion matrix.

- False Positive Rate (FPR) = FP / (FP+TN)
- Accuracy=(TP+TN)/ (TP+TN+FP+FN)
- Precision= TP/(TP+FP)
- Recall=TP/(TP+FN)
- F1-Score=2*Precision*Recall/(Precision+ Recall)

[10] http://crfpp.googlecode.com/svn/trunk/doc/index.html?source=navbar

[11] http://www.openpr.org.cn/index.php/NLP-Toolkit-for-Natural-Language-Processing/30-Layer-Based-Dependency-Parser/View-details.html

Confusion Matrix		System Result	
		Positive (With Errors)	Negative (Without Errors)
Gold Standard	Positive	**TP** (True Positive)	**FN** (False Negative)
	Negative	**FP** (False Positive)	**TN** (True Negative)

Table 1: Confusion Matrix

3.3 Experiment Design

There are some different settings in our previous experiments on the development set (the released training data) and we apply three of them to the final test file.

BIT Run1: All modules are employed except the abnormal POS detection and dependency relation matching. The threshold of the n-gram transfer probability at non-word retrieval step is set as 0.008. The frequency threshold of the "dependable" word is set as 80. That is to say the quasi non-word will not be retrieved if its "dependable" word appears less than 80 times in the dictionary.

BIT Run2: Abnormal POS detection and dependency relation matching are included.

BIT Run3: "De" is a frequently used word in Chinese texts. Due to the low parsing accuracy, plenty of "De" were wrongly replaced in our experiments. To avoid this type of noise, the heuristic rules about the correction of "De" are removed in Run3. Moreover, the transfer probability and the frequency threshold is changed to 0.001 and 100 respectively to tighten the retrieval.

3.4 Final Results

We get three evaluation results (shown in Table 2 and Table 3) from the organizer. Run1 and Run2 are the ones submitted to the Bake-off.

Considering that nearly two-thirds of the errors are wrong word errors, Run1 which doesn't employ any wrong word detection strategies performs poorly on recall. Another reason of the low recall is that the non-word detection module in our system lies on the assumption that there is no more than one wrong character in a non-word. In this way, words such as "劳刀" (唠叨) and "花鑽品" ("化妝品") are missed.

	Approaches	Resources and knowledge	Toolkits
Word segmentation	CRFs based sequential labeling	Sinica corpus	TagPinyin OpenCC CRF++ LDPar
POS tagging	CRFs based sequential labeling	Part of Penn CTB7.0	
Parsing	Layer-based dependency parsing	Part of Penn CTB7.0	
Non-word detection	Word segmentation n-gram based non-word retrieval	SIGHAN Bake-off 2013 test set Word base (Sinica corpus and Tsai's list of Chinese words) Training data released	
Non-word correction	Weighted votes	Word base Pinyin similar pronunciation character set similar shape character set POS tag	
Heuristic rules	Rule-based correction	Training set HIT-CIR Tongyici Cilin (Extended)	
Wrong word detection & correction	POS tagging Dependency parsing Abnormal POS detection Dependency relation matching	Word-POS base Dependency relation base	

Table 4: A summary of approaches and resources employed in our correction system

BIT Run1				
FPR	Accuracy	Precision	Recall	F1-Score
0.3352	Detection Level			
	0.4313	0.3710	0.1977	0.2580
	Correction Level			
	0.4115	0.3206	0.1582	0.2119
BIT Run2				
FPR	Accuracy	Precision	Recall	F1-Score
0.3277	Detection Level			
	0.4482	0.4061	**0.2241**	0.2888
	Correction Level			
	0.4303	0.3650	**0.1883**	0.2484

Table 2: The results of the submitted two runs

BIT Run3				
FPR	Accuracy	Precision	Recall	F1-Score
0.1582	Detection Level			
	0.5245	**0.5670**	0.2072	**0.3034**
	Correction Level			
	0.5122	**0.5359**	0.1827	**0.2725**

Table 3: The results of Run3

According to the results of Run2, wrong word correction based on the knowledge of POS tag and dependency relation shows positive effects both on precision and recall. Since only the POS tag is adopted to detect possible wrong words in the current strategy, the misusage of words which are in the same category will escape. "哪裡" and "那裡" is an typical example. Both of them act as pronouns at most of the time. A broader context and more complex semantic knowledge are required to distinguish them.

Management of the auxiliary word "De" is not given enough attention in our system. Although the corresponding rules designed are delicate and clear, many unexpected cases and poor performance of Chinese language analysis techniques make it not work well in practice. Results of Run3 reveal that the accuracy and precision are improved a lot when heuristic rules for correction of "De" are removed, although the recall decreases to some extent.

Results of Run3 also illustrate that the stricter thresholds for retrieval in non-word detection are helpful to improve the performance. This implies that the perplexity of non-words in this task is not very high and it is not a big problem to differentiate them from correct ones.

4. Conclusion

In this paper we propose a hybrid system for Chinese spelling mistake correction. The n-gram based non-word retrieval, abnormal POS tag based wrong word detection and dependency relation matching based wrong word correction are the key techniques of our system. All the approaches, linguistic resources and toolkits involved are gathered in Table 4.

To further improve the performance of our system, we will try to extend our work in the following aspects: 1) Make full use of the training data, such as modeling the correct and the incorrect syntactic structures of the data; 2) Apply semantic collocations to elevate the wrong word detection and correction precision.

Acknowledgments

Heyan Huang was supported by the National Program on Key Basic Research Project (973 Program) (No.2013CB329303) and the National Natural Science Foundation of China (No. 61132009). Ping Jian was supported by the National Natural Science Foundation of China (No. 61202244).

References

Chao-Huang Chang. 1995. A new approach for automatic Chinese spelling correction. In *Proceedings of Natural Language Processing Pacific Rim Symposium*, pages 278-283, Seoul, Korea.

Wanxiang Che, Zhenghua Li, and Ting Liu. 2010. LTP: A Chinese Language Technology Platform. In *Proceedings of the Coling 2010: Demonstration Volume*, pages 13-16, Beijing, China.

Ping Jian and Chengqing Zong. 2009. Layer-based Dependency Parsing. In *Proceedings of the 23rd Pacific Asia Conference on Language, Information and Computation (PACLIC 23)*, pages 230-239, Hong Kong.

Chao-Lin Liu, Min-Hua Lai, Kan-Wen Tien, Yi-Hsuan Chuang, Shih-Hung Wu, and Chia-Ying Lee. 2011. Visually and phonologically similar characters in incorrect Chinese words: Analyses, identification, and applications. In *ACM Transactions on Asian Language Information Processing (TALIP)*, 10(2): 1-39.

Joseph J. Pollock and Antonio Zamora. 1984. Automatic spelling correction in scientific and scholarly text. In *Communications of the ACM*, 27(4): 358-368.

Shih-Hung Wu, Chao-Lin Liu, and Lung-Hao Lee. 2013. Chinese Spelling Check Evaluation at SIGHAN Bake-off 2013. In *Proceedings of the 7th SIGHAN Workshop on Chinese Language Processing*, pages 35-42.

Nianwen Xue, Fei Xia, Fu-Dong Chiou, and Martha Palmer. 2005. The Penn Chinese TreeBank: Phrase Structure Annotation of a Large Corpus. *Natural Language Engineering*, 11(2): 207-238.

Lei Zhang, Changning Huang, Ming Zhou, and Haihua Pan. 2000. Automatic detecting/correcting errors in Chinese text by an approximate word-matching algorithm. In *Proceedings of the 38th Annual Meeting on Association for Computational Linguistics*, pages 248-254.

Extraction system for Personal Attributes Extraction of CLP2014

Zhen Wang
ERTIM-INALCO / 2, rue de Lille, 75007, Paris, France
wangzhen1027@gmail.com

Abstract

This paper presents the design and implementation of our extraction system for Personal Attributes Extraction in Chinese Text (task 4 of CLP2014). The objective of this task is to extract attribute values of the given personal name. Our extraction system employs a linguistic analysis following by a dependency patterns matching technique.

1 Introduction

This is the first year that we take part of in CLP's Personal Attributes Extraction in Chinese Text task. The goal of this task is to extract specific attributes values of given personals names, such as, birth_date, birth_city, children, title etc. from the collections of unstructured Chinese texts. We are required to fill an extracted result into a single attribute slot.

Our approach is based on dependency patterns matching process, which is similar to the works of Xu et al. (2013).

2 System Architecture

In order to accomplish the task, we have proceeded in four steps :

- a pre-processing module;
- an extraction treatment and alignment;
- an ontology alignment;
- a result generation.

Pre-processing module consists of a morphsyntactic analysis and a parsing. Morphosyntactic analysis is used for word segmentation and part of speech tagging. Operations are based on dictionnaries and linguistics rules. Unknown words, especially proper nouns are detected in this step.

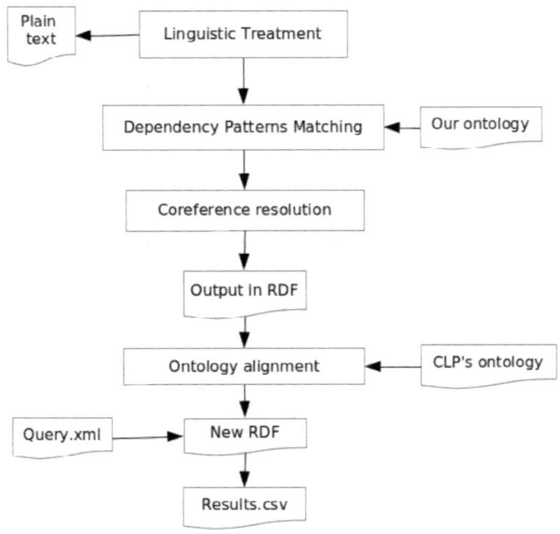

Figure 1: Process for task 4

A type, like "person", "location", "organization" or "unknown" for each proper noun is attributed. The other unknown words received several hypothetical categories, such as "noun", "verb", etc.. A statistical n-gram part of speech model is used for disambiguation. As a result, we only keep one analysis solution among whole solutions. This solution includes lemmas, POS tag, semantic properties and words positions. Our parsing uses dependency grammar. Based on words postions and categories, we build relations between two words and associate with a type, like SV for Suject-Verb,VO for Verb-Object, etc.. Negation and anaphora problems are treated after parsing. All segmentation and parsing results are reported into an XML file.

Extraction treatment uses reported patterns to match dependency relations in the XML file. The extracted informations are saved into an RDF format file. Alignment process is used to group same classes and to remove duplicates in RDF file. The RDF file has to be conform to our ontology.

Proceedings of the Third CIPS-SIGHAN Joint Conference on Chinese Language Processing, pages 186–188,
Wuhan, China, 20-21 October 2014

We created a software to align our ontology to CLP's. The idea is to generate a new RDF file by collecting personal name classes and personal attributes classes from all classes. Given person names is used to question the new RDF file. When a person name is matched to one of them in query, each attribut is generated as a line and saved into a CSV file.

2.1 Dependency patterns matching

Dependency patterns are used to extract information from the parsing results. A dependency pattern is composed of dependency relations elements and of a class of our ontology (see example in figure 2).

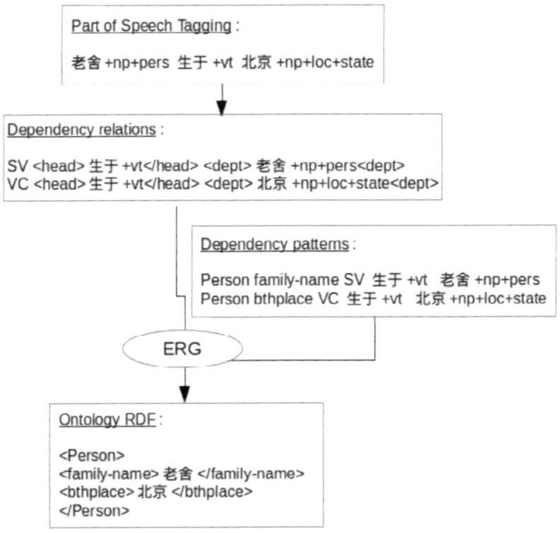

Figure 2: Process of extraction

ERG (Extraction Rule Generator) begins by getting a list of relations, then based on these relations, ERG selects the corresponding patterns. By using these patterns, ERG generates triplets RDF to represent the extracted informations. One matching between a relation and a pattern is enough to generate one triplet. The position of head or dependancy is assigned to be the triplet's ID. ERG repeats this process sentence by sentence. All triplets with same ID are grouped together in the end of process.

2.2 Coreference resolution

Coreference resolution is used to group equal elements, such as events, actions and named entities (persons, organizations, locations, objets, etc.). We make some attributes as decisive elements for equal elements identification. They can be personal family name, organization name or location name. For the equal elements, we change their ID to be the same.

2.3 Ontology alignment

In order to fill the slot, we have to transform our ontology(see example in figure 3) to CLP's. A software was created for this interest (see examples in table 1). After getting a personal named entity and its id, we search all classes containing this id and make these classes as sub-classes of the personal named entity. By aligning the classes with those in CLP's ontology, we transform our RDF result.

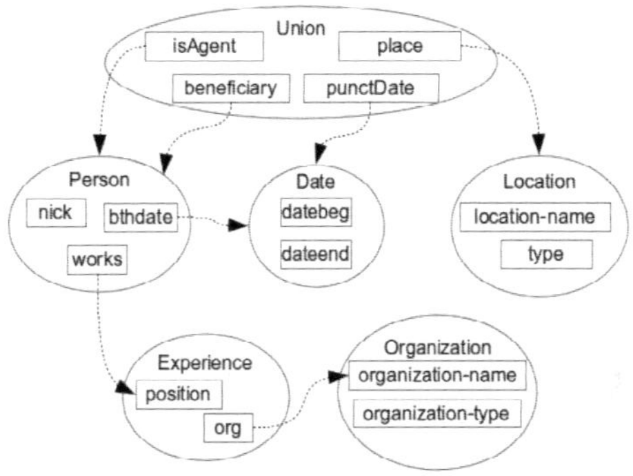

Figure 3: Example of our ontology and their links

CLP's ontology	Our ontology
PER:Alternate Names	Person:nick
PER:Age	Person:age
PER:Date of Birth	Person:bthdate
PER:City of Birth	Person:bthplace + Location:location-name + Location:type=city
PER:Spouses	Union:beneficiary=PER1 + Union:beneficiary=PER2

Table 1: Examples of ontology alignment

For some basic personal attributes, we have equal classes, so the alignment is easy. But for some others, we have to take two or more classes to align with one class of CLP's ontology. For instance, in order to fill the slot *PER:City of Birth*, we have to find in our RDF result that a *Person:familyname* is equal to a given name in query, and that it has a *bthplace* which is pointed to a *Location*. We have to ensure that the *type* of this *Location* is equal to "city". When all these conditions are fulfilled, the mentioned slot can be filled. Another example, in order to generate *PER:Spouses*, we have to find *Union* where there is two and only two *beneficiairy*.

The principal advantage of this step is to merge the named entities of different texts/files. Before the entity creation step, we check if it already exists in reported file.

2.4 Result generation

The objective of this step is to parse queries, create slots for each given personal name and to interrogate ontology in order to verify if it has a corresponding entity request and set all informations which are already integrated during the transformation step.

3 Results and error analysis

A lot of slots haven't been filled in this bake-off. Our single score is 0.0043 and SF value 0.004311. Here are the main dysfunctions : some personal names weren't identified because of morphsyntactic analysis: given name without family name, family name without given name, these are the cases that we have not treated yet; some relations between personal name and attribut haven't been established because of parsing. The main reason of a bad parsing is that the two elements (like personal name and attribute) are located in two differents clauses. Another reason is that anaphora between two sentences, omission of suject or possessive suject, are not solved yet. Some attributs haven't been extracted because extraction rules weren't created. Some slots have not been filled because of name matching between query and ontology, that did not work correctly. All foreign personal names with a " **dot** " were extracted in CSV because the matching between foreign personal names in query and in ontology did not work. The name is writen as "*given name* **dot** *family name*" in query but in ontology it is writen as "family name given name" which is the order used for chinese names but without the " **dot** ".

4 Conclusions

The paper presents our submission to the Personal Attributes Extraction in Chinese Text. Our system uses a linguistic analysis as pre-processing and an extration rule generation which employs a dependency patterns matching. In the future, we will improve our extraction rules and treat the relations between clauses. We will find a solution for anaphora problems between sentences. We also plan to expand the queries (see Xu et al. (2013)) and register the names similarity.

Acknowledgments

We would linke to thank the National Research Agency, the project for reference ANR-09-CSOSG-08-01, for their help in producing this work.

References

Sheng Xu, Chunxia Zhang, Zhendong Niu, Rongyue Mei, Junpeng Chen, Junjiang Zhang, and Hongping Fu. 2013. Bits slot-filling method for tac-kbp 2013. Technical report.

Extraction system for Personal Attributes Extraction of CLP2014

Zhen Wang
ERTIM-INALCO / 2, rue de Lille, 75007, Paris, France
wangzhen1027@gmail.com

Abstract

This paper presents the design and implementation of our extraction system for Personal Attributes Extraction in Chinese Text (task 4 of CLP2014). The objective of this task is to extract attribute values of the given personal name. Our extraction system employs a linguistic analysis following by a dependency patterns matching technique.

1 Introduction

This is the first year that we take part of in CLP's Personal Attributes Extraction in Chinese Text task. The goal of this task is to extract specific attributes values of given personals names, such as, birth_date, birth_city, children, title etc. from the collections of unstructured Chinese texts. We are required to fill an extracted result into a single attribute slot.

Our approach is based on dependency patterns matching process, which is similar to the works of Xu et al. (2013).

2 System Architecture

In order to accomplish the task, we have proceeded in four steps :

- a pre-processing module;
- an extraction treatment and alignment;
- an ontology alignment;
- a result generation.

Pre-processing module consists of a morphsyntactic analysis and a parsing. Morphosyntactic analysis is used for word segmentation and part of speech tagging. Operations are based on dictionnaries and linguistics rules. Unknown words, especially proper nouns are detected in this step.

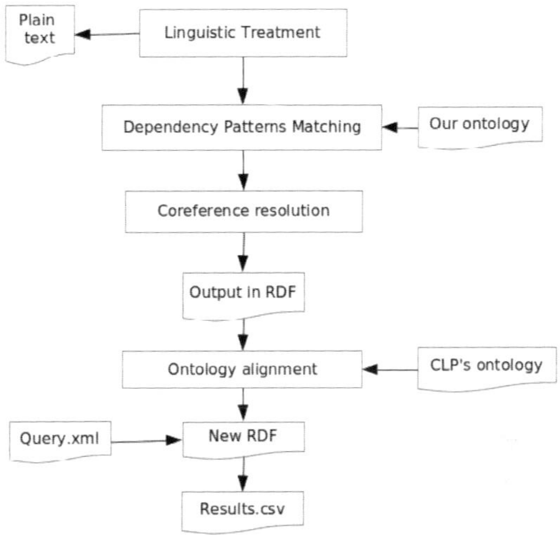

Figure 1: Process for task 4

A type, like "person", "location", "organization" or "unknown" for each proper noun is attributed. The other unknown words received several hypothetical categories, such as "noun", "verb", etc.. A statistical n-gram part of speech model is used for disambiguation. As a result, we only keep one analysis solution among whole solutions. This solution includes lemmas, POS tag, semantic properties and words positions. Our parsing uses dependency grammar. Based on words postions and categories, we build relations between two words and associate with a type, like SV for Suject-Verb,VO for Verb-Object, etc.. Negation and anaphora problems are treated after parsing. All segmentation and parsing results are reported into an XML file.

Extraction treatment uses reported patterns to match dependency relations in the XML file. The extracted informations are saved into an RDF format file. Alignment process is used to group same classes and to remove duplicates in RDF file. The RDF file has to be conform to our ontology.

Proceedings of the Third CIPS-SIGHAN Joint Conference on Chinese Language Processing, pages 189–191,
Wuhan, China, 20-21 October 2014

We created a software to align our ontology to CLP's. The idea is to generate a new RDF file by collecting personal name classes and personal attributes classes from all classes. Given person names is used to question the new RDF file. When a person name is matched to one of them in query, each attribut is generated as a line and saved into a CSV file.

2.1 Dependency patterns matching

Dependency patterns are used to extract information from the parsing results. A dependency pattern is composed of dependency relations elements and of a class of our ontology (see example in figure 2).

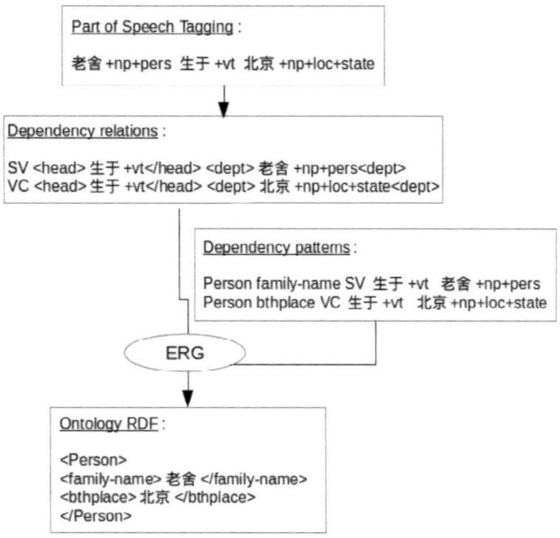

Figure 2: Process of extraction

ERG (Extraction Rule Generator) begins by getting a list of relations, then based on these relations, ERG selects the corresponding patterns. By using these patterns, ERG generates triplets RDF to represent the extracted informations. One matching between a relation and a pattern is enough to generate one triplet. The position of head or dependancy is assigned to be the triplet's ID. ERG repeats this process sentence by sentence. All triplets with same ID are grouped together in the end of process.

2.2 Coreference resolution

Coreference resolution is used to group equal elements, such as events, actions and named entities (persons, organizations, locations, objets, etc.). We make some attributes as decisive elements for equal elements identification. They can be personal family name, organization name or location name. For the equal elements, we change their ID to be the same.

2.3 Ontology alignment

In order to fill the slot, we have to transform our ontology(see example in figure 3) to CLP's. A software was created for this interest (see examples in table 1). After getting a personal named entity and its id, we search all classes containing this id and make these classes as sub-classes of the personal named entity. By aligning the classes with those in CLP's ontology, we transform our RDF result.

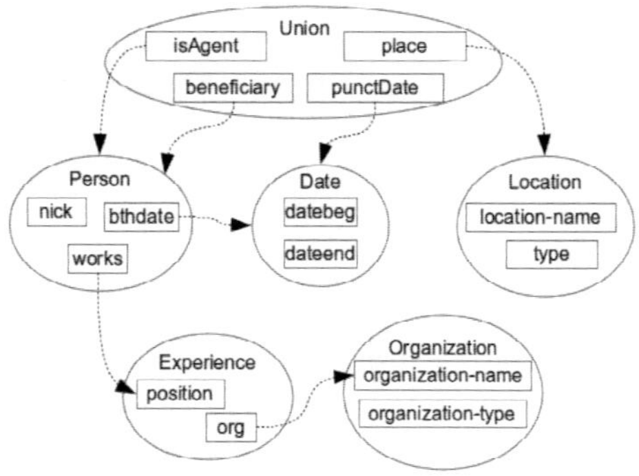

Figure 3: Example of our ontology and their links

CLP's ontology	Our ontology
PER:Alternate Names	Person:nick
PER:Age	Person:age
PER:Date of Birth	Person:bthdate
PER:City of Birth	Person:bthplace + Location:location-name + Location:type=city
PER:Spouses	Union:beneficiary=PER1 + Union:beneficiary=PER2

Table 1: Examples of ontology alignment

For some basic personal attributes, we have equal classes, so the alignment is easy. But for some others, we have to take two or more classes to align with one class of CLP's ontology. For instance, in order to fill the slot *PER:City of Birth*, we have to find in our RDF result that a *Person:familyname* is equal to a given name in query, and that it has a *bthplace* which is pointed to a *Location*. We have to ensure that the *type* of this *Location* is equal to "city". When all these conditions are fulfilled, the mentioned slot can be filled. Another example, in order to generate *PER:Spouses*, we have to find *Union* where there is two and only two *beneficiairy*.

The principal advantage of this step is to merge the named entities of different texts/files. Before the entity creation step, we check if it already exists in reported file.

2.4 Result generation

The objective of this step is to parse queries, create slots for each given personal name and to interrogate ontology in order to verify if it has a corresponding entity request and set all informations which are already integrated during the transformation step.

3 Results and error analysis

A lot of slots haven't been filled in this bake-off. Our single score is 0.0043 and SF value 0.004311. Here are the main dysfunctions : some personal names weren't identified because of morphsyntactic analysis: given name without family name, family name without given name, these are the cases that we have not treated yet; some relations between personal name and attribut haven't been established because of parsing. The main reason of a bad parsing is that the two elements (like personal name and attribute) are located in two differents clauses. Another reason is that anaphora between two sentences, omission of suject or possessive suject, are not solved yet. Some attributs haven't been extracted because extraction rules weren't created. Some slots have not been filled because of name matching between query and ontology, that did not work correctly. All foreign personal names with a " **dot** " were extracted in CSV because the matching between foreign personal names in query and in ontology did not work. The name is writen as "*given name* **dot** *family name*" in query but in ontology it is writen as "family name given name" which is the order used for chinese names but without the " **dot** ".

4 Conclusions

The paper presents our submission to the Personal Attributes Extraction in Chinese Text. Our system uses a linguistic analysis as pre-processing and an extration rule generation which employs a dependency patterns matching. In the future, we will improve our extraction rules and treat the relations between clauses. We will find a solution for anaphora problems between sentences. We also plan to expand the queries (see Xu et al. (2013)) and register the names similarity.

Acknowledgments

We would linke to thank the National Research Agency, the project for reference ANR-09-CSOSG-08-01, for their help in producing this work.

References

Sheng Xu, Chunxia Zhang, Zhendong Niu, Rongyue Mei, Junpeng Chen, Junjiang Zhang, and Hongping Fu. 2013. Bits slot-filling method for tac-kbp 2013. Technical report.

A Study on Personal Attributes Extraction Based on the Combination of Sentences Classifications and Rules

Nan-chang Cheng
Institute of Automation Chinese Academy of Sciences
Beijing, china
nanchang.cheng@nlpr.ia.ac.cn

Cheng-qing Zong
Institute of Automation Chinese Academy of Sciences
Beijing, china
cqzong@nlpr.ia.ac.cn

Min Hou
Communication University of China
Beijing, china
houmin@cuc.edu.cn

Yong-lin Teng
Communication University of China
Beijing, china
tengyonglin@cuc.edu.cn

Abstract

Personal attributes extraction plays a significant role in information mining, event tracing and personal name disambiguation. It mainly involves two problems, attribute recognition and decision making on whether this attribute belongs to the extracted person. Personal attributes generally involve named entities, which are recognized mainly by adjusting word segmentation software. As for those which cannot be recognized by word segmentation, the combination of feature words and rules can be used for their recognition. The combination of sentences classifications and rules is employed for attribute ownership decision. At first, all the sentences in the document are classified into those with attribute words and those without, with the latter omitted. The former are then classified into description sentences with one person and description sentences with more persons, according to the criterion that whether there are more than one person described in the sentence. According to statistics of description sentences with one person, anaphora resolution is not necessary, which reduces recognition errors from anaphora resolution failures. Minimum slicing is used for description sentences with more persons, and attribute ownership decision is made within the minimum language segment with the co-occurrence of both the person and the attribute. This method achieves 0.507388780 and 0.489505010 respectively in the lenient evaluation results and the strict evaluation results of SF_Value in CIPS-SIGHAN2014[1] Bakeoff, which turns out to be the best. The fact has shown that the method is effective.

1 Introduction

Attribute, characterized by its objectivity, is inherent in things(Zhuang, 2000). Personal attribute extraction aims at automatically extracting in unstructured texts specific attributes associated with the personal name, such as the character entity's date of birth, work units, spouses, children, education, title, etc. This plays a significant role in information mining, event tracing and personal name disambiguation. International TAC KBP has been conducted since 2009 (Bikel et al., 2009; McNamee et al., 2009), and CIPS-SIGHAN2014 has referred to and revised its Slot Filling tasks to design personal attribute extraction tasks in Chinese. There are six groups participating this bakeoff.

Personal attribute extraction mainly involves two problems, attribute recognition and decision making on whether this attribute belongs to the extracted person, and the latter can be called attribute ownership decision. Personal attributes are generally named entities, such as personal names, place names, organization names, temporal nouns, so named entity recognition technology is needed in attribute recognition. Although named entity recognition is one difficulty in natural language processing, there are plenty of experiences and methods we can draw upon as 30 years has witnessed its research since the introduction of Chinese word segmentation, as in (Sun et al., 1995; Zhao et al., 1999; Liao et al., 2004; Yu et al., 2006; Ye et al., 2007). Therefore, this paper focuses upon attribute ownership decision after a brief introduction to personal attribute extraction, since the former is more complicated with anaphora resolution and attribute ownership decision among more persons. Some of bakeoff papers

[1] http://www.cipsc.org.cn/clp2014/webpage/en/home_en.htm

Proceedings of the Third CIPS-SIGHAN Joint Conference on Chinese Language Processing, pages 192–201,
Wuhan, China, 20-21 October 2014

regarding filling slot have noticed these problems, as in (Bikel et al., 2009; Burman et al., 2012). In this paper, we propose attribute ownership decision through the combination of sentences classifications and rules in accordance with natural language features and the task requirements of our bakeoff. This method has achieved good results in the evaluation. The rest of the paper is organized as: Section 2 introduces main ideas, Section 3 presents the methods of personal attribute recognition, Section 4 emphasizes on and discusses the methods of personal attribute ownership decision, Section 5 is experimental results and Section 6 is conclusion.

2 Main ideas

Attribute recognition is mainly named entity recognition, which is attempted to be settled in word segmentation in our study. According to attribute recognition task requirements, the word segmentation software used in this study has been adjusted so that it can recognize most named entities. As for those which cannot be recognized by the software, the method of feature words together with rules has been employed. After attribute recognition, all the sentences in the document are classified into those with attribute words and those without, with the latter omitted. Therefore, attribute ownership decision is merely conducted to the sentences marked with attribute words.

Now that the anaphora of personal pronouns are widely used in most sentences, attribute ownership decision involves anaphora resolution, which means the determination of the antecedent of the anaphor(Wang, 2005). Anaphora resolution appears to be difficult in Chinese, far from being settled completely satisfactorily(Wang, 2002; Wang 2005). In order to decrease the reliance on anaphora resolution, we have studied the tested documents and found that the described person in most of them is the extracted character. When most sentences in a document describe the extracted person, it is not necessary to employ anaphora resolution. Anaphora resolution or some other methods are needed to find the attribute of the extracted person only for those sentences with more persons. In a small number of documents, there is only one extracted person within the whole text, such as "马伟明_T1.xml" and "白志东_T1.xml". As such, in attribute ownership decision, it should be determined whether there are more than two persons described in the sentence. In this way, the sentences marked with attribute words in the document will be classified as description sentences with one person and description sentences with more persons through some methods, which would decrease the reliance on anaphora resolution and so greatly improve decision precision by decreasing the recognition errors from anaphora resolution failures. The challenge here is how to determine those sentences with more persons, which will be expounded later.

3 Personal attribute recognition

Personal attribute recognition involves two jobs. One is to adjust word segmentation software in order to achieve full recognition of various types of named entities, and the other is to annotate feature words to ensure exact decision of attribute identity of some named entities.

3.1 Adjusting word segmentation software

Named entity recognition is mainly completed in word segmentation. The word segmentation software used is CUCBst, a dictionary and rule based software developed by Broadcasting Media Center, Communications University of China. The adjustment includes: adjustmenting tagging, adding words, and adjusting rules.

3.1.1 Adjustmenting Tagging

First, some tags are adjusted in the dictionary. Take some words associated with titles as an example. In the dictionary, there are items such as "程序员(programmer) n", "雕刻师(sculptor) n", "董事长(president) n", "发明家(inventor) n" and "检察长(chief-prosecutor) n". The tag of "n" within is adjusted to be "tt". For instance:

Example Sentence 1: 可见魏冉这位封建社会地主阶级的政治家，在完成秦王朝统一中国的事业中所起的作用。

Translation: As a feudal politician of landlord class, in the cause of uniting China by Qin dynasty, Wei Ran's role is clearly demonstrated.

Its tagged version is:

可见/c 魏冉/nr 这位/r 封建社会/ln 地主/n 阶

级/n 的/u 政治家/tt，/w 在/d 完成/v 秦王朝/t 统一/a 中国/gj 的/u 事业/n 中/f 所/u 起/v 的 /u 作用/n 。/w

Through the tagging adjustment, it is easy to recognize the title of the extracted person "魏冉 (Wei Ran)" is "政治家(statesman)". We also adjust the tagging of death reasons(sw), nations(gj), provincial cities(sh), cities and towns(sx). In addition, some feature words are annotated. For example, the feature words associated with character birth such as "生于(be born)", "出生(be born)" and "诞生(be born)" are annotated as "bir".

3.1.2 Adding words

There are two stages in adding words:

Stage One is to collect and sort dictionaries in system development, adding names such as titles, nations and places to the segmentation dictionary.

Stage Two is to add OOV words to the segmentation dictionary in evaluation period by implementing new words automatic recognized in evaluation corpus with manual intervention. It should be pointed out that some certain noun phrase is regarded as one word and then kept in the dictionary. These noun phrases are mainly organization titles, nicknames and titles such as "北平研究院物理研究所(Institute of Physics of Peking Academy of Sciences)", "罗彻斯特储蓄银行(Rochester Bank)", "橙县小姐(Miss Orange County)" and "名誉理事长(Honorary chairman)".

3.1.3 Adjusting rules

CUCBst segmentation system is characterized by coarse-grained segmentation and fine-grained segmentation, which is implemented by rules. We adjust some merging rules so that they can achieve better attribution recognition. For example:

Example Sentence 2: 斯托曼 1953 年出生于美国纽约曼哈顿地区的犹太人家庭。

Translation: Stallman was born of a Jewish family in Manhattan, New York, in 1953.

Its segmented version before the rule adjustment is:

coarse-grained segmentation：斯托曼/nr 1953 年/t 出生/v 于/p 美国纽约曼哈顿地区/ns 的/u 犹太人/n 家庭/n

fine-grained segmentation：斯托曼/nr 1953 年/t 出生/v 于/p 美国/ns 纽约/ns 曼哈顿/ns 地区/n 的/u 犹太人/n 家庭/n

In the coarse-grained segmentation version, "美国纽约曼哈顿地区", which includes two personal attributes in accordance with evaluation outline, country of birth and city of birth, is merged together. Further analyses and processes are needed for correct recognition. In the fine-grained segmentation version, "美国纽约曼哈顿地区" is divided into 4 words as "美国/ns 纽约/ns 曼哈顿/ns 地区/n", in which country of birth is correctly segmented. However, city of birth needs further processes by merging the following three words. Example Sentence 2's segmented version after the rule adjustment is:

斯托曼/nr 1953 年/t 出生/v 于/p 美国/gj 纽约曼哈顿地区/ns 的/u 犹太人/n 家庭/n

In this version, "美国纽约曼哈顿地区" is segmented into 2 words as "美国/gj 纽约曼哈顿地区/ns", which are country of birth and city of birth respectively. This makes the recognition and extraction of related attributes convenient.

3.2 Finding nearest named entity through the feature word

Although some specific tagging aimed for named entities and some personal attributes is conducted in word segmentation, it should be noted that not all tagged named entities are personal attributes. For example, 1998 is not always a person's date of birth, since it could be the date for an event or something else. Therefore, it is necessary to decide personal attribute through the feature word, and find nearest named entity through the feature word within the sentence. Take the example of time of birth:

Example Sentence 3: 张幼仪/nr 生于/bir 1900 年/t ，/w 比/p 徐志摩/nr 小/a 4/m 岁/q 。/w

Translation: Zhang Youyi was born in 1900, and she was four years younger than Xu Zhimo.

Example Sentence 4: 鲁桂珍/nr 1904 年/t 生于 /bir 南京/ns

Translation: In 1904, Lu Guizhen was born in Nanjing.

When segmented, "生于(be born)" is tagged as "bir", which means the word is a feature word associated with a person's birth. When there is "bir" in a sentence, the system will iterate before and after this feature word to find the nearest time noun, as in Example Sentence 3, 1900 is after the feature word and in Sentence 4, 1904 is before the feature word.

4 Deciding whether the attribute belongs to the extracted person

In this section, we first classify the sentences in two levels in order to decide the attribute ownership in the classified sentence. As for the description sentence with one person, decide whether the character is the extracted object. If not, just omit the sentence. As for the description sentence with more persons, decide personal attribute ownership by extracting the personal attribute within the minimum language segment with the co-occurrence of both the person and the attribute.

4.1 Sentence classification

Sentence classification involves two levels. First, the sentences are classified into sentences with or without attribute marks. Then, classify the sentences with attribute marks into those with one person and those with more persons.

4.1.1 Classifying all the sentences into two types

All the attributes and feature words are marked in word segmentation. In terms of these marks, all the sentences are classified into two types. Those without attribute marks will be directly omitted, whereas those with attribute marks will be kept for further processing.

4.1.2 Classifying the sentences with attribute marks into two types

The sentences with attribute marks are classified into those with one described person and those with 2 or more than 2 described persons. Character recognition is significant in this step. The forms to recognize characters include personal names, only surnames or first names, personal pronouns, zero form and kinship titles, in which personal names and kinship titles can be either antecedent or anaphora, the rest three can only be anaphora.

(1) personal names

Personal names are the most important feature to detect characters. For example:

Example Sentence 5. 1973 年 7 月 19 日，冯白驹在北京逝世。

Translation: On July 19, 1973, Feng Baiju passed away in Beijing.

Example Sentence 6. 次年 1 月，王文明病逝，冯白驹继任中共琼崖特委书记。

Translation: In January of the next year, Wang Wenming passed away, and Feng Baiju take Wang' place to be the Special Secretary of CPC in Qiongya.

Here, the number of personal names in the sentence will decide whether the sentence is the one with one described person. Example Sentence 5 is the sentence with one described person, for there is one personal name "冯白驹" within, whereas Example Sentence 6 is the sentence with more described persons, for there are two personal names within, "王文明" and "冯白驹".

(2) only surnames or first names

As for non-Chinese names, the whole name is used first and then generally the surname is used for anaphora. For example:

Example Sentence 7. 莫奈 1840 年 11 月 14 日出生于法国巴黎 45 街拉菲特第九郡，是阿道夫和路易斯的第二个儿子。（克劳德·莫奈）

Translation: Monet was born on November 14, 1840, in 45 Street, the 9th canton of Lafayette, Paris, France; and he was the second son of Adolf and Louis. (Claude Monet)

When using the surname would be confusing, first names will be used, as in the introduction to the twin brothers, "Mike Bryan" and "Bob Bryan", in Example Sentence 8.

例句 8. 等到鲍勃和迈克开始真正对网球产生了浓厚兴趣，也拿起球拍开始了网球生涯后，布莱恩夫妇又给他们订了个规矩：在 17 岁之前，这对双胞胎都不可以在比赛中对抗。

Translation: Until Bob and Mike really grew strong interests in tennis and began their tennis career, Bryans set up a catch for them. Before 17 years old, the twins were not permitted to compete in game.

Generally speaking, the whole name is used for the Chinese name. However, only surnames or first names could be used. For example:

Example Sentence 9. 七七事变后，日本人邀请他组建"中日友好协会"，梁意识到，要想不当汉奸，必须立即离开北平。（梁思成）

Translation: After Marco Polo Bridge Incident of 7th July 1937, the Japanese invited him to organize the "China-Japan Friendship

Association", Liang realized that he had to leave Peking immediately; otherwise he would be forced to become a traitor. (Liang Sichneg)

Example Sentence 10. 我与泽涵兄交往多了，与他的家人都处得很熟。（江泽涵）

Translation: After frequent contacts with Bro Zehan, I got well acquainted with his families. (Jiang Zehan)

When only surnames or first names are used, it is a little difficult to recognize them. Once recognized, it is as easy to decide whether there is one person or there are more persons in the sentence, as in the case of personal names.

(3) personal pronouns

Anaphora means that another component is used to refer to the prior component in order to avoid its repeat in the text(Xu 2003). There are three forms of anaphora, zero anaphora, pronominal anaphora and NP anaphora(Chen, 1987). In the personal attribute extraction, personal pronouns are anaphora with obvious forms and are used as one of the features to detect characters. For example:

Example Sentence 11. 江泽涵是中国数学会的创始人之一，从 1935 年该会成立时起，他就是副理事长。（江泽涵）

Translation: Jiang Zehan, one of the founders of the Chinese Mathematics Society, has been the vice chairman since the association was founded in 1935. (Jiang Zehan)

When the character is detected, a single personal pronoun (such as he, she, you and I) used in one sentence, even with several occurrences, will be regarded as only one person, for in one sentence, it is rare to use the same single personal pronoun to refer to different persons.

Generally the sentence with plural personal pronouns includes more persons. For example:

Example Sentence 12. 李约瑟一如既往忠于他的爱妻："执子之手、与子偕老，" 直到 1987 年德萝西 91 岁时去世，他们夫妇共同生活了整整 64 年。

Translation: Joseph Needham was always loyal to his beloved wife, just as the famous Chinese saying goes, "Holding your hand, lead our merry life till old". Until De Luoxi left at the age of 91 in 1987, the couple had lived together for a full 64 years.

(4) kinship titles

When the extracted person is introduced, some other related persons will be mentioned. Relatives, such as parents, the wife and brothers, are often mentioned. Besides, some other connections may also be mentioned, such as teachers, friends and leaders. The kinship titles have obvious form features and can be used for detecting characters in the sentence. For example:

Example Sentence 13. 布兰切特的降生充满了浪漫色彩，爸爸是美国前海军军官，军舰在澳洲墨尔本停靠时，与布兰切特的母亲相识。（凯特·布兰切特）

Translation: Blanchett birth is full of romance. His father, a former US Navy officer, met Blanchett mother when the warship docked in Melbourne, Australia. (Cate Blanchett)

In Example Sentence 13, there are three persons, "Blanchett", "father" and "mother".

In addition, we also find that when some attributes of the extracted person's teacher, student, friend or leader are described, this person's name will appear. However, when a teacher, a student or a professor is used in a general sense, he or she has little thing to do with attribute extraction, so he or she will not be regarded as a character. For example:

Example Sentence 14. 但法伊弗却透露，自己上高中的时候很不受欢迎，"我那时很高，很笨拙，老师曾经在我的成绩单上写过'米歇尔是班里个子最大的女孩'"。

Translation: But Pfeiffer has revealed that she was very unpopular in high school, "At that time, I am very tall but somehow clumsy, and my teacher once wrote on my report card 'Michelle is the tallest Girl in class'".

Example Sentence 15. 梅耶的死让很多人震惊，他的同事和学生认为他是一个非常有才华的科学家和教师。

Translation: Meyer's death shocked a lot of people, both his colleagues and students believed that he was a very talented scientist and teacher.

Example Sentence 16. 需要提出的是，卡罗瑟斯的学生 Paul J. Flory (1910-1985)，在总结研究卡罗瑟斯的基础上，出版了影响整个世界的《高分子化学原理》一书，该书依然是今天高分子领域主要的理论基础。

Translation: I must point out that Carothers' student Paul Flory (1910-1985), on the basis of summarizing research on Carothers, published "Principles of Polymer Chemistry", which shook the whole globe. The book is still the bible-like theoretical basis of today's realm of polymer.

"老师(the teacher)" in Example Sentence 14, "同事、学生(colleagues, students)" in Example Sentence 15 are used in a general sense, so both sentences are ones with one person. Instead, Example Sentence 16 makes clear the date of birth, date of death, and some other information, concerning Carothers' student, Paul J. Flory(with a specific name for the student), so the sentence is one with more persons.

4.2 Attribute ownership decision

By employing the above mentioned character recognition features to classify the sentences, we get two sentence sets, the description sentences with one person (including zero anaphora) and the description sentences with more persons.

4.2.1 The description sentences with one person

(1) affirming the extracted person

As for the sentences with personal names, including with only first names or surnames, the extracted persons' names, including first names or surnames, are used for the match. The difficulty lies in the sentences with personal pronouns and zero form. As mentioned above, most documents in the testing texts mainly describe extracted persons, thus when the description sentences with one person involve personal pronouns and zero form, it can be hypothesized that extracted persons are directly used as described persons. In order to test this hypothesis, we study the use of the third singular personal pronoun "他(he)" in all the sentences. Through automated recognition, we obtain 369 sentences with one person which have "他(he)". Then we identify all the sentences to see whether "他(he)" is the anaphora of the extracted person. Fig. 1 and Fig. 2 show the results.

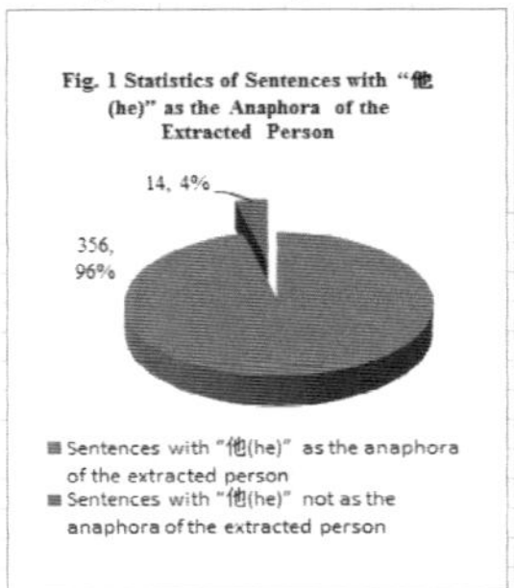

Fig. 1 Statistics of Sentences with "他(he)" as the Anaphora of the Extracted Person

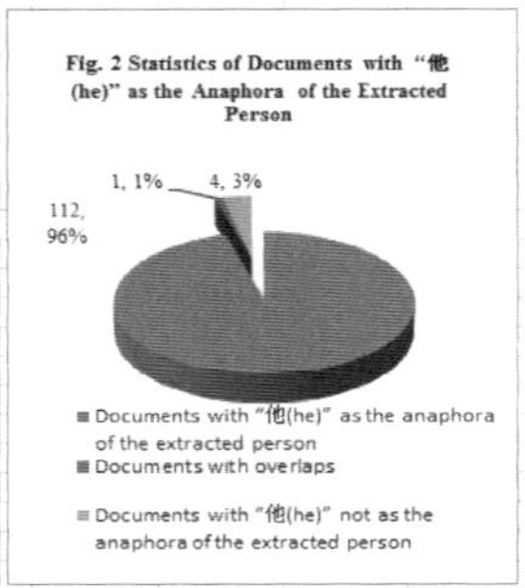

Fig. 2 Statistics of Documents with "他(he)" as the Anaphora of the Extracted Person

As illustrated in Fig. 1 and Fig. 2, 356 sentences, in 112 documents, with "他(he)" as the anaphora of the extracted person, account for 96 percent of all the sentences, whereas 14 sentences, in 5 documents, with "他(he)" not as the anaphora of the extracted person, account for only 4 percent of all the sentences. We study these 5 documents and find that the chiefly described person is not the extracted person in 3 documents, which are "鲁桂珍_T2.xml", "鲁桂珍_T3.xml" and "陈济棠_T3.xml". In "鲁桂珍_T2.xml" and "鲁桂珍_T3.xml", the chiefly described person is 鲁桂珍's husband, 李约瑟, not the extracted person, 鲁桂珍. In "陈济棠_T3.xml", he chiefly described person is 陈济棠's son, 陈树柏, not the extracted person, 陈济棠. In this document, there are 5 sentences with one person which have "他(he)". There are 4 sentences with "他(he)" not as the anaphora of the extracted person, while there is only one sentences with "他(he)" as the anaphora of the extracted person. Thus we call this document as one with overlaps. The other two documents are "马伟明_T3.xml" and "白志东_T3.xml" respectively. Although the chiefly described person is the extracted person in both documents, the narrative perspective is first-person perspective.

In addition, we also perform statistical analysis of the use of zero form. As there are a number of zero anaphora, 193 sentences with zero anaphora are randomly chosen from 126 documents. Then we identify all these sentences to see whether there is the anaphora of the extracted person. The results are shown in Fig. 3 and Fig. 4.

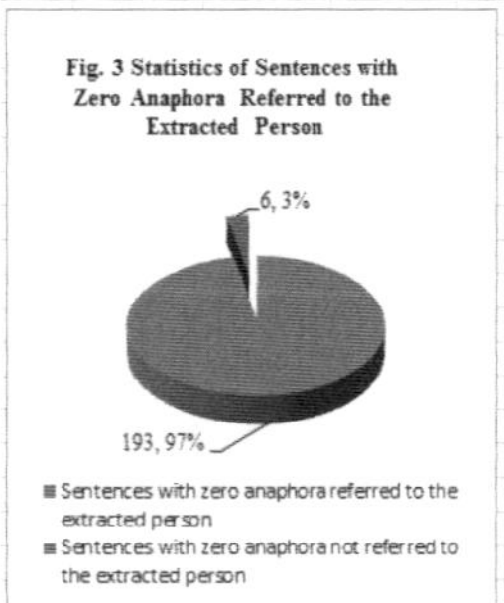

Fig. 3 Statistics of Sentences with Zero Anaphora Referred to the Extracted Person

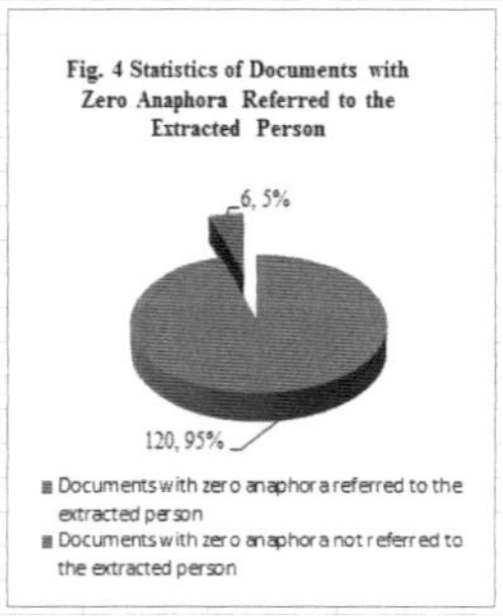

Fig. 4 Statistics of Documents with Zero Anaphora Referred to the Extracted Person

As illustrated in Fig. 3 and Fig. 4, zero anaphora shares similar use with the anaphora of the third singular pronoun "他(he)". By analyzing the documents with zero anaphora not referred to the extracted person, we find that the chiefly described person is not the extracted person.

However, there is no first-person perspective, which is quite different from the case of the third singular pronoun "他(he)".

The data above demonstrate that our hypotheses are in line with reality. If we have had classified the documents in terms of some features such as the chiefly described person and narrative perspectives and then classified the sentences in documents, we would have achieved better results.

(2) attribute extraction

The extracted character in the description sentence with one person is affirmed at first. If the character is not the extracted object, omit the sentence. If the character is the extracted object, attributes are extracted and put into different attribute lists in terms of marks. For example:

Example Sentence 17. 1943 年 11 月/t ，/w 白志东/nr 出生/bir 于/p 河北省/sh 乐亭县/sx。/w

Translation: In November, 1943, Bai Zhidong was born in Leting County, Hebei Province.

According to the feature word "出生(birth)" and attribute marks, the attributes of "1943 年 11 月(Nov. 1943)", "河北省(Hebei province)" and "乐亭县(Laoting county)" are put into such attribute lists as date of birth, province of birth and city of birth(including towns and villages) of the extracted person "白志东".

4.2.2 The description sentences with more persons

Attribute ownership decision in the description sentences with more persons turns out be the challenge of this evaluation task. For example:

Example Sentence 18. 李济深升为军长，陈济棠升任第十一师师长。（陈济棠）

Translation: Li Jishen was promoted to an army corps commander, and Chen Jitang was promoted to be the commander of eleventh division. (Chen Jitang)

In this sentence, "军长(army commander)" is the title of "李济深", while "师长(divisional commander)" is the title of "陈济棠", a person to be extracted. Attribute ownership decision requires us to correctly recognize "陈济棠" and then extract it. We mainly employ minimum slicing with the co-occurrence of the extracted person and the attribute and the nearest distance principle to decide attribute ownership, which will be expounded below.

(1) minimum co-occurrence slicing

When the person and the attribute co-occur in the same grammatical unit as minimum as possible, and there is only one person, the attribute belongs to the person. For example:

Example Sentence 19. 1947 年 4 月冀察热辽军区部队改编为东北民主联军第八纵队，黄永胜任司令，丁盛任二十四师师长，之后参加了辽沈战役。

Translation: In April, 1947, the troops of Ji-Cha-Re-Liao military region were reorganized as the 8th Army of the Northeast Democratic Coalition Force. Huang Yongsheng became the commander, and Ding Sheng took the post of commander of 24th division, then they took part in the Liaoning-Shenyang Campaign.

Example Sentence 20. 1935 年，蒋中正调张学良东北军剿共，西安出现以西北剿匪总司令部副总司令张学良、西安绥靖公署主任杨虎城和陕西省政府主席邵力子为首三种势力并存局面。（杨虎城）

Translation: In 1935, Chiang Kai-shek dispatched Zhang Xueliang's Northeast Army to conquer the communist power. There coexisted three powers in Xi'an, ie the power of Zhan Xueliang, who was the Vice Commander in chief of Northeast Anti-communist Army; the power of Yang Hucheng, who was the director of Xi'an Appeasement Administrative Office; and the power of Shao Lizi, who as the governor of Shaanxi provincial government. (Yang Hucheng)

In the two clauses of Example Sentence 19, "黄永胜任司令" and "丁盛任二十四师师长" means the title of "司令(commander)" belongs to "黄永胜", while the title of "师长(divisional commander)" belongs to "丁盛". In Example Sentence 20, "副总司令张学良", "主任杨虎城" and "主席邵力子" show that the person and the attribute co-occur in the same subject-predicate phrase.

(2) the nearest distance principle

When there is a long distance between the person and the attribute, and at the same time, there are more persons in the sentence, the attribute belongs to the person with the nearest distance.

Example Sentence 21. 钱三强的父亲钱玄同是中国近代著名的语言文字学家。（钱三强）

Translation: Qian Sanqiang's father, Qian Xuantong is a famous modern Chinese linguist.

(Sanqiang Qian)
Example Sentence 22. 我从小就知道江泽涵是北京大学一位鼎鼎大名的数学教授，却无缘见面，但他们的堂姐江冬秀我却在孩童时就见过。（江泽涵）
Translation: When I was young, I got to know that Jiang Zehan is a famous math professor of Peking University, but I had no luck to meet him; but I'd seen their cousin Jiang Dongxiu during my childhood. (Zehan Jiang)
Example Sentence 23. 薛万彻的二哥薛万淑，也战功显赫，历任右领军将军、梁郡公、畅武道行军总管。（薛万彻）
Translation: Xue Wanche's second brother, Xue Wanshu also made daring military exploits, who used to be a general of the right wing, Duke of Liang Jun, and Commander in Chief of Changwudao.(Wanren Xue)
In Example Sentence 21, the title "语言文字学家(linguist)" belongs to "钱玄同" instead of "钱三强", for the distance between the title "语言文字学家(linguist)" and the person "钱玄同" is smaller. The situations in Example Sentence 22 and Example Sentence 23 are also like this. It should be noted that the nearest distance principle is not always effective, as in the following example sentence.
Example Sentence 24. 中共四大后，彭述之以中央委员身份接替多病的蔡和森担任中央宣传部长，为了工作方便，蔡和森夫妇、彭述之夫妇等人一起住在宣传部的寓所。
Translation: After the 4th National Congress of CPC, as a member of the Central Committee of CPC, Peng Shuzhi take the place of Cai Hesen, who was sick, to be the minister of the State of Central Propaganda Ministry. In order to facilitate the work, both Hesens and Shuzhis lived in the apartments of Propaganda Ministry.
In Example Sentence 24, the title "部长(minister)" belongs to "彭述之", the person which has a longer distance. This sentence needs deeper syntax or semantic analysis, which is a little difficult to process at present.

4.2.3 anaphora resolution of person pronouns[2]

As for anaphora resolution in the description sentences with more persons, we mainly refer to the methods in (Wang, 2001; Wang, 2005). The extracted person is known, so its designation and sex can be annotated in advance, which facilitates anaphora resolution. For example:
Example Sentence 25 & 26：1940 年，钱三强取得了法国国家博士学位，又继续跟随第二代居里夫妇当助手。1946 年，他与同一学科的才女何泽慧结婚。
Translation: In 1940, Qian Sanqiang obtained his French national doctorate, and then he continued to follow Curies, the junior, as an assistant. In 1946, he married the talented girl He Zehui, who was learning the same subject.
As in Example Sentence 25, "居里夫妇" is plural, "他(He)" in Example Sentence 26 refers to "钱三强" in the preceding sentence, which is a male name in singular form.

4.3 Attribution extraction flowchart

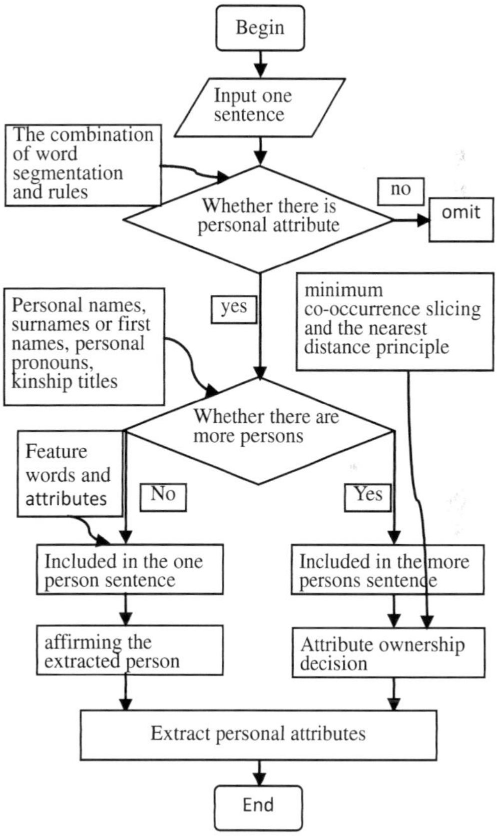

Fig. 5 the Flowchart of Personal Attribution Extraction

5 Experimental results

In this bakeoff, the performance of 6 groups attending the competition are shown in Table 1.

[2]Since there are few cases of reverse anaphora, it has not been considered in this text.

Our system is named as CASIA_CUC_PAES.

Table 1. The lenient and strict evaluation results

Team Id	lenient SF_Value	strict SF_Value
CIST-BUPT	0.363235496	0.352206490
ICTNET_002	0.277775207	0.273884523
WZ_v4	0.004311033	0.002491385
BLCU-yudong	0.308706661	0.292608955
Result-BUPT	0.071467108	0.035979785
CASIA_CUC_PAES	0.507388780	0.489505010

According to the evaluation results, our system achieves 0.507388780 and 0.489505010 respectively in the lenient evaluation results and the strict evaluation results of SF_Value in CIPS-SIGHAN2014 Bakeoff, which turns out to be the best. The fact has shown that our system is effective. However, 50 percent of SF_Value implies that there is still room to increase the system's efficiencies. The system performance could be improved in 3 aspects:

1. to establish the word segmentation system specific for personal attribute extraction.
2. to establish grammatical knowledge system regarding personal attribute extraction, For example, "我父亲住在北京(My father lived in Beijing)" is different from "我和父亲住在北京(My father and I live in Beijing)", with "我父亲" as a modifier-head construction in the former and "我和父亲" as a parallel construction in the latter.
3. to establish semantic knowledge system regarding personal attribute extraction, For example, in the sentence of "凯利与女演员劳里・莫顿结婚后居住于 Goatstown.(After wedding, Kerry and actress, Laurie Morton settled in Goatstown.)", certain semantic knowledge is needed to correctly extract the information that Laurie Morton is Kelly's wife.

6 Conclusion

This bakeoff is full of challenges with a number of personal attributes to be extracted. CUCBst, the word segmentation software, plays a significant role in named entity recognition, which provides a solid foundation for attribute extraction. The strategy of sentence classifications is employed in attribute ownership decision, which, though cannot solve all the problems, simplifies analyses. This strategy plays a role in improving precision in attribute ownership decision.

References

Bikel, D., Castelli, V., Florian, R., & Han, D. J. 2009, November. Entity linking and slot filling through statistical processing and inference rules. In *Proc. TAC 2009 Workshop*.

Burman, A., Jayapal, A., Kannan, S., Kavilikatta, M., Alhelbawy, A., Derczynski, L., & Gaizauskas, R. 2012. USFD at KBP 2011: Entity linking, slot filling and temporal bounding. *arXiv preprint arXiv*:1203.5073.

Chen Ping. 1987. Discourse Analysis of Chinese Zero Anaphora. *Studies of The Chinese Language*, 5: 363-378.

Kong Fang, Zhou Guodong, & Zhu Qiaoming. 2010. Survey on Coreference Resolution. *Computer Engineering*, 36(8): 33-36.

Liao Xiantao, Yu Haibin, & Qin Bing, Liu Ting. 2004. HMM combined with automatic rules-extracting for Chinese Named Entity recognition. *The second national student Workshop on Computational Linguistics*. Beijing:[s. n.], 2004: 232-237.

McNamee, P., & Dang, H. T. 2009, November. Overview of the TAC 2009 knowledge base population track. In *Text Analysis Conference (TAC)* (Vol. 17, pp. 111-113).

McNamee, P., Dang, H. T., Simpson, H., Schone, P., & Strassel, S. 2010, May. An Evaluation of Technologies for Knowledge Base Population. In *LREC*.

Sun Maosong, & Gao Haiyan. 1995. Identifying Chinese Names in Unrestricted Texts. *Journal of Chinese Information Processing*, 9(2), 16-27.

Sun, A., Grishman, R., Xu, W., & Min, B. 2011. New York University 2011 system for KBP slot filling. In *Proceedings of the Text Analytics Conference*.

Wang Houfeng, & Tingting He. 2001. Research on Chinese Personal Pronoun Anaphora Resolution. *Chinese Journal of Computers*, 24(2), 136-143.

Wang Houfeng, & Zheng Mei. 2005. Robust Pronominal Resolution within Chinese Text. *Journal of Software*, 16(5), 700-707.

Wang Houfeng. 2002. Computational Models and Technologies in Anaphora Resolution. *Journal of Chinese Information Processing*, 16(6), 9-17.

Wang Houfeng. 2005. On Anaphora Resolution

within Chinese Text. *Applied Linguistics*, (4), 113-119.

Xu Jiujiu. 2003. Anaphora in Chinese Texts. *China Social Sciences Publishing House*.

Ye Zheng, Lin Hongfei, & Shu Sui. 2007. Person Attribute Extracting Based on SVM. *Journal of Computer Research and Development*, (z2): 271-275.

Yu Hongkui, Zhang Huaping, & Liu Qun. 2006. Chinese named entity identification using cascaded hidden Markov model. *Journal on Communications*, 27(2).

Zhao Jun, Huang Changning. 1999. A Transformation-Based Model for Chinese BaseNP Recognition. *Journal of Chinese Information Processing*, 13(2): 1-7.

Zhuang Shouqiang. 1997. Difference and Relation Between Features and Attribute and its Significance in Scientific Research. *Studies In Dialectics of Nature*, 13(11): 44-48.

Chinese Spell Checking Based on Noisy Channel Model

Hsun-wen Chiu **Jian-cheng Wu** **Jason S. Chang**
Department of Institute of Information Systems and Applications
National Tsing Hua University
chiuhsunwen@gmail.com wujc86@gmail.com jason.jschang@gmail.com

Abstract

Chinese spell checking is an important component of many NLP applications, including word processors, search engines, and automatic essay rating. Compared to English, Chinese has no word boundaries and there are various Chinese input methods that cause different kinds of typos, so it is more difficult to develop spell checkers for Chinese. In this paper, we introduce a novel method for correcting Chinese typographical errors based on sound or shape similarity. In our approach, similar characters are automatically generated using Web corpora, and potential typos in a given sentence are then corrected using a channel model and a character-based language model in the noisy channel model. In the training phase, we estimate the channel probabilities for each character based on ngrams in Web corpus. At run-time, the system generates correction candidates for each character in the given sentence and selects the appropriate correction using the channel model and the language model.

1 Introduction

Spell checking is a necessary task for text processing of every written language, which involves automatically detecting and correcting typographical errors. However, compared to spell checkers for alphabetical languages (e.g., English or French), Chinese spell checkers are more difficult to develop because there are no word boundaries in Chinese writing system and errors may be caused by various Chinese input methods. In this thesis, we define typos as Chinese characters that are misused due to sound or shape similarity. Liu et al. (2011) show that people tend to unintentionally generate typos due to sound similarity (e.g., *索定 (suo ding) instead of 鎖定 (suo ding)) or shape similarity (e.g., *銷 定 (xiao ding) instead of 鎖定 (suo ding)). On the other hand, some typos found on the Web (e.g., forums or blogs) are used deliberately for the purpose of speed typing or just for fun. Therefore, spell checking is an important component for many applications, including computer-aided writing, search engines, and social media text normalization.

Very little work has been done on the task of Chinese spell checking. The methods proposed in the literature can be classified into two types: rule-based methods and statistical methods. Rule-based methods use knowledge resources, for example, dictionaries, confusion sets, and segmentation systems. Simple rule-based methods, however, have their limitations. The following sentence is a snippet collected from students' written essays which is correct .

> 為什麼你要如此地用功呢？如果我不用功，那以後我將趕不上自己所定的目標。(*wei she me ni yao ru ci di yong gong ne ？ru guo wo bu yong gong ，na yi hou wo jiang gan bu shang zi ji suo ding de mu biao* 。)

Unfortunately, based on simple rules the two characters 所 (*suo*) and 定 (*ding*) are likely to be regarded as typos of the dictionary word 鎖定 (*suo ding*) with identical pronunciation.

The data-driven, statistical spell checking approach appears to be more robust and perform better. Statistical methods typically use a large corpus to create a language model to validate the correction hypotheses. Intuitively, by using 自己所定的目標 (*zi ji suo ding de mu biao*), the three characters 所定的 (*suo ding de*) are a trigram with high probability in a monolingual corpus, we may determine the 所定 (*suo ding*) is not a typo after all. Table 1 shows the frequency and probability of 所定的 (*suo ding de*) and 鎖定的 (*suo ding de*).

Proceedings of the Third CIPS-SIGHAN Joint Conference on Chinese Language Processing, pages 202–209,
Wuhan, China, 20-21 October 2014

Trigrams	Freq.	LM prob.(log)
所定的 (*suo ding de*)	5	-0.70
鎖定的 (*suo ding de*)	2	-1.49

Table 1: Example trigrams with corresponding frequency and probability.

In this thesis, we propose a model using statistical approaches and model generates the most appropriate corrections in a given sentence. In the training phase, we automatically generate the channel model (confusion set). We use a Chinese spell checker to correct instances in the training data and estimate the channel probability of a typo condition on a correct character , then re-estimate the probability, and iterate until convergence.

At run-time, the checker corrects typos using a noisy channel model. Consider the following sentence.

> 為什麼你要如此地用功呢？如果我不用功，那以後我將趕不上自己**鎖**定的目標。(*wei she me ni yao ru ci di yong gong ne ？ru guo wo bu yong gong ， na yi hou wo jiang gan bu shang zi ji suo ding de mu biao* 。)

The checker generates correction candidates by the replacements of each character and confusable characters with channel probabilities in a beam search algorithm, then calculates the probability of correction hypotheses according to the language model and the channel model. Three correction candidates are shown in Table 2. Finally, the checker returns the correction with the highest score, e.g., the follow sentence:

> 為什麼你要如此地用功呢？如果我不用功，那以後我將趕不上自己**所**定的目標。(*wei she me ni yao ru ci di yong gong ne ？ru guo wo bu yong gong ， na yi hou wo jiang gan bu shang zi ji suo ding de mu biao* 。)

The rest of the paper is organized as follows. We describe the proposed model for automatically correcting the spelling typos in section 2. Section 3 presents the experimental data. We conclude in Section 4.

2 Method

Using fixed rule to correct typos in a given Chinese sentence (e.g., 自己鎖定的目標 *(zi ji suo ding de mu biao)*) does not work very well. Previous work typically corrects typos based on a set of detection rules. Unfortunately, the detection rules depend on a lot of resources, and can be at times unreliable. Typo positions usually are detected using heuristic rules based on Chinese dictionary, word segmentation and the frequency of the ngram. However, Chinese dictionary, and word segmentation have their limitations. For example, the segmentation result of the sentence "自己**鎖**定的目標" is "自己/**鎖**定/的/目標", the two characters 鎖 and 定 may or may not be considered as a word, depend on the segmentation system. To avoid the limitations of rule-based method, a promising approach for Chinese spell checking is to train a noisy channel model based on unannotated data, which containing many information.

Hypotheses
為什麼你要如此地用功呢？如果我不用功，那以後我將趕不上自己**所**定的目標。
為什麼你要如此地用功呢？如果我不用功，那以後我將趕不上自己**瑣**定的目標。
為什麼你要如此地用功呢？如果我不用功，那以後我將趕不上自己**鎖**定的目標。

Table 2: The three correction candidates of the given sentence.

In the rest of this section, we describe our solution to the problem of Chinese spell checking. We describe the process of training the channel model in Section 2.1. More specifically, we describe the method for limiting confusable characters in Section 2.1.1, and the use of ngrams in Section 2.1.2. We will also describe an Expectation-Maximization (*EM*) algorithms for estimating channel probabilities in Section 2.1.3. This algorithm relies on a set of confusable characters and ngrams. Finally in Section 2.2, we describe how to correct typos using the trained noisy channel model at run-time by combining channel model and language model.

2.1 Training Channel Model

We attempt to learn to develop a channel model from the ngrams of Web corpus for correcting Chinese spell typos.

Type	Sound	Shape
Full	所瑣索梭娑嗦縮 唆蓑簑數碩勺鑠 說朔爍帥率妁鎗 鎰鎳鎢鎬鎮鎊鎚 莎蟀鎔鎘	瑣銷鋇鏜鐺鑽貝 賞員賄煩鈔貼敗 狽盼贖賤賊損貽 貞負頁賽贊圓貧 財則
Limited	索瑣鎖所	贖鏜鎖

Table 3: The full confusion set and the limited confusion set of 鎖.

2.1.1 Limiting Confusable Characters

In the first stage of training the channel model, we limit the confusable characters based on the sound and shape similar characters, which containing unlikely confusable characters (as the full confusion set). For example, the full confusion set of 鎖 *(suo)* is shown in Table 3. Liu et al. (2011) analyzed erroneous Chinese character and found that more than 70% of typos were related to the phonologically similar characters, about 50% are visually similar, and almost 30% are both phonologically and visually similar. The goal of this method is to reduce the sizes of the confusion sets and improve the accuracy.

The input to this stage is a set of confusable characters. These confusable characters constitutes the full confusion set. We generate potential confusable characters by reducing some unlikely confusable relations and expanding the confusable characters slightly.

The output of this stage is confusion sets that can be used to correct ngrams for training channel model. Limited confusion set of 鎖 *(suo)*, automatically generated from the full confusion set is shown in Table 3. We can see that the limited confusion set minimize the confusable characters and select more likely characters. The limited confusion set is used to accurately correct ngrams and reduce the computational complexity.

Our method for limiting confusable characters can generate many characters, potentially including a significant number of characters that are not useful in correcting typos. We also remove some loosely similarly relations and expand the confusable characters slightly. For example, we remove all relations based on non-identical phonologically similarity. After that, we add the similarly sounding characters based on nasal consonant in Chinese phonetics (e.g., "ㄣ，ㄥ" *(en, eng)* and "ㄢ，ㄤ" *(an, ang)*), and retroflex consonant (e.g., "ㄙ，ㄕ" *(shi, si)* and "ㄔ，ㄘ" *(chi, chi)*). We also modify the shape similarity by comparing the characters in Cangjie codes *(倉頡碼)* to filter out confusable characters with low similarity. We retain character pairs differing from each other by at most one symbol in Cangjie codes that tend to be highly similar in shape. For example, the code of 徵 *(zheng)* and 微 *(wei)* are highly similar in shape, and their corresponding codes "竹人山土大" and "竹人山山大", differ only in one place.

Note that we do not attempt to estimate the channel probabilities of typos of a character at this point. In contrast, we only use sound or shape similarity to limit confusable characters, leading to more effective confusion set as the basis for subsequent probability estimation.

2.1.2 Retrieving Ngrams

In the second stage of the training phase, we retrieve ngrams (e.g., 所定目標 *(suo ding mu biao)*) possibly containing a typo characters (e.g., 所 *(suo)*) that can be corrected using the confusable characters (e.g., 所 *(suo)*, 鎖 *(suo)*, or 索 *(suo)*). Because estimating channel probabilities need a parallel corpus with typos annotated, we use an existing Chinese spell checker *CSC* to correct typos in the ngrams. We use ngrams generated based on collocates of high frequency words containing the confusable character. The procedure for retrieving and correcting ngrams consist of a number of steps, namely, generating collocates for words containing a specific character, filtering these collocates by frequency, producing the ngrams for the remaining collocates, and correcting these ngrams using *CSC*. Each step is described below in detail.

For this stage of the learning process, we use a collection of *(Word, Collocate)* pairs (e.g., (目標, 鎖定) *((mu biao, suo ding))*, (版面, 鎖定) *((ban mian, suo ding)))*. We generate the word from the corpus using word frequency and find corresponding collocates using Dice coefficient, which is a statistic association value used for comparing the relation of words and collocates. The collocates of each word are sorted according to the Dice coefficient. We retain at most *K* collocates per word to reduce the computational cost. We compute Dice coefficient using the following equation:

$$Dice(w,c) = \frac{2 \cdot freq_{(\mathrm{w})} \cdot freq_{(\mathrm{c})}}{freq_{(\mathrm{w})} + freq_{(\mathrm{c})}} \quad (1)$$

where $freq_{(w)}$ is the frequency of the word, and $freq_{(c)}$ is the frequency of the collocate. Take 鎖

Words	Collocates	Dice
鎖定	版面	.025
	單擊	.021
	防偷	.004
	目標	.004
	移動	.004
	已經	.002
	敬請	.001
	解除	.001

Words	Collocates	Dice
封鎖	衝出	.019
	長城	.017
	突破	.015
	嚴密	.007
	網絡	.002
	大陸	.001

Table 4: Two sample collocates of 鎖定 and 封鎖.

Typos	Texts	Count
所	中 所 定 目標	86
	依 所 定 目標	83
	達到 所 定 目標	44
	我們 所 定 的 目標	42
索	索 定 海珠 收	66
	索 定 起息日	93
	索 定 高清	40

Table 5: Sample texts of typo 所 and 索 of 鎖 from the corpus.

(suo) for instance, the words (e.g., 鎖定 *(suo ding)* and 封鎖 *(feng suo)*) and their corresponding collocates of words are shown in Table 4. The word 鎖定 *(suo ding)* has the highest Dice coefficient of 0.025 with the collocate 版面 *(ban mian)*, while 封鎖 *(feng suo)*) has the highest Dice coefficient of 0.019 with the collocate 衝出 *(chong chu)*.

For each *(Word, Collocate)* pair, we generate all possible potential ngrams *N* containing *Word* and *Collocate*. This stage of the learning process operates over a corpus of ngram words. The sample texts of the typos (所, 索, and 瑣) of 鎖 found in a

Words	Collocates	Characters	Instances
鎖定	目標	所	目標所定
封鎖	突破	索	突破封索
深鎖	眉頭	瑣	眉頭深瑣

Table 6: A sample of instances containing character 鎖 and potentially confusable characters.

corpus is shown in Table 5. We find the ngrams in the corpus with identical collocates and *Word* containing confusable characters (e.g., (所定, 目標)). Sample instances of character 鎖 is shown in Table 6. In this sample, we can find that 鎖 may be misused as confusable characters (e.g., 所, 索, 瑣) in the corpus with such information in the ngrams, we can generate typo pairs (e.g., [所, 鎖], [索, 鎖], [瑣, 鎖]). Finally, we correct the typos in these ngrams by using existing Chinese spell checker (In Section 2.1.3). With the typos and corrections, we can estimate the channel probabilities.

2.1.3 Correcting Ngrams and Training Channel Model

In the third and final stage of training, we correct the ngrams and train the channel model for supporting correction candidates. Figure **??** shows the algorithm for correcting ngrams using a Chinese spell checker and estimating the channel probabilities related to typo pairs. The procedure is repeated for all ngrams obtained in the previous stage until the channel probabilities converge.

We are given a set of ngrams as training data (described in Section 2.1.2). Recall that our goal is to estimate the channel model for each character, in the form of [original, correction, log channel probability] (e.g., [所, 鎖, -4.284] and [索, 鎖, -5.264]). In order to generate a parallel corpus, we need to provide representative ngrams to the training algorithm. The training set is created by retrieving the ngrams from *Word*s of each character and the corresponding *Collocate*s in the corpus.

We apply a previously developed Chinese spell checker(*CSC*) to correct ngrams. In this checker, we adopt the confusion set limited in Stage (1) to reduce the unlikely confusable characters and improve the accuracy for generating typo pairs. We combine the global error probability (GP) and local error probability (LP) to reliably estimate the channel probabilities (CP) using following equation:

$$CP(O,C) = W_{\text{GL}} \cdot GP + (1 - W_{\text{GL}}) \cdot LP(O,C) \tag{2}$$

where *O* is original character, *C* is corrected character, and W_{GL} is a weight for probability. The global error probability is a prior probability calculated from a development data set, which can instead the detection and avoid data sparse. The global error probability calculated by the follow-

Ngrams	Corrections	Typo Pairs
目標所定	目標所定	[目, 目], [標, 標]
		[所, 所], [定, 定]
突破封索	突破封鎖	[突, 突], [破, 破]
		[封, 封], [索, 鎖]
眉頭深瑣	眉頭深鎖	[眉, 眉], [頭, 頭]
		[深, 深], [瑣, 鎖]

Table 7: A sample of the typo pairs for 鎖.

ing equation.

$$GP(Devedata) = \left\{ \begin{array}{c} \frac{count(nochange)}{count(char)} \\ \frac{count(typos)}{count(char)} \end{array} \right\} \quad (3)$$

where *count(nochange)* is the count of corrected characters, *count(typos)* is the count of typos, and *count(char)* is the count of characters. The *Devedata* is the development data.

We use the Expectation-maximization algorithm to estimate the local error probabilities related to the confusion set. We initialize the confusion set with uniformed probability in the E-step and re-estimate the probability of each character in M-step until the local error probability converge. For each of the potentially confused ngram (e.g., 所定目標 *(suo ding mu biao)*, we attempt to find typos and corrections using *CSC* (Step (1)) and produce the typo pairs (Step (2)). The typo pairs are in the form of [Original, Correction]. The frequency is the count of how many times of the ngram occurs in the corpus. We estimate the local error probability based on nochange pair (e.g., [所, 所] *([suo, suo])*), and correction pair (e.g., [所, 鎖] *([suo, suo])*). In Table 7, we show a sample of the typo pairs in the ngrams of the character 鎖 *(suo)*.

Then we calculate the global error probability using the development data (Step (3)). In Step (4), the typo pairs are sorted according to the *Original*. For each [*Original, Correction*] pair, we calculate the local error probability of the *Original* conditioned on *Correction* (Step (5a)). The probability is calculated as follows:

$$LP(C_O, O) = \frac{count(O, C_O)}{count(O)} \quad (4)$$

As shown in Table 8, the total *count* of 所 *(suo)* is 6799532 + 529 + 235 = 6800296, the *count* of (索, 所) is 235, and the *LocalErrorProbability(索—所)* is calculated as follows:

Original	Correction	Frequency
所	所	6,799,532
所	匠	529
所	索	235
Total Frequency		6,800,296

Table 8: Sample of the typo pairs with frequency.

Original	Correction	Freq.	LP_{log}
所	所	6799532	-0.0001
所	匠	529	-9.4614
所	索	235	-10.2728
所	瑣	1	-15.7324
所	鎖	1	-15.7324

Table 9: The result of the local error probability with smoothing.

LocalErrorProbability(索—所) = Count(索, 所)) / Count(所) = 235/6800296 =0.0000346

However, we can not estimate that 所 *(suo)* as a typo of 瑣 *(suo)*, if *CSC* does not find [所, 瑣] *([suo, suo])*. In that case, we use smoothing algorithm to solve this problem. If a confusable character does not has a certain typo pair, we use add-one smoothing algorithm to deal with the unseen problem. For example, confusable characters (e.g., 瑣, 鎖) of 所 *(suo)* are not found in the corpus, so we add count one for them. Table 9 shows a confusion set of 所 *(suo)* and the corresponding smoothed local error probability.

We combine the global error probability and the local error probability to estimate the channel probabilities in Step (5b), and save the *Original*, *Correction*, and their channel probability in the channel model in Step (5c). Steps (1) through (5) are repeated to re-estimate the local error probability until the probabilities converge. The output of this stage of training is a channel model with reliable probabilities, automatically estimated using the confusable characters and ngrams based on collocates. A samples of the channel model for 所 *(suo)* is shown in Table 10.

2.2 Run-time Typo Correction

Once the channel model is automatically trained for each character, we store the model as a confusion set. We then correct a given sentence using the procedure shown in Figure **??** with the character-based language model and the channel model.

For each character in the given sentence of *n*

Original	Correction	Freq.	CP_{log}
所	所	6799532	-0.1416
所	匠	529	-2.2111
所	索	235	-4.4357
所	瑣	1	-10.4947
所	鎖	1	-10.4947

Table 10: A sample of the channel model for 所 *(suo)*.

Originals	Corrections	Ngrams	Score
自	自	()	0.0
己	己	(,自)	-2.6049
鎖	所	(自,己)	-2.6756
定	定	(己,所)	-5.1145
的	的	(所,定)	-6.3698
目	目	(定,的)	-5.1627
標	標	(的,目)	-5.7875
		(目,標)	-10.2282

Table 11: A sample of the hypotheses.

characters (e.g., 自己**鎖**定的目標 *(zi ji suo ding de mu biao)*), we correct typos as follows. In Step (1), the system initializes *n* stacks for the channel model, [*Character, Ngram, Score*]. In Step (2), the system replaces each character with the confusable characters (e.g., 所,索,瑣,鎖 *(suo, suo, suo, suo)*) in the channel model as the correction candidates. For each confusable characters, we create new hypotheses with a score, character ngram state, character, and correction candidates. In order to reduce computational complexity, we use beam search algorithm to replace each and calculate the score of sentences. The score in a hypothesis is calculated based on the channel model and the language model as follows.

$$S(hypothesis) = log(LP^{W_{\text{LC}}} \cdot CP^{(1-W_{\text{LC}})}) \quad (5)$$
$$= W_{\text{LC}} \cdot log(LP) + (1 - W_{\text{LC}}) \cdot log(CP) \quad (6)$$

where *LP* is language model probability, *CP* is channel probability, and W_{LC} is a weight parameter in channel model and language model. A sample hypothesis is shown in Table 11. In Step (3), the new hypothesis are stored in the stack and combined with the existing hypothesis in Step (4). If the stack has too many hypotheses, we prune the stack down to a fixed size in Step (5).

Finally in Step (6), we compare the score of all the hypotheses in the last stack, and output the correction candidate with the highest score as output.

	Sentences
Given	遇到逆竟時，我們必須勇於面對。
Corrected	遇到逆境時，我們必須勇於面對。
Given	人生難免會碰到的一些錯折。
Corrected	人生難免會碰到的一些挫折。

Table 12: A sample of the given sentences and corrections.

When there is no correction candidates with the highest score (e.g., score(自己所定的目標) = -10.2282), we output the given sentence. Table 12 shows three input sentences and the corresponding corrected sentences output. For example, 竟 *(jing)* is corrected as 境 *(jing)*, because 境 *(jing)* is the most appropriate for the context of 遇到逆 * 時 *(yu dao ni jing shi)*.

3 Experiment Setting

Our systems were designed to provide wide coverage spell checking for Chinese texts. As such, we trained our systems using the confusion set, a compiled corpus, Web-scale ngrams, and an existing Chinese spell checker. These resources are used for different purposes: the confusion sets provide the correction candidates; the compiled corpus provide the training data for the language model; Web-scale ngrams and the existing Chinese spell checker are used for training the channel model. We evaluate our systems on the sentence level. In this section, we present the details of data sources used in training(Section 3.1 to Section 3.4).

3.1 Confusion Set

The confusion sets we used are the same as in Liu et al. (2011) and provided for SIGHAN 7 Bake-off 2013: Chinese Spelling Check Shared Task. The confusion sets represent sound similarity and shape similarity between a typo and potential corrections.

There four categories of phonological similarity between two characters: identical sound and tone (*II*), identical sound but different tone (*ID*), similar sound and identical tone (*SI*), similar sound and different tone (*SD*), and identical radical and number of strokes (*RS*). A sample of sound-related confusion sets from SIGHAN 7 Bake-off 2013. In this sample, the confusion sets of 已 *(yi)*, 勇 *(yong)*, and 胡 *(hu)* contain a lot of unlikely con-

N-gram Types	Google Chinese 5-gram
Unigram	1,616,150
Bigram	281,107,315
Trigram	1,024,642,142
Fourgram	1,348,990,533
Fivegram	1,256,043,325

Table 13: The information of n-grams in Google Chinese 5-gram.

N-gram Types	Traditional Chinese 5-gram
Unigram	527,694
Bigram	102,092,428
Trigram	237,599,483
Fourgram	201,500,549
Fivegram	126,959,922

Table 14: The information of n-grams in Traditional Chinese 5-gram.

fusable characters. Examples of unlikely pairs include 已 *(yi)* and 肄 *(yi)* in *ID*, 勇 *(yong)* and 穩 *(wen)* in *SI*, 胡 *(hu)* and 馥 *(fu)* in *SD*. The shape-related confusion sets of 已 *(yi)*, 勇 *(yong)*, and 胡 *(hu)*. The confusion sets also contain loosely similarly relations, for instance, 已 *(yi)* and 圈 *(quan)* are not very similar visually.

In our work, we expand the sets slightly and also remove some unlikely confusable characters in order to improve the performance. We modify the confusion set using the pronunciation and Cangjie codes (倉頡碼). The process is described in detail in Section 2.1.1.

3.2 Google Chinese Web 5-gram

In 2010, *Google* published a Chinese Web 5-gram dataset based on public webpages through Linguistics Data Consortium (LDC).[1] Chinese Web 5-gram consists of Chinese word n-grams and their observed frequency counts generated from approximately 883 billion word tokens of text in publicly accessible Web pages. The Google Chinese Web 5-gram contains 30 GB (gzip compressed) of text files with n-grams ranging from unigrams (single words) to fivegrams. In this work, we used only the traditional Chinese 5-grams. Table 13 and Table 14 show the information of 5-grams in Google Chinese Web 5-gram and traditional Chinese Web 5-gram. We use the traditional Chinese Web 5-gram to retrieve ngrams (at most ten *Words*) in the training phase for estimate channel model probabilities. The advantage of using the Web ngram is that unlike a compiled corpus, it contains many typos.

3.3 Existing Chinese Spell Checker

We use an existing Chinese spell checker (*CSC*) we previously developed in 2013 (Chiu et al., 2013) with the training data described in (Wu et al., 2013). This *CSC* is based on a novel method for detecting and correcting Chinese typographical typos. The approach involves word segmentation, detection rules, and phrase-based machine translation. The error detection module detects typos by segmenting words and checking word and phrase frequency based on compiled and Web corpora. The phonological or morphological typographical typos found then are corrected by running a decoder based on the statistical machine translation model. The language model is trained using the word-based corpus using the SRILM (Stolcke et al., 2011) toolkit. The translation model is trained using the frequency of the word containing typos and the corrected word. The results show that the proposed system achieves high accuracy in error detecting and correcting. We use this Chinese spell checker to train the channel model and as a system to compared with the proposed method.

3.4 Sinica Corpus

"Academia Sinica Balanced Corpus of Modern Chinese", or "Sinica Corpus", is the first balanced Chinese corpus with part-of-speech tags. The size of the corpus we used is about 5 million words. The corpus is segmented according to the word segmentation standard proposed by the ROC Computational Linguistic Society. Each segmented word is manually tagged with a part of speech. Texts in the corpus are collected from different areas: Literature, Life, Society, Science, Philosophy, and Art. Table 15 shows the information about numbers of word, character, article, and percentage by area. We use Sinica Corpus (ignoring word segmentation) to train a character-based n-gram language model running the SRILM (Stolcke et al., 2011) toolkit. The sizes of the ngrams of the character-based language model is shown in Table 16

[1] `https://catalog.ldc.upenn.edu/LDC2010T06`

Areas	Word Token	Character	Article
Literature	777,050	1,169,801	1,385
Life	858,750	1,398,791	2,301
Society	1,610,997	2,711,720	3,246
Science	629,838	1,054,738	994
Philosophy	439,955	673,080	695
Art	474,340	781,415	518
Others	101,394	160,306	89
Total Count	4,892,324	7,949,851	9228

Table 15: The information of the word, character, article, and percentage in the area of sinica corpus.

Ngram Types	Ngram Count
Unigram	17,201
Bigram	741,739
Trigram	859,442
Fourgram	791,846
Fivegram	588,200

Table 16: The information of n-grams in character-based language model.

4 Conclusions and Future Work

Many avenues exist for future research and improvement of our system. For example, confusion sets can be automatically generated using Web-based character n-grams to improve correction performance. Part of speech tagging can be performed to provide more information for the noisy channel model. Named entities can be recognized in order to avoid false alarms. A supervised statistical classifier can be used to model channel probability more accurately. Additionally, an interesting direction to explore is using Web corpus in addition to a compiled corpus for correcting typos. Yet another direction of research would be to consider errors related to a missing or redundant character, or collect data from user to update channel probabilities dynamically.

In summary, we have introduced a novel method for Chinese spell checking. In our approach, the channel model is trained based the sound and shape similarity using Web corpus, and the potential typos in a given sentence is corrected using a noisy channel model. In the training phase, we limit the confusable characters, retrieve the ngrams from the Web corpus, and correct ngrams and estimate the channel probability. At run-time, our system generate the correction candidates and calculate their probabilities using the language model and channel model from a given sentence. The results prove that the channel probability we estimate for the noisy channel model are useful in Chinese spell checking.

References

[Chiu et al.2013] Hsun-wen Chiu, Jian-cheng Wu, and Jason S. Chang. 2013. Chinese spelling checker based on statistical machine translation. In *Sixth International Joint Conference on Natural Language Processing*, page 49.

[Liu et al.2011] C-L Liu, M-H Lai, K-W Tien, Y-H Chuang, S-H Wu, and C-Y Lee. 2011. Visually and phonologically similar characters in incorrect chinese words: Analyses, identification, and applications. *ACM Transactions on Asian Language Information Processing (TALIP)*, 10(2):10.

[Stolcke et al.2011] Andreas Stolcke, Jing Zheng, Wen Wang, and Victor Abrash. 2011. Srilm at sixteen: Update and outlook. In *Proceedings of IEEE Automatic Speech Recognition and Understanding Workshop*, page 5.

[Wu et al.2013] Shih-Hung Wu, Chao-Lin Wu, and Lung-Hao Lee. 2013. Chinese spelling check evaluation at sighan bake-off 2013. In *Proceedings of the 7th SIGHAN Workshop on Chinese Language Processing*, pages 35–42.

NTOU Chinese Spelling Check System in CLP Bake-off 2014

Wei-Cheng Chu and Chuan-Jie Lin
Department of Computer Science and Engineering
National Taiwan Ocean University
No 2, Pei-Ning Road, Keelung 202, Taiwan R.O.C.
{wcchu.cse, cjlin}@ntou.edu.tw

Abstract

This paper describes details of NTOU Chinese spelling check system participating in CLP-2014 Bakeoff. Confusion sets were expanded by using two language resources, Shuowen and Four-Corner codes. A new method to find spelling errors in legal multi-character words was proposed. Comparison of sentence generation probabilities is the main information for error detection and correction. A rule-based classifier and a SVM-based classifier were trained to identify spelling errors. Two formal runs were submitted, and the rule-based classifier achieved better performance.

1 Introduction

Automatic spell checking is a basic and important technique in building NLP systems. It has been studied since 1960s as Blair (1960) and Damerau (1964) made the first attempt to solve the spelling error problem in English. Spelling errors in English can be grouped into two classes: non-word spelling errors and real-word spelling errors.

A non-word spelling error occurs when the written string cannot be found in a dictionary, such as in *fly fron* Paris*. The typical approach is finding a list of candidates from a large dictionary by edit distance or phonetic similarity (Mitten, 1996; Deorowicz and Ciura, 2005; Carlson and Fette, 2007; Chen *et al.*, 2007; Mitten 2008; Whitelaw *et al.*, 2009).

A real-word spelling error occurs when one word is mistakenly used for another word, such as in *fly form* Paris*. Typical approaches include using confusion set (Golding and Roth, 1999; Carlson *et al.*, 2001), contextual information (Verberne, 2002; Islam and Inkpen, 2009), and others (Pirinen and Linden, 2010; Amorim and Zampieri, 2013).

Spelling error problem in Chinese is quite different. Because there is no word delimiter in a Chinese sentence and almost every Chinese character can be considered as a one-character word, most of the errors are real-word errors.

On the other hand, there is also an *illegal-character error* where a hand-written symbol is not a legal Chinese character (thus not collected in a dictionary). Such an error cannot happen in a digital document because all characters in Chinese character sets such as BIG5 or Unicode are legal.

There have been many attempts to solve the spelling error problem in Chinese (Chang, 1994; Zhang *et al.*, 2000; Cucerzan and Brill, 2004; Li *et al.*, 2006; Liu *et al.*, 2008). Among them, lists of visually and phonologically similar characters play an important role in Chinese spelling check (Liu *et al.*, 2011).

This bake-off is the second Chinese spell checking evaluation project. It includes two subtasks: error detection and error correction. The task is organized based on some research works (Wu *et al.*, 2010; Chen *et al.*, 2011; Liu *et al.*, 2011).

2 Replacement and Filtering

Figure 1 shows the architecture of our Chinese spelling checking system. A sentence under consideration is first word-segmented. Candidates of spelling errors are replaced by similar characters one by one. The newly created sentences are word segmented again. They are sorted according to sentence generation probabilities measured by word or POS bigram model. If a replacement results in a better sentence, spelling error is reported.

Proceedings of the Third CIPS-SIGHAN Joint Conference on Chinese Language Processing, pages 210–215,
Wuhan, China, 20-21 October 2014

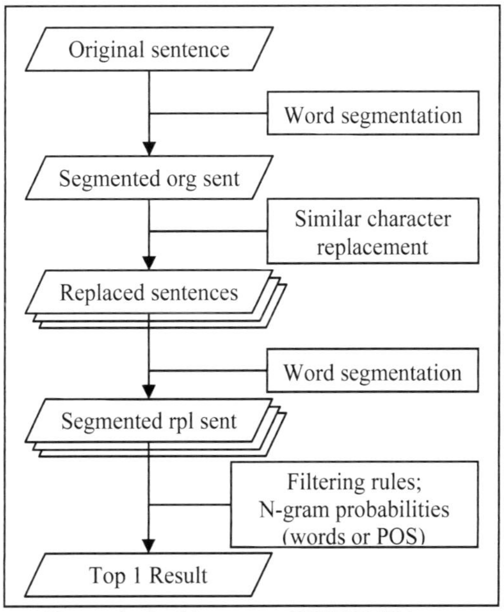

Figure 1. Architecture of NTOU Chinese Spelling Check System

In our experience, the confusion sets provided by the organizers do not cover all the cases in the development set. Two sources used to expend confusion sets are described in Section 2.1.

There are two kinds of spelling-error candidates in our system: one-character words and multi-character words. Their replacement procedures are different, as described in Section 2.2 and 2.3.

2.1 Confusion set expansion

In SIGHAN7 Bake-off 2013 Chinese Spelling Check task (Wu *et al.*, 2013), the organizers provided two kinds of confusion sets, phonologically similar characters and visually similar characters. We adopted all these confusion sets except the one consisting of characters having the same radical and the same number of strokes, because we do not think they are similar.

However, these confusion sets do not cover all the spelling error cases in the training data. We used two resources to expand the confusion sets. One is Showen and the other is the Four-Corner Encoding System.

Shuowen Jieji[1] (說文解字) is a dictionary of Chinese characters. Xu Shen (許慎), author of this dictionary, analyzed the characters according to the six lexicographical categories (六書). One major category is phono-semantic compound characters (形聲), which were created by combining a radical (形符) with a phonetic component (聲符). We collect characters with same phonetic components to expand confusion sets, because they are by definition phonologically and visually similar. For example, the following characters share the same phonetic component "寺" thus become confusion candidates (their actual pronunciation are given in brackets):

侍[si4]持[chi2]恃[shi4]特[te4]時[shi2]...

The Four-Corner System[2] (四角號碼) is an encoding system for Chinese characters. Digits 0~9 represent some typical shapes in character strokes. A Chinese character is encoded into 4 digits which represent the shapes found in its 4 corners. We collect characters in the same Four-Corner codes to expand confusion sets, because they are by definition visually similar. For example, the following characters are all encoded as 6080 in the Four-Corner System:

只囚貝足炅是員異買圓圜

2.2 One-character word replacement

After doing word segmentation on the original sentence, every one-character word is considered as candidate where error occurs. These candidates are one-by-one replaced by similar characters in their confusion sets to see if a new sentence is more acceptable.

Taking C1-1701-2 in the test set as an example. The original sentence is

...嬰兒個數卻特續下滑...

and it is segmented as

...嬰兒 個數 卻 特 續 下滑...

"卻", "特" and "續" are one-character words so they are candidates of spelling errors. The confusion set of the character "卻" includes 腳欲叩卸... and the confusion set of the character "特" includes 持時恃峙侍... Replacing these one-character words with similar characters one-by-one will produce the following new sentences.

...嬰兒個數腳特續下滑...
...嬰兒個數欲特續下滑...

[1] 說文解字
http://zh.wikisource.org/wiki/說文解字

2 四腳號碼列表
http://code.web.idv.hk/misc/four.php

... 嬰兒個數卻持續下滑...
... 嬰兒個數卻時續下滑...
......

2.3 Multi-character word replacement

Our observation on the training sets finds that some errors occur in multi-character words, which means that a string containing an incorrect character is also a legal word. Examples are "身手" (shen1-shou3, skills) versus "生手" (sheng1-shou3, amateur), and "人員" (ren2-yuan2, member) vs. "人緣" (ren2-yuan2, popularity).

To handle such kinds of spelling errors, we created confusion sets for all known words by the following method. The resource for creating word-level confusion set is Academia Sinica Balanced Corpus (ASBC for short hereafter, cf. 馬偉雲 *et al.*, 2001).

For each word appearing in ASBC, each character in the word is substituted with its similar characters one by one. If a newly created word also appears in ASBC, it is collected into the confusion set of this word. Take the word "人員" as an example. After replacing "人" or "員" with their similar characters, new strings 仁員, 壬員, ..., 人緣, and 人韻 are looked up in ASBC. Among them, only 人緣, 人猿, 人文, and 人備 are legal words thus collected in 人員's confusion set.

For each multi-character word, if it has a confusion set, similar words in the set one-by-one substitute the original word to see if a new sentence is more acceptable.

Take ID=00058 in the Bakeoff 2013 CSC Datasets as an example. The original sentence is

... 在教室裡只要人員好...

and it is segmented as

... 在 教室 裡 只要 人員 好...

where "教室", "只要", and "人員" are multi-character words with confusion sets. By replacing 教室 with 教士, 教師..., replacing 只要 with 祇要, 只有, and replacing 人員 with 人緣, 人猿..., the following new sentences will be generated.

... 在教士裡只要人員好...
... 在教師裡只要人員好...
... 在教室裡祇要人員好...
... 在教室裡只要人緣好...
... 在教室裡只要人猿好...

2.4 Filtering rules

Two filter rules are applied before error detection in order to discard apparently incorrect cases. The rules are defined as follows.

Rule 1: No error in person names

If a replacement results in a person name, discard it. Our word segmentation system performs named entity recognition at the same time. If the replacing similar character can be considered as a Chinese family name, the consequent characters might be merged into a person name. As most of the spelling errors do not occur in personal names, we simply ignore these replacements. Take C1-1701-2 as an example:

... 每 位 產 齡 婦女...

"魏" is phonologically similar to "位" and is a Chinese family name. The newly created sentence is segmented as

... 每 魏產齡(PERSON) 婦女...

where "魏產齡" is recognized as a person name. We will discard such a replacement.

Rule 2: Stopword filtering

For the one-character replacement, if the replaced (original) character is a personal anaphora (你 'you' 我 'I' 他 'he/she') or numbers from 1 to 10 (一二三四五六七八九十), discard the replacement. We assume that a writer seldom misspell such words. Take B1-0122-2 as an example:

... 我 會 在 二 號 出口 等 你...

Although "二" is a one-character word, it is in our stoplist therefore no replacement is performed on this word.

3 Error Detection and Correction

In our system, error detection and correction greatly rely on sentence generation probabilities. Therefore, all the newly created sentences should also be word segmented. If a new sentence results in a better word segmentation, it is very likely that the original character is misused and this replacement is correct. But if no replacement is better than the original sentence, it is reported as "no misspelling".

Three language models were used to measure sentence generation probabilities as described in Section 3.1. Two formal runs were output of two different classifiers, SVM-based and rule-based systems, as described in Section 3.2 and 3.3.

3.1 N-gram probabilities

The possibility of a sequence of words can be measured as sentence generation probability by language models. We used smoothed word-unigram, word-bigram and POS-bigram models in our experiments. The training corpus used to build language models is ASBC. As usual, we use log probabilities instead.

A basic hypothesis is that a "better" sentence often has higher probability than the original one. We define *preference scores* to capture such kind of features:

$$pref_M(S_{new}, S_{org}) = \frac{\log(\text{Prob}_M(S_{org}))}{\log(\text{Prob}_M(S_{new}))} - 1 \quad \text{(E1)}$$

where M is the language model (word-unigram model, *etc.*), S_{org} is the original sentence, S_{new} is the new sentence, and Prob(s) is the generation probability of sentence s. By this definition, a new sentence having higher probability than the original one will have a preference score larger than 0, and the higher the better.

3.2 SVM-based classifier

6 features defined in Table 1 were used to train a support vector machine classifier (Chang and Lin, 2011). Besides the preference scores of word-unigram, word-bigram, and POS-bigram probabilities, another kind of features reveals whether a new sentence has the highest preference score among all replacements.

Unfortunately, the developed classifier tends to label all replacements as positive. So we define a threshold so that the replacement is accepted only when SVM thinks the probability of assigning "positive" label is larger than 0.95.

#	Feature definition
1	Preference score of word-unigram prob.
2	Preference score of word-bigram prob.
3	Preference score of POS-bigram prob.
4	Is max of word-unigram prob. preference
5	Is max of word-bigram prob. preference
6	Is max of POS-bigram prob. preference

Table 1. Features for training SVM classifier

3.3 Rule-based classifier

According to our hypothesis of error detection, a correct sentence should have a positive preference score since it has higher generation probability. Moreover, if many replacements have positive preference scores, the correct one should have the highest score.

However, in our observations, sometimes replacing with a frequently-seen word may result in higher preference score, even if the replacement is incorrect. Therefore, we define three thresholds for each n-gram model, respectively, for stricter error detection. Thresholds were trained by using Bakeoff 2013 CSC Datasets (Wu *et al.*, 2013).

The rules of detecting and correcting errors are defined as follows.

1. If no replacement has positive preference scores, report "no error" in both error detection and correction subtasks.
2. Sort the replacements first by their word-bigram preference scores, and then by their word-unigram preference scores, and then by the POS-bigram preference scores.
3. If the top-1 replacement's preference scores are all larger than the thresholds (0.004 for word-unigram, 0.03 for word-bigram, and 0.001 for POS-bigram), report "with error" and output the replacing character and its location in the sentence as correction.

4 Performance

There are two judging correctness in this bakeoff: detection level and correction level.

The metrics are evaluated in both levels by the following metrics:

False-Positive Rate = FP / (FP+TN)
Accuracy = (TP+TN) / (TP+TN+FP+FN)
Precision = TP / (TP+FP)
Recall = TP / (TP+FN)
F1-Score= 2* Precision * Recall)/(Precision + Recall)

We submitted 2 formal runs based on two different classifiers. The first run was output by the rule-based classifier and the second run was output by the SVM-based classifier.

Table 2 and 3 illustrate the evaluation results of formal runs. As we can see, using the rule-based classifier performed better than the SVM-based classifier. Unfortunately none of them could achieve acceptable performance.

Run	FPAlarm	Accuracy	Precision	Recall	F1
Formalrun1_NTOU	**0.258**	**0.4652**	**0.4219**	**0.1883**	**0.2604**
Formalrun2_NTOU	0.9925	0.1045	0.1688	0.2015	0.1837

Table 2: Formal run performance in detection level.

Run	FPAlarm	Accuracy	Precision	Recall	F1
Formalrun1_NTOU	**0.258**	**0.4557**	**0.3965**	**0.1695**	**0.2375**
Formalrun2_NTOU	0.9925	0.0678	0.1143	0.1281	0.1208

Table 3: Formal run performance in correction level.

5 Conclusion

In this year, we tried to expand confusion sets in order to obtain larger coverage of similar characters. We also proposed a new method to find spelling errors in legal multi-character words. We submitted 2 formal runs based on the output of a rule-based classifier and a SVM-based classifier, respectively. The evaluation results showed that the rule-based classifier outperformed the SVM-based classifier, but neither of them achieved acceptable performance.

In the future, more features should be investigated and more decision rules should be discovered.

References

R.C. de Amorim and M. Zampieri. 2013. "Effective Spell Checking Methods Using Clustering Algorithms," *Recent Advances in Natural Language Processing*, 7-13.

C. Blair. 1960. "A program for correcting spelling errors," *Information and Control*, 3:60-67.

A. Carlson, J. Rosen, and D. Roth. 2001. "Scaling up context-sensitive text correction," *Proceedings of the 13th Innovative Applications of Artificial Intelligence Conference*, 45-50.

A. Carlson and I. Fette. 2007. "Memory-Based Context-Sensitive Spelling Correction at Web Scale," *Proceedings of the 6th International Conference on Machine Learning and Applications*, 166-171.

C.C. Chang and C.J. Lin. 2011. "LIBSVM: a library for support vector machines," *ACM Transactions on Intelligent Systems and Technology*, 2:27:1-27.

C.H. Chang. 1994. "A pilot study on automatic chinese spelling error correction," *Journal of Chinese Language and Computing*, 4:143-149.

Q. Chen, M. Li, and M. Zhou. 2007. "Improving Query Spelling Correction Using Web Search Results", *Proceedings of the 2007 Conference on Empirical Methods in Natural Language (EMNLP-2007)*, 181-189.

Y.Z. Chen, S.H. Wu, P.C. Yang, T. Ku, and G.D. Chen. 2011. "Improve the detection of improperly used Chinese characters in students' essays with error model," *Int. J. Cont. Engineering Education and Life-Long Learning*, 21(1):103-116.

S. Cucerzan and E. Brill. 2004. "Spelling correction as an iterative process that exploits the collective knowledge of web users," *Proceedings of EMNLP*, 293-300.

F. Damerau. 1964. "A technique for computer detection and correction of spelling errors." *Communications of the ACM*, 7:171-176.

S. Deorowicz and M.G. Ciura. 2005. "Correcting Spelling Errors by Modelling Their Causes," *International Journal of Applied Mathematics and Computer Science*, 15(2):275-285.

A. Golding and D. Roth. 1999. "A winnow-based approach to context-sensitive spelling correction," *Machine Learning*, 34(1-3):107-130.

A. Islam and D. Inkpen. 2009. "Real-word spelling correction using googleweb 1t 3-grams," *Proceedings of Empirical Methods in Natural Language Processing (EMNLP-2009)*, 1241-1249.

M. Li, Y. Zhang, M.H. Zhu, and M. Zhou. 2006. "Exploring distributional similarity based models for query spelling correction," *Proceedings of the 21st International Conference on Computational Linguistics and 44th Annual Meeting of the ACL*, 1025-1032.

W. Liu, B. Allison, and L. Guthrie. 2008. "Professor or screaming beast? Detecting words misuse in Chinese," *The 6th edition of the Language Resources and Evaluation Conference.*

C.L. Liu, M.H. Lai, K.W. Tien, Y.H. Chuang, S.H. Wu, and C.Y. Lee. 2011. "Visually and phonologically similar characters in incorrect Chinese words: Analyses, identification, and applications," *ACM Transactions on Asian Language Information Processing*, 10(2), 10:1-39.

R. Mitton. 1996. *English Spelling and the Computer*, Harlow, Essex: Longman Group.

R. Mitton. 2008. "Ordering the Suggestions of a Spellchecker Without Using Context," *Natural Language Engineering*, 15(2):173-192.

T. Pirinen and K. Linden. 2010. "Creating and weighting hunspell dictionaries as finite-state automata," *Investigationes Linguisticae*, 21.

S. Verberne. 2002. *Context-sensitive spell checking based on word trigram probabilities*, Master thesis, University of Nijmegen.

C. Whitelaw, B. Hutchinson, G.Y. Chung, and G. Ellis. 2009. "Using the Web for Language Independent Spellchecking and Autocorrection," *Proceedings Of Conference On Empirical Methods In Natural Language Processing* (*EMNLP-2009*), 890-899.

S.H. Wu, Y.Z. Chen, P.C. Yang, T. Ku, and C.L. Liu. 2010. "Reducing the False Alarm Rate of Chinese Character Error Detection and Correction," *Proceedings of CIPS-SIGHAN Joint Conference on Chinese Language Processing* (*CLP 2010*), 54-61.

S.H. Wu, C.L. Liu, and L.H. Lee. 2013. "Chinese Spelling Check Evaluation at SIGHAN Bake-off 2013," *Proceedings of the 7th SIGHAN Workshop on Chinese Language Processing* (*SIGHAN'13*), 35-42.

L. Zhang, M. Zhou, C.N. Huang, and H.H. Pan. 2000. "Automatic detecting/correcting errors in Chinese text by an approximate word-matching algorithm," *Proceedings of the 38th Annual Meeting on Association for Computational Linguistics*, 248-254.

馬偉雲, 謝佑明, 楊昌樺, 陳克健. 2001. "中文語料庫構建及管理系統設計," *Proceedings of the 14th Conference on Computational Linguistics and Speech Processing* (*ROCLING 14*), 1-17.

NCTU and NTUT's Entry to CLP-2014 Chinese Spelling Check Evaluation

Yih-Ru Wang
National Chiao Tung University
HsinChu, Taiwan
yrwang@mail.nctu.edu.tw

Yuan-Fu Liao
National Taipei University of Technology, Taipei, Taiwan
yfliao@ntut.edu.tw

Abstract

This paper describes our Chinese spelling check system submitted to SIGHAN Bake-off 2014 evaluation. The system's main components are still the conditional random field (CRF)-based word segmentation/part-of-speech (POS) tagger and tri-gram language model (LM) used last year. But we tried to refine the misspelling rules, decision-making threshold and improve LM rescoring speed to reduce false alarm rate and improve rescoring speed. Bake-off 2014 evaluation results show that one of our system (Run2) did achieve reasonable performance with about 0.485/0.468 accuracies and 0.226/0.180 F1 scores in the detection/correction metrics.

1 Introduction

Chinese spelling check could be treated as an abnormal word sequence detection problem. Therefore, word segmentation, part-of-speech (POS) parser and language models (LM) are usually adopted to correct the sentence (Bengio 2003).

Therefore, a Chinese spelling checker (Wang 2013) had been built by integrating our conditional random field (CRF)-based parser and a 100K tri-gram LM. Although, these two components are originally designed for automatic speech recognizer (ASR), the system did get some success on Bake-off 2013 evaluation (Wu 2013). These results have confirmed the generalization and sophistication of our parser and LM.

However, there are still many issues in our system. Especially, our system often produces a large amount of false alarms and requires very long processing time on Bake-off 2013 evaluation. Therefore, the focus of this report is on how to reduce the false alarm rate, reduce search space and increase computing speed.

2 Summary of the proposed system

The proposed system is an open-set Chinese spelling check system, i.e., no any training data prepared by the Bake-off 2014 evaluation organizers were used in the system.

The block diagram of our system is shown in Fig. 1. There are three main components in the system including (1) a misspelling rules frontend, (2) a CRF-based Chinese parser and (3) a 100k trigram LM.

Basically, our approach is to exchange potential error characters with their confusable ones and rescore the modified sentence using our CRF-based parser and tri-gram LM to see if the modified one could get better word segmentation result and higher LM score or not. By this way, potential spelling error could be detected and corrected.

In this scheme, the input text is first checked and corrected if there are some high frequency misspelled words in the rule-based replacement frontend. The sentence is then segmented into a word sequence using our CRF-based parser and scored with a tri-gram LM. Then each character in short words (less than 3 characters) is considered as a potential error character and is replaced with character that has similar shape or pronunciation. The modified sentence is further re-segmented and re-scored to get a LM score. This process is repeated until the best modification (with maximum LM score) is found.

It could be found that a lot of re-segmentation and re-scoring computations are required by this approach. These steps, especially the LM rescoring, are very time-consumption. Therefore, the computation of LM score should be done as efficient as possible.

In the following subsections, the architecture and performance of the CRF-based parser and LM modules will be further summarized for better understanding our approach.

Proceedings of the Third CIPS-SIGHAN Joint Conference on Chinese Language Processing, pages 216–219,
Wuhan, China, 20-21 October 2014

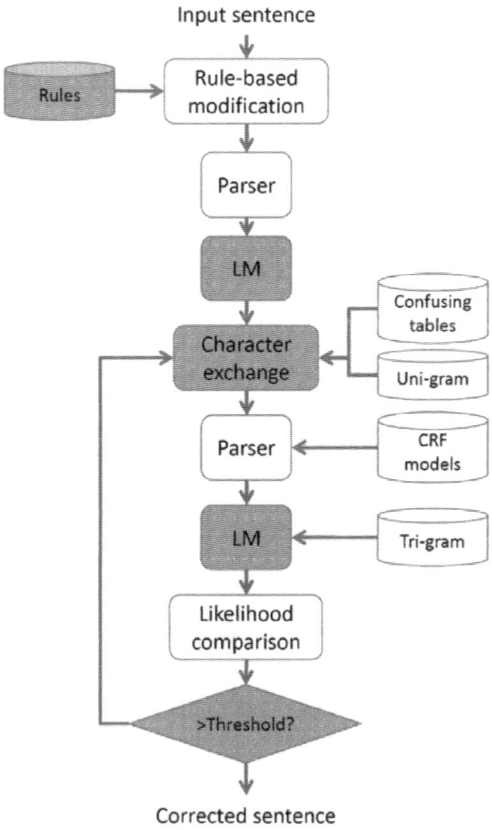

Fig. 1: The schematic diagram of the proposed Chinese spelling checker. Those shaded blocks had been improved for participating Bake-off 2014 evaluation.

2.1 CRF-based traditional Chinese parser

The block diagram of traditional Chinese parser is shown in Fig. 2. There are three blocks including (1) text normalization, (2) word segmentation and (3) POS tagging.

Both the word segmentation and POS tagging modules were based on CRF and trained using Sinica Balanced Corpus version 4.0[1]. The corpus had been manually checked and about 1% of inconsist word-segmentations were corrected. The word segmentation is basically implemented following Zhan's work (Zhao 2006), only the radix cues of the characters (in Chinese, "*bushu*") are add as new features (Wang 2013).

The F-measure of the word segmentation is 96.72% for the original database and 97.50% for the manually corrected corpus. The difference between precision and recall rates is less than 0.06%. About the parser, the accuracy of the 47-type POS tagging is 94.22%. According to these evaluation results, it is believed that our traditional Chinese parser is sophisticated enough.

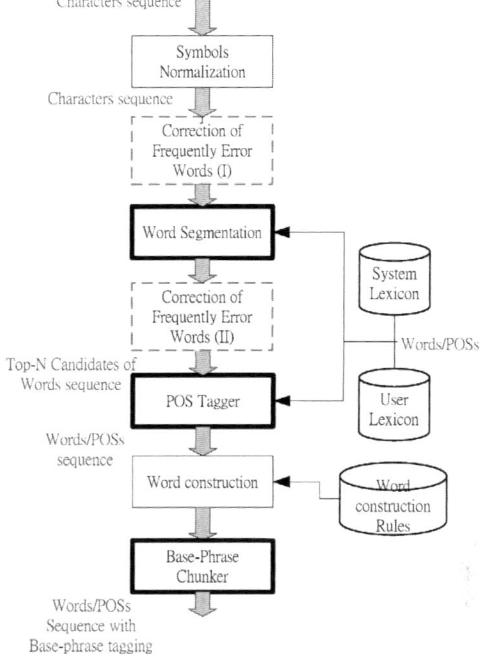

Fig. 2: The schematic diagram of the proposed Chinese parser.

2.2 LM construction

Four text corpora, the LDC Chinese Giga-byte[2], Sinica Balanced Corpus, CIRB030[3] (Chinese Information Retrieval Benchmark, version 3.03), the Taiwan Panorama Magazine[4] and context of Wikipedia (zh_tw version) were used to construct a 100k tri-gram LM.

There are in total 440 million words in the corpora. They were first parsed and post-processed (text normalization, word variation replacement, numbers into short-word conversion, etc.). Then, a 100k lexicon with most frequently words (without POS information) that have document frequency (DF) higher than a threshold was established. Finally, SRLIM toolkit (Stolcke 2000) version 1.7.0 was used to build a tri-gram LM for traditional Chinese.

This LM had been adopted to assist ASR and got significant improvement (Chen 2012), it is therefore a well-established LM.

[1] http://www.aclclp.org.tw/use_asbc_c.php
[2] https://catalog.ldc.upenn.edu/LDC2005T14
[3] http://www.aclclp.org.tw/use_cir.php
[4] http://www.aclclp.org.tw/use_gh_c.php (in Chinese)

3 System improvement

To speed up the rescoring computation and reduce the false alarm rate, several modifications had been done in this year's system. They are (1) misspelling rule expansion, (2) inline language model computation, (3) decision-making threshold and (4) potential error and exchange candidate selection. They are all shown as shaded blocks in Fig. 1.

3.1 Misspelling rule expansion

About 400 more (in total about 1000 now) high frequency error words were added into our misspelling rules. Those words are also collected from Internet. The new rules to replace error words are in general as follows (in Chinese):

腹漲 → 腹脹
行逕 → 行徑
幅射線 → 輻射線
檢查署 → 檢察署
排洩物 → 排泄物
可見一班 → 可見一斑
分道揚鏢 → 分道揚鑣
遺憾終身 → 遺憾終生

Fig. 3: Typical examples of misspelled Chinese word rules used in the frontend module.

3.2 Language model computation

The confusing tables used in the system includes many similar shape or pronunciation characters (Liu 2010). There are about 5400 characters in both the similar shape and pronunciation lists. Beside, each character has about 26 and 71 similar shape and pronunciation characters, respectively. The LM rescoring procedure is therefore very time-consuming. In fact, it is the major bottleneck of our system and often requires several days to finish the evaluation.

Two approaches had been tried to alleviate this problem. The first one is to change the format of LM file from an ASCII to a compressed binary one. The other one is to directly call SRILM's libraries instead of the executables in the rescoring program.

To call SRILM's library, three function calls (as shown in Fig. 2) were embedded into our main program to load LM, check word index/out-of-vocabulary (OOV) and compute LM score, respectively. By this way, the 100k tri-gram LM was loaded only once and therefore the LM rescoring time is significantly improved.

```
// srilm headers
#include "Ngram.h"

// srilm library -loolm -ldstruct -lmisc

// global variables
Vocab vocab;

Ngram*ngram;

//function calls
void srilm_init(const char* fname, int order) {
    File file(fname, "r", 0);
    assert(file);
    ngram = new Ngram(vocab, order);
    ngram->read(file, false);
    cerr << "Done\n";
  }

int srilm_getvoc(const char* word) {
    return vocab.getIndex((VocabString)word);
  }

float srilm_wordprob(int w, int* context) {
    return (float)ngram->wordProb(w, (VocabIndex*)context);
  }
```

Fig. 4: Application programming interface (APIs) for initialize SRILM, check word index/OOV and compute LM scores.

3.3 Decision-making threshold

In our scheme, each sentence is repeatedly modified, re-segmented and re-scored to find a word sequence with maximum LM score. However, the LM scores for different word segmentations in fact can't be compared fairly.

To alleviate this issue, a high score threshold was added into the decision-making logic. In other words, only those hypotheses that have significant LM score improvement were selected as candidates.

3.4 Error and exchange candidate selection

As mentioned in Section 3.2, for each potential error character there are many similar shape or pronunciation confusable ones. However, those tables may be over-completed.

To save some time, two heuristic rules that take advantage of a unigram model are applied. The first one is not to replace those high-frequency characters. The other one is to ignore those very low-frequency candidates. By this way, the search space is dramatically reduced. Bakeoff 2014 Evaluation Results

The goal of the checker is to return the locations of incorrect characters of an input sentence and suggest the correct characters. The criteria for judging correctness are: (1) Detection level: all locations of incorrect characters in a given passage should be completely identical with the gold standard. (2) Correction level: all locations and corresponding corrections of incorrect characters should be completely identical with the gold standard. There are in total 1,062 test sentences in the Bake-off 2014 evaluation.

4 Evaluation Results

Four configurations of our system (Run1~4) were tested. Run1 applied only the rule-based frontend. Run2~4 explored different search space and LM score threshold. The settings of the different runs are shown in Table 1. Among them, the search range of Run1~2 is very restricted and Run3~4 are much larger than others.

Run	Error	Candidate	Log
1	-	-	-
2	50~2000	100~4000	3.0
3	1~3000	1~5000	3.0
4	1~3000	1~5000	1.5

Table 1: Character frequency ranking range and LM score threshold settings for different Runs. Here "Error" and "Candidate" mean the character frequency ranking range to be considered as potential errors and as exchange candidates, respectively.

Table 2 show the all evaluation results. From Table 2, it can be found that Run1 and Run2 do have very low false alarm rate, but higher accuracy in both measures. The reason is that they only modified few errors with high confidence. On the other hand, Run3 and Run4 have higher recall rate and F1 scores but induce more false alarms. In summary, these results show our systems, especially Run1~2, are much conserved.

Run	F/P Rate	Detection Level				Correction Level			
		Acc.	Pre.	Rec.	F1	Acc.	Pre.	Rec.	F1
1	**0.038**	**0.513**	**0.630**	0.064	0.116	**0.509**	**0.600**	0.057	0.103
2	0.181	0.485	0.455	0.150	0.226	0.468	0.392	0.117	0.180
3	0.281	0.461	0.420	0.203	0.274	0.435	0.349	0.151	0.211
4	0.642	0.313	0.294	**0.267**	**0.280**	0.276	0.232	**0.194**	**0.211**

Table 2: Evaluation results of the proposed system on Bake-off 2014 Chinese spelling check task. The table shows the false positive (F/P) rate, accuracy (Acc.), precision (Pre.), recall (Rec.), and F1 score for both the detection and correction levels.

5 Conclusions

In this paper, several modifications have been made to improve our Chinese spelling check system. Evaluation results show that our systems have achieved reasonable performance. Especially, Run2 gains about 0.485/0.468 accuracies and 0.226/0.180 F1 scores in the detection/correction levels.

Experimental results also show that a machine learning-based spelling error detector/classifier should be added on top of parser and LM to further improve system's performance. Finally, our latest traditional Chinese parser is available online at http://parser.speech.cm.nctu.edu.tw.

Acknowledgments

This work was supported by the Ministry of Science and Technology, Taiwan, under the projects with contract MOST 103-2221-E-027-079 and MOST 103-2221-E-009-125-MY2.

References

Y. Bengio, R. Ducharme, P. Vincent, and C. Jauvin (2003), "A neural probabilistic language model, Journal of Machine Learning Research", 2003, No. 3(2), pp. 1137–1155.

Sin-Horng Chen, Jyh-Her Yang, Chen-Yu Chiang, Ming-Chieh Liu and Yih-Ru Wang (2012), "A New Prosody-Assisted Mandarin ASR System", IEEE Trans. on Audio, Speech and Language Processing, vol.20, no.6, pp.1669,1684, Aug. 2012.

Chao-Lin Liu, Min-Hua Lai, Kan-Wen Tien, Yi-Hsuan Chuang, Shih-Hung Wu, and Chia-Ying Lee (2011). Visually and phonologically similar characters in incorrect Chinese words: Analyses, identification, and applications, ACM Trans. Asian Lang. Inform. Process. 10, 2, Article 10 (June 2011).

A. Stolcke (2002), SRILM -- An Extensible Language Modeling Toolkit. Proc. Intl. Conf. on Spoken Language Processing, vol. 2, pp. 901-904, Denver.

Yih-Ru Wang, Yuan-Fu Liao, Yeh-Kuang Wu and Liang-Chun Chang (2013). Traditional Chinese Parser and Language Model-Based Chinese Spelling Checker. Proceedings of the 7th SIGHAN Workshop on Chinese Language Processing (SIGHAN'13), Nagoya, Japan, 14 October, 2013, pp. 69-73.

Shih-Hung Wu, Chao-Lin Liu, and Lung-Hao Lee (2013). Chinese Spelling Check Evaluation at SIGHAN Bake-off 2013. Proceedings of the 7th SIGHAN Workshop on Chinese Language Processing (SIGHAN'13), Nagoya, Japan, 14 October, 2013, pp. 35-42.

H. Zhao, C. N. Huang and M. Li (2006), "An Improved Chinese Word Segmentation System with Conditional Random Field", the Fifth SIGHAN Workshop on Chinese Language Processing 2006, pp. 108-117.

Chinese Spelling Error Detection and Correction Based on Language Model, Pronunciation, and Shape

Junjie Yu and Zhenghua Li
Provincial Key Laboratory for Computer Information Processing Technology
Soochow University, China
20144227010@stu.suda.edu.cn; zhli13@suda.edu.cn

Abstract

Spelling check is an important preprocessing task when dealing with user generated texts such as tweets and product comments. Compared with some western languages such as English, Chinese spelling check is more complex because there is no word delimiter in Chinese written texts and misspelled characters can only be determined in word level. Our system works as follows. First, we use character-level n-gram language models to detect potential misspelled characters with low probabilities below some predefined threshold. Second, for each potential incorrect character, we generate a candidate set based on pronunciation and shape similarities. Third, we filter some candidate corrections if the candidate cannot form a legal word with its neighbors according to a word dictionary. Finally, we find the best candidate with highest language model probability. If the probability is higher than a predefined threshold, then we replace the original character; or we consider the original character as correct and take no action. Our preliminary experiments shows that our simple method can achieve relatively high precision but low recall.

1 Introduction

Spelling check is a traditional and important preprocessing task for natural language processing, since spelling errors happen in written texts, such as short messages, emails, and so on. Lots of research has been devoted to English spelling error detection and correction. In English spelling error detection and correction, the errors can be classified into "non-word" error and "real-word" error (Kukich, 1992). Unlike English, Chinese words are not separated by space and all characters in Chinese are "real-word". Therefore, automatic word segmentation need to be applied in order to produce words (Zhang et al., 2000). There are many Chinese input methods (Zhang et al., 2005). Different input methods lead to different types of spelling errors. For example, input methods based on pinyin which usually lead to spelling errors of characters sharing similar pronunciations; while input methods based on radical methods usually lead to errors related to character shapes. Huang et al. (2007) proposed a learning model based on Chinese phonemic alphabet to detect Chinese spelling errors. Yeh et al. (2013) presented a method based on N-gram ranked inverted index list to deal with this problem.

2 System Architecture

Our system includes two cascaded components: spelling error detection and spelling error correction, as shown in Figure 1.

2.1 Resources

To train our language mode, we use a portion of Chinese Gigaword version 2.0 (LDC2009T14), which contains about 12 million traditional Chinese sentences. We do not split sentence into words, but treat each character as an individual unit. In other words, our language model is based on character. In order to take advantage of the context information, we train a new language model by reversing all sentences in the corpus. So, we will calculate twice for one character based on this two language models. And the total score is the combination of both.

As misspelled characters in a sentence can only be detected in word level, we construct a word dictionary which contains about 300 thousand words collected from Internet. And the SIGHAN organizer provides a dictionary including about 5000 Chinese characters with other characters in similar pronunciation or shape which can be used in candidate generation.

2.2 Spelling Error Detection

In spelling error detection phase, we propose two methods to deal with this problem. One is to gather the characters which get a low score

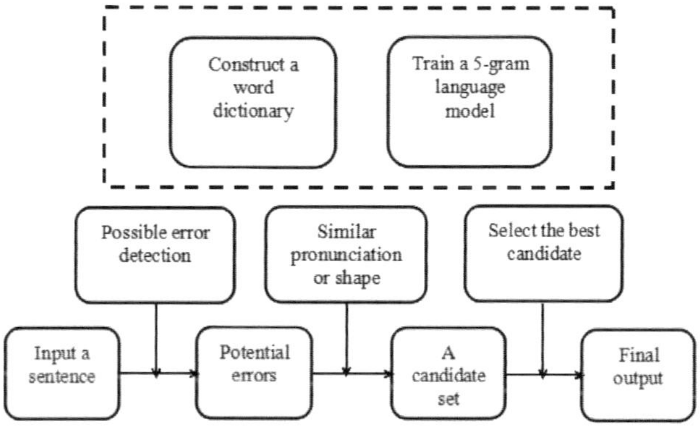

Figure 1: Framework of our proposed system

under language model. Another is to record any independent characters after automatic word segmentation. However, we find both will bring in lots of irrelevant characters though most errors have been discovered. Because Chen et al. (2011) find the average amount of errors in a learners' corpus for a student essay is only 2, we do not want to mark too many error characters to cause false-alarm problem heavily.

In order to make the best of the two methods, we prepare two steps to combine both. Step 1, we calculate the score of each character in a sentence by a forward-backward 5-gram language model. While the score is less than the threshold, the character and its location are sent to Step 2. To find as more errors as possible, we set the threshold in a quite tight value. However, this will result in more irrelevant characters which confuse the system. In Step 2, we need to filter the characters generated in Step 1. We will judge the character whether it can construct a word. Otherwise, we make the assumption that it may be a spelling error which means we are still not sure about it. Anyhow, we will send the results to next phase.

2.3 Spelling Error Correction

In spelling error correction phase, we firstly generate a candidate set for the error character. Characters of similar pronunciations are the most common source of spelling errors (Wu et al., 2013). But there still exist some errors from similar shape (Liu et al., 2011). So, the candidate generation is based on a similar pronunciation or shape dictionary. For more details about the dictionary, please refer to Yeh et al., (2013). Secondly, each character in the candidate set will be tested whether it can form a legal word with its neighbors. Here, the character which can construct a legal word with its neighbors will be left for calculating its score by the language model. After filtering, the number of candidates has been reduced which will bring two benefits: most candidates that have been cut are irrelevant characters and less candidates makes the system be more efficient. At last, the best candidate means one character gets the highest score under a forward-backward 5-gram language model and the score is higher than the threshold. If existing, the original character finally will be recognized as an error character and it will be replaced by the best candidate.

We only use the language model to choose the best candidate because we find that the language model can get a quite high accuracy if we can provide a suitable candidate set successfully.

3 Experimental Analysis

In this paper, we use 300 sentences from the final test of SIGHAN Bake-off 2013 as our training data and 1000 sentences provided by the SIGHAN organizer are our test data.

In our training data, there are 402 error characters in total. We first test the recall of the spelling error detection based on language model.

Function threshold	Language model	
	Recall(%)	#Characters
-4	26.67	2
-3	57.00	6
-2	86.67	18
-1	96.32	38

Table 1: Results on error detection

Table 1 shows that when threshold become tighter, the recall is higher. However, the average number of characters increases quickly. Average number of characters means how many

0	1	2	3	4	5	6	7	8	9	10	11	12	13	14	15	16
<s>	遇	到	逆	**竟**	時	,	我	們	必	須	勇	於	面	對	。	</s>

The size of window is 4, so, if the character "竟" is the target character, then it will generate such words:

逆竟 竟時 到逆竟 逆竟時 遇到逆竟 到逆竟時 遇到逆竟時

If the character in the window is a punctuation or the start or end of the sentence, the system will set the character be a new boundary.

Figure 2: Example to show how to construct a word

Run	False Positive Rate	Detection Level				Correction Level			
		Accuracy	Precision	Recall	F1	Accuracy	Precision	Recall	F1
1	0.2524	0.4539	0.3881	**0.1601**	**0.2267**	0.4426	0.3527	**0.1375**	**0.1978**
2	**0.032**	**0.5292**	**0.7385**	0.0904	0.1611	**0.5235**	**0.7119**	0.0791	0.1424

Table 2: Results of our error detection and correction subtask

characters are marked as error characters by our system. The average length of sentences in our training data is about 70 characters. When the threshold has been set to be -1, more than half of the characters in a sentence have been marked as errors on average. Though the recall is very high in this case, too many correct characters have been recognized as errors. So we prefer to give up the high recall rather than reserve too many irrelevant characters. As we mentioned in Section 2.2, the average number of spelling errors in a sentence is quite low. Threshold = -2 only leads to a slight reduce in recall but the average number of characters have been cut down by half.

As shown in Figure 1, we firstly prepare two resources: a forward-backward 5-gram language model and a word dictionary. As described in previous sections, such two resources will be applied into both spelling check detection and correction. Then, we start to detect the error characters in a sentence. For each character in a sentence, if its score which calculated by the forward-backward 5-gram language model is less than the threshold value, it will be sent to next phase. And the threshold is set at -2 as we discussed before. Next, we will test the character for constructing a word. We set the size of the window at 4 which means the target character can be combined with its neighbors at a distance of 4 characters. For example, Figure 2 describes the details.

After the target character is combined with its neighbors, we will look up the word dictionary. While none of combinations can be found in the word dictionary, we make the assumption that the target character may be an error. In this example, none of these 7 words can be found in word dictionary. So, the character "竟" in this sentence would be marked as an error and sent to next phase.

In spelling check correction phase, we first generate candidates by similar pronunciation or shape. Then the candidates are filtered by constructing a word. This time, we reserve the candidates which can construct a word with its neighbors. At last, the rest candidates will be ranked by language model. The best candidate with its score higher than threshold will replace the original character in the sentence. Here, the threshold is the same with the value in detection level.

4 Final Results

In this bake-off, there are 1000 sentences and all sentences contain at least more than one error. Table 2 shows that the F1 score is very low because we can only find a small portion of all errors. However, the false positive rate and precision is satisfactory especially for the false positive rate. Such results are consistent with our main idea that we choose to under-correct rather than over-correct.

We can see that the performance in detection level and correction level are similar. As described in previous sections, only when the best candidate has been found, we will make the conclusion that the target character is a spelling error. The performance in correction level only has a slight decrease compared with the detection level. But the unavoidable reality is that the recall is not good.

5 Conclusions

Based on n-gram language model and judging a character whether it can form a legal word with its neighbors, a simple approach is proposed to detect and correct the spelling errors in traditional Chinese text. To find the spelling errors in sentence, the language model and a word dictionary are both used. And in order to reduce the false positive rate, the system only treats the character as a spelling error when the best candidate has been found.

Acknowledgments

This work was supported by National Natural Science Foundation of China (Grant No. 61373095, 61333018).

Reference

Chen, Y. Z., Wu, S. H., Yang, P. C., & Ku, T. (2011). *Improve the detection of improperly used Chinese characters in students' essays with error model*. International Journal of Continuing Engineering Education and Life Long Learning, 21(1), 103-116.

Huang, C. M., Wu, M. C., & Chang, C. C. (2007). *Error detection and correction based on Chinese phonemic alphabet in Chinese text*. In Modeling Decisions for Artificial Intelligence (pp. 463-476). Springer Berlin Heidelberg.

Kukich, K. (1992). *Techniques for automatically correcting words in text*. ACM Computing Surveys (CSUR), 24(4), 377-439.

Liu, C. L., Lai, M. H., Tien, K. W., Chuang, Y. H., Wu, S. H., & Lee, C. Y. (2011). *Visually and phonologically similar characters in incorrect Chinese words: Analyses, identification, and applications*. ACM Transactions on Asian Language Information Processing (TALIP), 10(2), 10.

Wu, S. H., Liu, C. L., & Lee, L. H. *Chinese Spelling Check Evaluation at SIGHAN Bake-off 2013*. In Sixth International Joint Conference on Natural Language Processing (p. 35).

Yeh, J. F., Li, S. F., Wu, M. R., Chen, W. Y., & Su, M. C. (2013). *Chinese Word Spelling Correction Based on N-gram Ranked Inverted Index List*. In Sixth International Joint Conference on Natural Language Processing (p. 43).

Zhang, L., Huang, C., Zhou, M., & Pan, H. (2000). *Automatic detecting/correcting errors in Chinese text by an approximate word-matching algorithm*. In Proceedings of the 38th Annual Meeting on Association for Computational Linguistics (pp. 248-254). Association for Computational Linguistics.

ZHANG, Y. S., YU Shi-wen. (2006). *Summary of Text Automatic Proofreading Technology*. Application Research of Computers, 6.

Author Index

Association for Computational Linguistics
209 N. Eighth Street
Stroudsburg, Pennsylvania 18360

CURRAN ASSOCIATES INC
proceedings.com

EACL Workshop on Innovative Hybrid Approaches to the Processing of Textual Data 2012

Avignon, France
23-24 April 2012

ISBN: 978-1-62276-474-7